T0201413

The Science of Deep Learning

The Science of Deep Learning emerged from courses taught by the author that have provided thousands of students with training and experience for their academic studies, and prepared them for careers in deep learning, machine learning, and artificial intelligence in top companies in industry and academia.

The book begins by covering the foundations of deep learning, followed by key deep learning architectures. Subsequent parts on generative models and reinforcement learning may be used as part of a deep learning course or as part of a course on each topic. The book includes state-of-the-art topics such as Transformers, graph neural networks, variational autoencoders, and deep reinforcement learning, with a broad range of applications. The appendices provide equations for computing gradients in backpropagation and optimization, and best practices in scientific writing and reviewing.

The text presents an up-to-date guide to the field built upon clear visualizations using a unified notation and equations, lowering the barrier to entry for the reader. The accompanying website provides complementary code and hundreds of exercises with solutions.

Iddo Drori is a faculty member and associate professor at Boston University, a lecturer at MIT, and adjunct associate professor at Columbia University. He was a visiting associate professor at Cornell University in operations research and information engineering, and research scientist and adjunct professor at NYU Center for Data Science, Courant Institute, and NYU Tandon. He holds a PhD in computer science and was a postdoctoral research fellow at Stanford University in statistics. He also holds an MBA in organizational behavior and entrepreneurship and has a decade of industry research and leadership experience. His main research is in machine learning, AI, and computer vision, with 70 publications and over 5,100 citations, and he has taught over 35 courses in computer science. He has won multiple competitions in computer vision conferences and received multiple best paper awards in machine learning conferences.

The Science of Deep Learning

IDDO DRORI

Massachusetts Institute of Technology
Columbia University

CAMBRIDGE
UNIVERSITY PRESS

University Printing House, Cambridge CB2 8BS, United Kingdom

One Liberty Plaza, 20th Floor, New York, NY 10006, USA

477 Williamstown Road, Port Melbourne, VIC 3207, Australia

314–321, 3rd Floor, Plot 3, Splendor Forum, Jasola District Centre, New Delhi – 110025, India

103 Penang Road, #05–06/07, Visioncrest Commercial, Singapore 238467

Cambridge University Press is part of the University of Cambridge.

It furthers the University's mission by disseminating knowledge in the pursuit of education, learning, and research at the highest international levels of excellence.

www.cambridge.org
Information on this title: www.cambridge.org/highereducation/isbn/9781108835084
DOI: 10.1017/9781108891530

First published 2023

Printed in the United Kingdom by TJ Books Limited, Padstow, Cornwall, 2023

A catalogue record for this publication is available from the British Library.

ISBN 978-1-108-83508-4 Hardback

Additional resources for this publication at www.cambridge.org/drori

Contents

Part III Generative Models

Part V Applications

Preface

This book provides comprehensive and clear coverage of deep learning, which has transformed the field of artificial intelligence. The book is distinctive in that it uses a unified notation, high-quality illustrated figures and the most up-to-date material in the field, and is accompanied by hundreds of code samples, exercises, and solutions on each topic, automatically generated by program synthesis. *The Science of Deep Learning* emerged from courses taught by the author in the past five years that have provided thousands of students with training and experience for their academic studies, and prepared them for careers in deep learning, machine learning, and artificial intelligence in leading companies in industry and academia. The motivation for the book is to provide a guide to the field built upon clear visualizations using a unified notation and equations. The content is self-contained, using a unified language so that students, teachers, and researchers in academia and industry can use the book without having to overcome the barriers to entry of the specific language and notation of each topic. Introductory topics are represented using both basic linear algebra and graphs simultaneously, along with the corresponding algorithms.

Coverage

The material is presented in five main parts:

1. Part I, on the foundations of deep learning, includes Chapters 1–4, which covers core deep learning material on forward and backpropagation, optimization, and regularization.
2. Part II, on deep learning architectures, includes Chapters 5–8. This covers key architectures including convolutional neural networks (CNNs), recurrent neural networks (RNNs), long short-term memory (LSTMs), gated recurrent units (GRUs), graph neural networks (GNNs), and Transformers.
3. Part III, on generative models, comprises Chapters 9 and 10, which cover generative adversarial networks (GANs) and variational autoencoders (VAEs).
4. Part IV addresses reinforcement learning and deep reinforcement learning (Chapters 11 and 12).
5. Part V, on applications (Chapter 13), covers a broad range of deep learning

applications, which are also distributed among the chapters by topic and relevance.

6. Appendices provide equations for computing gradients in backpropagation and optimization, and best practices in scientific writing and reviewing.

Contribution

The book contributes to the literature in the field in that it uses rigorous math with a unified notation. In addition, over the past five years, during the course of instruction, advanced topics have been simplified to become part of the core, while bringing in new topics in the field as advanced topics. The key advantages of this book are that it is up-to-date, with the latest advances in the field including unique content; the math is rigorous, using a unified notation; and the book presents comprehensive algorithms and uses high-quality figures.

Audience and Prerequisite Knowledge

The book is intended for students and researchers in academia and industry, as well as lecturers in academia. The book is primarily intended for computer science undergraduate and graduate students, as well as advanced PhD students. This book has been used for teaching students mainly in computer science, electrical engineering, data science, statistics, and operations research. The required background is linear algebra and calculus. Optional background is machine learning and programming experience. The book is also applicable for a wide audience of students pursuing degrees in STEM fields with the required background. The book is useful for researchers in academia and industry, as well as data scientists and algorithm developers of artificial intelligence. Finally, the book may be used by lecturers in academia for teaching a course on deep learning, and chapters may be used in teaching topics in courses on machine learning, data science, optimization, and reinforcement learning at the undergraduate and graduate levels.

Usage

The first four parts of the book have been used as a textbook in courses on deep learning. The third part, on generative models, may be used as part of a course on unsupervised learning. The fourth part may be used as part of a course on reinforcement learning or deep reinforcement learning. Appendix A is useful for computing the gradients in backpropagation and optimization. Appendix B may be used in project-based courses for providing best practices in scientific writing and reviewing.

Acknowledgments

I developed the material for this book over the past five years while teaching a dozen deep learning classes. The book is now used as the new textbook in deep learning at Columbia University. I would like to thank Columbia University students that read each chapter before class and reported errata that I fixed and improved the book, MIT students and colleagues for reading the book and providing feedback, Leslie Goodman and Gary Daniel Smith for copy editing, Michal Solel Elnekave and Nikhil Singh, who were helpful in producing high-quality figures in Illustrator from sketches, and Maggie Jeffers and Lauren Cowles, my editors who encouraged me to see the book to completion. I wish to thank numerous colleagues, particularly Kyunghyun Cho and Claudio Silva of NYU, Nakul Verma and Itsik Pe'er of Columbia University, Tonio Buonassisi and Gilbert Strang of MIT, Dov Te'eni of Tel Aviv University, and Madeleine Udell and David Williamson of Cornell University. Finally, I'd like to thank my family, Adi, Danielle, Yael, Sharon, and Gilly, my sister Dr. Tali Drori Snir, mom Nili and special thanks to my dad, Prof. Israel Drori, who has published over a dozen books and gets to read my first one.

Abbreviations and Notation

Abbreviations

A2C	advantage actor–critic
A3C	asynchronous advantage actor–critic
AMV	Atlantic Multidecadal Variability
AVI	amortized variational inference
BBVI	black-box variational inference
BCE	binary cross entropy
BERT	bidirectional encoder representations from Transformers
BFGS	Broyden–Fletcher–Goldfarb–Shanno (correction)
CFD	computational fluid dynamics
CGAN	conditional GAN
CLIP	contrastive language-image pre-training
CNN	convolutional neural network
DAG	directed acyclic graph
DCGAN	deep convolutional generative adversarial network
DDPG	deep deterministic policy gradient
DDPM	denoising diffusion probabilistic model
DFP	Davidon–Fletcher–Powell (correction)
DMD	digital micromirror device
DQN	deep Q-network
ELBO	evidence lower bound
EMD	Earth mover's distance
ENSO	El Niño-Southern Oscillation
ESM	Earth system model
FID	Frechet inception distance
FKL	forward KL
GAE	generalized advantage estimation
GAN	generative adversarial network
GAT	graph attention network
GCN	graph convolutional network
GDA	Gradient descent ascent
GNN	graph neural network
GPT-3	generative pre-trained Transformer 3
GRU	gated recurrent unit
IID	independent and identically distributed

IR	impulse response
IS	inception score
JS	Jensen–Shannon (divergence)
KL	Kullback–Leibler
LSTM	long short-term memory
MAE	mean absolute error
MC	Monte Carlo
MCMC	Markov chain Monte Carlo
MCTS	Monte Carlo tree search
MDP	Markov decision process
MFVI	mean-field variational inference
MST	minimum spanning tree
NAS	neural architecture search
NPCC	negative Pearson correlation coefficient
NPG	natural policy gradient
OGDA	optimistic gradient descent ascent
PCA	principle component analysis
PPO	proximal policy optimization
ReLU	rectified linear unit function
RFIW	Recognizing Families in the Wild
RKL	reverse KL
RNN	recurrent neural network
seq2seq	sequence-to-sequence (models)
SGAN	semi-supervised GAN
SGD	stochastic gradient descent
SLM	spatial light modulator
SSP	single-source shortest paths
SSS	sea surface salinity
SST	sea-surface temperatures
TD	temporal difference
TRPO	trust region policy optimization
TSP	traveling salesman problem
UCB	upper confidence bound
VAE	variational autoencoder
VI	variational inference
VQ-VAE	vector quantized variational autoencoder
VRN	Volumetric Regression Network
VRP	vehicle routing problem
WGAN	Wasserstein GAN

Notation

General

$\mathbb{E}$	expectation
$\mathbb{R}$	real numbers
I	identity matrix
X^T	matrix transpose
$\|x\|_p$	ℓ_p norm of vector x
$\cap$	intersection
$\cup$	union
$\|$	concatenation of vectors
$\mathcal{N}(\mu, \sigma)$	Gaussian distribution with mean μ and standard deviation σ
$\nabla_x y$	gradient of y with respect to x

Neural Networks

α	learning rate
θ	learning parameter
ℓ	neural network layer index
W^ℓ	weight matrix of layer
z^ℓ	pre-activation vector of layer
Z^ℓ	pre-activation matrix of layer
a^ℓ	activation vector of layer
A^ℓ	activation matrix of layer
f^ℓ	non-linear activation function of layer
σ	sigmoid function
$\mathcal{L}$	loss function
$\mathcal{R}$	regularization function

Convolutional Neural Networks

$f \star g$	convolution of functions f and g

Sequence Models

x_t	input vector at time t
h_t	hidden vector at time t
y_t	output vector at time t
U	weight matrix applied to input vector shared across time
V	weight matrix applied to hidden vector shared across time
W	weight matrix applied to previous hidden vector shared across time

Graph Neural Networks

$\mathcal{G}$ graph
$\mathcal{V}$ graph nodes
$\mathcal{E}$ graph edges
$\mathcal{N}(i)$ neighbors of node i
A graph adjacency matrix
D graph diagonal degree matrix
L graph Laplacian matrix
L^{sym} symmetric normalized Laplacian matrix
L^{rw} random walk normalized Laplacian matrix
h^{ℓ} embedding vector of layer ℓ

Generative Models

$\mathcal{D}$ GAN discriminator
$\mathcal{G}$ GAN generator
D_{KL} Kullback–Leibler divergence
D_{JS} Jenson–Shannon divergence

Reinforcement Learning

s state
$\mathcal{S}$ set of states
a action
$\mathcal{A}$ set of actions
$T(s, a, s')$ transition function from state s and action a to next state s'
r reward
$R(s, a)$ reward for state s and action a
γ reward discount factor
g_t return at time step t
π policy
$\pi(a|s)$ probability of taking action a in state s under policy π
h horizon
$V_{\pi}^{h}(s)$ state value function with respect to policy π with horizon h of state s
$Q_{\pi}^{h}(s, a)$ action value function with respect to policy π with horizon h of state s and action a
$\pi^{\star}$ optimal policy
$V_{\star}(s)$ state value function with respect to optimal policy $\pi^{\star}$ for state s
$Q_{\star}(s, a)$ action value function with respect to optimal policy $\pi^{\star}$ for state s and action a

Part I

Foundations

1   Introduction

In the fifteenth century, the printing press revolutionized the world by overcoming the genomic bottleneck that allows for only two billion characters of our DNA to be passed on from generation to generation. The printed text allows for unlimited knowledge to be passed on between generations.

A common distinction between the capabilities of humans and machines is that humans are generalists and machines are specialists. The deep learning revolution has resulted in many specialized machine learning systems with super-human capabilities under the title AlphaX. A few noteworthy examples are AlphaGo (Silver et al., 2016) for playing Go, AlphaZero (Silver et al., 2017) for playing chess, AlphaHoldem (Zhao et al., 2022) for playing poker, AlphaD3M (Drori, Krishnamurthy, Rampin, Lourenco, One, Cho, Silva and Freire, 2018) for automated machine learning, AlphaStock (Wang, Zhang, Tang, Wu and Xiong, 2019) for trading stocks, AlphaStar (Vinyals et al., 2019) for playing multi-player strategy games, AlphaDogfight (Pope et al., 2021) for flying fighter jets, AlphaFold (Jumper et al., 2021) for protein structure prediction, and AlphaCode (Li et al., 2022) for competition-level code generation.

In contrast, recent deep learning Transformers, also called foundation models, trained with one trillion parameters, are generalists. Consider the task of learning a university-level course. A human may learn at most a few hundred courses with great effort during an entire lifetime, whereas a foundation model is soon able to learn all courses in days with super-human performance. Understanding such a machine is very different from that of a human.

Deep learning and artificial intelligence (AI) are revolutionizing the world again in the twenty-first century by overcoming the human perception of reality, which is limited by our brains and senses. Machines are revealing to humans insights and new understandings of reality, in which, by comparison, individual human capabilities are mundane.

1.1   Deep Learning

Deep learning is narrowly defined as optimizing neural networks that have many layers. In the broader sense, deep learning encompasses all methods, architectures, and applications involving neural network representations. Deep neural networks are inspired by neurons and their connections in the brain. The back-propagation algorithm is the most commonly used approach for optimizing deep neural networks. Backpropagation is based on computing gradients of a loss function using the chain rule in reverse mode differentiation. Backpropagation and gradient-based methods for optimizing neural networks are very different from biological learning mechanisms in the brain. Deep neural networks may also be optimized using genetic algorithms or Hebbian learning rules, which are inspired by learning in biological neural networks. This book focuses on the broad definition of deep learning, encompassing methods, architectures, and applications that use neural network representations optimized using backpropagation.

1.2   Outline

The book is divided into five parts: (1) *Foundations*, (2) *Architectures*, (3) *Generative Models*, (4) *Reinforcement Learning*, and (5) *Applications*.

1.2.1   Part I: Foundations: Backpropagation, Optimization, and Regularization

Part I, *Foundations*, consists of three chapters. Chapter 2 defines neural networks and presents forward propagation and backpropagation. Neural networks are defined as a composition of functions consisting of a linear and a non-linear part. The chapter defines the network inputs, pre-activations, non-linear activation functions, activation units, and outputs. These are used to introduce forward propagation in neural networks. Next, the chapter presents loss functions and their gradients, derivatives of non-linear activation functions, and the chain rule. These are used to explain backpropagation in a neural network, which is the cornerstone of training neural networks by gradient descent. Multiple examples illustrate the algorithms and provide the backpropagation derivations using the chain rule in reverse mode differentiation. Finally, the chapter presents initialization and normalization strategies for neural networks and the key deep learning software libraries and platforms.

Chapter 3 presents optimization in deep learning, focusing on gradient descent which iteratively finds a local minimum by taking steps in the direction of the steepest descent. Three main problems with training neural networks using gradient descent and their solutions are discussed: (1) the total loss function with respect to the neural network weights, which is a sum of many individual losses for many samples – the solution is mini-batch or stochastic gradient descent; (2) the derivative of the total loss, which is computed with respect to all of the network weights – the solution is backpropagation; and (3) the directions of gradients for consecutive time steps which follow optimized step sizes are orthogonal, forming a zig-zag pattern, which is slow, especially in flat regions. The solution is adaptive gradient descent methods that use previous gradients to determine the step size. Next, the chapter presents second-order methods, including practical quasi-Newton approaches. Finally, the chapter discusses gradient-free optimization approaches such as evolution strategies.

Chapter 4 presents regularization as a technique that can be used to prevent overfitting and explains generalization, bias, and variance. The chapter presents three methods for regularization: (1) adding a penalty term to the cost function – the penalty term is usually a function of the number of parameters in the model; (2) dropout, which is a technique that randomly sets several of the weights in a neural network to zero, which helps to prevent overfitting by reducing the variance of the network; and (3) data augmentation, which is a technique that involves modifying the input data to the neural network by applying random transformations. This technique also helps prevent overfitting by increasing the size of the training set.

1.2.2   Part II: Architectures: CNNs, RNNs, GNNs, and Transformers

Part II, *Architectures*, is about deep learning architectures and consists of four chapters. The first three chapters in this part present successful deep learning representations since they share weights across space, time, or neighborhoods.

Chapter 5 presents convolutional neural networks (CNNs), which are a type of neural network that is designed to recognize patterns in images. The network comprises a series of layers, with each layer performing a specific function. The first layer is typically a convolutional layer, which performs a convolution operation on the input image. The convolution operation is a mathematical operation that extracts information from the input image. The output of the convolutional layer is then passed to a pooling layer, which reduces the number of neurons in the network. Multiple convolutions and pooling layers are followed by a series of fully connected layers responsible for classification or other applications performed on the image. Convolutional neural networks perform well in practice across a broad range of applications since they share weights at multiple scales across space. Finally, the chapter describes CNN architectures such as residual neural networks (ResNets), DenseNets, and ODENets.

Chapter 6 introduces recurrent neural networks (RNNs), which share weights across time. This chapter describes backpropagation through time, its limitations, and the solutions in the form of long short-term memory (LSTM) and gated-recurrent unit (GRU). Next, the chapter describes sequence-to-sequence models, followed by encoder–decoder attention and self-attention and embeddings.

Chapter 7 presents graph neural networks (GNNs), which share weights across neighborhoods. The chapter begins with the definitions of graphs and their representations. Graph neural networks are introduced and applied to irregular structures such as networks. They are used for three tasks: (1) predicting properties of nodes; (2) predicting properties of edges; and (3) predicting properties of sub-graphs or properties of entire graphs.

The second part of the book concludes with Chapter 8, which covers state-of-the-art Transformers, also known as foundation models, which have become a mainstream architecture in deep learning. Transformers have disrupted various fields, including natural language processing, computer vision, audio processing, programming, and education. Large Transformer models currently consist of more than one trillion parameters, and the number of parameters of Transformers is increasing by orders of magnitude each year; it is on track to surpass the number of connections in the human brain. Transformers may be classified into three types of architectures: (1) autoencoding Transformers, which is a stack of encoders; (2) auto-regressive Transformers, which is a stack of decoders; and (3) sequence-to-sequence Transformers, which is a stack of encoders connected to a stack of decoders. New scalable deep learning architectures such as Transformers are revolutionizing how machines perceive the world, make decisions, and generate novel output.

1.2.3   Part III: Generative Models: GANs, VAEs, and Normalizing Flows

The task of classification maps a set of examples to a label. In contrast, generative models map a label to a set of examples. Part III, *Generative Models*, consists of two chapters.

Chapter 9 introduces generative adversarial network (GAN) theory, practice, and applications. The chapter begins by describing the roles of the generator and discriminator. Next, the advantages and limitations of different loss functions are described. Generative adversarial network training algorithms are presented, discussing the issues of mode collapse and vanishing gradients while providing state-of-the-art solutions. Finally, the chapter concludes with a broad range of applications of GANs.

Chapter 10 introduces variational inference and its extension to black-box variational inference used in practice for inference on large datasets. Both reverse Kullback–Leibler (KL) and forward KL approaches are presented. The chapter covers the variational autoencoder algorithm, which consists of an encoder neural network for inference and a decoder network for generation, trained end-to-end by backpropagation. The chapter describes how the variational approximation of the posterior is improved using a series of invertible transformations, known as normalizing flows, in both discrete and continuous domains. Finally, state-of-the-art examples of deep variational inference on manifolds are presented.

1.2.4   Part IV: Reinforcement Learning

Part IV covers *Reinforcement Learning*, a type of machine learning in which an agent learns by interacting with an environment.

Chapter 11 begins by defining a stateless multi-armed bandit, presenting the trade-off between exploration and exploitation. Next, the chapter covers basic principles of state machines and Markov decision processes (MDPs) with known transition and reward functions. Finally, the chapter presents reinforcement learning in which the transition and reward functions are unknown, and therefore the agent interacts with the environment by sampling the world. Monte Carlo sampling and temporal difference sampling are described with examples. The chapter concludes by presenting the Q-learning algorithm.

Chapter 12 presents deep reinforcement learning through value-based methods, policy-based methods, and actor–critic methods. Value-based methods covered include deep Q-networks and present prioritized replay. Policy-based methods described include policy gradients and REINFORCE. Next, the chapter covers actor–critic methods, including advantage actor–critic and asynchronous advantage actor–critic. Advanced hybrid approaches, such as natural policy gradient, trust region policy optimization, proximal policy optimization, and a deep deterministic policy gradient, are presented. Next, the chapter covers model-based reinforcement learning approaches, including Monte Carlo tree search (MCTS), AlphaZero, and world models. The chapter concludes by presenting imitation learning and exploration strategies for environments with sparse rewards.

1.2.5 Part V: Applications

The book concludes with Part V, which covers a dozen state-of-the-art applications of deep learning in a broad range of domains: autonomous vehicles, climate change and monitoring, computer vision, audio processing, voice swapping, music synthesis, natural language processing, automated machine learning, learning-to-learn courses, protein structure prediction and docking, combinatorial optimization, computational fluid dynamics, and plasma physics. Each deep learning application is briefly described, along with a visualization or system architecture.

1.2.6 Appendices

The first appendix, Matrix Calculus, defines the partial derivatives of a function with respect to variables and is helpful for gradient computations in backpropagation and optimization. The second appendix summarizes best practices in scientific writing and reviewing. A section on scientific writing addresses the abstract, introduction, related work, the structure of the text, figures, captions, results, discussion, and the reader's perspective and provides this book's style sheet. A section on reviewing explains the review process, including best practices for evaluating and rating scientific work and writing a rebuttal.

1.3 Code

Hundreds of Python functions are automatically generated on each topic for each chapter by program synthesis using deep learning. All of the code is made available on the book's website at `www.dlbook.org`.

1.4   Exercises

Each chapter has around a dozen human-generated theoretical and programming exercises and their solutions. In addition, hundreds of questions and solutions on each topic are automatically generated by program synthesis using deep learning. All questions and solutions are made available on the book's website at `www.dlbook.org`.

2 Forward and Backpropagation

2.1 Introduction

This chapter defines neural networks and presents forward propagation and back-propagation. Neural networks are defined as a composition of functions consisting of a linear and a non-linear part. The linear part is matrix multiplication, and the non-linear part is a non-linear activation function. We define the network inputs x, pre-activations z, non-linear activation functions f, activation units a, and outputs y. These are used to introduce forward propagation in a neural network. Next, we introduce loss functions and their gradients, derivatives of non-linear activation functions, and the chain rule. These are used to present backpropagation in a neural network, which is the cornerstone of training neural networks by gradient descent. Next, we present initialization and normalization strategies for neural networks. Finally, the chapter introduces the key deep learning software libraries and platforms.

2.2 Fully Connected Neural Network

A neural network as shown in Figure 2.1 is a composition of functions:

$$F^L(\dots F^1(F^0(x))) \tag{2.1}$$

F^ℓ represents layers $\ell = 0, \dots, L$, where each function F^ℓ consists of a linear part which is a matrix multiplication W (green) and non-linear part which is pointwise application of a non-linear function f (blue). Figure 2.2 shows a fully connected neural network. Each column of pre-activations is denoted by z^ℓ, which is the result of multiplying the input to the layer by a matrix W^{ℓ^T}. A non-linear function f is applied pointwise to the coefficients of the pre-activations z^ℓ to form activation units a^ℓ. Together, these operations form layer ℓ of the network. Layer $\ell = 0$ is the input layer with input example x and layer $\ell = L$ is the output layer with output y. The number of activation units in layer ℓ for $\ell = 0, \dots, L$ is denoted by n_ℓ where $L = 3$.

Layer ℓ contains pre-activations z^ℓ and activation units a^ℓ, inputs $x = a^0$, and outputs $y = a^L$, as shown in Figure 2.2. The input $x = a^0$ is a vector denoting a single sample. For example, if x is a color $w \times h$ image, then a^0 is flattened

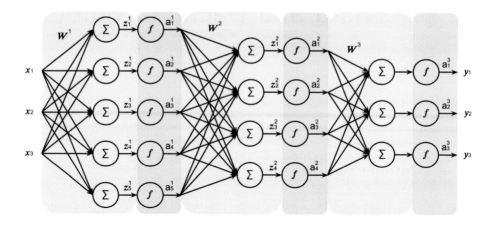

Figure 2.1 Three-layer fully connected neural network. Each layer of the network consists of a linear part (in green) and a non-linear part f (in blue). The inputs are a 3×1 vector $x = (x_1, x_2, x_3)^T$ which are multiplied by a 5×3 matrix W^{1^T} to produce a 5×1 vector of pre-activations $z^1 = (z_1^1, z_2^1, z_3^1, z_4^1, z_5^1)^T = W^{1^T} x$. A non-linear activation function f is applied point-wise to each element z_i^1 of the pre-activation vector to yield a 5×1 activation vector $a^1 = (a_1^1, a_2^1, a_3^1, a_4^1, a_5^1)^T$ such that $a_i^1 = f(z_i^1)$. Together, the linear part of matrix multiplication (in green) and non-linear part of point-wise non-linear activation function (in blue) form the first layer of the neural network. The output activations a^1 of the first layer serve as the inputs to the second layer of the network and the process is repeated. In the second layer the 5×1 activations a^1 are multiplied by the 4×5 weight matrix W^{2^T} to yield a 4×1 pre-activations vector $z^2 = W^{2^T} a^1$, which is passed through a pointwise non-linear activation function f to yield a 4×1 vector of activations $a^2 = f(z^2)$. The outputs a^2 of the second layer form the input to the third layer, which yields a 3×1 pre-activation vector $z^3 = W^{3^T} a^2$ followed by a 3×1 activation vector $a^3 = f(z^3)$, which constitute the outputs $y = a^3$ of the network.

and represented as a $3wh \times 1$ vector, where each color channel (red, green, and blue) constitutes wh coefficients. The layers of a neural network form a Markov chain, as shown in Figure 2.3, where each layer l depends only on the previous layer $l - 1$. In this example the input, pre-activations, activations, and output are represented by vectors.

The matrix $X = A^0$ is an $n_0 \times m$ matrix whose columns are examples a^{0i} for $i = 1 \ldots m$. The matrix $A^0 = \begin{bmatrix} a^{01} \cdots a^{0m} \end{bmatrix}$ has n_0 rows, which are features, and m columns, which are examples. The output $\hat{y} = a^L$ is a vector for a single example and the matrix $\hat{Y} = A^L$ is a matrix of outputs for m examples. Here, $A^L = [a^{31}, \ldots, a^{3m}]$ for $L = 3$ and m examples. For layer ℓ, A^ℓ is an $n_\ell \times m$ matrix.

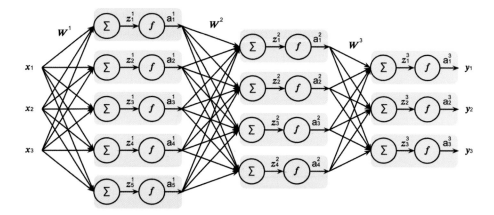

Figure 2.2 Fully connected neural network. Each layer of the network consists of multiple nodes (orange). In this example, the input is a 3×1 vector x which is considered layer 0 with $n_0 = 3$ nodes. The first hidden layer consists of $n_1 = 5$ nodes. The second layer has $n_2 = 4$ nodes, and the third layer with $n_3 = 3$ nodes in this example is the output y.

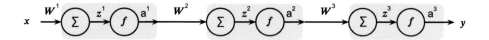

Figure 2.3 Neural network layers form a Markov chain with operations on vectors. Starting from the input vector $x = a^0$, which is considered layer $\ell = 0$, each layer $\ell = 1, \ldots, L$ consists of a pre-activation vector $z^\ell = W^{\ell^T} a^{\ell-1}$ and activation vector $a^\ell = f(z^\ell)$ and only depends on the previous layer output vector $a^{\ell-1}$. The output is $y = a^L$, where $L = 3$ in this example denotes the number of layers.

2.3   Forward Propagation

Forward propagation of activations from layer $\ell - 1$ to layer ℓ is a mapping F^ℓ from $A^{\ell-1}$ to A^ℓ:

$$A^\ell = F^\ell(A^{\ell-1}) \tag{2.2}$$

where each F^ℓ is composed of two parts: a linear function and a non-linear function. The linear function is defined as:

$$Z^\ell = W^{\ell^T} A^{\ell-1} + b^\ell \tag{2.3}$$

where W^ℓ is an $n_{\ell-1} \times n_\ell$ matrix of weights for layer ℓ, W^{ℓ^T} is the $n_\ell \times n_{\ell-1}$ transpose of W^ℓ and b^ℓ is an $n_\ell \times 1$ bias vector for layer ℓ. Both act on all examples.

We absorb the bias vector b^ℓ into W^{ℓ^T} by appending it as the last column, making W^{ℓ^T} an $n_\ell \times (n_{\ell-1} + 1)$ matrix, and appending a 1 to the activation vector $a^{\ell-1}$ or equivalently appending a row of 1s to the activation matrix, making $A^{\ell-1}$ an $(n_{\ell-1}+1) \times m$ matrix. Without loss of generality we continue to use the notation of W^{ℓ^T} and $A^{\ell-1}$ to denote the augmented matrix and vector. For example, if $W^\ell = \begin{pmatrix} w_{11} & w_{12} \\ w_{21} & w_{22} \\ w_{31} & w_{32} \end{pmatrix}$ and $A^{l-1} = \begin{pmatrix} a_1 \\ a_2 \\ a_3 \end{pmatrix}$ and $b^l = \begin{pmatrix} b_1 \\ b_2 \end{pmatrix}$, then

$$W^{\ell^T} A^{\ell-1} + b^\ell = \begin{pmatrix} w_{11} & w_{21} & w_{31} \\ w_{12} & w_{22} & w_{32} \end{pmatrix} \begin{pmatrix} a_1 \\ a_2 \\ a_3 \end{pmatrix} + \begin{pmatrix} b_1 \\ b_2 \end{pmatrix} = \begin{pmatrix} w_{11}a_1 + w_{21}a_2 + w_{31}a_3 + l \\ w_{12}a_1 + w_{22}a_2 + w_{32}a_3 + l \end{pmatrix}$$

$$= \begin{pmatrix} w_{11} & w_{21} & w_{31} & b_1 \\ w_{12} & w_{22} & w_{32} & b_2 \end{pmatrix} \begin{pmatrix} a_1 \\ a_2 \\ a_3 \\ 1 \end{pmatrix}$$

Equation 2.3 is then rewritten as matrix multiplication:

$$Z^\ell = W^{\ell^T} A^{\ell-1} \tag{2.4}$$

The non-linear part is a non-linear activation function f^ℓ, for layer ℓ, which operates on each element of the matrix Z^ℓ separately:

$$A^\ell = f^\ell(Z^\ell) \tag{2.5}$$

2.3.1   Algorithm

Unrolling the forward propagation for the network shown in Figure 2.3, we get:

$$\hat{Y} = A^3 = f^3(W^{3^T} f^2(W^{2^T} f^1(W^{1^T} X))) \tag{2.6}$$

If f is the identity then F is linear in x.

Algorithm 2.1 provides the forward propagation pseudocode.

Algorithm 2.1 Forward propagation.

---

   given initial weights $W^1, \ldots, W^L$
   given data example vector x^1
   for each layer $\ell = 1, \ldots, L$ **do**:
     $x^{\ell+1} = f^\ell(W^{\ell^T} x^\ell)$

2.3.2   Example

As an example of forward propagation, consider the neural network shown in Figure 2.4 with input vector $x = [x_1, x_2, x_3]^T$.

The 3×1 input is $x = a^0$ and the 3×2 weight matrix of the first layer is

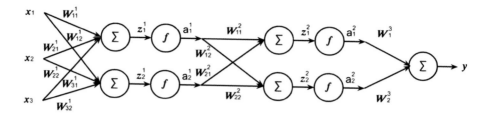

Figure 2.4 Neural network example. The input to the network is a 3×1 vector $x = (x_1, x_2, x_3)^T$.

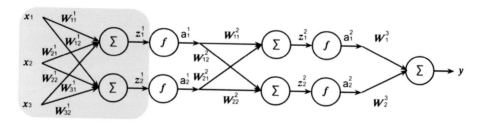

Figure 2.5 Example of forward propagation in a neural network. The 3×1 input vector x is multiplied by a 2×3 matrix W^{1^T} to form a 2×1 pre-activations vector $z^1 = W^{1^T}x$, which is the linear part (in green) of the first layer of the network.

$W^1 = \begin{pmatrix} w_{11}^1 & w_{12}^1 \\ w_{21}^1 & w_{22}^1 \\ w_{31}^1 & w_{32}^1 \end{pmatrix}$. The 3×1 input is multiplied by the 2×3 transpose W^{1^T}

to yield the 2×1 pre-activations z^1, as shown in Figure 2.5:

$$z^1 = \begin{pmatrix} z_1^1 \\ z_2^1 \end{pmatrix} = W^{1^T}x = \begin{pmatrix} w_{11}^1 & w_{21}^1 & w_{31}^1 \\ w_{12}^1 & w_{22}^1 & w_{32}^1 \end{pmatrix} \begin{pmatrix} x_1 \\ x_2 \\ x_3 \end{pmatrix} = \begin{pmatrix} w_{11}^1 x_1 + w_{21}^1 x_2 + w_{31}^1 x_3 \\ w_{12}^1 x_1 + w_{22}^1 x_2 + w_{32}^1 x_3 \end{pmatrix}$$

(2.7)

The pre-activation vector z^1 is followed by a non-linear function f^1 applied pointwise to yield the activation vector $a^1 = [a_1^1, a_2^1]^T$ of the first layer, as shown in Figure 2.6:

$$a^1 = \begin{pmatrix} f(z_1^1) \\ f(z_2^1) \end{pmatrix} = \begin{pmatrix} a_1^1 \\ a_2^1 \end{pmatrix}$$

(2.8)

Next, as shown in Figure 2.7, the activation vector a^1 of the first layer is multiplied by the 2×2 weight matrix W^{2^T} of the second layer:

$$z^2 = W^{2^T}a^1 = \begin{pmatrix} w_{11}^2 & w_{21}^2 \\ w_{12}^2 & w_{22}^2 \end{pmatrix} \begin{pmatrix} a_1^1 \\ a_2^1 \end{pmatrix} = \begin{pmatrix} w_{11}^2 a_1^1 + w_{21}^2 a_2^1 \\ w_{12}^2 a_1^1 + w_{22}^2 a_2^1 \end{pmatrix} = \begin{pmatrix} z_1^2 \\ z_2^2 \end{pmatrix}$$

(2.9)

followed by a non-linear function f of the second layer applied pointwise to yield

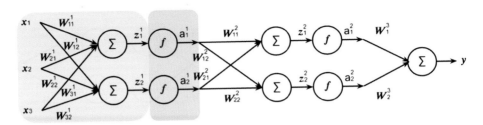

Figure 2.6 Example of forward propagation in a neural network highlighting the first layer of the network. After the linear part (in green), the 2×1 pre-activation vector z^1 is passed through a point-wise non-linear activation function f to form a 2×1 activation vector a^1 (in blue). Together, the linear part (in green) and a non-linear part (in blue) constitute the first layer of the network.

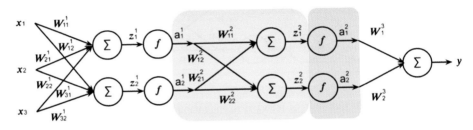

Figure 2.7 Example of forward propagation in a neural network highlighting the second layer of the network. The outputs of the first layer a^1 are multiplied by the weight matrix W^{2T} to form the 2×1 pre-activation vector $z^2 = W^{2T} a^1$ (in green), which is passed through a pointwise non-linear activation function f to form a 2×1 activation vector $a^2 = f(z^2)$ (in blue). Together, the linear part (in green) and a non-linear part (in blue) constitute the second layer of the network.

the activation vector a^2 of the second layer:

$$a^2 = \begin{pmatrix} f(z_1^2) \\ f(z_2^2) \end{pmatrix} = \begin{pmatrix} a_1^2 \\ a_2^2 \end{pmatrix} \tag{2.10}$$

Finally, the activation vector a^2 of the second layer is multiplied by the weight matrix W^{3T} of the third layer to yield the output y, as shown in Figure 2.8:

$$y = \begin{pmatrix} w_1^3 & w_2^3 \end{pmatrix} \begin{pmatrix} a_1^2 \\ a_2^2 \end{pmatrix} = w_1^3 a_1^2 + w_2^3 a_2^2 \tag{2.11}$$

In this example, the network output is a real value used for regression rather than classification, and therefore the last layer does not consist of a non-linear activation function. Next, various non-linear activation functions are described.

2.3.3   Logistic Regression

As a second example of forward propagation in a general computation graph, we consider simple logistic regression, which is defined when the log-odds of the

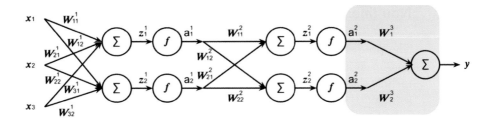

Figure 2.8 Example of forward propagation in a neural network highlighting the third layer of the network. In this example, the network output is a real value used for regression rather than classification and therefore the last layer consists only of multiplication of the 2×1 activations a^2 by a 1×2 weight matrix W^{3^T} to yield a scalar output $y = W^{3^T} a^2$ (in green) and does not include a non-linear activation function.

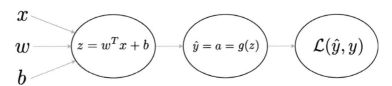

Figure 2.9 Logistic regression computation graph forward propagation.

class is a linear function:

$$f(x) = \log \left(\frac{p(x)}{1 - p(x)} \right) = w^T x \tag{2.12}$$

which yields the sigmoid:

$$p(x) = \frac{1}{1 + e^{-f(x)}} \tag{2.13}$$

which may represent mapping the input to a probability in $(0, 1)$. Therefore, fitting a logistic regression model to data involves computing the likelihood that each example belongs to a class given the weights:

$$g(x, w) = \begin{cases} p(x), & \text{if } x \in C \\ 1 - p(x), & \text{if } x \notin C \end{cases} \tag{2.14}$$

Next, we sum $\sum_i g(x^i, w)$ for all examples $i = 1, \ldots, m$, so that the model over all possible weights w which gives the largest sum is the maximum likelihood model. Stacking logistic regression functions results in a highly non-linear parametric function, which is a neural network.

In our example, the inputs to the graph are the variables x, w, and the bias b if not absorbed into the weights, and the output is $\mathcal{L}(y, f(x, w, b))$ where $a = f(x, w, b) = g(w^T x + b)$ and $\mathcal{L}(y, a) = -y \log a - (1 - y) \log(1 - a)$, as shown in Figure 2.9.

2.4   Non-linear Activation Functions

The pre-activation z of a neural network may be followed by a differentiable non-linear activation function $f : \mathbb{R} \mapsto \mathbb{R}$. Typical non-linear activation functions include the sigmoid, hyperbolic tangent, rectified linear unit (ReLU), Swish, and softmax.

2.4.1   Sigmoid

For a probability $p(x)$ the log-odds is defined by:

$$\log \frac{p(x)}{1 - p(x)} \tag{2.15}$$

For example, for a probability $\frac{1}{2}$ the odds are 50:50 or 1, and the log-odds is 0. For a probability of 0.9, the odds are 90:10 or 9, and the log-odds equal 2.19. A linear classifier is given by:

$$f_w(x) = w^T x \tag{2.16}$$

Setting the log-odds to be a linear classifier:

$$\log \frac{p(x)}{1 - p(x)} = w^T x \tag{2.17}$$

and solving for $p(x)$ results in the sigmoid function. The sigmoid function shown in Figure 2.10 maps the input z to $(0, 1)$ by:

$$f(z) = \frac{1}{1 + e^{-z}} \tag{2.18}$$

The function asymptotes at $\lim_{z \to \infty} f(z) = 1$ and $\lim_{z \to -\infty} f(z) = 0$, and crosses zero at $f(0) = 0.5$. The sigmoid function is commonly used in logistic regression for building a classifier by taking the sigmoid of linear regression.

2.4.2   Hyperbolic Tangent

The hyperbolic tangent function *tanh* shown in Figure 2.11 maps the input z to $(-1, 1)$ by:

$$f(z) = \frac{e^z - e^{-z}}{e^z + e^{-z}} \tag{2.19}$$

The function asymptotes at $\lim_{z \to \infty} f(z) = 1$ and $\lim_{z \to -\infty} f(z) = -1$, and crosses zero at $f(0) = 0$.

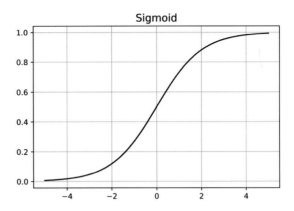

Figure 2.10 Sigmoid function: $f(z) = \frac{1}{1+e^{-z}}$ crosses zero at $f(0) = 0.5$ and asymptotes at $\lim_{z \to \infty} f(z) = 1$ and $\lim_{z \to -\infty} f(z) = 0$.

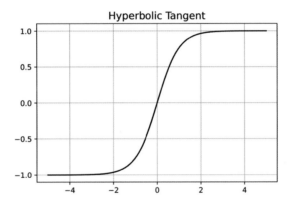

Figure 2.11 Hyperbolic tangent function: $f(z) = \frac{e^z - e^{-z}}{e^z + e^{-z}}$ crosses zero at $f(0) = 0$ and asymptotes at $\lim_{z \to \infty} f(z) = 1$ and $\lim_{z \to -\infty} f(z) = -1$.

2.4.3 Rectified Linear Unit

The ReLU, shown in Figure 2.12, maps negative values to zero:

$$g(z) = z_+ = \max(0, z) \tag{2.20}$$

If g is a ReLU non-linear activation function $\text{ReLU}(x) = \max\{0, x\}$, then f is continuous and piecewise linear in x and the graph of f consists of hyper-planes with folds.

The leaky ReLU shown in Figure 2.13 is defined for $\alpha \geq 0$ by:

$$g(z) = z_+ - \alpha z_- = \max(0, z) - \alpha \max(0, -z) \tag{2.21}$$

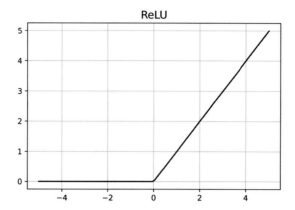

Figure 2.12 Rectified linear unit (ReLU) function.

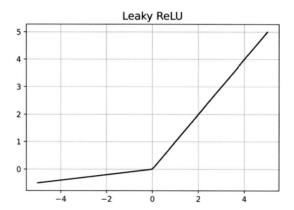

Figure 2.13 Leaky ReLU function.

2.4.4   Swish

The Swish function, shown in Figure 2.14, is a non-linear activation function found by automatically searching the space of activation functions (Ramachandran et al., 2017) for a function with good performance which empirically outperforms the ReLU. It is defined by $f(x) = x\sigma(\beta x)$ where σ is the sigmoid function. As $\lim_{\beta \to \infty} f(x)$ the Swish becomes the ReLU; however, unlike the ReLU, which has a stepwise derivative, the Swish has a smooth derivative for various values of β.

2.4.5   Softmax

For binary classification the labels are $y^i \in \{0,1\}$ for example i. For multiple classes, the labels are $y^i \in \{1, 2, \ldots, k\}$ for example i. The softmax function

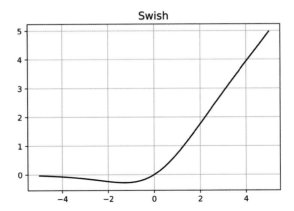

Figure 2.14 Swish function with $\beta = 1$.

extends logistic regression from binary to multi-class classification:

$$f_w(x) = \begin{pmatrix} p(y=1|x;w) \\ \vdots \\ p(y=k|x;w) \end{pmatrix} = \frac{1}{\sum_{c=1}^{k} e^{w_c^T x}} \begin{pmatrix} e^{w_1^T x} \\ \vdots \\ e^{w_k^T x} \end{pmatrix} \tag{2.22}$$

The softmax is a non-linear activation function used in the last layer L for multi-class classification. The softmax function is a generalization of the sigmoid function, from scalars to vectors, mapping a vector $z \in R^k$ to a vector $f(z) \in [0,1]^k$ which sums to 1: $\sum_{c=1}^{k} f(z)_c = 1$, where k is the number of classes. The softmax function for class i is given by:

$$f^L(z^L)_i = \frac{e^{z_i^L}}{\sum_{c=1}^{k} e^{z_c^L}} \tag{2.23}$$

The softmax is used for multi-class classification and computes a probability in $(0,1)$ for each class $c = 1, \ldots, k$, which sum to 1.

2.5 Loss Functions

Compare output $f(x) = \hat{y} = a^L$ with ground truth label y for an input x. For example, consider the probability of an image being an object. Compare all outputs $f(X) = \hat{Y} = A^L$ with all ground truth labels Y for all inputs X. The loss function for a single input example and output label is $\mathcal{L}(y, F(x))$. The average loss over all examples, or cost, is:

$$\frac{1}{m} \sum_{i=1}^{m} \mathcal{L}(y^i, \hat{y}^i) \tag{2.24}$$

Our goal is to minimize the loss function so that the predictions agree with

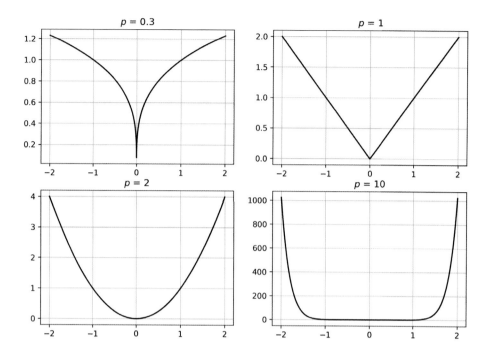

Figure 2.15 Loss functions $|y - a|^p$ for various values of p with $y = 0$.

the ground truth. The loss function space may be highly non-linear as a function space of the network weights. The weights constitute a point in a high-dimensional space, and moving in that space corresponds to changing the classifier and hence the predicted labels.

Given the weights of the network W and forward propagating the inputs x through the network to get the output labels $\hat{y}^i = F(x^i, W)$ our goal is to find weights W such that:

$$\underset{W}{\text{minimize}}\frac{1}{m}\sum_{i=1}^{m}\mathcal{L}(y^i, F(x^i, W)) \tag{2.25}$$

A common regularization term $\mathcal{R}(W)$ may be added to the loss function to prefer simple models and avoid overfitting.

In general, the loss function is not convex with respect to W; therefore, solving Equation 2.25 does not guarantee a global minimum. We therefore use gradient descent to find a local minimum.

Common loss functions are the mean squared error, with $\mathcal{L}(y^i, \hat{y}^i)$ defined by:

$$\mathcal{L}(y^i, \hat{y}^i) = (y^i - \hat{y}^i)^2 \tag{2.26}$$

The loss function $|y - a|^p$ for various values of p with $y = 0$ is shown in Figure 2.15.

The logistic regression loss is defined by:

$$\mathcal{L}(y^i, \hat{y}^i) = -y^i \log(\hat{y}^i) - (1 - y^i) \log(1 - \hat{y}^i) \tag{2.27}$$

which is the special case for binary classification $k = 2$:

$$\mathcal{L}(y^i, \hat{y}^i) = -\sum_{c=1}^{k} I\{y^i = k\} \log p(y = k | x^i, W) \tag{2.28}$$

for k classes, where I is the indicator function such that $I\{\text{true}\} = 1$ and $I\{\text{false}\} = 0$, and $p(y = k | x^i, W)$ is a softmax coefficient. For the special case of logistic regression, the mean squared error is not convex, whereas the logistic regression loss is convex.

2.6 Backpropagation

The goal of backpropagation is to efficiently compute the derivatives of the total loss function with respect to all of the network weights. Backpropagation, also known as automatic reverse differentiation, efficiently computes the gradient of a function F with respect to all of the parameters $\frac{\partial F}{\partial W^\ell}$ for all ℓ.

Once the output x^ℓ of the last layer is computed by forward propagation, the loss between the ground truth labels y and network output is minimized:

$$\underset{W}{\text{minimize}} \mathcal{L}_W(x^\ell, y) \tag{2.29}$$

Denote the application of a single layer of the network by:

$$x^{\ell+1} = f(W^{\ell T} x^\ell) \tag{2.30}$$

Then, differentiating both sides, we get:

$$dx^{\ell+1} = f'^\ell(dW^\ell x^\ell + W^\ell dx^\ell) \tag{2.31}$$

and in vector and matrix form:

$$dx = DdW + Ldx \tag{2.32}$$

where dx is a vector of derivatives, D is a diagonal matrix, L is a lower triangular matrix, and dW is the derivative with respect to the network weights. Solving for dx, we get:

$$(I - L)dx = DdW \tag{2.33}$$

and, therefore:

$$dx = (I - L)^{-1} DdW \tag{2.34}$$

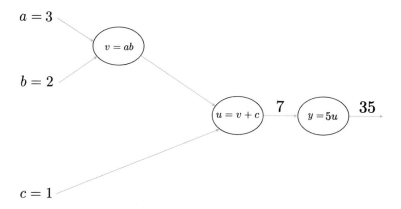

Figure 2.16 Computation graph forward propagation.

2.7   Differentiable Programming

Backpropagation is a special case of differentiable programming (Wengert, 1964; Bellman et al., 1965) for neural networks. Derivatives of variables corresponding to nodes in a computational directed acyclic graph (DAG) can be computed with respect to the output using the chain rule in two opposite directions. Differentiation in a forward pass through the graph using the chain rule results in the partial derivative of the output with respect to a single input variable, whereas differentiation in a backward pass using the chain rule results in the partial derivative of the output with respect to all input variables, namely the gradient, in a single pass. This $O(n)$ factor in computational efficiency is significant in data science, in a similar fashion to the $\log(n)$ factor of the fast Fourier transform to convolution in signal processing and has broad implications. First is the special case of backpropagation in neural networks (Rumelhart et al., 1986), namely computing the gradient of the loss function with respect to the weights in a single backward pass. Perhaps most importantly, any number of complex differentiable functions can be composed into a computational DAG, and optimized using differentiable programming.

2.8   Computation Graph

2.8.1   Example

We begin with a simple toy example illustrating forward and backpropagation using a computation graph. The inputs to the graph shown in Figure 2.16 are three constants $a = 3$, $b = 2$, and $c = 1$. Nodes in the graph denote arithmetic operations. The graph computes the output $f(a, b, c) = y = 5u = 5(v + c) = 5(ab + c) = 35$ by propagating the input forward through the nodes.

Next, we compute the derivatives of the output with respect to each input by

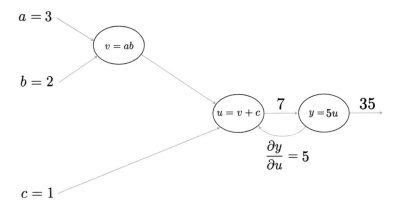

Figure 2.17 Computation graph backward propagation, third layer.

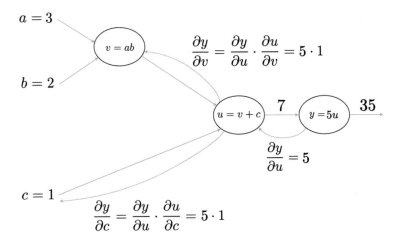

Figure 2.18 Computation graph backward propagation, second layer.

applying the chain rule of differentiations. As shown in Figure 2.17, beginning with $y = 5u$ the derivative with respect to the intermediate value u is $\frac{dy}{du} = 5$.

The derivative of y with respect to intermediate value v is $\frac{dy}{dv} = \frac{dy}{du}\frac{du}{dv} = 5 \times 1 = 5$ and the derivative of y with respect to the input c is $\frac{dy}{dc} = \frac{dy}{du}\frac{du}{dc} = 5 \times 1 = 5$, as shown in Figure 2.18.

Finally, the derivative of y with respect to the inputs a and b are respectively $\frac{dy}{da} = \frac{dy}{dv}\frac{dv}{da} = 5 \times 2 = 10$ and $\frac{dy}{db} = \frac{dy}{dv}\frac{dv}{db} = 5 \times 3 = 15$, as shown in Figure 2.19. Notice that the computation at each node is local. Each node receives an input from the next layer, performs a local computation of its partial derivative, and provides output to the previous layer. This allows us to build complex graphs consisting of many simple local computations. The deep learning frameworks TensorFlow and PyTorch perform such simple local computations on complex graphs.

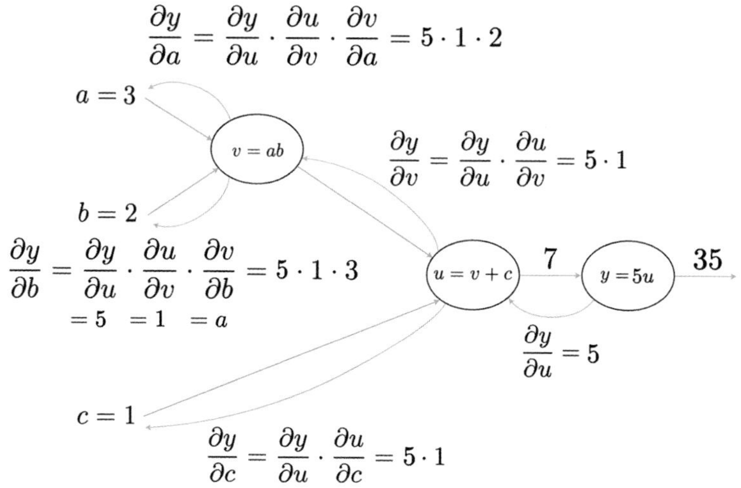

$\frac{\partial y}{\partial a} = \frac{\partial y}{\partial u} \cdot \frac{\partial u}{\partial v} \cdot \frac{\partial v}{\partial a} = 5 \cdot 1 \cdot 2$
$a = 3$
$v = ab$
$\frac{\partial y}{\partial v} = \frac{\partial y}{\partial u} \cdot \frac{\partial u}{\partial v} = 5 \cdot 1$
$b = 2$
$\frac{\partial y}{\partial b} = \frac{\partial y}{\partial u} \cdot \frac{\partial u}{\partial v} \cdot \frac{\partial v}{\partial b} = 5 \cdot 1 \cdot 3$
$= 5 \quad = 1 \quad = a$
$u = v + c$
7
$y = 5u$
35
$\frac{\partial y}{\partial u} = 5$
$c = 1$
$\frac{\partial y}{\partial c} = \frac{\partial y}{\partial u} \cdot \frac{\partial u}{\partial c} = 5 \cdot 1$

Figure 2.19 Computation graph backward propagation, first layer.

x
w
b
$z = w^T x + b$
$\hat{y} = a = g(z)$
$\mathcal{L}(\hat{y}, y)$
$\frac{\partial L}{\partial a}$

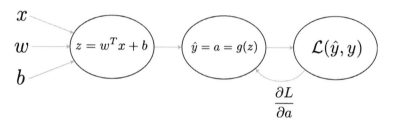

Figure 2.20 Logistic regression computation graph backpropagation, third layer.

2.8.2 Logistic Regression

As a second example, we consider backpropagation in logistic regression. We first compute the derivative of the loss with respect to the predicted output $\frac{d\mathcal{L}}{da}$, as shown in Figure 2.20.

Next we compute the derivative of the loss with respect to z such that $\frac{d\mathcal{L}}{dz} = \frac{d\mathcal{L}}{da}\frac{da}{dz}$, as shown in Figure 2.21.

Finally, we compute the derivative of the loss with respect to the weights w

x
w
b
$z = w^T x + b$
$\hat{y} = a = g(z)$
$\mathcal{L}(\hat{y}, y)$
$\frac{\partial L}{\partial z} = \frac{\partial L}{\partial a} \cdot \frac{\partial a}{\partial z}$
$\frac{\partial L}{\partial a}$

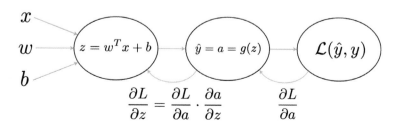

Figure 2.21 Logistic regression computation graph backpropagation, second layer.

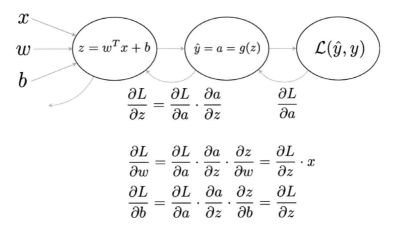

Figure 2.22 Logistic regression computation graph backpropagation.

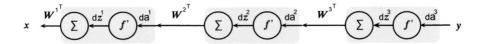

Figure 2.23 Backpropagation.

such that $\frac{d\mathcal{L}}{dw} = \frac{d\mathcal{L}}{dz}\frac{dz}{dw}$ and $\frac{d\mathcal{L}}{db} = \frac{d\mathcal{L}}{dz}\frac{dz}{db}$, as shown in Figure 2.22, all by applying the chain rule. Plugging in the derivative $\frac{d\mathcal{L}}{da} = -\frac{y}{a} + \frac{1-y}{1-a}$, and setting $a = g(z) = \frac{1}{1+e^{-z}}$ to be the sigmoid function, we plug in the local value $\frac{da}{dz} = \frac{e^z}{(1+e^z)^z} = g(z)(1-g(z))$ and reach the derivatives of the output with respect to each of the input variables.

2.8.3 Forward and Backpropagation

In a neural network, forward propagation maps the activations from layer $\ell - 1$ forward to layer ℓ by matrix multiplications followed by an elementwise non-linear activation function. The forward mapping from $A^{\ell-1} \to A^\ell$ is given by:

$$Z^\ell = W^{\ell T} A^{\ell-1} \tag{2.35a}$$

$$A^\ell = f^\ell(Z^\ell) \tag{2.35b}$$

which means that each activation layer A^ℓ is a function $F(A^{\ell-1}, W^{\ell T})$ of the previous activation layer $A^{\ell-1}$ and a weight matrix W^ℓ, as shown in Figure 2.3.

Backpropagation maps the derivatives from layer ℓ back to layer $\ell - 1$ with respect to both activations and weights, as shown in Figure 2.23.

Given $\frac{\partial \mathcal{L}}{\partial A^\ell}$, our goal is to compute the partial derivative of the loss with respect to the previous layer's activations $\frac{\partial \mathcal{L}}{\partial A^{\ell-1}}$ and with respect to the weights $\frac{\partial \mathcal{L}}{\partial W^\ell}$.

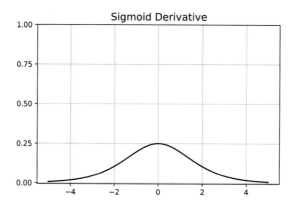

Figure 2.24 Sigmoid derivative.

Using $\frac{\partial \mathcal{L}}{\partial A^\ell}$ and $\frac{\partial \mathcal{L}}{\partial Z^\ell}$, the backward mapping from $\frac{\partial \mathcal{L}}{\partial A^\ell} \rightarrow \frac{\partial \mathcal{L}}{\partial A^{\ell-1}}$ is given by:

$$\frac{\partial \mathcal{L}}{\partial Z^\ell} = \frac{\partial \mathcal{L}}{\partial A^\ell} \times f'^\ell(Z^\ell) \tag{2.36a}$$

$$\frac{\partial \mathcal{L}}{\partial A^{\ell-1}} = (W^\ell)^T \frac{\partial \mathcal{L}}{\partial Z^\ell} \tag{2.36b}$$

which follows from the chain rule for differentiation:

$$\frac{\partial \mathcal{L}}{\partial Z^\ell} = \frac{\partial \mathcal{L}}{\partial A^\ell} \frac{\partial A^\ell}{\partial Z^\ell} \tag{2.37}$$

and

$$\frac{\partial \mathcal{L}}{\partial A^{\ell-1}} = \frac{\partial \mathcal{L}}{\partial Z^\ell} \frac{\partial Z^\ell}{\partial A^{\ell-1}} \tag{2.38}$$

Next, we differentiate the loss with respect to the weights. Since $A^\ell = F(A^{\ell-1}) = f^\ell(Z^\ell) = f^\ell(W^{\ell T} A^{\ell-1})$, therefore by the chain rule we have:

$$\frac{\partial \mathcal{L}}{\partial W^\ell} = \frac{\partial \mathcal{L}}{\partial A^\ell} \frac{\partial F(A^{\ell-1})}{\partial W^\ell} = \frac{\partial \mathcal{L}}{\partial A^\ell} \frac{\partial f^\ell(W^{\ell T} A^{\ell-1})}{\partial W^\ell} = \frac{\partial \mathcal{L}}{\partial A^\ell} f'^\ell(A^{\ell-1})^T \tag{2.39}$$

Finally, the weights W^ℓ are updated using $\frac{\partial \mathcal{L}}{\partial W^\ell}$ by:

$$W^\ell = W^\ell - \alpha \frac{\partial \mathcal{L}}{\partial W^l} \tag{2.40}$$

2.9   Derivative of Non-linear Activation Functions

The derivative of the sigmoid function is:

$$f'(z) = \frac{e^z}{(1 + e^z)^2} = f(z)(1 - f(z)) \tag{2.41}$$

as shown in Figure 2.24. The sigmoid derivative is computed efficiently by using the sigmoid itself.

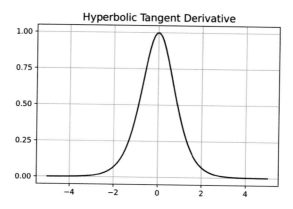

Figure 2.25 Hyperbolic tangent derivative.

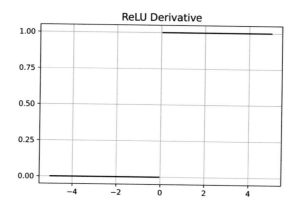

Figure 2.26 Rectified linear unit (ReLU) derivative.

The derivative of the hyperbolic tangent function is:

$$f'(z) = \frac{4}{(e^{-z} + e^{z})^2} = 1 - f(z)^2 \tag{2.42}$$

as shown in Figure 2.25. The hyperbolic tangent derivative is computed efficiently using the hyperbolic tangent function.

The derivative of the ReLU is defined for $z \neq 0$:

$$f'(z) = \begin{cases} 0, & \text{if } z < 0 \\ 1, & \text{if } z > 0 \end{cases} \tag{2.43}$$

as shown in Figure 2.26. The derivative of the ReLU is not defined at zero, though for practical purposes, machine floating-point numbers may not be exactly zero. If they are, we add a tiny offset to define the derivative. The derivative of the ReLU is either 0 or 1, which is significantly simpler than the derivatives of the sigmoid and tanh activation functions.

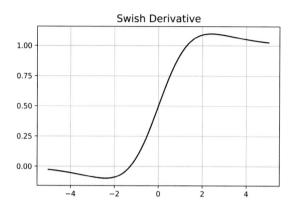

Figure 2.27 Swish derivative for $\beta = 1$.

Similarly, the derivative of the leaky ReLU is defined for $\alpha \geq 0$ and $z \neq 0$ by:

$$f'(z) = \begin{cases} \alpha, & \text{if } z < 0 \\ 1, & \text{if } z > 0 \end{cases} \tag{2.44}$$

While similar to the ReLU, the Swish function (Ramachandran et al., 2017) has the advantage that its derivative is well defined and smooth:

$$f'(z) = \sigma(\beta z) + \beta z \sigma(1 - \sigma(\beta z)) \tag{2.45}$$

as shown in Figure 2.27.

2.10   Backpropagation Algorithm

Given an input example and a ground-truth label, we perform the following three steps iteratively:

1. Forward propagation: Forward propagate the activations through all layers from input to output, reaching a prediction.
2. Compute loss function: Compute the error between the prediction and ground truth.
3. Backpropagation: Use the chain rule for differentiation for backpropagating the gradients through the layers in the opposite direction from the output to the input.
4. Update the weights.

Algorithm 2.2 provides pseudocode for training a neural network using stochastic gradient descent (SGD) using forward and backpropagation.

Algorithm 2.2 Training a neural network by SGD using forward and backpropagation.

---

for $i = 1, \ldots, n$ do
    randomly sample an input–label pair $(x = a_0, y)$
    for each layer $\ell = 1, \ldots, L$ do:
        $z^\ell = W^\ell a^{\ell-1}$
        $a^\ell = f^\ell(z^\ell)$
    for each layer $\ell = L, \ldots, 1$ do:
        $\frac{\partial \mathcal{L}(y, F(x,W))}{\partial z^\ell} = \frac{\partial \mathcal{L}(y, F(x,W))}{\partial a^\ell} \times f'^\ell(z^\ell)$
        $\frac{\partial \mathcal{L}(y, F(x,W))}{\partial W^\ell} = \frac{\partial \mathcal{L}(y, F(x,W))}{\partial z^\ell} a^{\ell-1}$
        $W^\ell = W^\ell - \alpha \frac{\partial \mathcal{L}}{\partial W^\ell}$

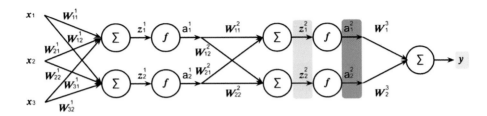

Figure 2.28 Backpropagation example: third layer.

2.10.1 Example

As an example of backpropagation, consider the neural network shown in Figure 2.4 with sigmoid non-linear activation functions in the first and second layers, $f^1 = f^2 = \sigma$. First, as shown in Figure 2.28, the derivative of the output $y = w_1^3 a_1^2 + w_2^3 a_2^2$ is computed with respect to z_1^2:

$$\frac{\partial y}{\partial z_1^2} = w_1^3 \frac{\partial a_1^2}{\partial z_1^2} = w_1^3 \sigma(z_1^2)(1 - \sigma(z_1^2)) = w_1^3 a_1^2 (1 - a_1^2) \tag{2.46}$$

and z_2^2, such that the derivative of the output y with respect to z^2 is:

$$\frac{\partial y}{\partial z^2} = \frac{\partial y}{\partial a^2} \frac{\partial a^2}{\partial z^2} = \begin{pmatrix} w_1^3 a_1^2 (1 - a_1^2) \\ w_2^3 a_2^2 (1 - a_2^2) \end{pmatrix} \tag{2.47}$$

Next, as shown in Figure 2.29, the derivative of the output y with respect to z^1 is computed by using the value $\frac{\partial y}{\partial z^2}$ of the derivative of the output y with respect to z^2, which was previously computed, and the chain rule:

$$\frac{\partial y}{\partial z^1} = \frac{\partial y}{\partial z^2} \frac{\partial z^2}{\partial z^1} = \frac{\partial y}{\partial z^2} \frac{\partial z^2}{\partial a^1} \frac{\partial a^1}{\partial z^1} = \begin{pmatrix} w_{11}^2 & w_{12}^2 \\ w_{21}^2 & w_{22}^2 \end{pmatrix} \frac{\partial y}{\partial z^2} a^1 (1 - a^1) \tag{2.48}$$

Finally, as shown in Figure 2.30, the derivative of the output y is computed with respect to each of the weight matrix coefficients of the first layer by using

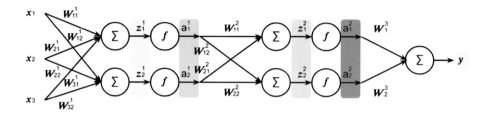

Figure 2.29 Backpropagation example: second layer.

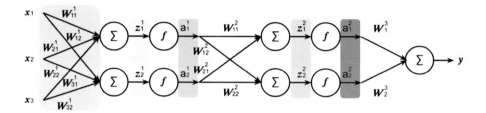

Figure 2.30 Backpropagation example: first layer.

the value $\frac{\partial y}{\partial z^1}$ of the derivative of the output y with respect to z^1, which was previously computed:

$$\frac{\partial y}{\partial w_{11}^1} = \frac{\partial y}{\partial z^1}\frac{\partial z^1}{\partial w_{11}^1} = \frac{\partial y}{\partial z^1}\begin{pmatrix} x_1 \\ 0 \end{pmatrix} \tag{2.49}$$

In a single backward pass, the derivatives of the output y with respect to each of the network weights are computed efficiently by a series of local computations using the chain rule for differentiation.

2.11   Chain Rule for Differentiation

We define the chain rule for differentiation for two and three functions in one dimension and two functions in higher dimensions.

2.11.1   Two Functions in One Dimension

First, consider the simple case of the derivative of the composition of two functions in one dimension:

$$(f \circ g)' = (f' \circ g)g' \tag{2.50}$$

which is:

$$f(g(x))' = f'(g(x))g'(x) \tag{2.51}$$

Therefore, for $y = g(x)$ and $z = f(y) = f(g(x))$ we get:

$$\frac{dz}{dx} = \frac{dz}{dy}\frac{dy}{dx} = f'(y)g'(x) = f'(g(x))g'(x) \qquad (2.52)$$

2.11.2 Three Functions in One Dimension

Next, consider the case of the derivative of the composition of three functions in one dimension:

$$(f \circ g \circ h)' \qquad (2.53)$$

which is:

$$f(g(h(x)))' = f'(g(h(x)))g(h(x))' = f'(g(h(x)))g'(h(x))h'(x) \qquad (2.54)$$

Let $y = f(u)$ and $u = g(v)$ and $v = h(x)$; then we get:

$$\frac{dy}{dx} = \frac{dy}{du}\frac{du}{dv}\frac{dv}{dx} \qquad (2.55)$$

2.11.3 Two Functions in Higher Dimensions

Let $f : \mathbb{R}^m \to \mathbb{R}^k$ and $g : \mathbb{R}^n \to \mathbb{R}^m$. Let $z = f(y)$ and $y = g(x)$. Then $z = f(g(x))$ maps the $n \times 1$ vector x to the $k \times 1$ vector z through the $m \times 1$ vector y.

For $f : \mathbb{R}^n \to \mathbb{R}^m$ and $y = f(x)$ mapping an $n \times 1$ vector x to an $m \times 1$ vector y, for example by multiplying by A, is an $m \times n$ matrix such that $y = Ax$. Define the Jacobian matrix as:

$$J_f = \begin{bmatrix} \frac{\partial f}{\partial x_1} & \cdots & \frac{\partial f}{\partial x_n} \end{bmatrix} = \begin{bmatrix} \frac{\partial f_1}{\partial x_1} & \cdots & \frac{\partial f_1}{\partial x_n} \\ \vdots & \ddots & \vdots \\ \frac{\partial f_m}{\partial x_1} & \cdots & \frac{\partial f_m}{\partial x_n} \end{bmatrix} \qquad (2.56)$$

and $J_{ij} = \frac{\partial f_i}{\partial x_j}$.

For example, for the function:

$$y = \begin{bmatrix} y_1 \\ y_2 \end{bmatrix} = \begin{bmatrix} f_1(x_1, x_2) \\ f_2(x_1, x_2) \end{bmatrix} = \begin{bmatrix} x_1^2 x_2 \\ 5x_1 + \sin(x_2) = f(x_1, x_2) \end{bmatrix} \qquad (2.57)$$

The Jacobian is:

$$J_f = \begin{bmatrix} 2x_1 x_2 & x_1^2 \\ 5 & \cos(x_2) = f(x_1, x_2) \end{bmatrix} \qquad (2.58)$$

and in the general case, in a similar fashion to the chain rule in one dimension in Equation 2.50, the chain rule in higher dimensions is:

$$J_{f \circ g}(x) = J_f(g(x))J_g(x) \qquad (2.59)$$

For $z = f(y) = (f_1(y), \ldots, f_k(y))$ and $y = g(x) = (g_1(x), \ldots, g_m(x))$ applying the chain rule we get:

$$\frac{\partial(z_1, \ldots, z_k)}{\partial(x_1, \ldots, x_n)} = \frac{\partial(z_1, \ldots, z_k)}{\partial(y_1, \ldots, y_m)} \frac{\partial(y_1, \ldots, y_m)}{\partial(x_1, \ldots, x_n)} \tag{2.60}$$

which is Equation 2.52 in higher dimensions.

Storing and computing the Jacobian of large matrices in neural networks is very inefficient. Therefore, we use the expressions derived in Equations 2.36 and 2.39.

2.12   Gradient of Loss Function

For a neural network, given a single training example, consider the loss function $\mathcal{L}(y, F(x, W))$. Writing $\partial\mathcal{L} = \partial\mathcal{L}(y, F(x, W))$ then by the chain rule of differentiation for the output $\mathcal{L}$ we get:

$$\delta^{\mathcal{L}} = \frac{\partial\mathcal{L}(y, F(x, W))}{\partial z^L} = \frac{\partial\mathcal{L}(y, F(x, W))}{\partial a^L} \times f'^L(z^L) \tag{2.61}$$

and for a squared error loss:

$$\mathcal{L}(y, F(x, W)) = \frac{1}{2}\|y - F(x, W)\|_2^2 \tag{2.62}$$

where the derivative in Equation 2.61 is $\delta^L = -(y - a^L) \times f'^L(z^L)$.

2.13   Gradient Descent

A practical method for minimizing the loss function is gradient descent. Gradient descent iteratively finds a local minimum by taking steps in the direction of the steepest descent, as shown in Algorithm 2.3. It does not guarantee to find a global minimum, and two different starting points may result in two different local minima. Local minimum points are rare in high dimensions since they require that the partial derivatives in all dimensions be zero. Therefore, having saddle points or plateaus in high dimensions is more common than a local minimum.

Algorithm 2.3 Gradient descent.

---

given a starting point $x \in \mathrm{dom} f$
repeat:
    determine descent direction $-\nabla f(x)$
    choose scalar α
    update $x := x - \alpha\nabla f(x)$
until stopping criterion is satisfied

Given m training examples, the gradient of the loss function with respect to the weights is given by:

$$\frac{\partial \mathcal{L}}{\partial W^\ell} = \frac{1}{m} \sum_{i=1}^{m} \frac{\partial \mathcal{L}(y^i, F(x^i, W))}{\partial W^\ell} \qquad (2.63)$$

The gradient descent update is then given by $W^\ell := W^\ell - \alpha \frac{\partial \mathcal{L}}{\partial W^\ell}$ for layers $\ell = 1, \ldots, L-1$.

2.14 Initialization and Normalization

Given input x, a standard practice is to normalize the data to the standard score by $x = \frac{x-\mu}{\sigma}$ where $\mu = \frac{1}{n} \sum_{i=1}^{n} x_i$ is the mean and $\sigma^2 = \frac{1}{n} \sum_{i=1}^{n} (x_i - \mu)^2$ is the variance. Input normalization improves the convergence of gradient descent, turning narrow ravines in the loss function into even level sets. In a similar fashion, batch normalization (Ioffe and Szegedy, 2015) normalizes each batch of input for each layer of the network, making the optimization landscape smoother (Santurkar et al., 2018).

Gradient descent methods require an initial value for the weights; however, since the layers are symmetric with respect to the weights into each activation we cannot initialize to zero. Therefore, a common practice is to initialize the weights to small random values by using a normal distribution $\frac{N(0,1)}{\sqrt{(n)}}$, where n is the number of connections into an activation unit. Another common initialization is a normal distribution with zero mean and variance $\sigma^2 = 2/(n_{l-1} + n_l)$, where n_{l-1} and n_l are the number of activation units in the previous and current layers of the weights (Glorot and Bengio, 2010).

2.15 Software Libraries and Platforms

The most notable and commonly used deep learning platforms are the open-source libraries PyTorch (Paszke et al., 2017) from Facebook and TensorFlow (Abadi et al., 2016) from Google. Both libraries implement automatic differentiation on general computation graphs. Keras (Chollet, 2015) is a high-level API based on TensorFlow that allows rapid prototyping.

2.16 Summary

This chapter presents forward and backpropagation in neural networks using linear algebra, calculus, and algorithms. Multiple examples illustrate the algorithms and provide the backpropagation derivations using the chain rule in reverse mode differentiation. Key advantages of backpropagation are:

- Efficiency: It allows computing derivatives of the total loss function with respect to all network weights in linear time in a single backward pass.
- Extendable: Backpropagation in neural networks is a special case of differentiable programming and extends to a general computation graph with nodes representing differentiable functions.
- Gradient-based learning: Backpropagation minimizes a total loss function by updating the neural network parameters based on the gradients of the total loss with respect to each of the parameters. Stochastic gradient descent, described in the next chapter, is key in neural network optimization.

3 Optimization

3.1 Introduction

Why have a basic understanding of the optimization under the hood of deep learning? A key reason is that different algorithms perform differently, and understanding their performance is important in practice.

An optimization goal when training neural networks is to minimize the loss function. The loss function measures the error between the output of the network, such as predictions, and target values, such as ground-truth values. The optimization problem is that of finding the minimum of a function:

$$\underset{x \in \mathcal{X}}{\text{minimize}} f(x) \qquad (3.1)$$

for x in a feasible set $\mathcal{X}$. The point $x^\star = \underset{x}{\text{argmin}} f(x)$ is a local minimum of the function if there exists $\delta > 0$ such that $f(x^\star) \leq f(x)$ for all x where $\|x^\star - x\| \leq \delta$. In the case of neural networks, f may be the loss function and x the parameters of the network, and the optimization goal is to find the parameter values x^* that minimize the loss $f(x)$.

The optimization problem for neural networks is usually solved using gradient descent, an iterative method for finding a local minimum of a function. It starts with an initial point and, at each iteration, updates the parameter values in the direction of the negative gradient. Gradient descent converges to a local minimum of the loss function if the learning rate is small enough. The gradient descent algorithm may be implemented using backpropagation, which is an efficient way to compute the gradient of a loss function with respect to the parameters of a neural network.

3.2 Overview

3.2.1 Optimization Problem Classes

Optimization methods may be coarsely divided into two important classes: convex and non-convex optimization problems, as shown in Figure 3.1. Convex optimization problems are a tiny subset of non-convex problems (and may, in turn, be finely classified into linear programs, quadratic programs, second-order cone pro-

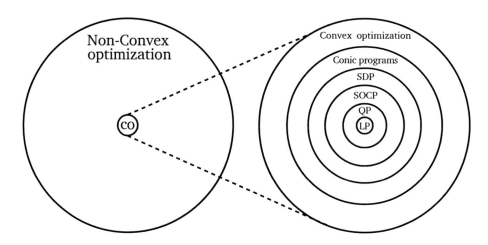

Figure 3.1 Optimization problem classes.

grams, semidefinite programs, and conic programs, each subsuming the other). A set S is convex if for any points $x, y \in S$ the line that connects them is in the set $\alpha x + (1 - \alpha)y \in S$ for all $\alpha \in (0, 1)$. A function f is convex if the set of points above the function graph is convex: $f(\alpha x + (1 - \alpha)y) \leq \alpha f(x) + (1 - \alpha)f(y)$. The maximum of convex functions is convex, and a convex function is the maximum of its tangent functions. A convex optimization problem is defined for a convex function over a convex set. Perhaps most importantly, the set of points that are a minimum of a convex problem is convex, which means that any local minimum is a global minimum. Unfortunately, training neural networks involves optimizing non-convex optimization problems, so a local minimum will, in general, not be a global minimum.

The most common non-convex optimization methods are gradient descent and quasi-Newton methods. Gradient descent is a method for minimizing a function f by taking steps proportional to the negative of the gradient of f. The gradient descent algorithm proceeds by iteratively updating the variables in proportion to their partial derivatives with respect to the objective function. This algorithm converges to a local minimum, but it may converge slowly or not if the function is not convex.

Quasi-Newton methods are a family of algorithms that use Newton's method to approximate the gradient descent algorithm. Newton's method is an iterative procedure for finding the roots of a function by computing successive approximations. The quasi-Newton methods use a Taylor expansion to approximate the derivative of f at a given point. The algorithm then uses this approximation to compute the next step in the gradient descent algorithm. This approach converges much faster than gradient descent, but it does not guarantee that the algorithm will converge to a global minimum.

3.2.2 Optimization Solution Methods

In this chapter, we will review three types of optimization solution methods for non-convex optimization problems, based on the degree of derivatives they use:

- First-order methods depend on first derivatives, including gradient descent, which is the most simple and commonly used. Gradient descent is a first-order method and the simplest optimization method. It is based on the gradient of the cost function, which is calculated by taking partial derivatives of the cost function with respect to all of the weights and biases in the network. The gradient descent algorithm starts with an initial guess for all of the weights and biases in the network. Then it iteratively updates these values by moving in a direction that reduces error. We compute a gradient vector in each iteration, which points in a direction that reduces error. We then move a small step in that direction and repeat until we have moved far enough to reduce error significantly.

- Second-order methods depend on first derivatives and their rate of change. These include Newton's method (which is impractical for directly optimizing neural networks) and quasi-Newton methods (practical for optimizing neural networks). These methods have faster convergence than first-order methods but, even so, are less frequently used. Quasi-Newton methods are based on approximating the Hessian matrix of the function to be optimized. The Hessian matrix is a square matrix of second derivatives, and it is costly to compute directly. Quasi-Newton methods approximate the Hessian using a diagonal approximation or an approximation that only depends on first derivatives. The most common quasi-Newton method used for neural network optimization is Broyden–Fletcher–Goldfarb–Shanno (BFGS).

- Evolution strategies: Instead of optimizing an individual point toward a local minimum, evolution strategies consider multiple points sampled from a probability distribution, which progress as a group toward the minimum. The algorithm is a variant of the genetic algorithm, with the main difference being that instead of using a population of individuals, it uses a population of points. The points are generated from a probability distribution over the search space. The probability distribution is updated during the optimization process, and each point is evaluated for its fitness. The points are then sorted by fitness and used to form a new population for the next iteration.

3.2.3 Derivatives and Gradients

The derivative $f'(x)$ of a univariate function f at x is the rate of change of the function at x:

$$f'(x) = \frac{df(x)}{dx} \tag{3.2}$$

which is the slope of the tangent line to the function at x. The second derivative is the rate of change of the first derivative. The second derivative at x is defined

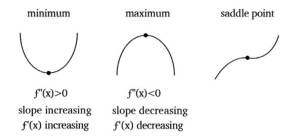

Figure 3.2 Extreme points of a function where the derivative is zero.

by:

$$f''(x) = \frac{df'(x)}{dx} = \frac{d^2 f}{dx^2} \tag{3.3}$$

A univariate function f for which the first derivative $f'(x) = 0$ can be classified as one of the three types of extreme points, as shown in Figure 3.2: (1) a point $x^\star$ is a local minimum if the first derivative is zero $f'(x) = 0$ and the second derivative is positive $f''(x) > 0$; (2) a point $x^\star$ is a local maximum if the first derivative is zero $f'(x) = 0$ and the second derivative is negative $f''(x) < 0$; (3) a point $x^\star$ is a saddle-point if the first and second derivatives are zero $f'(x) = 0$ and $f''(x) = 0$. The gradient $\nabla f(x)$ of a multivariate function $f(x_1, \ldots, x_n)$ is the vector in which each component is the partial derivative of f with respect to that component:

$$\nabla f(x) = \left(\frac{\partial f(x)}{\partial x_1}, \ldots, \frac{\partial f(x)}{\partial x_n} \right) \tag{3.4}$$

The Hessian $\nabla^2 f(x)$ of a multivariate function f is the matrix of the second partial derivatives of the function:

$$\nabla^2 f(x) = \begin{bmatrix} \frac{\partial^2 f(x)}{\partial x_1 \partial x_1} & \cdots & \frac{\partial^2 f(x)}{\partial x_1 \partial x_n} \\ \vdots & \ddots & \vdots \\ \frac{\partial^2 f(x)}{\partial x_n \partial x_1} & \cdots & \frac{\partial^2 f(x)}{\partial x_n \partial x_n} \end{bmatrix} \tag{3.5}$$

Similar to the univariate function, for a multivariate function the point $x^\star$ is a local minimum if the gradient of the function is zero $\nabla f(x) = 0$ and the Hessian $\nabla^2 f(x)$ is positive definite.

3.2.4   Gradient Computation

The derivative of a function can be computed numerically or analytically. When it is available, the analytic derivation is exact and fast, whereas the numerical computation is approximate and slow. We, therefore, derive the analytic gradient for training neural networks and use the numerical gradient computation only for checking our implementation. There are several numerical finite difference approximations of the derivative, the most common being the forward difference:

$$f'(x) \approx \frac{f(x + \varepsilon) - f(x)}{\varepsilon} \tag{3.6}$$

backward difference:

$$f'(x) \approx \frac{f(x) - f(x - \varepsilon)}{\varepsilon} \tag{3.7}$$

and (two-sided) central difference, which is their average:

$$f'(x) \approx \frac{f(x + \varepsilon) - f(x - \varepsilon)}{2\varepsilon} \tag{3.8}$$

Compared with the analytic derivation, the numeric approximation using the central difference is helpful for debugging purposes when training a neural network. In practice, we replace $J(\theta, x)$ with the loss of the neural network and compute its derivative.

3.3 First-Order Methods

First-order methods use the gradient $g_t = \nabla f(x_t)$ to direct the search towards a local minimum. We begin with gradient descent, in which we follow the direction of the steepest descent.

3.3.1 Gradient Descent

Gradient descent minimizes a function based on iterative steps in the direction of steepest descent, which is the opposite direction of the gradient, as shown in Algorithm 3.1.

Algorithm 3.1 Gradient descent.

---
given objective function $f(x)$
given starting point $x_1 \in \mathbf{dom} f$
given learning rate α
while not converged **do**:
    $g_t = \nabla f(x_t)$ gradient
    $x_{t+1} = x_t - \alpha g_t$ update

At every descent step, we compute the function's gradient and update the value x in the negative direction scaled by the learning rate α. So long as the gradient is not zero, this improves for a smooth function and a sufficiently small step size. Gradient descent terminates once a stopping criterion is met. The stopping criteria may be set to a fixed number of iterations, or once the change in the function values between successive iterations $f(x_{t+1}) - f(x_t)$ is smaller than either a constant threshold $s = \varepsilon$ or threshold which depends on the function magnitude $s = \varepsilon \|f(x_t)\|$, or once the gradient magnitude is smaller than a threshold $\|g_t\| < s$.

Our primary choices in gradient descent methods are determining the descent direction based on past gradients and choosing the step size. Gradient descent is a simple and basic optimization algorithm most commonly used to train machine learning models, specifically neural networks.

Consider the special case of applying gradient descent to logistic regression. The objective function is:

$$\mathcal{J} = \frac{1}{n} \sum_{i=1}^{n} \mathcal{L}(\hat{y}^i, y^i) + \frac{\lambda}{2} \|w\|^2 \tag{3.9}$$

where $\hat{y}^i = \sigma(w^T x^i + b)$ is the sigmoid of the dot product between the parameter vector w^T and the input point x^i plus the bias term b. Using the negative log likelihood loss:

$$\mathcal{L}(\hat{y}^i, y^i) = -y^i \log(\hat{y}^i) - (1 - y^i) \log(1 - \hat{y}^i) \tag{3.10}$$

the gradient of the optimization objective with respect to the weight vector w is:

$$\frac{\partial \mathcal{J}}{\partial w} = \frac{1}{n} \sum_{i=1}^{n} (\hat{y}^i - y^i) x^i + \lambda w \tag{3.11}$$

and the gradient of the optimization objective with respect to the bias b is:

$$\frac{\partial \mathcal{J}}{\partial b} = \frac{1}{n} \sum_{i=1}^{n} (\hat{y}^i - y^i) \tag{3.12}$$

We can then use gradient descent to find the optimal parameters.

When optimizing neural networks, the algorithm minimizes the total loss function $f(x) = \mathcal{L}(x)$ based on a step in the direction of steepest descent:

$$x_{t+1} = x_t - \alpha_t \nabla \mathcal{L}(x) \tag{3.13}$$

In neural networks the total loss function is the sum of errors in classifying each of the training examples. Examples of loss functions are the square loss:

$$\mathcal{L}(x) = \frac{1}{m} \sum_{i=1}^{m} \|f(x, a^i) - y^i\|^2 \tag{3.14}$$

for weights x, examples a^i, and ground-truth labels y^i; the hinge loss function is:

$$\mathcal{L}(x) = \frac{1}{m} \sum_{i=1}^{m} \max(0, 1 - tf(x)) \tag{3.15}$$

where $t = 1$ or $t = -1$ for classification, and the cross-entropy loss is:

$$\mathcal{L}(x) = -\frac{1}{m} \sum_{i=1}^{m} y^i \log(\hat{y}^i) + (1 - y^i) \log(1 - \hat{y}^i) \tag{3.16}$$

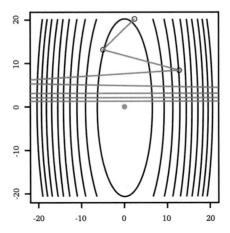

Figure 3.3 When the step size is too big, gradient descent may diverge and never converge.

where $\hat{y}$ is the prediction.

There are two main computational problems with the gradient descent algorithm applied to optimizing deep neural networks. The first problem is that the total loss function $\mathcal{L}(x)$ with respect to the neural network weights x is the sum of many individual losses $\mathcal{L}(x, a^i)$, one for each training example a^i:

$$\mathcal{L}(x) = \frac{1}{m} \sum_{i=1}^{m} \mathcal{L}(x, a^i) \tag{3.17}$$

and therefore computing the gradient with respect to the total loss is computationally expensive. The problem is solved by using only a mini-batch of samples at each step or random samples, also known as stochastic gradient descent (SGD), which we will discuss further. The second problem is computing the derivative of the total loss with respect to all network weights x, as there are many weights. The backpropagation algorithm solves this second problem.

3.3.2 Step Size

Having computed or approximated the gradient of the function f at x, our next task is to choose the learning rate α for updating x. Notice that the step size $\alpha\|g_t\|$ is the product of the learning rate α and the gradient vector length $\|g_t\|$. If the step size is too big, then the optimization may never converge, as shown in Figure 3.3. On the other hand, if the step size is too small, convergence may be very slow, as shown in Figure 3.4. When the step size is just right, gradient descent converges nicely to a local minimum in a relatively short time, as shown in Figure 3.5.

The learning rate α is an important hyperparameter in training neural networks and may control how quickly the model learns. The learning rate may

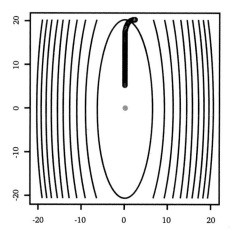

Figure 3.4 When the step size is too small, gradient descent convergence may be slow.

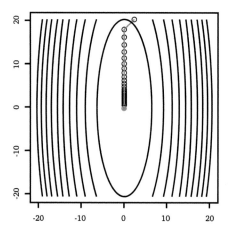

Figure 3.5 When the step size is just right, gradient descent converges nicely to a local minimum.

be manually set to a small constant in most cases. However, we may want to decrease the learning rate as training progresses to prevent overfitting for a vast dataset or training on a GPU. This can be done by reducing the learning rate by constant amounts or by using an adaptive learning rate schedule, decreasing the learning rate by a decay factor as a function of iteration t:

$$\alpha_t = \alpha_1 \frac{1}{1 + t\beta} \tag{3.18}$$

for β close to 0; or by exponential decay setting

$$\alpha_t = \alpha_1 \gamma^t \tag{3.19}$$

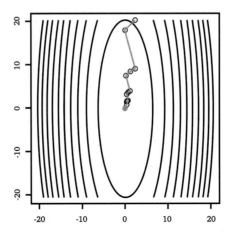

Figure 3.6 Gradient descent convergence path using a backtracking line search step size.

for γ close to 1; or by setting

$$\alpha_t = \alpha_1 \exp^{-\beta t} \qquad (3.20)$$

Backtrack line search: A simple and practical algorithm for computing an adaptive step size is the backtrack line search algorithm. The algorithm continuously halves α until a criterion is met, such as decreasing the value of the function:

$$f(x_{t+1}) \leq f(x_t) + \beta \alpha g_t \qquad (3.21)$$

for $\beta \in [0, 1]$. The result of backtrack line search is shown in Figure 3.6.

Exact line search: An alternative is to optimize for the best step size along the negative gradient direction $d_t = -\frac{g_t}{\|g_t\|}$:

$$\underset{\alpha}{\text{minimize}} f(x_t + \alpha d_t) \qquad (3.22)$$

Computing the derivatives of this optimization function may be performed by setting the derivative to zero:

$$\nabla f(x_t + \alpha d_t)^T d_t = 0 \qquad (3.23)$$

where $\nabla_{d_t} f(x_t) = \nabla f(x_t)^T d_t$. Since $d_{t+1} = -\frac{g_{t+1}}{\|g_{t+1}\|}$ and the next gradient is $g_{t+1} = \nabla f(x_t + \alpha d_t)$ we get:

$$d_{t+1} = -\frac{\nabla f(x_t + \alpha d_t)}{\|\nabla f(x_t + \alpha d_t)\|} \qquad (3.24)$$

and therefore $d_{t+1}^T d_t = 0$, which means that the directions of the gradients for consecutive steps t and $t+1$ which follow optimized step sizes α_t are perpendicular, forming a zig-zag pattern. Optimizing for the exact step size is computationally expensive, and rarely used in practice.

3.3.3   Mini-Batch Gradient Descent

In mini-batch gradient descent, the cost function is computed for each example in a mini-batch of examples, and then the weights are updated using these gradients. The size of the mini-batch can be fixed or variable. Mini-batch methods are a natural way to parallelize the gradient computation since the gradient can be computed in parallel on each of the k subsets. The mini-batch method is also more robust to outliers since it is less likely that all k subsets will contain an outlier.

The standard error of a sample mean $\hat{\mu}$ of a population mean μ is given by $SE(\hat{\mu}) = \frac{\sigma}{\sqrt{n}}$ where σ is the standard deviation of the population and the size n is the number of observations of the sample. To see this, note that if $x_1 \dots x_n$ are n independent samples, then the variance of $T = \sum_i x_i$ is $n\sigma^2$. The variance of the sample mean $\hat{\mu} = \frac{T}{n}$ is $\frac{\sigma^2}{n}$ and the standard deviation of $\hat{\mu}$ is $\frac{\sigma}{\sqrt{n}}$. This motivates us to estimate the gradient from samples rather than the entire dataset. For example, estimating the gradient from 100 samples instead of from 10,000 samples reduces the standard error of the mean only by a factor of 10, while reducing computation time and memory by a factor of 100. Optimization algorithms that use the entire dataset are termed batch methods. In contrast, mini-batch methods use a sample of the data, splitting the data into $\frac{n}{k}$ disjoint sets of size k.

3.3.4   Stochastic Gradient Descent

Stochastic gradient descent (Robbins and Monro, 1951) is a special case of mini-batch methods in which the mini-batch is of size 1, using a single random sample a^i at a time:

$$x_{t+1} = x_t - \alpha_t \nabla_x \mathcal{L}(x_t, a^i) \tag{3.25}$$

where the learning rate, or step-size parameter, α_t is dependent on iteration t and $\nabla f_i(x_t) = \nabla_x \mathcal{L}(x_t, a^i)$, as shown in Algorithm 3.2.

Algorithm 3.2 Stochastic gradient descent.

---

given objective function $f(x)$
given starting point $x_1 \in \mathbf{dom} f$
given $\{\alpha_t\}_{t=1}^T$ learning rates
while not converged **do**:
    Randomly shuffle training set $a^1, \dots, a^n$
    for $i = 1, \dots, n$ **do**:
        $g_t = \nabla f_i(x_t)$ gradient of a single sample i
        $x_{t+1} = x_t - \alpha_t g_t$ update

Two differences between the SGD and gradient descent algorithms are that (1) in SGD, we approximate the gradient using a single sample i by ∇f_i instead of all samples by ∇f, and (2) the learning rate α_t is dependent upon the iterations t rather than being a fixed α. SGD is also suitable as an online method for handling a stream of data one example at a time. Notice that near saddle-points, the gradient is close to zero, and therefore the step size in gradient descent may be too small to be efficient. A common practice is to add noise ε_t to the gradient descent update:

$$x_{t+1} = x_t - \alpha_t g_t + \varepsilon_t \tag{3.26}$$

where $\varepsilon_t \sim \mathcal{N}(0, \sigma_t)$. Stochastic gradient descent is by itself a noisy estimate of the true gradient, which increases the chances of finding a global minimum. Saddle-points in which the gradient is close to zero may cause gradient descent to make a step which is too small. To alleviate this problem we can add noise $\varepsilon_t \sim \mathcal{N}(0, \sigma_t)$ to the update in gradient descent $x_{t+1} = x_t - \alpha g_t + \varepsilon_t$ with σ_t decreasing in time t. Fortunately, the noisy estimate of the gradient in SGD eliminates the need to add noise to the gradient update, and also has the advantage of being a very efficient approximation of the gradient. Averaging the outputs of multiple steps of SGD, also known as stochastic weight averaging (Izmailov et al., 2018), improves generalization. In practice, SGD may be implemented by going though a random ordering of the training examples. A training epoch amounts to a pass through the training data. The data are then re-randomized for the next epoch, and so on, until convergence.

Since training neural networks may be a very time-consuming process, stochastic gradient descent is often used in practice. This means that we sample the gradient value at a new point and then update our parameters using this sample. If we want to use a mini-batch of samples, we need to compute the gradient over the mini-batch. An excellent property of SGD is that these samples are unbiased estimators of the actual gradient. This means that if we repeat updating the parameters for many iterations, we will eventually get close to the optimal parameters.

3.3.5   Adaptive Gradient Descent

The third problem with gradient descent is that it takes many steps in flat regions since the directions of the gradients in consecutive iterations for optimal step sizes are perpendicular, forming a slow zig-zag pattern.

A solution is to use the gradients from previous steps for faster convergence. Adaptive gradient descent methods use gradients from earlier steps to compute the current update. A critic of adaptive gradient descent methods (Wilson et al., 2017) shows that they may result in solutions that are different from that of gradient descent and SGD. A motivation for using the gradients computed in previous iterations to affect the current update is to move faster along dimensions of low curvature and slower along dimensions with oscillations.

3.3.6   Momentum

One of the simplest adaptive gradient descent methods is called gradient descent with momentum. The idea is to add a fraction of the previous step's gradient to the current step's update, where the fraction is a parameter that is tuned. This results in faster convergence in flat regions and slower convergence in steep regions.

The momentum vector accumulates gradients from previous iterations for computing the current gradient (Sutskever et al., 2013). In a weighted moving average the weights decrease arithmetically, normalized by the sum of weights:

$$a_t = \frac{na_t + (n-1)a_{t-1} + \cdots + a_{t-n+1}}{n + (n-1) + \cdots + 1} \tag{3.27}$$

For $s_t = \sum_{i=t-n+1}^{t} a_i$ we have $s_{t+1} = s_t + a_{t+1} - a_{t-n+1}$. Therefore:

$$\begin{aligned} a_{t+1} &= \frac{na_{t+1} + (n-1)a_t + \cdots + a_{t-n+2}}{n + (n-1) + \cdots + 1} \\ &= a_t + \frac{na_{t+1} - a_t - \cdots - a_{t-n+1}}{n + (n-1) + \cdots + 1} = a_t + \frac{na_{t+1} - s_{t,n}}{\frac{n(n+1)}{2}} \end{aligned} \tag{3.28}$$

In an exponentially weighted moving average the weights decrease exponentially:

$$\begin{aligned} m_t &= \alpha a_t + (1-\alpha)m_{t-1} \\ &= \alpha a_t + (1-\alpha)(\alpha a_{t-1} + (1-\alpha)(\alpha a_{t-2} + (1-\alpha)(\cdots))) \\ &= \alpha(a_t + (1-\alpha)a_{t-1} + (1-\alpha)^2 a_{t-2} + \cdots) \end{aligned} \tag{3.29}$$

and by unrolling the telescopic sum, the weight of a_{t-i} is $\alpha(1-\alpha)^i$.

Setting a to be the gradient and choosing the parameter $\beta = 1 - \alpha \in [0,1)$ close to 1, and step sizes $\{\alpha_t\}_{t=1}^T$, we compute the gradient for each iteration using momentum as an exponentially weighted moving average of gradients:

$$\begin{aligned} g_t &= \nabla f(x_t) \\ m_t &= \beta m_{t-1} + g_t \\ x_{t+1} &= x_t - \alpha_t m_t \end{aligned} \tag{3.30}$$

The special base of $\beta = 0$ reduces to gradient descent. The first problem with momentum is that the step sizes may not decrease once we have reached close to the minimum that may cause oscillations, which can be remedied by using Nesterov momentum (Dozat, 2016) that replaces the gradient with the gradient after computing momentum (Dozat, 2016):

$$\begin{aligned} g_t &= \nabla f(x_t - \alpha\beta m_{t-1}) \\ m_t &= \beta m_{t-1} + g_t \\ x_{t+1} &= x_t - \alpha_t m_t \end{aligned} \tag{3.31}$$

3.3.7 Adagrad

A second problem with momentum is that it updates all components of x_t using the same learning rate α. Therefore, adaptive subgradient descent, or Adagrad (Duchi et al., 2011), uses adaptive updates for different components of the learning rate, making the method less sensitive to α:

$$g_t = \nabla f(x_t)$$
$$s_t = \beta s_{t-1} + g_t^2 \qquad (3.32)$$
$$x_{t+1} = x_t - \alpha_t \frac{g_t}{\sqrt{s_t} + \varepsilon}$$

where $g_t^2 = g_t \odot g_t$ is a pointwise multiplication. If g_t^2 is large then $\frac{1}{\sqrt{s_t}+\varepsilon}$ is small. This is a limitation since the learning rate may be monotonically decreasing, decaying to zero $\lim_{s_t \to \infty} \frac{1}{\sqrt{s_t}+\varepsilon} = 0$.

Improvements upon Adagrad for overcoming this limitation include RMSProp and AdaDelta:

- RMSProp (Tieleman and Hinton, 2012) is Adagrad using a weighted moving average, replacing:

$$s_t = \beta s_{t-1} + g_t^2 \qquad (3.33)$$

with

$$s_t = \beta s_{t-1} + (1 - \beta)g_t^2 \qquad (3.34)$$

- AdaDelta (Zeiler, 2012) is Adagrad using an exponential decaying average of square updates without a learning rate, replacing:

$$x_{t+1} = x_t - \alpha_t \frac{1}{\sqrt{s_t} + \varepsilon} g_t \qquad (3.35)$$

with:

$$x_{t+1} = x_t - \frac{\sqrt{u_t} + \varepsilon}{\sqrt{s_t} + \varepsilon} g_t$$
$$u_{t+1} = \gamma u_t + (1 - \gamma)\Delta x^2 \qquad (3.36)$$

where $\Delta x^2 = (x_{t+1} - x_t) \odot (x_{t+1} - x_t)$ is a pointwise multiplication.

3.3.8 Adam: Adaptive Moment Estimation

Adaptive moment estimation, or Adam (Kingma and Ba, 2014), combines the best of both momentum updates and Adagrad-based methods, as shown in Algorithm 3.3. Like momentum updates, Adam does not rely on a pre-specified learning rate, but it also does not suffer from the same flaw of overfitting the initial stage of training. Typical hyperparameter values are $\beta_1 = 0.9$ and $\beta_2 = 0.99$.

Several improvements upon Adam include the following:

- NAdam (Dozat, 2016) is Adam with Nesterov momentum.

Algorithm 3.3 Adam: Adaptive moment estimation.

given starting point $x_1 \in \mathbf{dom} f$
given learning rates $\{\alpha_t\}_{t=1}^{T}$
given decay rates $\beta_1, \beta_2 \in [0, 1)$ close to 1
given small $\varepsilon > 0$
init $m_0 = 0$, $v_0 = 0$
while not converged **do**:
$\qquad g_t = \nabla f(x_t)$ gradient
$\qquad m_t = \beta_1 m_{t-1} + (1 - \beta_1) g_t$ first momentum
$\qquad v_t = \beta_2 v_{t-1} + (1 - \beta_2) g_t^2$ second momentum
$\qquad x_{t+1} = x_t - \alpha_t \frac{m_t}{\sqrt{v_t} + \varepsilon}$ update

---

- Yogi (Zaheer et al., 2018) is Adam with an improvement to the second momentum term, which is rewritten as:

$$v_t = v_{t-1} - (1 - \beta_2)(v_{t-1} - g_t^2) \tag{3.37}$$

and replaced with:

$$v_t = v_{t-1} - (1 - \beta_2)\mathrm{sign}(v_{t-1} - g_t^2) g_t^2 \tag{3.38}$$

- AMSGrad (Reddi et al., 2018) is Adam with the following improvement:

$$\hat{v}_t = \max(\hat{v}_{t-1}, v_t)$$
$$x_{t+1} = x_t - \frac{\alpha_t m_t}{\sqrt{\hat{v}_t}} \tag{3.39}$$

3.3.9   Hypergradient Descent

Hypergradient descent (Baydin et al., 2018) performs gradient descent on the learning rate within gradient descent. This improves the convergence of the various gradient descent methods and may be applied to any adaptive stochastic gradient descent method. Computing the derivative of f with respect to α_t is used to update:

$$h_t = \frac{\partial f(x_t)}{\partial \alpha} = g_t^T \frac{\partial}{\partial \alpha}(x_{t-1} - \alpha g_{t-1})$$
$$\alpha_{t+1} = \alpha_t - \beta h_t = \alpha_t + \beta g_t^T g_{t-1} \tag{3.40}$$

Algorithm 3.4 shows the application to gradient descent.

The above methods are usually used with annealing schedules, which provide a schedule of the learning rate, and are applied when the network's performance does not improve. The schedule may lower the learning rate when the optimization gets stuck in a local minimum and increase the learning rate when the network is progressing well.

Algorithm 3.4 Hypergradient descent.

---
given objective function $f(x)$
given starting point $x_1 \in \textbf{dom} f$
given starting learning rate α_1
given hypergradient learning rate β
while not converged **do**:
$\quad g_t = \nabla f(x_t)$ gradient
$\quad h_t = \frac{\partial f(x_t)}{\partial \alpha_t}$ gradient
$\quad \alpha_{t+1} = \alpha_t - \beta h_t$ update
$\quad x_{t+1} = x_t - \alpha_{t+1} g_t$ update

3.4   Second-Order Methods

First-order methods are easier to implement and understand but have a slower convergence rate than second-order methods. Second-order methods use the first and second derivatives of a univariate function or the gradient and Hessian of a multivariate function to compute the step direction and size. Second-order methods approximate the objective function using a quadratic, resulting in faster convergence than first-order methods. The second-order information allows us to identify a local minimum among extreme points.

3.4.1   Newton's Method

Newton's method for zero values or for finding roots of a function finds a first-order approximation:

$$f'(x_t) = \frac{f(x_t)}{x_t - x_{t+1}} \tag{3.41}$$

$$x_{t+1} = x_t - \frac{f(x_t)}{f'(x_t)} \tag{3.42}$$

as shown in Figure 3.7. Newton's method is an iterative process. To find the root of a function, the method takes the sample point and guesses a function value at that position. It then makes a new guess based on the current guess at the function value.

Similarly, Newton's method for optimization or for finding roots of the derivative of a function finds a second-order approximation:

$$x_{t+1} = x_t - \frac{f'(x_t)}{f''(x_t)} \tag{3.43}$$

as shown in Figure 3.8. Newton's method is a modification of the secant method applicable for finding the zero of the derivative of a function at a special point. This special point is a point where the function's derivative is equal to zero. This is the method that is used by Newton's technique for optimization.

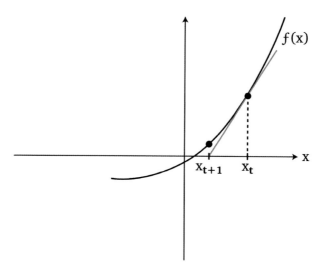

Figure 3.7 First-order fit: line.

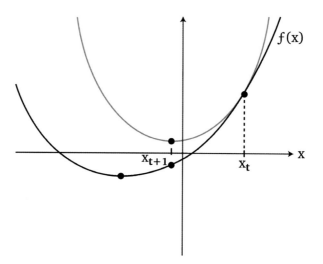

Figure 3.8 Second-order fit: quadratic.

Our goal is to find x which minimizes the objective function f:

$$x^\star = \operatorname*{argmin}_x f(x) \tag{3.44}$$

Given x_t we would like to take a step toward x_{t+1} that is closer to $x^\star$:

$$f'(x_{t+1}) \approx f'(x_t) + f''(x_t)(x_{t+1} - x_t) \tag{3.45}$$

such that $f'(x_{t+1}) = 0$, resulting in Equation 3.43, defined for $f''(x_t) \neq 0$.

3.4.2 Second-Order Taylor Approximation

The relationship between a function and its derivative is defined by:

$$f(b) - f(a) = \int_a^b f'(x)\, dx \tag{3.46}$$

and therefore:

$$f(x + h) - f(x) = \int_0^h f'(x + a)\, dx \tag{3.47}$$

and the Taylor series of f around x is:

$$
\begin{aligned}
f(x + h) &= f(x) + \int_0^h f'(x + a)\, dx \\
&= f(x) + \int_0^h \left(f'(x) + \int_0^a f''(x + b)\, db \right) da = \cdots \\
&= f(x) + \frac{f'(x)}{1!} h + \frac{f''(x)}{2!} h^2 + \cdots = \sum_{n=0}^{\infty} \frac{f^{(n)}(x)}{n!} h^n
\end{aligned}
\tag{3.48}
$$

Plugging in a for x, and $(x - a)$ for h, results in the Taylor series of $f(x)$ around a, given by:

$$f(x) = \sum_{n=0}^{\infty} \frac{f^{(n)}(a)}{n!} (x - a)^n = f(a) + \frac{f'(a)}{1!}(x - a) + \frac{f''(a)}{2!}(x - a)^2 + \cdots \tag{3.49}$$

The second-order Taylor approximation of a univariate function by a quadratic is:

$$f(x) \approx f(a) + f'(a)(x - a) + f''(a)\frac{1}{2}(x - a)^2 \tag{3.50}$$

To find the minimum, we set the derivative with respect to x to zero and get:

$$f'(x) \approx f'(a) + f''(a)(x - a) = 0 \tag{3.51}$$

and solving for x:

$$x = a - \frac{f'(a)}{f''(a)} \tag{3.52}$$

which is the update of Newton's method, and is defined when $f''(a) \neq 0$.

For a multivariate function $f : \mathbb{R}^n \to \mathbb{R}$ the approximation of the Taylor expansion is:

$$f(x) \approx f(a) + \nabla f(a)(x - a)^T + \frac{1}{2}(x - a)^T \nabla^2 f(a)(x - a) \tag{3.53}$$

Denoting the gradient g and Hessian H:

$$\nabla f(a) = g$$

$$\nabla^2 f(a) = \left(\frac{\partial^2 f(a)}{\partial x_i \partial x_j} \right)_{i,j} = H \tag{3.54}$$

Table 3.1 Comparison of properties of gradient descent vs. Newton's method.

	Gradient descent	Newton's method
Order	First	Second
Convergence	Linear	Quadratic
Memory	$O(n)$	$O(n^2)$
Computation	$O(n)$	$O(n^3)$
Conditioning	Degrades	
Robustness		More sensitive

we get

$$f(x) \approx f(a) + (x-a)g + \frac{1}{2}(x-a)^T H(x-a) \tag{3.55}$$

Regrouping the second-order, first-order, and constant terms we get:

$$q(x) = \frac{1}{2}x^T H x + (g - Ha)^T x + c \tag{3.56}$$

Since the gradients $\nabla_x b^T x = b$ and $\nabla_x x^T A x = (A + A^T)x$, and since the Hessian is a symmetric matrix, solving for a critical point of the function by setting its gradient to zero results in:

$$\nabla q(x) = Hx + (g - Ha) = 0 \tag{3.57}$$

The solution is $x^\star = a - H^{-1}g$, which is the Newton–Raphson update rule:

$$x_{t+1} = x_t - H_t^{-1} g_t \tag{3.58}$$

Notice that replacing the Hessian H with the identity I matrix times a scalar α reduces Newton's method to the special case of gradient descent since $x_{t+1} = x_t - \alpha g_t$.

For a deep neural network:

$$g_t = \frac{1}{m} \nabla_\theta \sum \mathcal{L}(y^i, \hat{y}^i)$$

$$H_t = \frac{1}{m} \nabla_\theta^2 \sum \mathcal{L}(y^i, \hat{y}^i) \tag{3.59}$$

$$\theta_{t+1} = \theta_t - H^{-1} g_t$$

Table 3.1 and Figure 3.9 compare gradient descent with Newton's method.

If the second derivative is unknown, we can approximate it by using the first derivatives:

$$f''(x) \approx \frac{f'(x) - f'(a)}{x - a} \tag{3.60}$$

which brings us to quasi-Newton methods, described next.

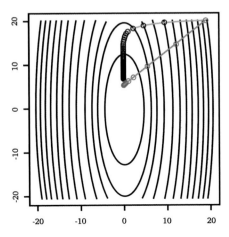

Figure 3.9 Comparison of convergence path of gradient descent vs. Newton's method (illustrated by a shorter line through the function's level sets).

3.4.3   Quasi-Newton Methods

Quasi-Newton methods, which provide an iterative approximation to the inverse Hessian H^{-1}, avoid computing the second derivatives, avoid inverting the Hessian and may also avoid storing the Hessian matrix. Quasi-Newton methods typically converge faster than Newton methods. For a convex quadratic function:

$$f(x) = \frac{1}{2}x^T H x + b^T x + c \tag{3.61}$$

where the Hessian H is positive definite, it holds that:

$$\nabla f(x) = Hx + b$$
$$\nabla^2 f(x) = H \tag{3.62}$$

Therefore, the Hessian satisfies:

$$\nabla f(x) - \nabla f(y) = H(x - y) \tag{3.63}$$

Multiplying both sides by $Q = H^{-1}$, we get the secant condition:

$$Q(\nabla f(x) - \nabla f(y)) = x - y \tag{3.64}$$

If the matrix Q satisfies the secant condition and the function f can be approximated by a quadratic function, then its inverse Hessian would be approximated by Q. We initialize $Q_0 = I$ to the identity and iteratively update the matrix, satisfying:

$$Q_{t+1}(\nabla f(x_{t+1}) - \nabla f(x_t)) = x_{t+1} - x_t \tag{3.65}$$

To define the iterative updates, we first define the differences:

$$\delta_t = x_{t+1} - x_t$$
$$h_t = g_{t+1} - g_t = \nabla f(x_{t+1}) - \nabla f(x_t) \tag{3.66}$$

and let $z_t = Q_t h_t$. Next, we update the inverse Hessian approximation using the following three methods: SR1, DFP, or BFGS. These methods are similar in that they all begin by initializing the inverse Hessian to the identity matrix and then iteratively updating the inverse Hessian. These three update rules differ in that their convergence properties improve upon one another. The first method, called an SR1 update, is a rank one correction and is defined by:

$$Q_{t+1} = Q_t + \frac{(\delta_t - z_t)(\delta_t - z_t)^T}{(\delta_t - z_t)^T h_t} \tag{3.67}$$

The second method for updating the inverse Hessian approximation is the Davidon–Fletcher–Powell (DFP) correction (Davidon, 1991; Fletcher and Powell, 1963) and is defined by:

$$Q_{t+1} = Q_t + \frac{\delta_t \delta_t^T}{h_t^T \delta_t} - \frac{z_t z_t^T}{h_t^T z_t} \tag{3.68}$$

The third method updates the inverse Hessian approximation by the BFGS correction, defined by:

$$Q_{t+1} = Q_t + \frac{(z_t \delta_t^T) + (z_t \delta_t^T)}{h_t^T z_t} - \left(1 + \frac{h_t^T \delta_t}{h_t^T z_t}\right) \frac{z_t z_t^T}{h_t^T z_t} \tag{3.69}$$

In summary, quasi-Newton methods avoid computing the inverse Hessian H^{-1} matrix and instead iteratively approximate. Each iteration involves $O(n^2)$ operations, without $O(n^3)$ operations such as solving linear systems or matrix–matrix operations. The iterative algorithm is robust, with fast convergence.

Storing the inverse Hessian approximation matrix itself for large dimensions may be prohibitive. Therefore, limited memory BFGS (L-BFGS) (Liu and Nocedal, 1989) avoids storing the inverse Hessian approximation by unrolling the approximation and using limited memory for storing updates. The L-BFGS approximates BFGS by storing only the last updates of δ_t, h_t, and z_t. Finally, quasi-Newton methods are easy to implement.

3.5   Evolution Strategies

Rather than incrementally improving a single point toward a local minimum, evolution strategies use a probability distribution and many sample points in the search space or parameter space to find a local minimum, which may be easily distributed. An advantage of using a probability distribution is that it allows the algorithm to escape local minima. The cross-entropy method stores a probability distribution over the search space and samples points from this probability distribution. The algorithm proceeds iteratively: Each iteration samples from the probability distribution and then updates the probability distribution to fit the best samples by the cross-entropy. Typically, a multivariate normal distribution is used as the probability distribution, maintaining a mean vector and covariance matrix. Neural evolution strategies use a probability distribution over the search space as well; however, instead of fitting the probability distribution to the best samples, it uses gradient descent where the gradient is computed from the samples (Salimans et al., 2017). Covariance matrix adaptation (Hansen, 2006) stores a covariance matrix and updates a probability distribution iteratively based on samples from a multivariate Gaussian distribution.

3.6   Summary

Gradient descent iteratively finds a local minimum by taking steps in the direction of the steepest descent. Three main problems with training neural networks using gradient descent and their solutions are:

- The total loss function with respect to the neural network weights is a sum of many individual losses for many samples. The solution is mini-batch or SGD.
- The derivative of the total loss is computed with respect to all network weights. The solution is backpropagation.
- The directions of gradients for consecutive time steps which follow optimized step sizes are orthogonal, forming a zig-zag pattern, which is slow, especially in flat regions. The solution is adaptive gradient descent.

Specifically, adding momentum avoids the zig-zag directions when using the optimal step size and improves progress toward the local minimum. Adaptive methods update the learning rate in each dimension individually and are combined with momentum. Stochastic gradient descent approximates the gradient by random samples, which is highly efficient for training neural networks with many examples, and its randomness improves optimization. Using the second derivative speeds up convergence, and quasi-Newton methods approximate the second derivative when unavailable or approximate the inverse Hessian, avoiding its computation and storage. In contrast to gradient descent methods, which advance a single point toward a local minimum, evolution strategies update a probability distribution, from which multiple points are sampled, lending itself to a highly efficient distributed computation.

4 Regularization

4.1 Introduction

Regularization is a technique that helps prevent overfitting by penalizing the complexity of the network. In this chapter, we will describe three forms of regularization: (1) penalty term, which is adding a penalty term to the cost function, which encourages the model to decrease the weights and has fewer parameters and a simpler structure; (2) dropout, which randomly removes a percentage of neurons in each layer from the network – this causes the network to be less accurate but also makes it more robust to overfitting; and (3) data augmentation, which generates new training data points that are similar to the existing training data points, though not identical. Overfitting occurs when a model is too closely tailored to the training data and does not generalize well to unseen data; augmentation may avoid overfitting and allow the model to generalize better to new data.

Overfitting data, as shown in Figure 4.1, happens when the model is too complex and captures noise in the data. To avoid overfitting, we may (1) add a penalty term to the loss function; (2) use dropout, which is a regularization technique that randomly sets some of the network activations to zero; or (3) augment the data. These three methods are all forms of regularization whose goal is to prevent the network from overfitting the training data.

Figure 4.2 shows the improvement in image classification performance as efficient methods were developed for training deeper neural networks. This figure shows the error of the best-published network for each year, while Figure 4.3 shows the corresponding number of neural network layers. As shown in the figures, the error decreases as the number of neural network layers increases. This continues until a certain depth, at which adding residual connections between layers is required to continue this trend and avoid vanishing gradients.

4.2 Generalization

Training data is a sample from a population. We want our neural network model to generalize well to unseen test data drawn from the same population. Specifically, the generalization gap G is defined as the difference between the expected

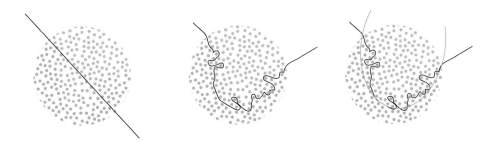

Figure 4.1 Underfitting (left): The model is not complex enough to capture the underlying pattern in the data. Overfitting (center): The model is too complex and captures noise in the data. Regularization (right): The green line represents a model which is neither too simple nor too complex. Regularization helps prevent overfitting by penalizing the complexity of the model.

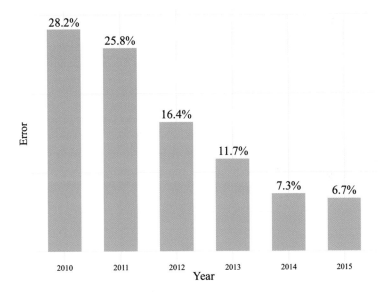

Figure 4.2 ImageNet classification error by year.

loss when sampling from the population $\mathcal{P}$, which the test error may approximate, and the empirical loss, which is the training error of the training samples (x^i, y^i) for $i = 1, \ldots, m$:

$$G(f(X, W)) = \mathbb{E}_{(X,Y)\sim\mathcal{P}}(\mathcal{L}(y^i, f(x^i, W)) - \frac{1}{m}\sum_{i=1}^{m}\mathcal{L}(y^i, f(x^i, W)))) \quad (4.1)$$

We can use the generalization gap to measure how well our neural network model fits the training data. If the generalization gap is low, the neural network model is a good fit for the training data. If the generalization gap is high, the neural network may be overfitting.

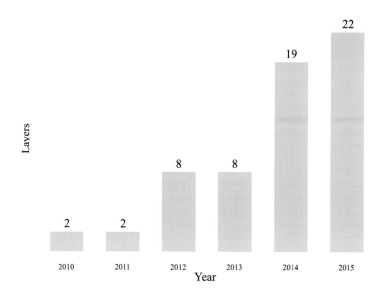

Figure 4.3 Number of neural network layers for corresponding best models on ImageNet by year.

Learning curves plot the test accuracy as a function of the amount of training data (X, Y) for various models. Adding more training data (X, Y) increases the generalization accuracy up to a limit, reducing the generalization gap as expected $\mathbb{E}_{(X,Y)\sim\mathcal{P}}$ by Equation 4.1.

4.3 Overfitting

A neural network model tailored to training data and does not generalize well to unseen test data has a high generalization error and is said to be overfitting the data. The training error decreases as we increase the network complexity for a given dataset, and the test error also decreases until a certain point and then increases due to overfitting. If we increase the network complexity even further, then at the limit, the test error begins to decrease again, a phenomenon that is known as double descent (Belkin et al., 2019). Unless we have sufficient data, a very complex neural network may fit the training data very well at the expense of a poor fit to the test data, resulting in a large gap between the training error and test error, which is overfitting. Since training data is a population sample, it may be overfitting; applying our model to test data is the way to detect overfitting.

4.4   Cross Validation

Cross validation allows us to compute the mean and variance of the generalization error. We randomly split the data into k folds and iteratively take the training data to be $k-1$ out of k folds for building a model that is tested on the remaining fold. After testing each model, we compute the mean and variance of the generalization error over all k models.

The mean generalization error is the average generalization error over all k models and is a good indicator of how well a model performs on unseen data. A common practice is to use cross validation to select hyperparameters for training a model. For example, when training a neural network with stochastic gradient descent (SGD), we can use cross validation to find the optimal learning rate and momentum. We can also use cross validation to select features for building a model. We can build many models with different subsets of features and then compute their mean and variance of the generalization error to determine which subset performs best.

4.5   Bias and Variance

Practical steps in training neural networks include reducing bias by training a deeper and wider network and reducing variance by obtaining more data or by regularization. Our goal is to reduce both bias and variance. In order to reduce the bias, we can train a deeper and wider network with more parameters to learn from the training data. In other words, a deeper and wider network can learn more complex functions from the training data. In order to reduce the variance, we can obtain more data or use regularization. The more data we have, the less variance in our model. Regularization is a method of preventing overfitting by penalizing complex models.

4.6   Vector Norms

We define vector norms before discussing regularization using different norms. For all vectors x, y and scalars α: (1) all vector norms of a non-zero vector are a positive scalar; (2) norms maintain the triangle inequality; and (3) all vectors and scalars have a rescaling property, as follows:

1. $\|x\| \geq 0$ and $\|x\| = 0$ iff $x = 0$
2. $\|x + y\| \leq \|x\| + \|y\|$
3. $\|\alpha x\| = |\alpha| \|x\|$

Special norms are illustrated in Figure 4.4; these are the ℓ_1 norm defined as:

$$\|x\|_1 = |x_1| + \cdots + |x_n| = \sum_{i=1}^{n} |x_i| \tag{4.2}$$

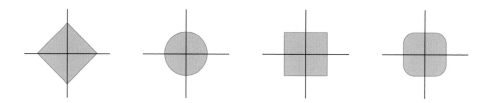

Figure 4.4 Unit circle $\{x \in \mathbb{R}^2 : \|x\| = 1\}$ for each vector norm: ℓ_1, ℓ_2, ℓ_∞, ℓ_p.

the ℓ_2 norm:

$$\|x\|_2 = \sqrt{x_1^2 + \cdots + x_n^2} = \sqrt{\sum_{i=1}^{n} x_i^2} \tag{4.3}$$

and the ℓ_∞ norm:

$$\|x\|_\infty = \max_i(|x_1|, \ldots, |x_n|) = \max_i |x_i| \tag{4.4}$$

which is the maximum norm – the maximum possible distance between any two vectors. The ℓ_∞ norm is also the maximum of all norms. More generally, we may define the ℓ_p norm by:

$$\|x\|_p = \left(\sum_{i=1}^{n} (\|x_i\|^P)\right)^{\frac{1}{p}} \tag{4.5}$$

for $1 \leq p \leq \infty$. Notice that the number of non-zero elements in a vector, often informally referred to as the ℓ_0 "norm," is not a norm by the properties above.

4.7   Ridge Regression and Lasso

We formulated machine learning as an optimization objective of the general form:

$$J(\theta) = \frac{1}{m} \sum_{i=1}^{m} \mathcal{L}(f_\theta(x^i, y^i)) + \lambda \mathcal{R}(\theta) \tag{4.6}$$

We may make multiple design choices regarding this general optimization objective: (1) define the hypothesis class or model denoted by the function $f_\theta(x^i, y^i)$ and it's parameters θ; (2) define the loss function denoted by $\mathcal{L}$; and (3) define the type of regularization function $\mathcal{R}(\theta)$. For example, choosing a linear model with a squared loss function and an ℓ_2 regularization term results in the objective:

$$J_{\text{ridge}}(\theta) = \frac{1}{m} \sum_{i=1}^{m} (\theta^T x^i - y^i)^2 + \lambda\|\theta\| \tag{4.7}$$

also known as ridge regression, where $\lambda > 0$ is a regularization hyperparameter. Ridge regression is a form of linear regression that penalizes the squared distance between the predicted and observed values, which may also be written in matrix form as:

$$J_{\text{ridge}}(\theta) = \frac{1}{m}(X\theta - Y)^T(X\theta - Y) + \lambda\|\theta\| \tag{4.8}$$

where X is a $d \times m$ matrix whose columns are the data points, and Y is an $n \times 1$ vector of labels. To find the minimum, we compute the derivative of the loss with respect to the parameters θ:

$$\nabla_\theta J_{\text{ridge}} = \frac{2}{m}X^T(X\theta - Y) + 2\lambda\theta \tag{4.9}$$

and set the gradient to zero:

$$\nabla_\theta J_{\text{ridge}} = \frac{1}{m}X^TX\theta - \frac{1}{m}X^TY + \lambda\theta = 0 \tag{4.10}$$

which has an analytic solution:

$$\theta = (X^TX + n\lambda I)^{-1}X^TY \tag{4.11}$$

A different choice of objective is called Lasso, which is a linear regression model that penalizes the absolute value of the difference between the prediction and the mean.

4.8   Regularized Loss Functions

Regularized loss functions is used in neural networks to prevent overfitting. This type of regularization is also called weight decay for its effect of decreasing the weights. Regularized loss functions are used to penalize the network for large weights and large activations. A regularization term $\mathcal{R}(W)$ is added to the loss function:

$$\frac{1}{m}\sum_{i=1}^{m}\mathcal{L}(y^i, f_W(x^i)) + \mathcal{R}(W) \tag{4.12}$$

where $\mathcal{R}(W) = \lambda\|W\|_p$ for a regularization parameter $\lambda > 0$, which is a scalar and an ℓ_p norm. The regularization parameter λ controls how much we want to penalize large weights. If $\lambda = 0$, then no regularization occurs. If $\lambda = 1$, then all weights are penalized equally. A value between 0 and 1 gives us a trade-off between fitting complex models and fitting simple models. The value of the hyperparameter λ may be set by cross validation. Specifically, by splitting the training data into multiple folds k, training $k-1$ folds and validating on the kth fold for a set of possible λ values. This results in k values of the loss for each different value of λ. We can then compute the average of the k losses for each λ value, and choose the best λ for our data.

Common types of regularization are ℓ_1 and ℓ_2. The effect of each of these norms when used for regularizing fully connected neural networks may be interactively

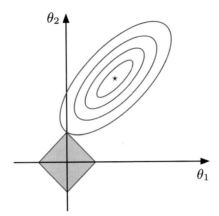

Figure 4.5 ℓ_1 regularization. The solution is called a sparse solution since the diamond shape of the ℓ_1 norm intersects with the loss function on a sharp point where coefficients are zero. In this example $\theta_1 = 0$.

visualized (Smilkov and Carter, n.d.). Setting $p = 1$ results in the ℓ_1 norm, and is called ℓ_1 regularization. The effect of ℓ_1 regularization is a solution with zero coefficients, also called a sparse solution, since the diamond shape of the norm, as shown in Figure 4.5, intersects with the loss function on a sharp point where coefficients are zero.

Setting $p = 2$ results in the ℓ_2 norm, called ℓ_2 regularization. The difference between ℓ_1 and ℓ_2 regularization is that ℓ_1 regularization is a penalty on the sum of absolute weights, which promotes sparsity, whereas ℓ_2 regularization is a penalty on the sum of the squares of the weights.

The effect of adding a regularization term to a neural network loss may be observed directly by the change in the update step of SGD. Consider the gradient of the ℓ_2 regularized loss with respect to a single random sample in SGD:

$$\mathcal{L}(y^i, f_W(x^i)) + \lambda \|W\|^2 \tag{4.13}$$

The weight update is then:

$$\begin{aligned}
W_{t+1} &= W_t - \alpha \nabla_{W_t}(\mathcal{L}(y^i, f_{W_t}(x^i)) + \lambda \|W_t\|^2) \\
&= W_t(1 - 2\alpha\lambda W_t) - \alpha \nabla_{W_t}(\mathcal{L}(y^i, f_{W_t}(x^i))
\end{aligned} \tag{4.14}$$

which demonstrates the effect of shrinking the weights.

4.9   Dropout Regularization

Dropout is a regularization technique used in neural networks to prevent over-fitting (Srivastava et al., 2014). It is a technique that randomly removes a percentage of the neurons in each layer from the network. This causes the network to be less accurate, making it more robust to overfitting.

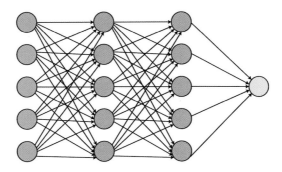

Figure 4.6 Fully connected neural network.

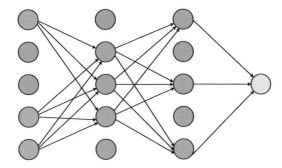

Figure 4.7 Dropout regularization. Activations are randomly removed with probability p at training time.

Activations are randomly set to zero during training. Testing is done without dropout. For layer l, set dropout probability p_l. For each activation $a_j^l = a_j^l I_j^l$ for $j = 1, \ldots, n_l$, where:

$$I_j^l = \begin{cases} 0 & \text{with probability } p_l \\ \frac{1}{1-p_l} & \text{with probability } 1 - p_l \end{cases} \tag{4.15}$$

such that activations that remain stand in for activations dropped out.

Figure 4.6 shows a fully connected neural network before dropout. Figure 4.7 shows the network after dropout where activations (in red) are randomly removed with probability p at training time. The dropout rate p is a hyperparameter.

4.9.1 Random Least Squares with Dropout

Dropout is not unique to neural networks and was used earlier in least squares. Random least squares with dropout is equivalent to ridge regression:

$$\mathcal{L}_I(\beta) = \frac{1}{2} \sum_{i=1}^{m} (y_i - \sum_{j=1}^{k} X_{i,j} I_{i,j} \beta_j)^2 \tag{4.16}$$

where

$$I_{i,j} = \begin{cases} 0 & \text{with probability } p \\ \frac{1}{1-p} & \text{with probability } 1-p \end{cases} \tag{4.17}$$

set:

$$\mathbb{E}\left(\frac{\partial \mathcal{L}_I(\beta)}{\partial \beta}\right) = -X^T y + X^T X \beta + \frac{p}{1+p} D\beta = 0 \tag{4.18}$$

with $D = \text{diag}\{\|x_1\|^2, \ldots, \|x_k\|^2\}$. The solution is $\hat{\beta} = (X^T X + \frac{p}{1+p} D)^{-1} X^T y$, which is ridge regression.

4.9.2   Least Squares with Noise Input Distortion

Least squares with noise input distortion is also equivalent to ridge regression:

$$\mathcal{L}_N(\beta) = \frac{1}{2} \sum_{i=1}^{m} (y_i - \sum_{j=1}^{k} (X_{i,j} + n_{i,j})\beta_j)^2 \tag{4.19}$$

We add random noise to the prediction $N(0, \lambda)$, by setting:

$$\mathbb{E}\left(\frac{\partial \mathcal{L}_N(\beta)}{\partial \beta}\right) = -X^T y + X^T X \beta + \lambda \beta = 0 \tag{4.20}$$

where $\mathbb{E}(n_{i,j}^2) = \lambda$. The solution is $\hat{\beta} = (X^T X + \frac{p}{1+p}\lambda)^{-1} X^T y$, which is ridge regression.

4.10   Data Augmentation

Data augmentation is the process of generating new data points by transforming existing ones. This is done to improve the performance of machine learning algorithms. For example, if a dataset has many images of cars, data augmentation might generate new images by rotating them or changing their color. The augmented training data is then used to train a neural network.

Data augmentation may be used to reduce overfitting. Overfitting occurs when a model is too closely tailored to the training data and does not generalize well to new data. Data augmentation can be used to generate new training data points that are similar to the existing training data points but are not identical copies. This helps the model avoid overfitting and generalizing better to new data. Since data augmentation adds more data for training, it may be used as a regularization technique for reducing variance in models.

We augment the training data by replacing each example pair (x_i, y_i) with a collection $\{x_i^{*b}, y_i\}_{b=1}^{B}$, where each x_i^{*b} is a version of x_i. Transformations commonly used for data augmentation include rotation, reflection, translation, shear, crop, color transformation, and added noise.

4.11 Batch Normalization

Exploding gradients is a problem that may occur when training a neural network. They occur when the gradient of the cost function with respect to the network's weights is too large. This can cause the weights to change too quickly and cause the neural network to diverge. Vanishing gradients is a phenomenon in neural networks where the gradient of the error function becomes small or zero. This means that the network cannot learn anymore and is stuck at a local minimum. Covariate shift occurs in neural networks when the magnitudes of the inputs to a layer change during training, making it challenging to learn the weights of a subsequent layer while accounting for the change in magnitude of the inputs.

Batch normalization is a technique for training neural networks that are used to counteract the problems of exploding and vanishing gradients, as well as covariate shift. It does this by scaling the input data by a factor of $\frac{1}{\sqrt{n}}$, where n is the batch size. This makes the gradient values more stable and prevents them from changing too quickly.

4.12 Summary

Regularization is a technique that can be used to prevent overfitting. Regularization can be achieved by adding a penalty term to the cost function. The penalty term is usually a function of the number of parameters in the model. Dropout and data augmentation are also forms of regularization in neural networks because these methods help to prevent overfitting. Dropout is a technique that randomly sets several weights in a neural network to zero. This technique helps to prevent overfitting by reducing the variance of the network. Data augmentation is a technique that involves modifying the input data to the neural network by applying random transformations. This technique also helps prevent overfitting by increasing the size of the training set.

Part II

Architectures

5 Convolutional Neural Networks

5.1 Introduction

The first step in the visual pathway is the retina, which consists of a layer of photoreceptor cells: the rods and cones. The retina's output is an optic nerve consisting of one million fibers connected to regions of the brain. Each of these regions is connected in turn to other regions. The primary visual cortex reacts to low-level visual stimuli such as oriented lines. Hubel and Wiesel won the Nobel Prize for mapping the function of receptor cells along the visual pathways of cats from the retina to the cortex (Hubel and Wiesel, 1968). Processing proceeds in a hierarchical fashion of layers (Felleman and Van Essen, 1991). Fukushima introduced the Neocognitron architecture (Fukushima, 1988), which led to the development of modern convolutional neural networks (CNNs). Initially, computer vision researchers handcrafted filters, whereas optimizing CNNs automatically calculates the weights of filter banks in multiple layers by backpropagation. Similarly, deep learning researchers initially handcrafted CNN architectures, whereas neural architecture search (NAS) automatically finds CNN architectures from basic layers and building blocks by optimization. Finally, computational power allows generating entire wirings of graph neural networks (GNNs) and vast amounts of data allow training vision Transformer networks without handcrafting the inductive bias into the network architecture. Convolutional neural networks are a special case of these vision Transformer networks, which supersede CNN performance on common tasks and benchmarks. Today, 60 years after Hubel and Wiesel's (1959) discoveries, there is an understanding of the visual pathways in the human brain, and common neural networks trained on millions of images outperform humans in visual recognition.

5.1.1 Representations Sharing Weights

The most successful deep learning representations share weights: CNNs, described in this chapter, share weights across space; recurrent neural networks (RNNs), described in Chapter 6, share weights across time; and GNNs, described in Chapter 7, share weights across neighborhoods.

In a fully connected neural network, as presented in Chapter 2, the dimension of the matrix of weights between two layers with n activation units each is the multiplication of the layer sizes, $n \times n$. Performing a computation with time complexity square in the number of activation units in a layer $O(n^2)$ is prohibitive for wide layers. Images are regular grids of pixels, and it is beneficial to perform the same operation locally on different parts of the image. Using a local filter and sharing these weights spatially across the image reduces the number of weights to a constant.

Convolutional neural networks reduce the number of weights by sharing weights for different parts of an image. They may learn many sets of weights, namely multiple filters, for each layer in the neural network, thereby capturing multiple features such as edges, corners, and textures. Each layer captures features at different scales, from low-level features, such as edges, through mid-level features, such as textures, to high-level features, such as entire objects.

When we process data of a particular type, such as images with locality, or when the mapping between input and output spaces has known properties, such as invariance to transformations, incorporating this inductive bias into the neural network architecture, for example, in the form of a CNN, makes sense. For example, image pixels depend on neighboring pixels or fragments, and objects are detected or classified with the same label under affine transformations.

5.2 Convolution

Convolution is the process of multiplying two functions together. A very simple example of convolution is multiplying an image with a kernel. The convolution kernel is a function that is typically represented by a small matrix that operates on the image. Specifically, the kernel is applied to the image by local pointwise multiplication of the image with the kernel and by summing the contributions. The convolution of an image with a kernel is a weighted average of the image.

5.2.1 One-Dimensional Convolution

The definition of the discrete one-dimensional convolution of two functions f and g is:

$$(f \star g)(i) = \sum_{u=-s}^{s} g(u)f(i-u) \tag{5.1}$$

Figure 5.1 illustrates the process of sliding a 3×1 filter k over a 10×1 input x, and for each position multiplying corresponding values of the input with the filter and taking their sum, resulting in an output value. For example, $y_{u+1} = \sum_{i=1}^{3} k_i x_{i+u-1}$ for $u = 1, \ldots, 8$, where we omit the reflection of the filter.

Convolution padding may be performed so that the output size is the same as the input size. Figure 5.2 illustrates zero-padding by padding the boundaries with zeros. Figure 5.3 illustrates reflection-padding by padding the boundaries using values that are a reflection of the signal.

Input:

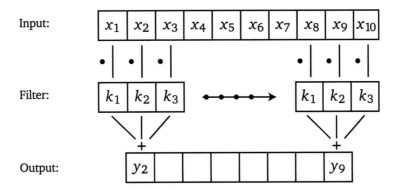

Filter:

Output:

Figure 5.1 One-dimensional convolution.

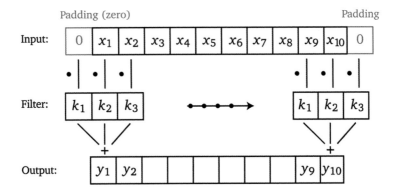

Figure 5.2 One-dimensional convolution with zero-padding.

Filtering with the identity kernel, for example $k = [0, 1, 0]$, results in the output being equal to the input, as shown in Figure 5.3. Filtering with an averaging kernel, for example, $k = \frac{1}{3}[1, 1, 1]$, results in the output is equal to a local average of the input. Notice that we normalize the filter by dividing each filter coefficient by the sum of the coefficients.

Filters are commonly used for blurring or sharpening a signal. For example, the filter kernel $k = \frac{1}{4}[1, 2, 1]$ approximates a Gaussian blur, whereas the filter kernel $k = [-1, 2, -1]$ sharpens the signal.

Figure 5.4 shows an example of a one-dimensional convolution, with a bias of $+1$, followed by applying a non-linear function, the rectified linear unit (ReLU) function, pointwise.

5.2.2 Matrix Multiplication

Convolution is a linear operation that may be represented by matrix multiplication. In one dimension we represent a filter k using a Toeplitz matrix (Böttcher

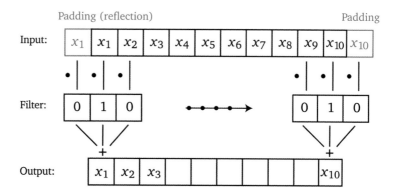

Figure 5.3 One-dimensional convolution with the identity filter.

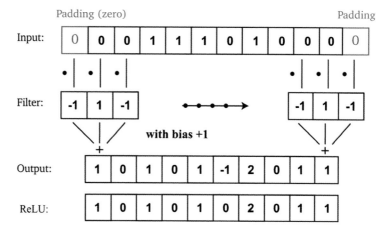

Figure 5.4 Example of one-dimensional convolution with bias, followed by a ReLU.

and Grudsky, 2005) such that the matrix–vector product Kx is the convolution operation $k \star x$. The matrix K may be expressed as a linear combination of diagonal matrices, with 1s on the diagonal, multiplied by the filter weights. For a 3×1 filter $k = (k_1, k_2, k_3)^T$: The first matrix S_1 has 1s on the diagonal below the main diagonal and is multiplied by the filter coefficient k_1; the second matrix S_2 has 1s on the main diagonal and is multiplied by k_2; and the third matrix S_3 has 1s on the diagonal above the main diagonal and is multiplied by k_3:

$$y = k \star x = Kx = \sum_{i=1}^{3} k_i S_i x \qquad (5.2)$$

The derivative of the output y with respect to each of the kernel weights is:

$$\frac{dy}{dk_i} = S_i x \qquad (5.3)$$

For example, convolution of a filter $k = (k_1, k_2, k_3)^T$ with a signal $x = (x_1, \ldots, x_5)^T$ expressed as $y = k \star x$ is equivalent to multiplication $y = Kx$ by a band diagonal matrix K called a Toeplitz matrix, with the kernel k replicated along the diagonal and all other elements zero:

$$
\begin{bmatrix} y_1 \\ y_2 \\ y_3 \end{bmatrix} = \begin{bmatrix} k_1 & k_2 & k_3 & 0 & 0 \\ 0 & k_1 & k_2 & k_3 & 0 \\ 0 & 0 & k_1 & k_2 & k_3 \end{bmatrix} \begin{bmatrix} x_1 \\ x_2 \\ x_3 \\ x_4 \\ x_5 \end{bmatrix}
\tag{5.4}
$$

In this case the input dimension is 5, whereas the output dimension is 3. To have the input and output dimensions be the same, we pad the signal x. One form of padding is zero-padding by adding zeros to the beginning and end of the signal and adding the corresponding rows and columns of the matrix:

$$
\begin{bmatrix} y_1 \\ y_2 \\ y_3 \\ y_4 \\ y_5 \end{bmatrix} = \begin{bmatrix} k_1 & k_2 & k_3 & 0 & 0 & 0 & 0 \\ 0 & k_1 & k_2 & k_3 & 0 & 0 & 0 \\ 0 & 0 & k_1 & k_2 & k_3 & 0 & 0 \\ 0 & 0 & 0 & k_1 & k_2 & k_3 & 0 \\ 0 & 0 & 0 & 0 & k_1 & k_2 & k_3 \end{bmatrix} \begin{bmatrix} 0 \\ x_1 \\ x_2 \\ x_3 \\ x_4 \\ x_5 \\ 0 \end{bmatrix}
\tag{5.5}
$$

Padding results in inputs and outputs of equal dimensions, which may be convenient to work with.

In this case we perform convolution of the filter with the signal by sliding the filter across the signal one step, or stride, at a time. We can also perform the convolution with different strides, for example with a stride of two in which case the kernel matrix is $\begin{bmatrix} k_1 & k_2 & k_3 & 0 & 0 \\ 0 & 0 & k_1 & k_2 & k_3 \end{bmatrix}$. Increasing the stride to two decreases the output length by a factor of two. Overall, the number of weights to be considered is reduced significantly, from the entire matrix dimensions to just the kernel's size. In contrast, in a fully connected neural network, the number of weights between two adjacent layers is the multiplication of the number of activation units in the layers.

5.2.3 Two-Dimensional Convolution

The two-dimensional convolution of a filter f with a signal g is defined as:

$$
(f \star g)(i, j) = \sum_{u=-s}^{s} \sum_{v=-s}^{s} g(u, v) f(i - u, j - v)
\tag{5.6}
$$

A two-dimensional input X representing an image may be represented as a regular two-dimensional grid with local connectivity of each pixel connected to its neighbors, as shown in Figure 5.5.

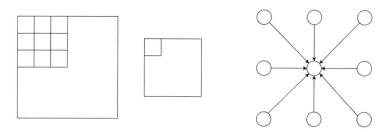

Figure 5.5 Regular two-dimensional grid.

Input:

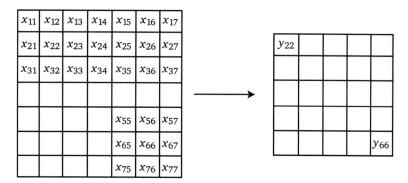

Filter:

$$y_{22} = k_{11}x_{11} + k_{12}x_{12} + k_{13}x_{13} + \ldots + k_{33}x_{33}$$

Figure 5.6 Two-dimensional convolution.

For such a two-dimensional input X representing an image, we first flatten X into a vector x by concatenating the rows of X into a single vector x. The convolution of the two-dimensional filter K with the two-dimensional input X is equivalent to a matrix–vector multiplication. For example, for a 3×3 filter k and a 7×7 image X flattened into a vector x, the result of convolution is a 5×5 image Y, as shown in Figure 5.6, where each coefficient is a linear combination of nine products of the kernel weights centered upon the corresponding image position.

For example, the value of the output y_{22} computed by centering the filter k on input x_{22} is:

$$y_{22} = k_{11}x_{11} + k_{12}x_{12} + k_{13}x_{13} + \cdots + k_{33}x_{33}. \tag{5.7}$$

As another example, consider the matrix form of the convolution of a two-dimensional 3×3 filter:

$$k = \begin{bmatrix} k_{11} & k_{12} & k_{13} \\ k_{21} & k_{22} & k_{23} \\ k_{31} & k_{32} & k_{33} \end{bmatrix} \tag{5.8}$$

with a 5×5 image:

$$x = \begin{bmatrix} x_{11} & x_{12} & x_{13} & x_{14} & x_{15} \\ x_{21} & x_{22} & x_{23} & x_{24} & x_{25} \\ x_{31} & x_{32} & x_{33} & x_{34} & x_{35} \\ x_{41} & x_{42} & x_{43} & x_{44} & x_{45} \\ x_{51} & x_{52} & x_{53} & x_{54} & x_{55} \end{bmatrix} \tag{5.9}$$

which is expressed as multiplication of a block Toeplitz matrix K:

$$K = \begin{bmatrix} K_1 & K_2 & K_3 & 0 & 0 \\ 0 & K_1 & K_2 & K_3 & 0 \\ 0 & 0 & K_1 & K_2 & K_3 \end{bmatrix} \tag{5.10}$$

whose blocks are themselves Toeplitz matrices K_i for $i = 1, 2, 3$:

$$K_i = \begin{bmatrix} k_{i1} & k_{i2} & k_{i3} & 0 & 0 \\ 0 & k_{i1} & k_{i2} & k_{i3} & 0 \\ 0 & 0 & k_{i1} & k_{i2} & k_{i3} \end{bmatrix} \tag{5.11}$$

with the flattened vector representation $x = (x_{11}, \dots, x_{55})^T$ of the image. Increasing the stride from one to two in each dimension decreases the output size by a factor of two in each dimension. Similarly to one-dimensional convolution, padding can be done with zeros, as shown in Figure 5.7, or reflected values in two-dimensions, as shown in Figure 5.8.

Figure 5.9 shows an example of two-dimmensional convolution followed by applying the ReLU. The result of this operation is finding a value of 1 surrounded by zeros.

Considering that an image may contain millions of pixels, the number of weights between layers using a fully connected network may increase to billions, whereas sharing all weights using a CNN results in a small constant number of weights. Between every two layers of the CNN we can learn multiple two-dimensional filters, and for each filter have a constant number of weights. The convolution of a filter with each local neighborhood of the image results in a response that captures diverse features from multiple filters and features at multiple scales from multiple network layers.

Before convolutional neural networks, image filters were manually designed for specific purposes. Examples of well-known filters include the box filter, approximation of Gaussian blur, sharpen filter, horizontal and vertical Sobel edge detection, and Prewitt edge detection. A discrete approximation of the Gaussian filter is given by a two-dimensional matrix. For a 3×3 discrete approximation,

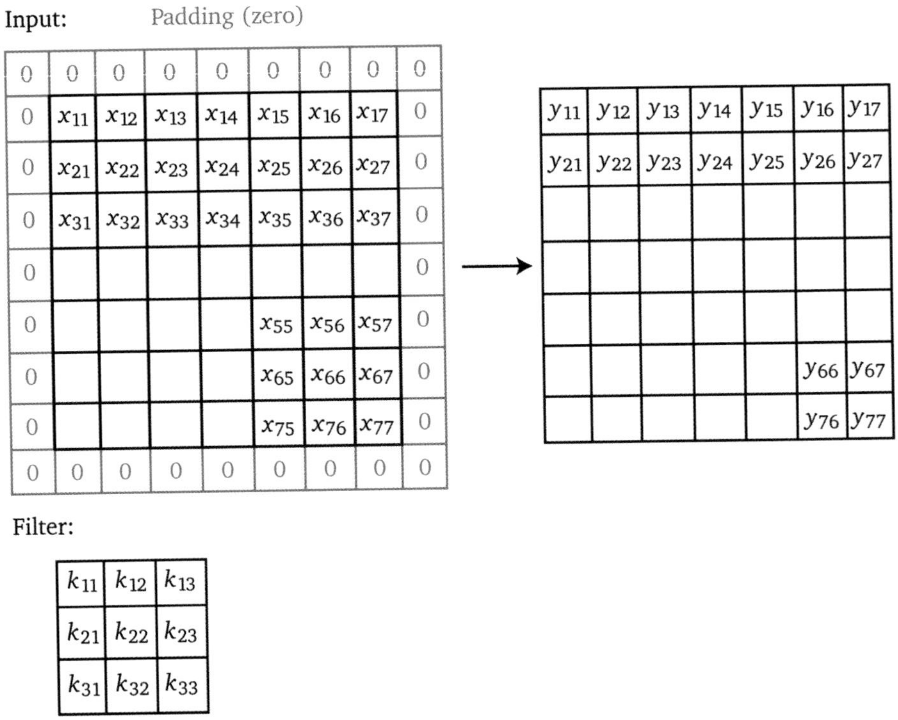

Input: Padding (zero)

0	0	0	0	0	0	0	0	0
0	x_{11}	x_{12}	x_{13}	x_{14}	x_{15}	x_{16}	x_{17}	0
0	x_{21}	x_{22}	x_{23}	x_{24}	x_{25}	x_{26}	x_{27}	0
0	x_{31}	x_{32}	x_{33}	x_{34}	x_{35}	x_{36}	x_{37}	0
0								0
0					x_{55}	x_{56}	x_{57}	0
0					x_{65}	x_{66}	x_{67}	0
0					x_{75}	x_{76}	x_{77}	0
0	0	0	0	0	0	0	0	0

y_{11}	y_{12}	y_{13}	y_{14}	y_{15}	y_{16}	y_{17}
y_{21}	y_{22}	y_{23}	y_{24}	y_{25}	y_{26}	y_{27}
					y_{66}	y_{67}
					y_{76}	y_{77}

Filter:

k_{11}	k_{12}	k_{13}
k_{21}	k_{22}	k_{23}
k_{31}	k_{32}	k_{33}

Figure 5.7 Two-dimensional convolution with zero-padding.

the filter coefficients are:

$$\frac{1}{16}\begin{bmatrix} 1 & 2 & 1 \\ 2 & 4 & 2 \\ 1 & 2 & 1 \end{bmatrix} = \frac{1}{4}\begin{bmatrix} 1 \\ 2 \\ 1 \end{bmatrix} \otimes \frac{1}{4}\begin{bmatrix} 1 & 2 & 1 \end{bmatrix} \tag{5.12}$$

5.2.4   Separable Filters

In special cases such as the approximation of a Gaussian filter, above, two-dimensional convolution is equivalent to the outer product of two one-dimensional filters, as shown in Figure 5.10. In such cases the computation is more efficient: Performing two one-dimensional convolutions of size k with an image of size $n \times n$ takes time $O(n^2 k)$, whereas performing one two-dimensional convolution of size $k \times k$ takes time $O(n^2 k^2)$.

5.2.5   Properties

The convolution operation is commutative, associative, distributive, and differentiable:

- Commutative: $f \star g = g \star f$

Input: Padding (reflection)

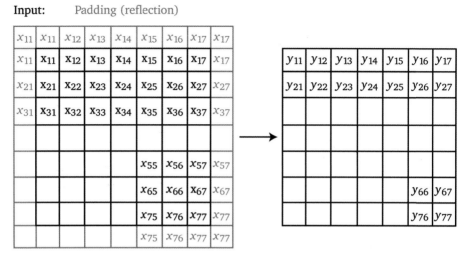

Filter:

k_{11}	k_{12}	k_{13}
k_{21}	k_{22}	k_{23}
k_{31}	k_{32}	k_{33}

Figure 5.8 Two-dimensional convolution with reflection-padding.

- Associative: $f \star (g \star h) = (f \star g) \star h$
- Distributive: $f \star (g + h) = f \star g + f \star h$
- Differentiation: $\frac{d}{dx}(f \star g) = \frac{df}{dx} \star g = f \star \frac{dg}{dx}$

5.2.6   Composition

Repeated convolutions with a small kernel are equivalent to a single convolution with a large kernel; however, they are more efficient. For example, two repeated convolutions with a 3×3 kernel may be equivalent and more efficient than a 2D convolution with a 5×5 kernel, and three repeated convolutions with a 3×3 kernel may be equivalent and more efficient than 2D convolution with a 7×7 kernel. An example of inputs and outputs of a repeated convolution with a 3×3 kernel are shown in Figure 5.11.

5.2.7   Three-Dimensional Convolution

Images are often represented by three color channels of red, green, and blue (RGB). Two-dimensional convolution can be performed on each channel separately, as shown in Figure 5.12, or a three-dimensional filter can be convolved

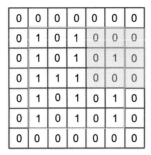

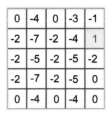

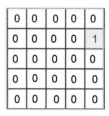

ReLU

Figure 5.9 Two-dimensional convolution followed by a ReLU.

with the 3D volume consisting of the three channels, as shown in Figures 5.13 and 5.14.

5.3   Layers

5.3.1   Convolution

Convolution of an $n \times n \times 3$ color image with a $k \times k \times 3$ filter, with padding, results in an $n \times n$ output, as shown in Figure 5.15. Convolution of an $n \times n \times 3$ color image with four such filters, with padding, results in an $n \times n \times 4$ volume of activations, as shown in Figure 5.16. Convolution of an $n \times n \times 3$ color image with f filters, with padding, results in an $n \times n \times f$ volume of activations, as shown in Figure 5.17.

Each set of such filtering operations constitutes the linear part of a convolution layer. Repeated filtering may increase the number of channels. As described next, a common way to reduce the spatial dimension is by pooling.

5.3.2   Pooling

Pooling is an operation that reduces the dimensionality of the input by taking a function value from a set of locations. Max pooling takes the maximum over image patches, for example over 2×2 grids of neighboring pixels $m = \max\{x_1, x_2, x_3, x_4\}$, reducing dimensionality to half in each spatial dimension, as shown in Figure 5.18.

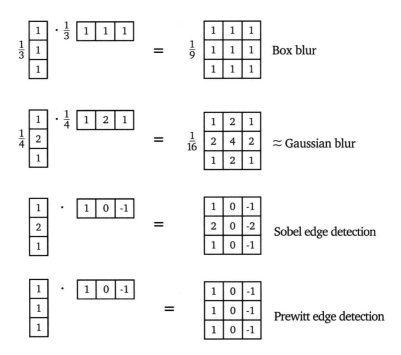

Figure 5.10 Two-dimensional convolution with separable filters.

One-Dimensional Convolution
One-dimensional convolution with f filters also allows reducing the number of channels, as shown in Figure 5.19.

5.4 Example

Combining the above components in sequential layers of convolution and non-linear functions followed by pooling results in a very simple CNN architecture, as shown in Figure 5.20. In this example, the input is a 28×28 grayscale image, and the output is 1 of 10 classes, such as the digits 0–9. The first convolutional layer consists of 32 filters, such as 5×5 filters applied to the image with padding, which yields a $28 \times 28 \ times32$ volume. Next, a non-linear function, such as the ReLU, is applied pointwise to each element in the volume. The first convolution layer of the network shown in Figure 5.20 is followed by a 2×2 max pooling operation that reduces dimensionality to half in each spatial dimension, to $14 \times 14 \times 32$. The second convolutional layer increases dimensionality to $14 \times 14 \times 64$ by applying a second set of 64 filters, such as 3×3 filters, and the second pooling layer reduces dimensionality, again to half in each dimension, to $7 \times 7 \times 64$. The

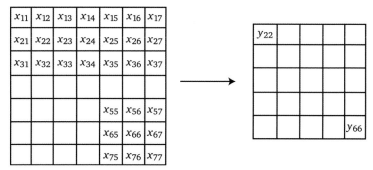

Convolution with 3 x 3 kernel

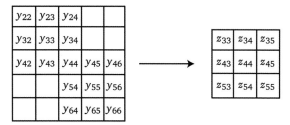

Convolution with 3 x 3 kernel

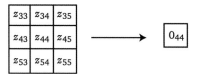

Convolution with 3 x 3 kernel

Figure 5.11 Repeated convolutions with a 3×3 kernel are equivalent to a single convolution with a 7×7 kernel, and more efficient.

resulting volume is then flattened to form a $3,136$ dimensional vector which is fed into two fully connected layers. The first fully connected layer consists of $1,024$ activations, followed by a second fully connected layer with 10 activations, one for each output class.

5.5   Architectures

Convolutional Neural Network
We composed a CNN using filters and convolutional and pooling layers. The simple convolutional neural network example described above consists of a few convolutional layers. The Neocognitron (Fukushima, 1988) introduced CNNs.

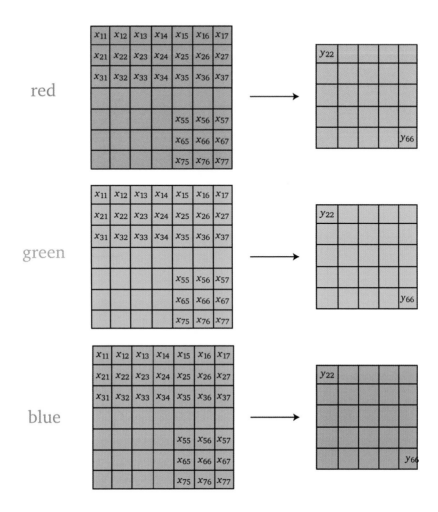

Figure 5.12 Two-dimensional convolution with three channels.

A deeper network of eight layers may resemble the cortical visual pathways in the brain (Cichy et al., 2016). Early implementations of CNN architectures were handcrafted for specific image classification tasks. These include LeNet (LeCun et al., 2010), AlexNet (Krizhevsky et al., 2012), VGGNet (Simonyan and Zisserman, 2014), GoogLeNet (Szegedy et al., 2015) and Inception (Szegedy et al., 2016). Figure 5.21 schematically illustrates a CNN with multiple layers and the connections between volumes of activations.

ResNet

The deep residual neural network (ResNet) architecture (He et al., 2016a,b), introduced skip connections between consecutive layers, as shown in Figure 5.22. Skip connections allow training deeper neural networks by avoiding vanishing gradients. The ResNet architecture enables training very deep neural networks

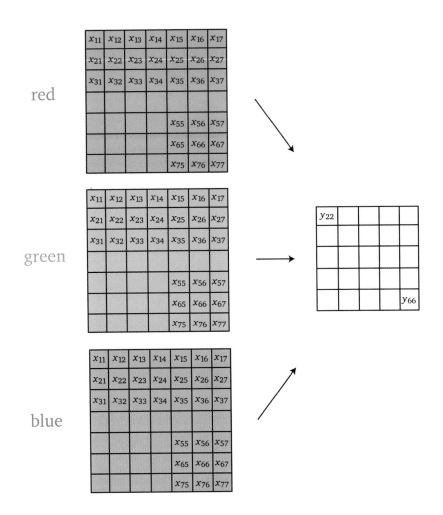

Figure 5.13 Three-dimensional convolution with three channels.

with hundreds of layers. The original ResNet with skip connections between layers is shown in Figure 5.23. In a neural network, the activations are the layer outputs:

$$a^{l+1} = f(W^l, a^l) \qquad (5.13)$$

where f is the non-linear function, W^l the weights of layer l, and a^l, the input activations to layer l. In a ResNet, due to the skip connections, the activations are the sum of the previous activations and the layer outputs:

$$a^{l+1} = a^l + f(W^l, a^l) \qquad (5.14)$$

Adding a new layer to a neural network with a skip connection does not reduce its representation power. Adding a residual layer results in the network representing all the functions that the network was able to represent before adding the

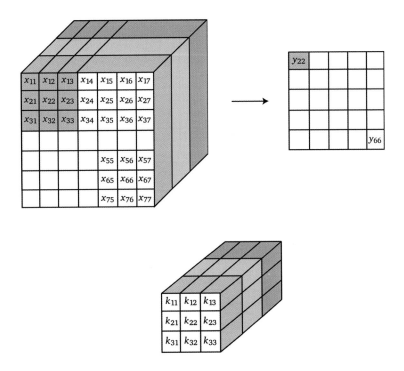

Figure 5.14 Three-dimensional convolution.

layer plus additional functions, thus increasing the space of functions. A neural network is a composition of functions f with a linear part and a non-linear part. For a three-layer network, the composition is:

$$F(x) = f(f(f(x))) \tag{5.15}$$

A ResNet is a composition of functions where each function is the sum $f(x) + x$, and each layer represents a residual $f(x) - x$. For a three-layer ResNet the function is:

$$F(x) = f(f(f(x) + x) + (f(x) + x)) + f(f(x) + x) + (f(x) + x) \tag{5.16}$$

DenseNet

A DenseNet (Huang, Liu, van der Maaten and Weinberger, 2017) layer concatenates the input x and output $f(x)$ of each layer to form the next layer $[f(x), x]$. Since a neural network is a composition of functions this results in a dense connection between each layer and its previous layers. For a three-layer network the composition is:

$$F(x) = f([f([f(x), x]), [f(x), x]]), f([f(x), x]), [f(x), x] \tag{5.17}$$

Figure 5.24 shows a block diagram of a DenseNet.

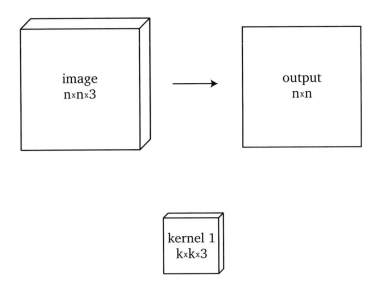

Figure 5.15 Convolution layer with one filter.

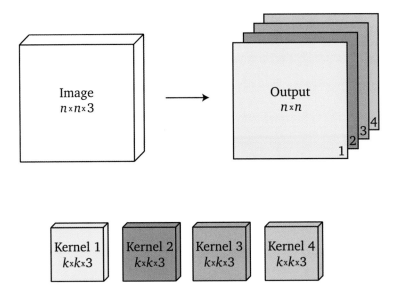

Figure 5.16 Convolution layer with four filters.

SENet

Squeeze and excitation networks, or SENet (Hu et al., 2018), take into account the relationships between channels by weighting the channels of layers.

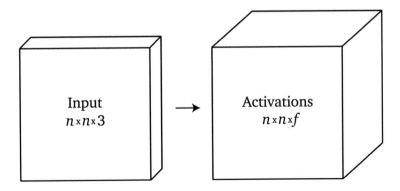

Figure 5.17 Convolution layer with f filters.

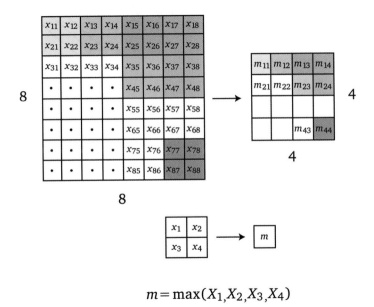

$$m = \max(X_1, X_2, X_3, X_4)$$

Figure 5.18 Max pooling.

MobileNets
MobileNets (Howard et al., 2017) are CNNs with a lightweight backbone and high performance geared toward mobile phones. MobileNet improvements include separable convolution filters, bottleneck blocks, and inverted residual blocks. ShuffleNets (Zhang, Zhou, Lin and Sun, 2018) optimize the CNN architecture for computation and memory access and allow for parallel computation (Ma et al., 2018).

ODENet
ODENet (Chen, Rubanova, Bettencourt and Duvenaud, 2018) introduce a continuous formulation for CNNs equivalent to any number of layers.

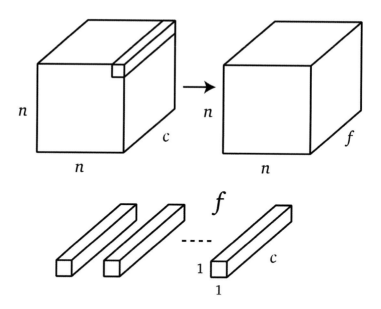

Figure 5.19 Convolution layer with one-dimensional filters.

Invertible Networks
Invertible residual neural networks (Behrmann et al., 2019) use the same network for both analysis and synthesis. An invertible ResNet is used for both classification and generation in the inverse direction.

Space–Time CNNs
Convolutional neural networks may be extended from input images to video by processing multiple video frames simultaneously, as shown in Figure 5.25.

5.6   Applications

Convolutional neural networks have broad applications in computer vision and beyond. Such a wide range of applications means that any architectural advance impacts multiple application domains. The applications in computer vision include classification, recognition, localization, counting, object detection, segmentation, image completion, and pose estimation. Beyond computer vision, CNNs are used to efficiently represent data that may be represented as an array or volume.

For example, in game playing, AlphaZero (Silver et al., 2017) uses a ResNet as the representation of the board, pieces, and their possible moves. A policy $\pi(a|s)$, which is the probability of any action a taking place given any board state s is represented by an $8 \times 8 \times 73$ volume, as shown in Figure 5.26. There

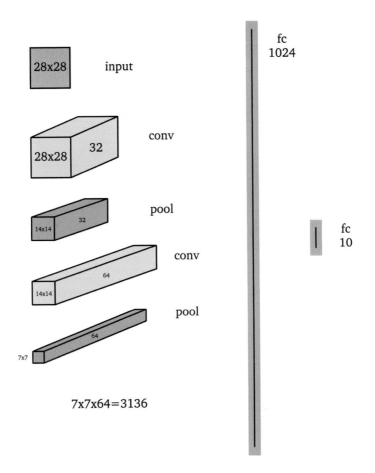

Figure 5.20 Convolutional neural network. Input is a 28×28 grayscale image, and the output is 1 of 10 classes, such as the digits 0–9. The first convolutional layer consists of 32 filters, such as 5×5 filters applied to the image with padding, which yields a $28 \times 28 \ times32$ volume. Next, a non-linear function, such as the ReLU, is applied pointwise to each element in the volume. This is followed by a 2×2 max pooling operation, which reduces dimensionality to half in each spatial dimension, to $14 \times 14 \times 32$. The second convolutional layer increases dimensionality to $14 \times 14 \times 64$ by applying a second set of 64 filters, such as 3×3 filters, and the second pooling layer reduces dimensionality, again to half in each dimension, to $7 \times 7 \times 64$. The resulting volume is then flattened to form a $3,136$ dimensional vector which is fed into two fully connected layers. The first fully connected layer consists of $1,024$ activations, followed by a second fully connected layer with 10 activations, one for each output class.

are 8×8 board positions from which to pick up a piece. Figure 5.27 shows that in chess, there are 56 queen moves in 8 possible directions times seven maximum steps, eight knight moves marked by blue squares, and nine under promotions, for a total of 73 possibilities.

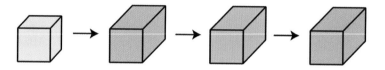

Figure 5.21 Convolutional neural network activations.

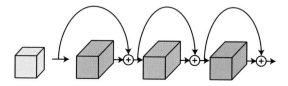

Figure 5.22 Residual neural network (ResNet) activations with skip connections between layers.

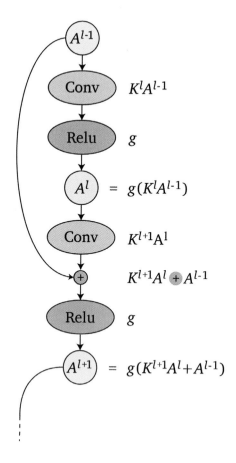

Figure 5.23 Residual neural network (ResNet).

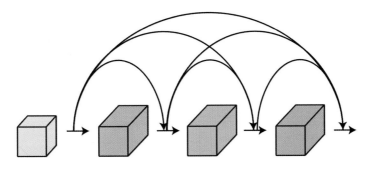

Figure 5.24 Dense neural network (DenseNet).

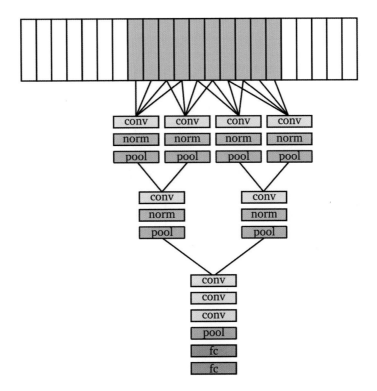

Figure 5.25 Space–time CNN.

5.7   Summary

In summary, CNNs are a type of neural network designed to recognize patterns in images. The network comprises a series of layers, with each layer performing a specific function. The first layer is typically a convolutional layer, which performs

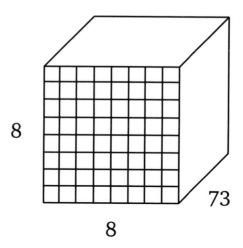

Figure 5.26 AlphaZero board and move representation.

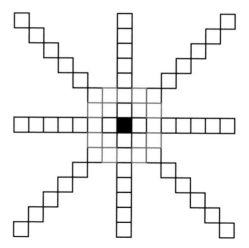

Figure 5.27 AlphaZero chess move representation.

a convolution operation on the input image. The convolution operation is a mathematical operation that extracts information from the input image. The output of the convolutional layer is then passed to a pooling layer, which reduces the number of neurons in the network. Multiple convolutions and pooling layers are followed by a series of fully connected layers responsible for the classification or other applications performed on the image. Convolutional neural networks perform well in practice across a broad range of applications since they share weights at multiple scales across space.

6 Sequence Models

6.1 Introduction

Time series may be used for representing any temporal sequence, such as a sentence of words, video of image frames, or audio spectrogram. There are many questions we can answer about sequences using deep learning. Applications using sequence models include machine translation, protein structure prediction, DNA sequence analysis, speech recognition, music synthesis, image captioning, sentiment classification, video action recognition, handwriting recognition, self-driving cars, and many other applications involving time series. In a similar fashion that representations for images share weights across space, many deep learning representations for sequences share weights across time.

6.2 Natural Language Models

Language models are among the most common sequence models and therefore we begin with their description. Representing language requires a natural language model which may be a probability distribution over strings. We begin the presentation of language models, starting from the simplest model and increasing model complexity to reach recurrent neural networks (RNNs), which model long-term dependencies.

6.2.1 Bag of Words

Perhaps the simplest model of language is a multi-set, also known as a bag of words. In a bag of words we count how prevalent each term x is in a single document d, which is the term frequency $TF(x, d)$. Words are commonly normalized to lowercase and stemmed by removing their suffixes; common stopwords (such as a, an, the, etc.) are removed. The inverse document frequency may be used to boost terms that are rare in an entire corpus of documents. The inverse document frequency of a word appearing in a document and of a word not appearing in a document measure together the entropy of the word:

$$IDF(x) = 1 + \log\left(\frac{\text{total number of documents}}{\text{number of documents containing } x}\right) \tag{6.1}$$

The product of the term frequency and the inverse document frequency may be used to form a vector $TFIDF(x, d) = TF(x, d) \times IDF(x)$ and used for measuring similarity between a query and a document. *TFIDF* can be used as weighting in search and data mining. A bag of words representation does not preserve order information. For example, representing the sentence "Alice sent a message to Bob" as a bag of words does not distinguish between the sender and receiver of the message, and has an equivalent representation as the sentence "Bob sent a message to Alice."

6.2.2   Feature Vector

In contrast to a bag of words, using a feature vector to represent a sentence preserves order information. A limitation of a feature vector representation is that it requires learning each word order separately, even if two sentences are equivalent, such as the sentences "Alice sent a message on Sunday" and "On Sunday Alice sent a message," which may be inefficient.

6.2.3   N-grams

A sequence of n adjacent words is called an n-gram. A bag of words is the 1-gram or unigram model in which $p(x_1, \ldots, x_n) \approx \prod p(x_i)$. A Markov model is a 2-gram or bi-gram model in which $p(x_n|x_1, \ldots, x_{n-1}) \approx p(x_n|x_{n-1})$. The probability of a word given the previous word may be computed by counting $p(x_n|x_{n-1}) = \frac{\text{count}(x_{n-1}x_n)}{\text{count}(x_{n-1})}$. Usually 3-,4-,5- or k-gram models are computed $p(x_n|x_1, \ldots, x_{n-1}) \approx p(x_n|x_{n-1}, \ldots, x_{n-k+1})$ and stored, given a large corpus.

6.2.4   Markov Model

The special case of a bi-gram is a Markov model given by $p(x_n|x_{n-1}, \ldots, x_1) \approx p(x_n|x_{n-1})$ and does not model long-term dependencies. For example, in the sentence "Alice and Bob communicate. Alice sent Bob a message," the probability of the last word "message," given a Markov model, depends only on the previous word "a," which does not provide much information, rather than taking into account the relevant prefix that "Alice and Bob communicate." A limitation of a Markov model is that it does not model long-term dependencies.

6.2.5   State Machine

A state machine is defined by a set of possible states $\mathcal{S}$, a set of possible inputs $\mathcal{X}$, a transition function $f : \mathcal{S} \times \mathcal{X} \mapsto \mathcal{S}$ that maps from state and input to state, a set of possible outputs $\mathcal{Y}$, a mapping $g : \mathcal{S} \mapsto \mathcal{Y}$ from states to outputs, and an initial state s_0. An example of a state machine is shown in Figure 6.1.

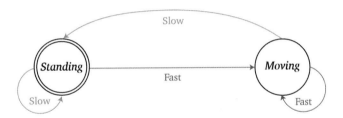

Figure 6.1 State machine example. Possible states are $\mathcal{S} = \{standing, moving\}$, a set of possible inputs are $\mathcal{X} = \{\text{slow}, \text{fast}\}$, transition function $f : \mathcal{S} \times \mathcal{X} \mapsto \mathcal{S}$ denoted by arrows, mapping g that in this example is the identity, and an initial state $s_0 = standing$.

Starting from the initial state s_0 we iteratively compute:

$$s_t = f(s_{t-1}, x_t)$$
$$y_t = g(s_t) \tag{6.2}$$

for time steps $t \geq 1$. For a sequence of inputs x_t the outputs y_t are of the form:

$$y_t = g(f(\ldots(f(f(s_0, x_1), x_2), \ldots), x_t)) \tag{6.3}$$

Recurrent neural networks are state machines with specific definitions of transition function f and mapping g, in which the states, inputs and outputs are vectors.

6.2.6   Recurrent Neural Network

Recurrent neural networks both maintain word order and model long-term dependencies by sharing parameters across time. They allow for the example inputs and the label outputs to be of different lengths. Bidirectional RNNs model both forward and backward sequence dependencies, and deep RNNs use multiple hidden layers. The limitation of plain RNNs is that they are difficult to train since the error signals flowing back in time explode or vanish. Therefore, the hidden units are replaced by simple gates that are easily trained.

6.3   Recurrent Neural Network

An RNN processes input sequences $x_1, \ldots, x_t$ via hidden units $h_0, h_1, \ldots, h_t$ to form outputs $y_1, \ldots, y_t$ by sharing parameter matrices U, W, V across time:

$$h_t = f(h_{t-1}, x_t) = g(Wh_{t-1} + Ux_t)$$
$$y_t = Vh_t \tag{6.4}$$

as shown in Figure 6.2, where the matrices U, W, V are shared across all time steps t. Each component of the sequence, x_t, h_t, y_t is a vector. The matrices U are applied to the input units x_t and the transformed input Ux_t serves as input to the

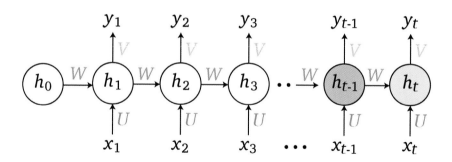

Figure 6.2 Recurrent neural network (RNN): forward propagation, sharing weights across time.

hidden unit h_t. The matrices W are applied to the recurrent hidden units h_{t-1} and the transformed hidden unit Wh_{t-1} serves as an input to the next hidden unit h_t. The matrices V are applied to the hidden units h_t and the transformed hidden unit Vh_t serves as an input to the predicted output y_t. The function g is a non-linear pointwise operation such as the tanh activation function. The matrices W and U may be concatenated to form a matrix $[W; U]$ and the hidden units h_{t-1} and input units x_t may be concatenated to form a single column vector $[h_{t-1}; x_t]^T$, resulting in a single matrix–vector multiplication followed by the non-linear function g for updating the hidden state h_t.

6.3.1   Architectures

Recurrent neural networks map input sequences to output sequences of varying lengths. This mapping may be a one-to-many, many-to-one, or a many-to-many mapping. A one-to-many mapping from x_1 to $y_1, \ldots, y_t$ is shown in Figure 6.3. An example of such a mapping applied to image captioning is receiving the representation of an image by a convolutional neural network (CNN) as an input vector x_1 for generating a sequence of words as output $y_1, \ldots, y_t$, describing the image.

A many-to-one mapping from $x_1, \ldots, x_t$ to y_t is shown in Figure 6.4. An example of such a mapping applied to sentiment classification is taking a sequence of word representations $x_1, \ldots, x_t$ as input for computing a number y_t which denotes the sentiment of the input sentence. This can be applied to a book or to restaurant reviews, where the input is the review in words, each word represented by an embedding as described in Section 6.8, and the output is the number of stars in the rating.

A many-to-many mapping from $x_1, \ldots, x_t$ to $y_1, \ldots, y_t$ is shown in Figure 6.5. An example of such a mapping applied to video action classification maps a sequence, which is the representations of video frames given by a CNN, to a sequence of classes, which is used for classifying the action in the video. A many-to-many model can also be used for named entity recognition, for example by

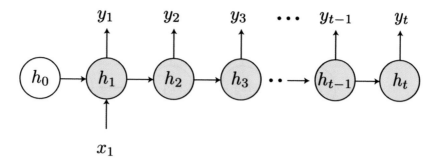

Figure 6.3 Recurrent neural network with a one-to-many mapping, which may be used in image captioning.

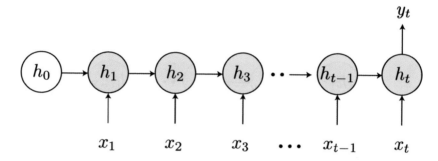

Figure 6.4 Recurrent neural network with a many-to-one mapping, which may be used in sentiment classification.

denoting the output corresponding to named entities as 1 and 0 otherwise, and learning the many-to-many mapping given multiple labeled sentences.

A many-to-many mapping can also be used in an encoder–decoder architecture, as shown in Figure 6.6 and described in Section 6.6. Mapping between sequences of words may be used in machine translation, in which the input sequence that is a sentence in one language is encoded and then decoded to an output sentence in another language.

6.3.2 Loss Function

To complete our definition of the RNN architecture requires incorporating a loss function, so that we can train our models, as shown in Figure 6.7.

The loss is a function of the predicted outputs o_t, and ground-truth labels y_t, as shown in Figure 6.8, and may be the cross-entropy loss. Using a softmax activation function we define the total loss between the softmax of the predicted values $\hat{y}_t = \text{softmax}(o_t)$, and ground-truth labels y_t as the sum of losses in individual time steps $\mathcal{L} = \sum_t \mathcal{L}_t$. Specifically, we defined the hidden units, outputs,

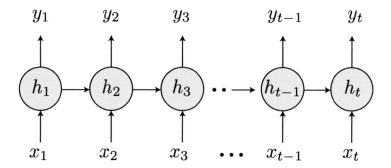

Figure 6.5 Recurrent neural network with a many-to-many mapping, which may be used in action recognition and named entity recognition.

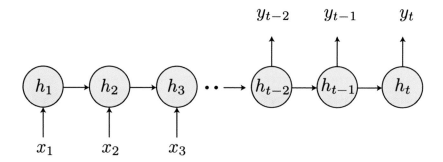

Figure 6.6 Recurrent neural network with a many-to-many mapping using an encoder–decoder architecture which may be used in machine translation.

predictions, and ground-truth value for each time step t by:

$$
\begin{aligned}
h_t &= g(W h_{t-1} + U x_t) \\
o_t &= V h_t \\
\hat{y}_t &= \text{softmax}(o_t) \\
y_t &= \text{ground-truth label}
\end{aligned}
\tag{6.5}
$$

Given input sequences x^i and predicted sequences $\hat{y}^i$ for $i = 1, \dots, m$, each pair of inputs and predicted outputs of length l_i, and ground-truth outputs y^i, define a loss of a single sequence as the sum of element losses where each element may be a character or word:

$$
\mathcal{L}_{\text{sequence}}(\hat{y}^i, y^i) = \sum_{t=1}^{l_i} \mathcal{L}_{\text{element}}(\hat{y}_t^i, y_t^i)
\tag{6.6}
$$

and the total loss over all sequences as the sum of sequence losses:

$$
\mathcal{L}_{\text{total}}(\hat{y}, y) = \sum_{i=1}^{m} \mathcal{L}_{\text{sequences}}(\hat{y}^i, y^i)
\tag{6.7}
$$

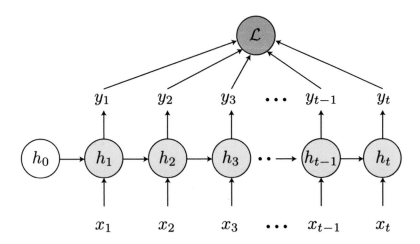

Figure 6.7 Recurrent neural network total loss.

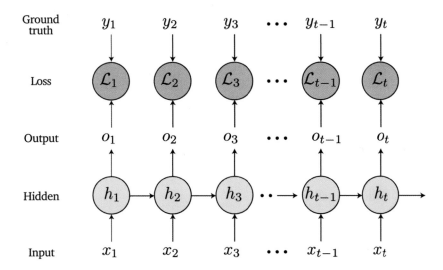

Figure 6.8 Recurrent neural network individual losses.

where $\hat{y}^i = F_\theta(x^i)$ is the prediction of the RNN for input x^i with network parameters θ.

6.3.3 Deep RNN

Stacking multiple hidden layers and connecting them:

$$h_t^l = g(W^l h_{t-1}^l + U^l h_t^{l-1}) \tag{6.8}$$

for layers $l = 1, \ldots, L$, results in a deep RNN, as shown in Figure 6.9. Matrices W^l, U^l for each layer l are shared across all time steps t.

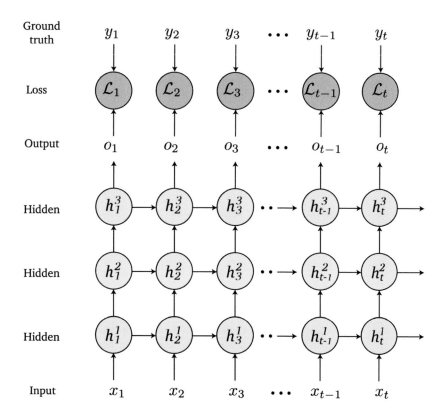

Figure 6.9 Deep recurrent neural network.

6.3.4   Bidirectional RNN

Often the output depends both on past and future values of the sequence. For example, in speech and handwriting recognition a word or character may depend both on previous and following words or characters. We therefore define a bidirectional RNN by:

$$
\begin{aligned}
h_t &= g(Wh_{t-1} + Ux_t)\\
\bar{h}_t &= g(\bar{W}\bar{h}_{t+1} + Ux_t)\\
o_t &= V[h_t; \bar{h}_t]^T
\end{aligned}
\tag{6.9}
$$

where the hidden units h_t move forward in time using the shared matrix W, and the hidden units $\bar{h}_t$ move backward in time from using the shared matrix $\bar{W}$, as shown in Figure 6.10. The inputs x_t are fed into both the forward hidden units h_t and backward hidden units $\bar{h}_t$, and in turn both the forward and backward hidden units are fed into the output o_t.

Stacking multiple bidirectional hidden layers results in a deep bidirectional RNN, as shown in Figure 6.11.

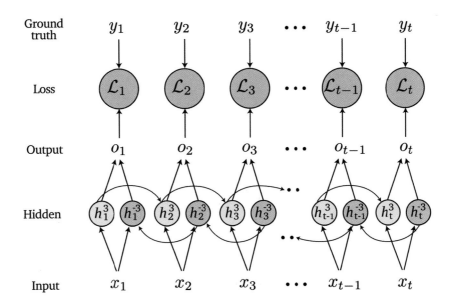

Figure 6.10 Bidirectional recurrent neural network.

6.3.5   Backpropagation Through Time

Having defined the RNN architectures and loss function, our goal is to train the RNN. Neural networks are trained using the backpropagation algorithm, and RNNs are trained using backpropagation through time. Given a non-linear activation function g such as the tanh activation function, and softmax loss, the loss for element or time step j may be defined as $\mathcal{L}_{\text{element}}(y_j, \hat{y}_j) = -y_j \log \hat{y}_j$ and the total loss of the sequence:

$$\mathcal{L}_{\text{sequence}}(y, \hat{y}) = \sum_{j=1}^{l} \mathcal{L}_{\text{element}}(y_j, \hat{y}_j) = -\sum_{j=1}^{l} y_j \log \hat{y}_j \qquad (6.10)$$

as illustrated in Figure 6.12.

Expressing the gradient of a sequence loss $\mathcal{L}_{\text{sequence}}(\hat{y}, y)$ with respect to all RNN weights θ by the sum of gradients of element losses and then using the chain rule results in:

$$\frac{d\mathcal{L}_{\text{sequence}}(\hat{y}, y)}{d\theta} = \sum_{j=1}^{l} \frac{d\mathcal{L}_{\text{element}}(\hat{y}_j, y_j)}{d\theta} = \sum_{j=1}^{l} \sum_{t=1}^{l} \frac{\partial \mathcal{L}_{\text{element}}(\hat{y}_j, y_j)}{\partial h_t} \frac{\partial h_t}{\partial \theta} \qquad (6.11)$$

Taking the derivatives of the loss for time t with respect to the matrix V only depends on time t. For example:

$$\frac{\partial \mathcal{L}_3}{\partial V} = \frac{\partial \mathcal{L}_3}{\partial \hat{y}_3} \frac{\partial \hat{y}_3}{\partial V} = \frac{\partial \mathcal{L}_3}{\partial \hat{y}_3} \frac{\partial \hat{y}_3}{\partial z_3} \frac{\partial z_3}{\partial V} \qquad (6.12)$$

where $z_3 = V h_3$. However, the derivative for time step t with respect to W also

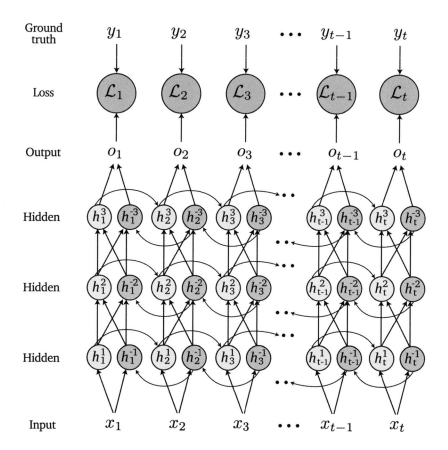

Figure 6.11 Deep bidirectional recurrent neural network.

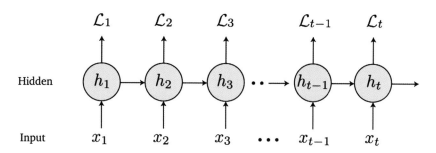

Figure 6.12 Recurrent neural network losses.

depends on the previous time step $t - 1$, which in turn depends on $t - 2$; for example:

$$\frac{\partial \mathcal{L}_3}{\partial W} = \frac{\partial \mathcal{L}_3}{\partial \hat{y}_3} \frac{\partial \hat{y}_3}{\partial h_3} \frac{\partial h_3}{\partial W} = \sum_{i=1}^{3} \frac{\partial \mathcal{L}_3}{\partial \hat{y}_3} \frac{\partial \hat{y}_3}{\partial h_3} \frac{\partial h_3}{\partial h_i} \frac{\partial h_i}{\partial W} \tag{6.13}$$

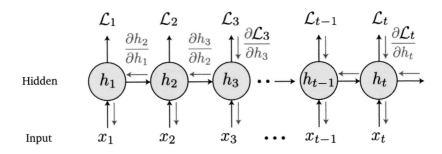

Figure 6.13 Recurrent neural network: backpropagation through time.

where $h_3 = \tanh(W h_2 + U x_3)$, as shown in Figure 6.13. Since:

$$\frac{\partial h_3}{\partial h_1} = \frac{\partial h_3}{\partial h_2}\frac{\partial h_2}{\partial h_1} \qquad (6.14)$$

we get:

$$\frac{\partial \mathcal{L}_3}{\partial W} = \sum_{i=1}^{3} \frac{\partial \mathcal{L}_3}{\partial \hat{y}_3}\frac{\partial \hat{y}_3}{\partial h_3}\left(\prod_{j=i+1}^{3}\frac{\partial h_j}{\partial h_{j-1}}\right)\frac{\partial h_i}{\partial W} \qquad (6.15)$$

where the product in parentheses in Equation 6.15 equals $\prod W^T \text{diag}(\tanh'(h_{t-1}))$. Thus, backpropagation through time involves raising the matrix W^T to a high power. Therefore, if the eigenvalues are less than 1 the corresponding terms will vanish, whereas if they are greater than 1 they will explode. While exploding gradients may be handled by clipping, vanishing gradients make plain RNNs difficult to train.

Backpropagation through time is described in pseudocode in Algorithm 6.1. Notice that the last line of the backpropagation loop involves a matrix multi-plication with W^T, which means that performing the loop results in taking the kth power of the matrix, which is equivalent to the analytic derivation. Thus, backpropagation in time will result in the eigenvalue of the matrix being either less than 1, in which case the gradient will vanish, or more than 1, in which case the gradients will explode.

Algorithm 6.1 RNN backward propagation through time.

> **for** $t = k, \ldots, 1$ **do:**
> $\quad do_t = e'(o_t)\frac{d\mathcal{L}(z_t;y_t)}{dz_t}$
> $\quad dV = dV + do_t h_t^T$
> $\quad dh_t = dh_t + V^T do_t$
> $\quad dz_t = g'(z_t)dh_t$
> $\quad dU = dU + dz_t x_t^T$
> $\quad dW = dW + dz_t h_{t-1}^T$
> $\quad dh_{t-1} = W^T dz_t$

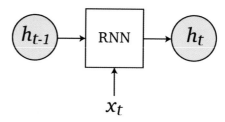

Figure 6.14 Recurrent neural network: hidden unit.

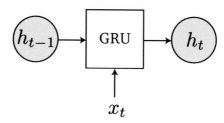

Figure 6.15 Gated recurrent unit inputs and output.

In summary, RNNs allow us to process variable-length sequences and model long-term dependencies by sharing parameters across time. Each hidden state depends on the corresponding input and current state, as shown in Figure 6.14.

An input may alter the network at a later time step. The main limitation of plain RNNs is that training is difficult and results in vanishing and exploding gradients. The solution is to model the hidden units using gates, which are easy to train, such as the long short-term memory (LSTM) (Hochreiter and Schmidhuber, 1997) and gated recurrent unit (GRU) (Cho et al., 2014), as described next.

6.4   Gated Recurrent Unit

The GRU (Cho et al., 2014) is simple and easy to train. It has the same inputs and outputs as the RNN. At each time step t the GRU receives as input the current state x_t and the hidden state h_{t-1} of the previous time step, and outputs the hidden state h_t at time t, as shown in Figure 6.15.

Gated recurrent units are placed one after the other, sequentially, where the hidden state output h_t of one unit serves as the hidden state input of the following unit, as shown in Figure 6.16. In a similar fashion to the RNN, the weights from the current states and from the hidden states are shared across time.

The GRU consists of an update gate z_t, a reset gate r_t and a candidate $\tilde{h}_t$, as shown in Figure 6.17.

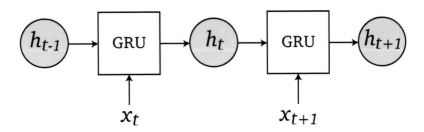

Figure 6.16 Gated recurrent units used sequentially with the outputs of one unit serving as the input to the next.

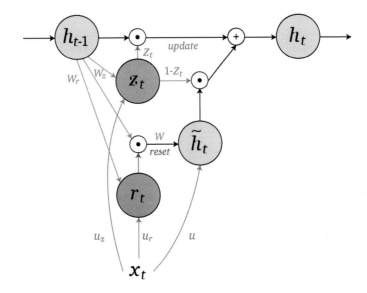

Figure 6.17 Gated recurrent unit.

The GRU gates are defined by:

$$
\begin{aligned}
z_t &= \sigma(W_z h_{t-1} + U_z x_t) && \text{update gate} \\
r_t &= \sigma(W_r h_{t-1} + U_r x_t) && \text{reset gate} \\
\tilde{h}_t &= \phi(W(r_t \odot h_{t-1}) + U x_t) && \text{candidate} \\
h_t &= z_t \odot h_{t-1} + (1 - z_t) \odot \tilde{h}_t && \text{output}
\end{aligned}
\tag{6.16}
$$

As an analogy, consider the input x_t to be the weather today, the hidden unit h_{t-1} to be the clothes we wore yesterday, $\tilde{h}_t$ to be the candidate clothes we prepared to wear today and h_t to be the actual clothes we wear today. Usually, we wear clothes based on the weather, based on what we wore yesterday, and based on our mood or what we prepared to wear today. The update and reset gates determine to what extent we take into account these factors: Do we ignore

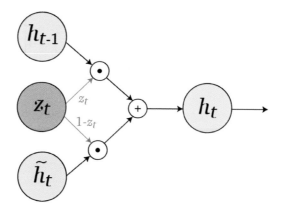

Figure 6.18 Gated recurrent unit update gate used for interpolation. The current hidden state h_t is a linear interpolation of the previous hidden state h_{t-1} and the new candidate $\tilde{h}_t$ based on the value of z_t, $h_t = z_t \odot h_{t-1} + (1 - z_t) \odot \tilde{h}_t$.

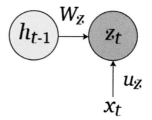

Figure 6.19 Gated recurrent unit update gate $z_t = \sigma(W_z h_{t-1} + U_z x_t)$.

the weather x_t completely? Do we forget what we wore yesterday h_{t-1}? And do we take into account our candidate clothes we prepared $\tilde{h}_t$, and to what extent?

6.4.1   Update Gate

The activation h_t at time t is a linear interpolation between the previous activation h_{t-1} and the current candidate $\tilde{h}_t$, which is controlled by an update gate z_t:

$$h_t = z_t \odot h_{t-1} + (1 - z_t) \odot \tilde{h}_t \qquad (6.17)$$

as shown in Figure 6.18.

The update gate z_t is a non-linear function, a sigmoid, of a combination of the current state x_t and the previous hidden state h_{t-1}:

$$z_t = \sigma(W_z h_{t-1} + U_z x_t) \qquad (6.18)$$

as shown in Figure 6.19.

If the update gate is set to $z_t = 0$, then the output is the new candidate, as shown in Figure 6.20.

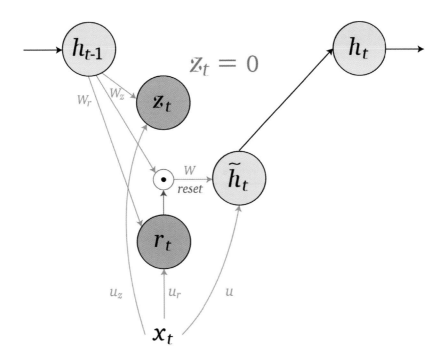

Figure 6.20 Gated recurrent unit with update gate set to $z_t = 0$. The current hidden state h_t is the new candidate $\tilde{h}_t$, $h_t = \tilde{h}_t = \phi(W(r_t \odot h_{t-1}) + Ux_t)$.

If the update gate is set to $z_t = 1$, then the output is the previous hidden state, ignoring both the candidate and current state altogether, as shown in Figure 6.21.

6.4.2 Candidate Activation

The candidate activation $\tilde{h}_t$ is a non-linear function, a $\phi = \tanh$, of a combination of the current state x_t and the previous hidden state h_{t-1} modulated by the reset gate r_t:

$$\tilde{h}_t = \phi(W(r_t \odot h_{t-1}) + Ux_t) \tag{6.19}$$

as shown in Figure 6.22.

6.4.3 Reset Gate

The reset gate r_t is a non-linear function, a sigmoid, of a combination of the current state x_t and the previous hidden state h_{t-1}:

$$r_t = \sigma(W_r h_{t-1} + U_r x_t) \tag{6.20}$$

as shown in Figure 6.23.

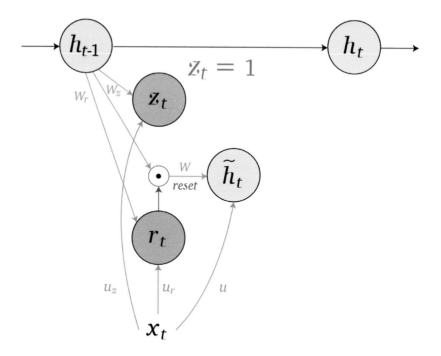

Figure 6.21 Gated recurrent unit with update gate set to $z_t = 1$. The current hidden state h_t equals the previous hidden state h_{t-1}, $h_t = h_{t-1}$, ignoring both the current state x_t and the new candidate $\tilde{h}_t$.

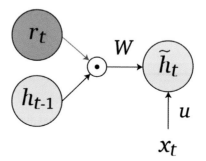

Figure 6.22 Gated recurrent unit candidate activation is a non-linear function of a combination of the current state x_t and previous hidden state h_{t-1} modulated by the reset gate r_t, $\tilde{h}_t = \phi(W(r_t \odot h_{t-1}) + Ux_t)$.

If the reset gate is set to $r_t = 0$ then the candidate $\tilde{h}_t$ is a function of the current state x_t such that $\tilde{h}_t = \phi(Ux_t)$, forgetting the previous hidden state h_{t-1}, as shown in Figure 6.24.

If the reset gate is set to $r_t = 1$ then the candidate is a function of the previous hidden state h_{t-1}, ignoring the current state x_t, as shown in Figure 6.25.

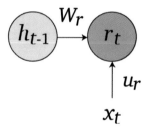

Figure 6.23 Gated recurrent unit reset gate $r_t = \sigma(W_r h_{t-1} + U_r x_t)$.

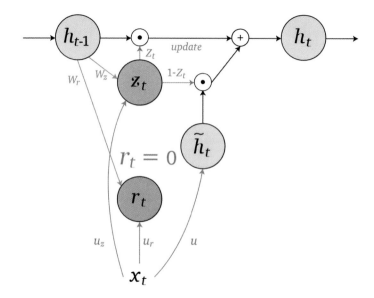

Figure 6.24 Gated recurrent unit with reset gate set to $r_t = 0$. The candidate is a function of the current state $\tilde{h}_t = \phi(U x_t)$.

6.4.4   Function

If $z_t = 0$ and $r_t = 0$ then the output hidden state is only dependent on the current state $\phi(U x_t)$, forgetting the previous hidden state h_{t-1}, as shown in Figure 6.26.

If $z_t = 0$ and $r_t = 1$, as shown in Figure 6.27, then the GRU is reduced to an RNN, as shown in Figure 6.28.

The GRU avoids the RNN problem of vanishing or exploding gradients by an addition before the output, as highlighted in Figure 6.29, which interrupts the repeated multiplication during backpropagation through time.

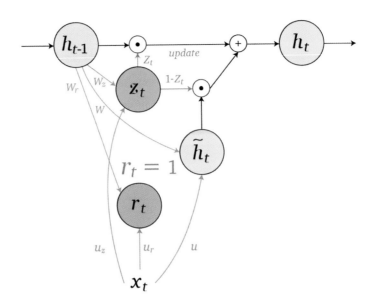

Figure 6.25 Gated recurrent unit with reset gate set to 1, $r_t = 1$. The candidate $\tilde{h}_t$ is a function of the previous hidden state h_{t-1} ignoring the current state x_t such that $\tilde{h}_t = \phi(W h_{t-1} + U x_t)$.

6.5   Long Short-Term Memory

The long short-term memory (Hochreiter and Schmidhuber, 1997) was introduced two decades before the GRU (Cho et al., 2014). The LSTM is easy to train, and includes an additional input and output compared with the RNN and GRU. At each time step t the LSTM receives as input the current state x_t, the hidden state h_{t-1}, and memory cell c_{t-1} of the previous time step, and outputs the hidden state h_t and memory cell c_t at time t, as shown in Figure 6.30. The memory cells propagate information from the previous state to the next, whereas the hidden states determine the way in which that information is propagated.

The LSTM units are placed one after the other, sequentially, where the hidden state h_t and memory cell c_t outputs of one unit serve as the hidden state and memory cell inputs of the following unit, as shown in Figure 6.31. In a similar fashion to the RNN and GRU, the weights from the current states and from the hidden states, as well as the weights from the memory cells, are shared across time.

The LSTM consists of a forget gate f_t, an input gate i_t, an output gate o_t, and a candidate memory $\tilde{c}_t$, as shown in Figure 6.32.

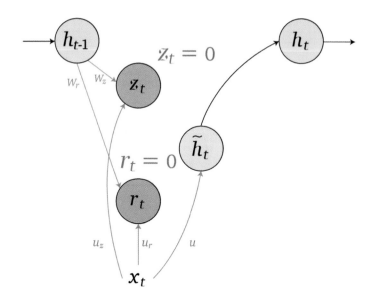

Figure 6.26 Gated recurrent unit with update gate set to $z_t = 0$, and reset gate set to $r_t = 0$. The output hidden state h_t does not take into account the previous hidden state h_{t-1}, such that $h_t = \tilde{h}_t = \phi(Ux_t)$.

The LSTM gates are defined by:

$$
\begin{aligned}
f_t &= \sigma(W_f h_{t-1} + U_f x_t) && \text{forget gate} \\
i_t &= \sigma(W_i h_{t-1} + U_i x_t) && \text{input gate} \\
o_t &= \sigma(W_o h_{t-1} + U_o x_t) && \text{output gate} \\
\tilde{c}_t &= \phi(W h_{t-1} + U x_t) && \text{candidate memory} \\
c_t &= f_t c_{t-1} + i_t \tilde{c}_t && \text{memory cell} \\
h_t &= o_t \phi(c_t) && \text{output gated memory}
\end{aligned}
\tag{6.21}
$$

6.5.1 Forget Gate

The forget gate f_t is a non-linear function, a sigmoid, of a combination of the current state x_t and the previous hidden state h_{t-1}:

$$
f_t = \sigma(W_f h_{t-1} + U_f x_t) \tag{6.22}
$$

as shown in Figure 6.33.

If $f_t = 0$ then the previous memory cell c_{t-1} is ignored, as shown in Figure 6.34.

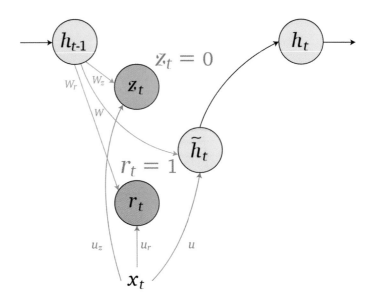

Figure 6.27 Gated recurrent unit with update gate set to $z_t = 0$, and reset gate set to $r_t = 1$. The GRU is reduced to an RNN such that $h_t = \tilde{h}_t = \phi(Wh_{t-1} + Ux_t)$.

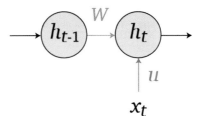

Figure 6.28 Gated recurrent unit reduced to an RNN when the update gate is set to $z_t = 0$ and the reset gate is set to $r_t = 1$, such that $h_t = \phi(Wh_{t-1} + Ux_t)$.

6.5.2   Input Gate

The input gate i_t is a non-linear function, a sigmoid, of a combination of the current state x_t and the previous hidden state h_{t-1}:

$$i_t = \sigma(W_i h_{t-1} + U_i x_t) \tag{6.23}$$

shown in Figure 6.35.

If $i_t = 0$ then the new candidate memory $\tilde{c}_t$ is ignored, as shown in Figure 6.36.

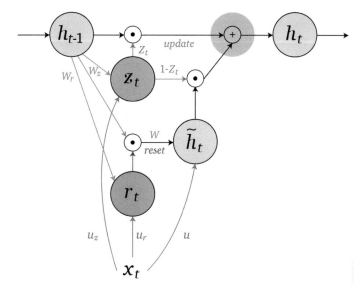

Figure 6.29 Gated recurrent unit addition before output, as highlighted, avoids the vanishing or exploding gradient problem during training, interrupting the repeated multiplication during backpropagation through time.

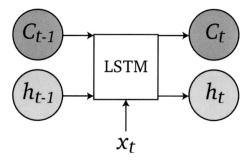

Figure 6.30 The LSTM inputs and outputs.

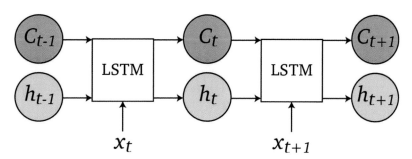

Figure 6.31 The LSTM units used sequentially, with the outputs of one unit serving as inputs to the next.

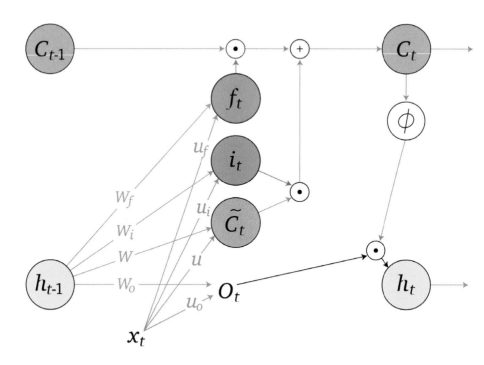

Figure 6.32 Long short-term memory.

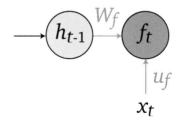

Figure 6.33 The LSTM forget gate $f_t = \sigma(W_f h_{t-1} + U_f x_t)$.

6.5.3   Memory Cell

The memory c_t is updated by partially forgetting the previous memory c_{t-1} and adding the new candidate memory $\tilde{c}_t$:

$$c_t = f_t c_{t-1} + i_i \tilde{c}_t \tag{6.24}$$

as shown in Figure 6.37.

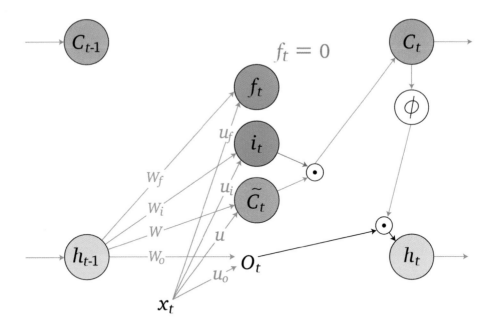

Figure 6.34 The LSTM forget gate set to $f_t = 0$, ignoring previous memory cell c_{t-1}.

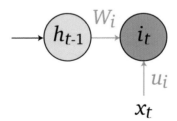

Figure 6.35 The LSTM input gate $i_t = \sigma(W_i h_{t-1} + U_i x_t)$.

6.5.4 Candidate Memory

The new candidate memory $\tilde{c}_t$ is a non-linear function, a sigmoid, of a combination of the current state x_t and the previous hidden state h_{t-1}:

$$\tilde{c}_t = \sigma(W h_{t-1} + U x_t) \tag{6.25}$$

as shown in Figure 6.38.

6.5.5 Output Gate

The output gate o_t is a non-linear function, a sigmoid, of a combination of the current state x_t and the previous hidden state h_{t-1}:

$$o_t = \sigma(W_o h_{t-1} + U_o x_t) \tag{6.26}$$

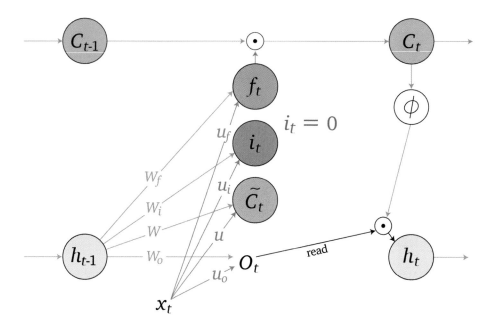

Figure 6.36 The LSTM input gate set to $i_t = 0$, ignoring new candidate memory $\tilde{c}_t$.

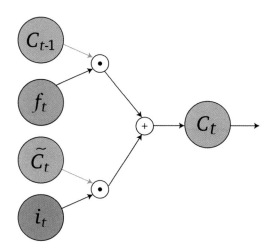

Figure 6.37 The LSTM interpolation of previous memory c_{t-1} and new candidate memory $\tilde{c}_t$ by forget gate f_t and input gate i_t, such that $c_t = f_t c_{t-1} + i_t \tilde{c}_t$.

as shown in Figure 6.39. The hidden state at time t is a pointwise multiplication of the output o_t and a non-linear function, a tanh of new memory cell c_t:

$$h_t = o_t \phi(c_t) \tag{6.27}$$

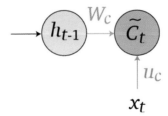

Figure 6.38 The LSTM candidate memory $\tilde{c}_t$ is a function of the previous hidden state h_{t-1} and the current state x_t, such that $\tilde{c}_t = \sigma(W h_{t-1} + U x_t)$.

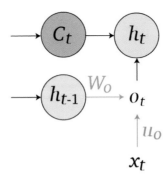

Figure 6.39 The LSTM output gate $\tilde{c}_t = \sigma(W h_{t-1} + U x_t)$.

6.5.6 Peephole Connections

Notice that the LSTM unit performs a read after write, as shown in Figure 6.40. This is avoided by adding peephole connections from the previous memory cell c_{t-1} or c_t:

$$\begin{aligned}
f_t &= \sigma(W_f h_{t-1} + P_f c_{t-1} + U_f x_t) & \text{forget gate} \\
i_t &= \sigma(W_i h_{t-1} + P_i c_{t-1} + U_i x_t) & \text{input gate} \\
o_t &= \sigma(W_o h_{t-1} + P_o c_t + U_o x_t) & \text{output gate}
\end{aligned} \tag{6.28}$$

as shown in Figure 6.41.

6.5.7 GRU vs. LSTM

Comparing the addition before the new hidden state h_t in the GRU as highlighted in Figure 6.29 with the addition before the new memory cell c_t in the LSTM as highlighted in Figure 6.42, both units avoid repeated multiplications that cause vanishing or exploding gradients by a similarly positioned addition.

Comparing the interpolation of the new candidate in the GRU as highlighted in Figure 6.43 with the interpolation of the new memory cell in the LSTM as highlighted in Figure 6.44 shows that the update gate z_t controls the amount

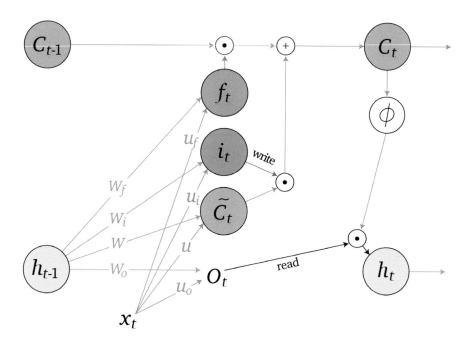

Figure 6.40 The LSTM read after writing.

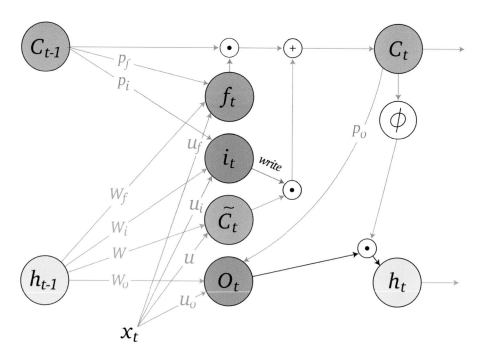

Figure 6.41 The LSTM with peepholes.

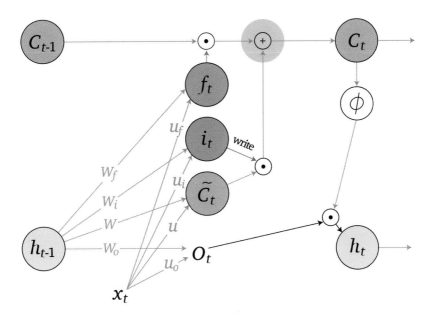

Figure 6.42 The LSTM addition, as highlighted, avoiding repeated multiplication, which causes vanishing or exploding gradients.

of the new candidate to pass in the GRU, whereas the input gate controls the amount of the new candidate memory to pass in the LSTM. Interpolation in the GRU is controlled by a single parameter z_t, whereas in the LSTM interpolation is controlled by two separate parameters i_t and f_t.

Comparing the GRU reset gate controlling the candidate hidden state, as highlighted in Figure 6.45, with the LSTM input gate controlling the candidate memory cell, as highlighted in Figure 6.46, shows the modulation of the candidate in both units.

Finally, an empirical evaluation of 10,000 architectures (Jozefowicz et al., 2015) for these units demonstrates that the best results are obtained by similar GRU variants. In summary, perhaps the exact gate configuration is less important than its overall structure and function.

6.6 Sequence to Sequence

Building a language model involves a distribution over words in the language. In applications such as machine translation, question answering, story synthesis, and protein structure prediction, it is important to generate entire sequences. In these applications the long-term dependencies between words in the vocabulary, sentences and even paragraphs are important. Sequence-to-sequence (seq2seq) models (Sutskever et al., 2014) consider entire sequences, or sentences, as inputs and outputs. Seq2seq models consist of an encoder and a decoder. The encoder is

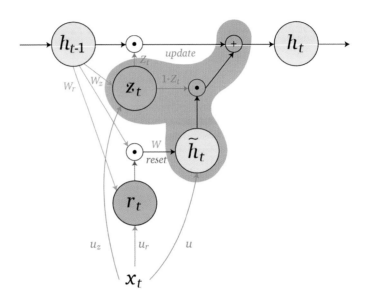

Figure 6.43 Gated recurrent unit candidate interpolation by $z_t \odot \tilde{h}_t$.

a GRU or LSTM, which may be bidirectional and deep, which encodes the input sequence $(x_1, \ldots, x_s)$ into a context vector as output $z = \mathrm{encoder}(x_1, \ldots, x_s)$. The decoder is also a GRU or LSTM that receives the context vector z as input, as the first hidden state vector, and generates an output sequence $(y_1, \ldots, y_t) = \mathrm{decoder}(z)$. The encoder and decoder models are trained end-to-end such that:

$$(y_1, \ldots, y_t) = \mathrm{decoder}(\mathrm{encoder}(x_1, \ldots, x_s)) \tag{6.29}$$

6.7   Attention

When humans translate or write sentences and paragraphs we do not store a representation of the entire sentence or paragraph before we begin its translation. When writing sentences and paragraphs we edit different parts of the sentence, going back to other parts. These processes are not only sequential and back-to-back as in the encoder–decoder architecture described earlier. A simple form of attention is applied to regression. Given samples x_i, y_i of a function, we can estimate the value $y = f(x)$ by weighting each y_i as a function of $\alpha(x, x_i)$, which decreases the farther apart x and x_i are. For example, we can estimate:

$$y = f(x) = \sum_i \alpha(x, x_i) y_i \tag{6.30}$$

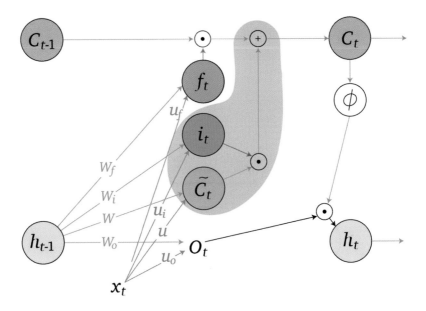

Figure 6.44 The LSTM candidate memory interpolation by $i_t \odot \tilde{c}_t$.

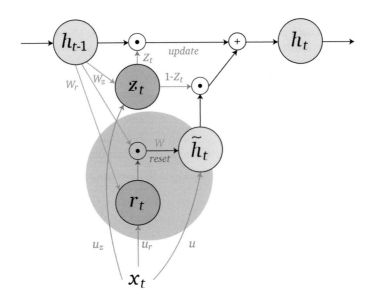

Figure 6.45 Gated recurrent unit reset r_t and candidate hidden state $\tilde{h}_t$.

where in attention x is called the query, x_i is called a key, and y_i is a value. A specific choice is using kernel k as a local weighting function:

$$\alpha(x, x_i) = \frac{k(x, x_i)}{\sum_j k(x, x_j)} y_i \qquad (6.31)$$

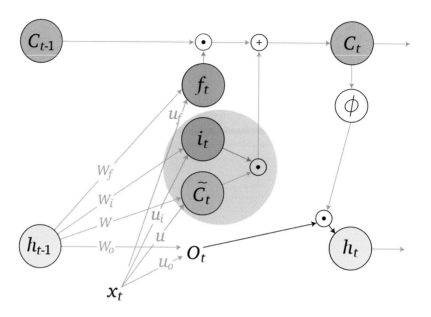

Figure 6.46 The LSTM input i_t and candidate memory $\tilde{c}_t$.

also known as the Nadaraya–Watson estimator (Nadaraya, 1964; Watson, 1964). More recently, seq2seq models have been improved by models of attention. Seq2seq models incorporating attention have different parts of the output sequence pay attention to different parts of the input sequence (Bahdanau et al., 2015; Luong et al., 2015). Instead of having the decoder receive as input the encoder's output in a sequential process, the decoder takes into account the entire encoding sequence, as shown in Figure 6.47. The input to the decoder hidden units are context vectors c_i for each time step i computed as:

$$c_i = \sum_j \alpha_{i,j} [h_j; \bar{h}_j]^T \tag{6.32}$$

for a bidirectional LSTM. The weights $\alpha_{i,j}$ sum to 1, $\sum_j \alpha_{i,j} = 1$, and are the amount of attention the output word o_i gives the input word x_j:

$$\alpha_{i,j} = \frac{\exp(s_{i,j})}{\sum_k \exp(s_{i,j})} \tag{6.33}$$

where $s_{i,j}$ is a function of the encoder hidden units $[h_t; \bar{h}_t]^T$ and decoder hidden units $\tilde{h}_{t-1}$. The decoder hidden units $\tilde{h}_t$ are a function of the context vectors c_t and output at the previous time step o_{t-1}. This form of attention is also known as encoder–decoder attention. Self-attention (Lin, Feng, Santos, Yu, Xiang, Zhou and Bengio, 2017) improves upon the encoding process by having each word in a sequence, in the encoder, consider the effect of all other words in the sequence. A self-attention matrix is then used to represent the embedding, where each entry i, j corresponds to the self-attention of word i to j in the same sequence.

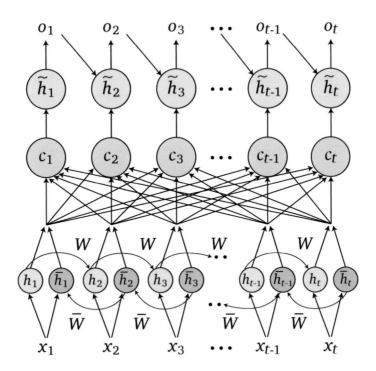

Figure 6.47 Machine translation with attention.

6.8   Embeddings

The representation of the input to our sequence model is an important decision, and for language we would like a meaningful representation for words. If we simply represent words in a language by one-hot encoding $x_i = (0, \ldots, 0, 1, 0, \ldots, 0)^T$ then there will be no meaning to the relationship between words, since in this simple representation two words x_i and x_j are either the same when their dot product is 1, $x_i^T x_j = 1$, or different when their dot product is 0, $x_i^T x_j = 0$. For example, using a one-hot representation of the words man, woman, king, queen and ball, all words will either be the same or different based on their dot product, without modeling any relationship between the words. In contrast, in language there are relationships and similarity between words such as synonyms and negations, as well as analogies. Therefore, we would like to use a representation of words that allows us to model their relationships, by learning a word embedding trained using a neural network (Bengio et al., 2003). Word embeddings can be used to model analogies $A : A' :: B : B'$, answering questions such as *man* is to *woman* like *king* is to ?, for which the answer is *queen*. We would like similar words to be close in a low-dimensional embedding space. Moreover, often we perform analysis using a limited training set in scope or breadth, whereas we would like to use representations that allow for transfer learning from a very large corpus with a broad vocabulary. Transfer learning from a pre-trained model is useful in many applications such as sentiment analysis, named entity recognition, text summarization, and parsing.

Next, we define the notion of an embedding and its training. For words in a vocabulary V represented by one-hot encoded $|V|$ dimensional vectors w, we learn an $n \times |V|$ dimensional embedding matrix E such that $x = Ew$ is the n-dimensional vector embedding of w. Using the embedding and cosine similarity between embedded words, we can find analogies such as $x_{man}{:}x_{woman}{::}x_{king}{:}?$ by:

$$\underset{x}{\mathrm{argmax}} = \mathrm{similarity}(x, x_{king} - x_{man} + x_{woman}) \qquad (6.34)$$

using the cosine similarity of two word representations x_i and x_j defined as:

$$\mathrm{cosine\ similarity}(x_i, x_j) = \frac{x_i^T x_j}{\|x_i\|_2 \|x_j\|_2} \qquad (6.35)$$

to find $x = x_{queen}$. To learn the embedding E, we use a large unsupervised corpus of sentences, which we turn into supervised training pairs by considering target words and their surrounding contexts. The embedding will represent each word in the corpus w_i by its embedding $x_i = Ew_i$. The skip-gram model (Mikolov, Chen, Corrado and Dean, 2013) randomly selects a context word w_c, while ensuring coverage of all words, and then randomly selects a target word w_t in a window around the context. Next, a neural network maps each context word w_c to its embedding $x_c = Ew_c$ and maps the embedding to a fully connected output layer o followed by a softmax mapping to the probabilities of all words in the vocabulary to the target word w_t:

$$p(w_t|w_c) = \frac{e^{\theta_c^T x_c}}{\sum_{j=1}^{|V|} e^{\theta_j^T x_c}} \qquad (6.36)$$

The network is trained by minimizing the loss between the softmax probabilities and the true targets, solving for the embedding matrix E weights and the network parameters θ end-to-end by backpropagation. In practice, the efficiency of training the skip-gram model is improved by using negative sampling and a hierarchical softmax (Mikolov, Sutskever, Chen, Corrado and Dean, 2013). Finally, the embedding is used in the various tasks by computing the embedding of individual words $x_t = Ew_t$, which serve as inputs to a sequence model.

Word embeddings have been extended to sentence embeddings (Kiros et al., 2015) and paragraph embeddings (Le and Mikolov, 2014). Embedding from language models (ELMo; (Peters et al., 2018)) represents word vectors as the hidden states of deep bidirectional LSTMs pre-trained on a very large corpus.

6.9   Introduction to Transformers

Transformers, described in detail in Chapter 8, are based only on attention mechanisms (Vaswani et al., 2017) without using RNNs or CNNs. The transformer consists of a stack of encoders connected to a stack of decoders. The input to the first encoder is a word embedding and a position embedding. Each encoder consists of a self-attention layer and a neural network passing its output as input to the next encoder in the stack of encoders. Each decoder contains a self-attention layer, followed by an encoder–decoder attention layer, followed by a neural network. Each decoder passes its output as input to the next decoder in the stack of decoders. Using self-attention in the encoders and both encoder–decoder and self-attention in the decoders results in state-of-the-art results in machine translation. The transformer architecture does not use RNNs nor CNNs, which results in faster training time. A limitation of the Transformer architecture is that it processes the entire sequence at once, which may be a very long sequence of words. Recent Transformer models split a long sequence of words into segments and add a recurrent layer between Transformers, allowing processing fixed-sized inputs while modeling long-term relationships. The position of words is required for computing the attention score. Therefore, the Transformer uses an absolute position embedding, whereas the Transformer XL that breaks the sequence into segments embeds the relative distance between words.

6.10   Summary

This chapter introduces RNNs and their extension to bidirectional and deep RNNs. We present backpropagation through time, its limitations, and the solutions in the form of LSTM and GRU. The chapter describes seq2seq models, followed by encoder–decoder attention and self-attention. Finally, the chapter presents word embeddings and their extension to sentences and paragraphs. Convolutional neural networks share weights across space, while RNNs share weights across time. Chapter 7 presents graph neural networks (GNNs), which share weights across neighborhoods.

7 Graph Neural Networks

7.1 Introduction

Graphs are the mathematical representation of networks. Networks describe interactions between entities; for example, a social network of friends, bonds between atoms in a molecule or protein, the internet of web pages, the cellular communication network between users, a financial transaction network between bank clients, protein-to-protein interaction networks, or the neural networks between neurons in our brains. Specifically, the human brain consists of around 100 billion neurons (for comparison, the cat brain consists of around one billion neurons) with 100 trillion connections between neurons. Each neuron is connected to 5,000–200,000 other neurons, and there are around 10,000 different types of neurons. Perhaps most importantly, around 1,000 neurons are generated each day of our lives. Modeling such networks requires a dynamic graph structure.

Each node in a network may have an associated feature vector, as shown in Figure 7.1. For example, in a graph representing a molecule or protein, the nodes are the atoms, the bonds between atoms are the edges, and each node has an associated feature vector of atom properties. In a social network, each node may represent a user. The edges are connections between users. Each node may have a feature vector, including the user's age, gender, status, country, occupation, interests, likes, etc.

Network data is often messy or incomplete, and therefore we would like to be

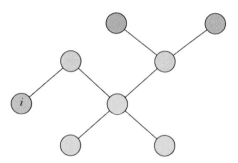

Figure 7.1 A graph with nodes. Each node $i \in \mathcal{V}$ is associated with a feature vector $v_i \in \mathcal{R}^n$.

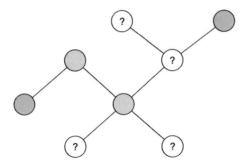

Figure 7.2 Graph node classification. The goal is to classify the uncolored nodes to one of two classes, green or blue.

able to perform operations on graphs, such as completing missing information in the graph. Common tasks on networks include node classification for predicting the type of nodes, as shown in Figure 7.2, link prediction for predicting whether two nodes are connected, finding clusters for detecting communities, and measuring the similarity between nodes for embedding node features into a low-dimensional space. Specifically, we will use deep learning for performing three key operations on graphs:

1. Node prediction: predicting a property of a graph node.
2. Link prediction: predicting a property of a graph edge. For example, in a social network, we can predict whether two people will become friends.
3. Graph or sub-graph prediction: predicting a property of the entire graph or a sub-graph. For example, given a graph representation of a protein, we can predict its function as an enzyme or not. Given a molecule represented as a graph, we can predict whether it will bind to a given receptor.

Notice that if we only have node information and the task is edge prediction, we may pool the information from the graph nodes. Similarly, if we only have edge information and the task is node prediction, we may pool information from the graph edges.

A fundamental property common to neural network representations that work well is that they all share weights. Chapter 5 on convolutional neural networks (CNNs) describes neural networks applied to images of fixed size and regular grids, sharing weights across space, as shown on the left of Figure 7.3, by using a CNN or ResNet or ODENet. Chapter 6, on sequence models, describes neural networks applied to sequences, sharing weights across time, as shown in the center of Figure 7.3, by using a recurrent neural network (RNN), long short-term memory (LSTM), or gated recurrent unit (GRU). In this chapter, we describe graph neural networks (GNNs), applied to networks or general graphs sharing weights across neighborhoods, as shown in the right of Figure 7.3. A key insight in GNNs is that, similarly to CNNs or RNNs, nodes in the graph may aggregate information from neighboring nodes.

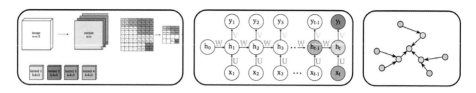

Figure 7.3 Neural network representations sharing weights. A CNN shares weights across space (left); an RNN shares weights across time (center); and a GNN shares weights across neighborhoods (right).

7.2   Definitions

We begin with basic graph definitions. A graph $\mathcal{G} = (\mathcal{V}, \mathcal{E})$ contains a set of n vertices (or nodes) $\mathcal{V}$ and a set of m edges $\mathcal{E}$ between vertices. The edges of the graph can either be undirected or directed.

A common duality of modeling problems in computer science is using graph theory by a graph representation or linear algebra by a matrix representation. Moving back and forth between graph theory and linear algebra allows us to apply algorithms from both.

Two basic graph representations are an adjacency matrix and adjacency list. An adjacency matrix A of dimensions $n \times n$ is defined such that:

$$A_{i,j} = \begin{cases} 1, & \text{if there is an edge between vertices } i \text{ and } j \\ 0, & \text{otherwise} \end{cases} \tag{7.1}$$

If the edges have weights then the 1s in the adjacency matrix are replaced with edge weights $w_{i,j}$. For an undirected graph the matrix A is symmetric.

The adjacency matrix of the example graph in Figure 7.4 with 9 nodes and 11 edges is the 9×9 matrix:

$$A = \begin{bmatrix} 0 & 1 & 1 & 1 & 0 & 0 & 0 & 0 & 0 \\ 1 & 0 & 0 & 1 & 1 & 0 & 0 & 0 & 0 \\ 1 & 0 & 0 & 1 & 0 & 0 & 0 & 0 & 0 \\ 1 & 1 & 1 & 0 & 1 & 1 & 0 & 0 & 0 \\ 0 & 1 & 0 & 1 & 0 & 0 & 0 & 0 & 0 \\ 0 & 0 & 0 & 1 & 0 & 0 & 1 & 0 & 0 \\ 0 & 0 & 0 & 0 & 0 & 1 & 0 & 1 & 1 \\ 0 & 0 & 0 & 0 & 0 & 0 & 1 & 0 & 0 \\ 0 & 0 & 0 & 0 & 0 & 0 & 1 & 0 & 0 \end{bmatrix} \tag{7.2}$$

where the number of 1s in matrix A is twice the number of edges in the graph.

Notice that different permutations of the node labels result in different adjacency matrices. In contrast, an adjacency list of the edges in the graph is invariant to node permutations. Storing an adjacency matrix takes $O(n^2)$ mem-

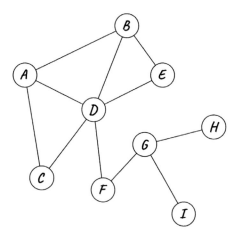

Figure 7.4 Example graph with 9 nodes and 11 edges.

ory, where n is the number of nodes in the graph; storing an adjacency list takes only $O(m + n)$, where m is the number of edges in the graph.

The degree of a node represents the number of edges incident to that node, and the average degree of a graph is the average degree over all its nodes $\frac{1}{n}\sum_{i=1}^{n} d_i$, which equals $\frac{2m}{n}$ for an undirected graph and $\frac{m}{n}$ for a directed graph. In a complete undirected graph, there is an edge between every two vertices for a total of $\frac{n(n-1)}{2}$ edges.

The degree matrix D of the adjacency matrix A is a diagonal matrix such that:

$$D_{i,i} = \text{degree}(v_i) = d_i = \sum_{j=1}^{n} A_{i,j} \tag{7.3}$$

The neighbors of a node $i \in V$ are its adjacent nodes $\mathcal{N}(i)$, and the degree of a node is its number of neighbors $d_i = |\mathcal{N}(i)|$. The degree matrix of the graph in Figure 7.4 is the 9×9 diagonal matrix:

$$D = \begin{bmatrix} 3 & 0 & 0 & 0 & 0 & 0 & 0 & 0 & 0 \\ 0 & 3 & 0 & 0 & 0 & 0 & 0 & 0 & 0 \\ 0 & 0 & 2 & 0 & 0 & 0 & 0 & 0 & 0 \\ 0 & 0 & 0 & 5 & 0 & 0 & 0 & 0 & 0 \\ 0 & 0 & 0 & 0 & 2 & 0 & 0 & 0 & 0 \\ 0 & 0 & 0 & 0 & 0 & 2 & 0 & 0 & 0 \\ 0 & 0 & 0 & 0 & 0 & 0 & 3 & 0 & 0 \\ 0 & 0 & 0 & 0 & 0 & 0 & 0 & 1 & 0 \\ 0 & 0 & 0 & 0 & 0 & 0 & 0 & 0 & 1 \end{bmatrix} \tag{7.4}$$

In a regular graph, each node has the same number of neighbors, which is the degree of a node.

The graph Laplacian matrix L is the difference between the degree matrix and adjacency matrix $L = D - A$. The Laplacian matrix of the example graph in Figure 7.4 is given by the matrix:

$$L = D - A = \begin{bmatrix} 3 & -1 & -1 & -1 & 0 & 0 & 0 & 0 & 0 \\ -1 & 3 & 0 & -1 & -1 & 0 & 0 & 0 & 0 \\ -1 & 0 & 2 & -1 & 0 & 0 & 0 & 0 & 0 \\ -1 & -1 & -1 & 5 & -1 & -1 & 0 & 0 & 0 \\ 0 & -1 & 0 & -1 & 2 & 0 & 0 & 0 & 0 \\ 0 & 0 & 0 & -1 & 0 & 2 & -1 & 0 & 0 \\ 0 & 0 & 0 & 0 & 0 & -1 & 3 & -1 & -1 \\ 0 & 0 & 0 & 0 & 0 & 0 & -1 & 1 & 0 \\ 0 & 0 & 0 & 0 & 0 & 0 & -1 & 0 & 1 \end{bmatrix} \tag{7.5}$$

The adjacency matrix and the degree matrix are symmetric, and therefore, the Laplacian matrix is symmetric. Normalizing the Laplacian matrix makes diagonal elements equal 1 and scales off-diagonal entries. The graph symmetric normalized Laplacian matrix is:

$$L^{\text{sym}} = D^{-\frac{1}{2}} L D^{-\frac{1}{2}} = I - D^{-\frac{1}{2}} A D^{-\frac{1}{2}} \tag{7.6}$$

where $D^{-\frac{1}{2}}$ is a diagonal matrix with entries $D_{i,i}^{-\frac{1}{2}} = \frac{1}{\sqrt{d_i}}$. Nodes without neighbors are not normalized to avoid division by zero. The symmetric normalized Laplacian matrix elements are given by:

$$L_{i,j}^{\text{sym}} = \begin{cases} 1, & \text{if } i = j \text{ and } d_i \neq 0 \\ -\frac{1}{\sqrt{d_i d_j}}, & \text{if } i \neq j \text{ and node } i \text{ is adjacent to node } j \\ 0, & \text{otherwise} \end{cases} \tag{7.7}$$

The symmetric normalized Laplacian matrix of the example graph in Figure 7.4 is given by the matrix:

$$L^{\text{sym}} = \begin{bmatrix} 1 & -\frac{1}{3} & -\frac{1}{\sqrt{6}} & -\frac{1}{\sqrt{15}} & 0 & 0 & 0 & 0 & 0 \\ -\frac{1}{3} & 1 & 0 & -\frac{1}{\sqrt{15}} & -\frac{1}{\sqrt{6}} & 0 & 0 & 0 & 0 \\ -\frac{1}{\sqrt{6}} & 0 & 1 & -\frac{1}{\sqrt{10}} & 0 & 0 & 0 & 0 & 0 \\ -\frac{1}{\sqrt{15}} & -\frac{1}{\sqrt{15}} & -\frac{1}{\sqrt{10}} & 1 & -\frac{1}{\sqrt{10}} & -\frac{1}{\sqrt{10}} & 0 & 0 & 0 \\ 0 & -\frac{1}{\sqrt{6}} & 0 & -\frac{1}{\sqrt{10}} & 1 & 0 & 0 & 0 & 0 \\ 0 & 0 & 0 & -\frac{1}{\sqrt{10}} & 0 & 1 & -\frac{1}{\sqrt{6}} & 0 & 0 \\ 0 & 0 & 0 & 0 & 0 & -\frac{1}{\sqrt{6}} & 1 & -\frac{1}{\sqrt{3}} & -\frac{1}{\sqrt{3}} \\ 0 & 0 & 0 & 0 & 0 & 0 & -\frac{1}{\sqrt{3}} & 1 & 0 \\ 0 & 0 & 0 & 0 & 0 & 0 & -\frac{1}{\sqrt{3}} & 0 & 1 \end{bmatrix} \tag{7.8}$$

which is a symmetric matrix.

The random walk normalized Laplacian matrix is a transition matrix for a random walk on a graph with non-negative weights and is defined as:

$$L^{\text{rw}} = D^{-1} L = I - D^{-1} A \tag{7.9}$$

where D^{-1} is a diagonal matrix with entries $D_{i,i}^{-1} = \frac{1}{d_i}$. The random walk normalized Laplacian matrix elements are given by:

$$
L_{i,j}^{\mathrm{rw}} =
\begin{cases}
1, & \text{if } i = j \text{ and } d_i \neq 0 \\
-\frac{1}{d_i}, & \text{if } i \neq j \text{ and node } i \text{ is adjacent to node } j \\
0, & \text{otherwise}
\end{cases}
\tag{7.10}
$$

The random walk normalized Laplacian matrix of the example graph in Figure 7.4 is given by the matrix:

$$
L^{\mathrm{rw}} =
\begin{bmatrix}
1 & -\frac{1}{3} & -\frac{1}{3} & -\frac{1}{3} & 0 & 0 & 0 & 0 & 0 \\
-\frac{1}{3} & 1 & 0 & -\frac{1}{3} & -\frac{1}{3} & 0 & 0 & 0 & 0 \\
-\frac{1}{2} & 0 & 1 & -\frac{1}{2} & 0 & 0 & 0 & 0 & 0 \\
-\frac{1}{5} & -\frac{1}{5} & -\frac{1}{5} & 1 & -\frac{1}{5} & -\frac{1}{5} & 0 & 0 & 0 \\
0 & -\frac{1}{2} & 0 & -\frac{1}{2} & 1 & 0 & 0 & 0 & 0 \\
0 & 0 & 0 & -\frac{1}{2} & 0 & 1 & -\frac{1}{2} & 0 & 0 \\
0 & 0 & 0 & 0 & 0 & -\frac{1}{3} & 1 & -\frac{1}{3} & -\frac{1}{3} \\
0 & 0 & 0 & 0 & 0 & 0 & -1 & 1 & 0 \\
0 & 0 & 0 & 0 & 0 & 0 & -1 & 0 & 1
\end{bmatrix}
\tag{7.11}
$$

which is not symmetric and each row sums to zero. The matrices L^{rw} and L^{sym} are similar and therefore have the same eigenvalues.

A graph with n nodes has n eigenvectors with eigenvalues that are non-negative since the Laplacian matrix L has non-negative eigenvalues. A sub-graph of a graph is a subset of edges and all their nodes in the graph. If there is at least one path between each pair of nodes in the sub-graph, it is a connected component. The number of zero eigenvalues of the Laplacian matrix of a graph is the number of its connected components.

A walk on a graph begins with a node $i \in V$ and ends with a node $j \in V$ and traverses a sequence of edges and nodes between nodes i and j. If the nodes are distinct, the walk is a path; if the edges are distinct, the walk is a trail. In the matrix, A^k, which is the adjacency matrix to the power of k, each entry $A_{i,j}^k$ is the number of walks of length k in the graph between the node in row i and the node in column j.

Graph nodes may consist of features x. For example, a binary feature x for the graph shown in Figure 7.4 may be defined by appending a column to the

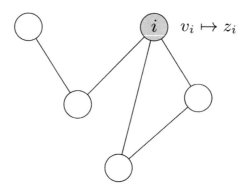

Figure 7.5 Graph node embedding. A node $i \in V$ with associated feature vector $v_i \in \mathcal{R}^n$ which is embedded into a low-dimensional space $z_i \in \mathcal{R}^d$ by an embedding $f : v_i \mapsto z_i$.

adjacency matrix:

$$\begin{bmatrix} A & B & C & D & E & F & G & H & I & x \\ 0 & 1 & 1 & 1 & 0 & 0 & 0 & 0 & 0 & 0 \\ 1 & 0 & 0 & 1 & 1 & 0 & 0 & 0 & 0 & 1 \\ 1 & 0 & 0 & 1 & 0 & 0 & 0 & 0 & 0 & 1 \\ 1 & 1 & 1 & 0 & 1 & 1 & 0 & 0 & 0 & 0 \\ 0 & 1 & 0 & 1 & 0 & 0 & 0 & 0 & 0 & 0 \\ 0 & 0 & 0 & 1 & 0 & 0 & 1 & 0 & 0 & 1 \\ 0 & 0 & 0 & 0 & 0 & 1 & 0 & 1 & 1 & 0 \\ 0 & 0 & 0 & 0 & 0 & 0 & 1 & 0 & 0 & 0 \\ 0 & 0 & 0 & 0 & 0 & 0 & 1 & 0 & 0 & 1 \end{bmatrix} \tag{7.12}$$

or, for example, a graph in which the nodes are papers, the edges are the other papers they cite, and the features are the paper abstract or the language embedding of the abstract.

Most graphs are sparse, with fewer edges than square nodes $m \ll n^2$; therefore, adjacency lists are an alternative representation for efficient storage. A linked list represents each vertex and all its edges and adjacent vertices.

7.3   Embeddings

An example of embedding a node in a graph into $\mathcal{R}^n$ is an embedding such that similar nodes in the graph along with their features are embedded to nearby nodes in the embedding space. Our embedding objective may not be limited to similarity and may be defined with respect to other properties of the graph and embedding space. We define an encoder f of a node $i \in V$, such that $f(i)$ is the embedding of the node feature vector v_i as shown in Figure 7.5.

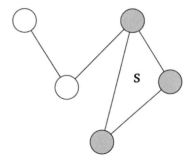

Figure 7.6 Sub-graph embedding by taking the sum of the embeddings of the nodes in the sub-graph.

If each node $i \in \mathcal{V}$ has an associated feature vector v_i then a node embedding, maintaining similarity, maps node feature vectors v_i to vectors z_i in a low-dimensional space such that the similarity between nodes i and j, denoted by $s(i,j)$, is maintained in the embedding space. For example, we may optimize for the similarity between nodes i and j, such that their similarity $s(i,j)$ is maintained after the embedding $f(i)^T f(j)$, where f denotes the encoder which embeds node feature vectors.

A shallow node embedding uses an $n \times 1$-dimensional one-hot encoding e_i of each node i to look up the embedded node. The one-hot encoding e_i of a node $i \in V$ is an $n \times 1$ zero vector except for a single 1 in position i. An embedding matrix W of dimensionality $d \times n$, where d is the dimensionality of a node feature vector v_i and n is the number of nodes, is formed such that each column of W is the embedding of a different node. Multiplying the $d \times n$ embedding matrix W by the $n \times 1$ one-hot encoded vector e_i representing a node i results in We_i, which is the $d \times 1$ ith column of the matrix W representing the node in the embedding space. This results in a problem with shallow embeddings: they do not share weights. As demonstrated earlier, the success of neural networks stems from representations sharing weights across space in CNNs or across time in RNNs. This motivates the sharing of weights by aggregating graph neighborhoods in GNNs, as described in Section 7.5.

We may embed a sub-graph $S \in \mathcal{G}$, either by taking the sum of the embeddings of the nodes in the sub-graph $\sum_{i \in S} f(i)$, or by taking a representative node j of the sub-graph and setting the sub-graph embedding to be $f(j)$ as shown in Figures 7.6 and 7.7.

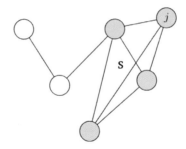

Figure 7.7 Sub-graph embedding by taking a representative node of the sub-graph.

7.4   Node Similarity

7.4.1   Adjacency-based Similarity

In node embeddings we define pairwise node similarity and optimize an embedding to approximate similarities. Going beyond shallow node embeddings, we can define different measures of similarity. For example, we define the similarity between nodes i and j to be the weight on the edge between them, $s(i,j) = A_{i,j}$, where A is the weighted adjacency matrix. We then find the matrix W with dimensions $d \times n$ which minimizes the loss:

$$\mathcal{L} = \sum_{(i,j) \in \mathcal{V} \times \mathcal{V}} \|f(i)^T f(j) - A_{i,j}\|^2 \tag{7.13}$$

over all pairs of nodes in the graph.

7.4.2   Multi-hop Similarity

The first ring of neighbors of a node, as shown in Figure 7.8, is the node's neighborhood. Let A denote the adjacency matrix of 1-hop neighbors, A^2 denote the adjacency matrix of 2-hop neighbors and in general A^k the adjacency matrix of k-hop neighbors. Then, we can minimize the loss:

$$L = \sum_{(i,j) \in \mathcal{V} \times \mathcal{V}} \|f(i)^T f(j) - A_{i,j}^k\|^2 \tag{7.14}$$

7.4.3   Overlap Similarity

Another measure of similarity is the overlap between node neighborhoods, as shown in Figure 7.9. Suppose nodes i and j share common nodes in the social network of mutual friends. We can then minimize the loss function measuring the overlap between neighborhoods:

$$L = \sum_{(i,j) \mathcal{V} \times \mathcal{V}} \|f(i)^T f(j) - S_{i,j}\|^2 \tag{7.15}$$

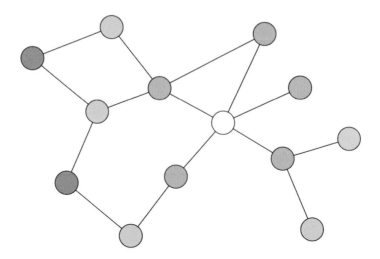

Figure 7.8 Graph neighborhoods. Given a root node shown in white, the 1-hop ring of neighbors is shown in blue, the 2-hop neighbors are shown in green, and the 3-hop neighbors are in purple.

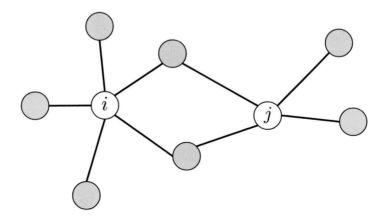

Figure 7.9 Mutual nodes (shown in purple) are the overlap between node neighborhoods of nodes i and j.

where $S_{i,j}$ measures the overlap between the neighbors $\mathcal{N}(i)$ of node i and neighbors $\mathcal{N}(j)$ of node j. The overlap may be measured using the overlap coefficient $\frac{|\mathcal{N}(i) \cap \mathcal{N}(j)|}{\min\{|\mathcal{N}(i)|, |\mathcal{N}(j)|\}}$ or Jaccard similarity $\frac{|\mathcal{N}(i) \cap \mathcal{N}(j)|}{|\mathcal{N}(i) \cup \mathcal{N}(j)|}$.

7.4.4 Random Walk Embedding

We can define an embedding using a random walk from nodes in the graph, as shown in Figure 7.10. A random walk in a graph begins with a node $i \in V$ and

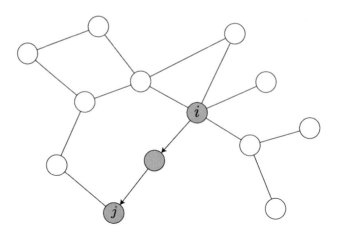

Figure 7.10 Graph random walk (shown in blue) consists of the nodes on a random path starting from node $i \in V$ and ending in node $j \in V$.

repeatedly walks to one of its neighbors $\mathcal{N}(i)$ with probability $\frac{1}{d(i)}$ for t steps until reaching an end at node j on the graph.

Running random walks may start from each graph node i multiple times. We collect all the nodes visited for each node in the walk, and then optimize the embedding defined by:

$$f(i)^T f(j) \propto P(i \text{ and } j \text{ co-occur on the random walk}) = p(i|j) \qquad (7.16)$$

which is the probability that we reach node j starting a random walk from node i.

Using the loss function:

$$\mathcal{L} = \sum_{i \in \mathcal{V}} \sum_{j \in \mathcal{N}(i)} -\log p(j|f(i)) \qquad (7.17)$$

where $p(j|f(i))$ is given by the softmax:

$$p(j|f(i)) = \frac{\exp(f(i)^T f(j))}{\sum_{j \in \mathcal{N}(i)} \exp(f(i)^T f(j))} \qquad (7.18)$$

DeepWalk (Perozzi et al., 2014) uses a skip-gram model of random walks on a graph to classify nodes of a graph. Node2vec (Grover and Leskovec, 2016) uses a random walk on a graph based on both the current node i and the previous nodes that led to node i. Instead of moving from node i to another node with probability $\frac{1}{d(i)}$, node2vec defines a random walk with probability based on the length of the shortest path between the previous node and the next node. LINE (Tang et al., 2015) embeds graph nodes into a low-dimensional space applied to the task of node classification and link prediction.

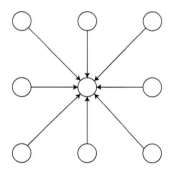

Figure 7.11 Regular graph structure representing neighboring pixels of an image.

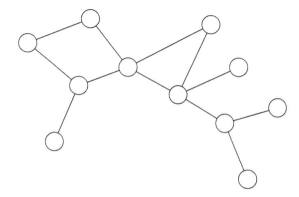

Figure 7.12 Irregular graph structure of real-world graphs representing networks.

7.4.5   Graph Neural Network Properties

A CNN has a regular grid structure, as shown in Figure 7.11, which is suitable for images; however, it is not suitable for real-world graphs, which have irregular structure, as shown in Figure 7.12.

A naive approach for representing a general graph is to concatenate each node's feature vectors to the adjacency matrix and encode each node by the corresponding row of the adjacency matrix and its features. A fully connected network architecture given a node's row in the adjacency matrix and features is unsuitable for graph representation. Having such a vector representation be the input to a fully connected neural network has numerous limitations. In such a naive network, the number of parameters is linear in the size of the graph, the network is dependent on the order of the nodes, and it does not accommodate dynamic graphs. We want to be able to add or remove nodes to real-world graphs, such as the social network, without changing the network architecture. The desired properties of our graph neural network architecture are that the number of parameters is independent of the graph size, scaling to graphs with billions of nodes, that the

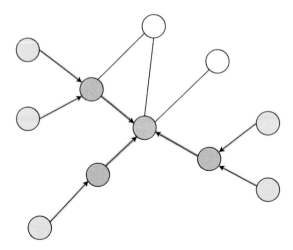

Figure 7.13 Each node aggregates information from its ring of neighbors.

network is invariant to node ordering, that the operations be local depending on neighborhoods, that the model accommodates any graph structure, and that once we learn the properties of one graph, we can transfer them to a new unseen graph.

7.5   Neighborhood Aggregation in Graph Neural Networks

We consider GNNs that take into account neighbors of each node, aggregating information from neighboring nodes similar to breadth-first search (BFS); and the other graph neural network which considers chains from a node, similar to depth-first search (DFS). In the first architecture, we consider each node in the graph and pick up the graph from that node as the root, allowing all other nodes to dangle, building a computation graph where that node is the root. Once we determine the node computation graph, we will propagate and transform information from its neighbors, its neighbors' neighbors, and so on, as shown in Figure 7.13, where each node consists of a vector containing the features of the node.

Most GNNs are based on aggregating information into each node from its neighboring nodes in a layer ℓ and combining that information with the node features in that layer:

$$h_i^\ell = \text{combine}^\ell \{h_i^{\ell-1}, \text{aggregate}^\ell \{h_j^{\ell-1}, j \in \mathcal{N}(i)\}\} \tag{7.19}$$

where h_i^ℓ is the feature representation of node i at layer ℓ.

Consider the graph shown in Figure 7.14. We generate embeddings based on local neighborhoods and aggregate information from neighbors using the neural

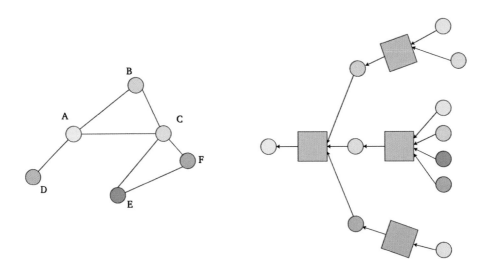

Figure 7.14 A computational graph is constructed for each node, aggregating its neighbors and in turn from each neighbor.

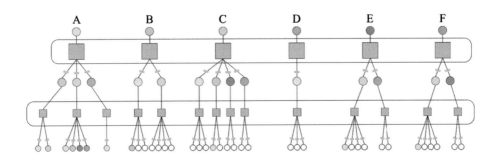

Figure 7.15 Computational graphs starting from each node in the graph, sharing weights between different computational graphs for all 1-hop neighbors, 2-hop neighbors, and 3-hop neighbors. The roots of the computational graphs for each node form the last layer of the GNN, whereas the leaves and their node features form the first layer.

network. Consider node A; its neighbors are nodes B, C, and D, and in turn B's neighbors are nodes A and C, C's neighbors are nodes A, B, E, and F, and D's neighbor is node A.

Next, we consider each node in turn and generate a computation graph for each node where that node is the root. Finally, we will share the aggregation parameters across all nodes for every layer of neighbors, as shown in Figure 7.15.

The gray boxes in each layer in Figure 7.15 represent aggregation parameters, denoted in the special case below by shared matrices W^ℓ and B^ℓ for layer ℓ, such that the aggregation boxes in each layer are identical and shared across nodes.

In summary, the nodes have embeddings at each layer, and the network shares aggregation parameters across all nodes in a layer.

We denote the feature vector of a node i by $h_i^0 = x_i$. A feature vector h_i^ℓ will be an aggregation of the feature vectors $h_j^{\ell-1}$ of the neighbors $j \in \mathcal{N}(i)$ of i and the feature vector $h_i^{\ell-1}$ of the previous layer embedding. An example of a choice of aggregation and combination function is:

$$h_i^\ell = \sigma \left(W^\ell \sum_{j \in \mathcal{N}(i)} \frac{h_j^{\ell-1}}{|\mathcal{N}(i)|} + B^\ell h_i^{\ell-1} \right) \tag{7.20}$$

where h_i^ℓ is the ℓth layer embedding of i, σ is a non-linear activation function and $\sum_{j \in \mathcal{N}(i)} \frac{h_j^{\ell-1}}{|\mathcal{N}(i)|}$ is the average of neighbors in the previous layer embedding. We have two types of weight matrices: W^ℓ is a matrix of weights for neighborhood embeddings, and B^ℓ is a matrix of weights for self-embedding. These matrices are shared for each layer ℓ across all nodes.

7.5.1   Supervised Node Classification Using a GNN

For the task of node classification, given m labeled nodes i with labels y^i we train a GNN by minimizing the objective:

$$\frac{1}{m} \sum_{i=1}^m \mathcal{L}(y^i, \hat{y}^i) \tag{7.21}$$

where the predictions $\hat{y}^i$ are the softmax of the node representations at the last layer.

7.6   Graph Neural Network Variants

7.6.1   Graph Convolution Network

A graph convolution network (GCN; Kipf and Welling (2017)) has a similar formulation using a single matrix for both the neighborhood and self-embeddings normalized by the product of square roots of node degrees:

$$\begin{aligned}
h_i^\ell &= \sigma \left(W^\ell \sum_{j \in i \cup \mathcal{N}(i)} \frac{\hat{A}_{i,j}}{\sqrt{\hat{d}_j \hat{d}_i}} h_j^{\ell-1} \right) \\
&= \sigma \left(\sum_{j \in \mathcal{N}(i)} \frac{\hat{A}_{i,j}}{\sqrt{\hat{d}_j \hat{d}_i}} W^\ell h_j^{\ell-1} + \frac{1}{\hat{d}_i} W^\ell h_i^{\ell-1} \right)
\end{aligned} \tag{7.22}$$

where $\hat{A} = A + I$ is the adjacency matrix including self-loops, $\hat{d}_i$ is the degree in the graph with self-loops, and σ is a non-linear activation function. Aggregation is defined by the term on the left and the combination on the right.

An equivalent formulation (Wu et al., 2019) is given by:

$$H^{\ell+1} = \hat{D}^{-\frac{1}{2}} \hat{A} \hat{D}^{-\frac{1}{2}} H^\ell W^\ell \tag{7.23}$$

where $\hat{D}_{i,i} = \sum_j \hat{A}_{i,j}$.

7.6.2   GraphSAGE

GraphSAGE (Hamilton et al., 2017) concatenates the neighborhood embedding and self-embedding:

$$h_i^\ell = \sigma([W^\ell \text{aggregate}(\{h_j^{\ell-1}, j \in \mathcal{N}(i)\}), B^\ell h_i^{\ell-1}]) \tag{7.24}$$

The graph neighborhood aggregation function can be the mean, pooling, or an LSTM sequence model:

$$\text{Mean aggregation:} \quad \sum_{j \in \mathcal{N}(i)} \frac{h_j^{\ell-1}}{|\mathcal{N}(i)|} \tag{7.25}$$

$$\text{Pooling:} \quad \gamma(\{Qh_j^{\ell-1}, j \in \mathcal{N}(i)\}) \tag{7.26}$$

$$\text{LSTM:} \quad \text{LSTM}([h_j^{\ell-1}, j \in \pi(\mathcal{N}(i))]) \tag{7.27}$$

and the network learns the parameters for aggregating information.

In the training process, we have an output embedding after L layers $e_i = h_i^L$ and we learn the weight matrices W^ℓ for the neighborhood embedding and B^ℓ for self-embedding. We define a neighborhood aggregation function and a loss function on embedding and train on a set of nodes generating embeddings for nodes.

This is useful since once we train the GNN, and compute the aggregation parameters, namely the weight matrices, we can generalize to new nodes. We generate a computation graph for a new node and transfer the weight matrices to the new node and compute a forward pass for prediction. In addition, given an entire new graph, we can transfer the aggregation weight matrices computed on one graph to a new graph and compute the forward pass to perform prediction.

7.6.3   Gated Graph Neural Networks

The second architecture, similar to DFS, shares weights across all the layers in each computation graph, instead of sharing weights across neighborhoods. In gated graph neural networks (Li et al., 2016) nodes aggregate messages from neighbors using a neural network, and similar to RNNs parameter sharing is across layers:

$$m_i^\ell = W \sum_{j \in \mathcal{N}(i)} h_j^{\ell-1} \tag{7.28}$$

$$h_i^\ell = \text{GRU}(h_i^{\ell-1}, m_i^\ell) \tag{7.29}$$

7.6.4   Graph Attention Networks

In graph attention networks (GATs) (Veličković et al., 2018) we use attention-based neighborhood aggregation. The attention function adaptively controls the contribution of neighbor j to node i:

$$h_i^\ell = \sigma \left(\sum_{j \in i \cup \mathcal{N}(i)} \alpha_{i,j} W h_j^{\ell-1} \right) \tag{7.30}$$

where $\alpha_{i,j}$ are the attention coefficients that define a distribution over node i and its neighbors $k \in \mathcal{N}(i)$ using the softmax:

$$\alpha_{i,j} = \frac{\exp(e_{i,j})}{\sum_{k \in i \cup \mathcal{N}(i)} \exp(e_{i,k})} \tag{7.31}$$

and $e_{i,j}$ is a function of $h_i^{\ell-1}$ and $h_j^{\ell-1}$:

$$e_{i,j} = \text{ReLU}(v^T(W h_i^{\ell-1} || W h_j^{\ell-1}) \tag{7.32}$$

where $||$ is the concatenation operation, and v and W are a learned vector and weight matrix. When using multiple attention heads, h_i^ℓ is the aggregation of multiple contributions, each of the form of Equation 7.30.

7.6.5   Message-Passing Networks

In a similar fashion to using aggregation and combination, a message-passing graph neural network is defined by messages between nodes across edges (aggregation) and node updates (combination):

$$h_i^\ell = \text{update}^\ell(h_i^{\ell-1}, \sum_{j \in \mathcal{N}(i)} \text{message}^\ell(h_i^{\ell-1}, h_j^{\ell-1}, e_{i,j})) \tag{7.33}$$

7.7   Applications

Graph neural networks are used in a wide range of applications, including (1) image retrieval; (2) computer vision for scene understanding (Santoro et al., 2017); (3) computer graphics for 3D shape analysis (Monti et al., 2017) and for learning point-cloud representations (Wang, Sun, Liu, Sarma, Bronstein and Solomon, 2019); (4) social networks for link prediction; (5) recommender systems and few-shot learning (Garcia and Bruna, 2018); (6) combinatorial optimization (Ma et al., 2020); (7) physics for learning the dynamics and interactions of physical objects (Battaglia et al., 2016; Chang et al., 2017; Watters et al., 2017; Sanchez-Gonzalez et al., 2018; Van Steenkiste et al., 2018); (8) chemistry for molecule classification (Duvenaud et al., 2015; Gilmer et al., 2017), defining a graph in which molecules are nodes and edges represent bonds between molecules, and

molecule design (Jin et al., 2018); (9) biology for drug discovery, protein function prediction, and protein–protein interactions; (10) for representing computer
programs; (11) in natural language processing; (12) for traffic applications such
as ride hailing and flight classification; and (13) in stock trading.

7.8   Software Libraries, Benchmarks, and Visualization

PyTorch Geometric (Fey and Lenssen, 2019) is a library for deep learning on
graphs in PyTorch. DGL (Wang, Yu, Gan, Zhaoogle, Gai, Ye, Li, Zhou, Huang,
Zheng, Lin, Ma, Deng, Guo, Zhang and Huang, 2020) is an optimized library
for deep learning on graphs in PyTorch and MXNet. OGB (Liu et al., 2020) is a
collection of benchmark datasets, data-loaders and evaluators for deep learning
on graphs.

7.9   Summary

Graph neural networks (Hamilton et al., 2017; Kipf and Welling, 2017; Veličković
et al., 2018; Xu et al., 2019) are applied to irregular structures such as networks
represented by graphs. They commonly share weights across neighborhoods, similar to how CNNs share weights across space and RNNs share weights across
time. Graph neural networks are used for three main tasks: (1) predicting properties of particular nodes, (2) predicting edges between nodes, and (3) predicting
properties of sub-graphs or entire graphs.

8   Transformers

8.1   Introduction

This chapter presents Transformer models, which have state-of-the-art performance across many tasks and datasets in a broad range of domains, including natural language processing, computer vision, audio processing, and program synthesis. The largest Transformer-based language model to date consists of around a trillion parameters. These models are trained using vast unlabeled corpora. Replacing labels are objectives based on context at multiple resolutions: where words occur in a sentence, whether sentences follow each other, and where sentences occur in a document. Very large Transformer-based models and improvements in usage of unlabeled data have led to results that supersede the largest available supervised counterparts and significant progress in real-world applications.

Transformers are based only on attention mechanisms (Vaswani et al., 2017) without using RNNs or CNNs. Transformers may be classified into three types of architectures: (1) autoencoding Transformers, which is a stack of encoders; (2) auto-regressive Transformers, which is a stack of decoders; or (3) sequence-to-sequence Transformers, which is a stack of encoders connected to a stack of decoders. In the latter case, the input to the first encoder is a word embedding and a position embedding. Each encoder consists of a self-attention layer and a neural network passing its output as input to the next encoder in the stack of encoders. Each decoder contains a self-attention layer, followed by an encoder–decoder attention layer, followed by a neural network. Each decoder passes its output as input to the next decoder in the stack of decoders. Using self-attention in the encoders and both encoder–decoder and self-attention in the decoders results in state-of-the-art results in machine translation. The Transformer architecture does not use RNNs or CNNs, which results in faster training time.

8.2 General-Purpose Transformer-Based Architectures

8.2.1 BERT

Bidirectional encoder representations from Transformers (Devlin et al., 2019), known as BERT, is a general-purpose Transformer-based architecture that achieves state-of-the-art performance on many natural language processing tasks and datasets:

- multi-genre natural language inference of sentence entailment, contradiction, or neutral pairs (Williams et al., 2018);
- Quora question pairs which classifies semantically equivalent sentences (Chen, Zhang, Zhang and Zhao, 2018);
- question natural language inference of labeled question–answer pairs (Wang, Singh, Michael, Hill, Levy and Bowman, 2019);
- Stanford sentiment treebank of movie review sentiments (Socher et al., 2013);
- corpus of linguistic acceptability of sentences (Warstadt et al., 2019);
- semantic textual similarity benchmark (Cer et al., 2017);
- Microsoft research paraphrase corpus annotating semantically equivalent sentences (Dolan and Brockett, 2005);
- recognizing a textual entailment task of bidirectional entailment (Bentivogli et al., 2009);
- Winograd NLI dataset for language inference (Morgenstern and Ortiz, 2015);
- Stanford question answering dataset (SQuAD) (Rajpurkar et al., 2016);
- CoNLL 2003 named entity recognition (NER) dataset (Sang and Meulder, 2003);
- situations with adversarial generations (SWAG) dataset of common-sense sentence completion (Zellers et al., 2018).

The BERT architecture is a deep bidirectional autoencoding Transformer. In BERT, each input word, or token, is represented by a token embedding, a segment embedding, and a position embedding. Next, a small fraction of all tokens in each sentence is randomly masked, and the goal of encoding self-attention is to complete the masked words. In addition, BERT learns to predict whether the relationship between two consecutive sentences is random or not, which is useful for question answering by concatenating the two sentences in random order with a separator token between them. Finally, the output sentence is represented using the hidden state of a classification token, which serves as input to a classifier that is fine-tuned on top of BERT.

8.3 Self-Attention

Sequence models, described in Chapter 6, perform computations on the input sequentially, whereas Transformers perform computations in parallel. Transformers are based on self-attention (Vaswani et al., 2017), which generates a representation for each word in the input in parallel. We begin by representing n words in a sentence using word embedding so that each embedded word is a d-dimensional vector $x_i \in \mathbb{R}^d$ and the sentence $X = [x_1, \ldots, x_n]^T \in \mathbb{R}^{n \times d}$ is an $n \times d$ matrix. This representation does not take into account the surroundings of the word in a specific sentence. Therefore, for a sentence with n words, self-attention computes n self-attention representations $A_1, \ldots, A_n$ for the n words. This computation is performed in parallel.

For each embedded word $x_i \in \mathbb{R}^d$ we compute a query $q_i \in \mathbb{R}^d$, a key $k_i \in \mathbb{R}^d$ and a value $v_i \in \mathbb{R}^d$, represented as row vectors (of matrices X, Q, K, and V), by linearly projecting X into three d-dimensional spaces of keys, queries, and values:

$$Q = XW^Q, \quad K = XW^K, \quad V = XW^V \tag{8.1}$$

where Q, K, V are $n \times d$-dimensional matrices whose rows i are the queries $q_i = x_i W^Q$, keys $k_i = x_i W^K$, and values $v_i = x_i W^V$ for each embedded word. $X \in \mathbb{R}^{n \times d}$ is the $n \times d$ matrix representing the sequence, or sentence, of embedded words, and W^Q, W^K, and W^V are learned $d \times d$ matrices. We compute the inner product between q_i and k_j for each $j = 1, \ldots, n$. Next, we compute the softmax multiplied by word values v_i to get the self-attention representation $A_i \in \mathbb{R}^d$ for embedded word x_i:

$$A_i(q, K, V) = \sum_{i=1}^{n} \frac{\exp(qk_i)}{\sum_j \exp(qk_j)} v_i \tag{8.2}$$

which may be summarized for all words $i = 1, \ldots, n$ as:

$$A(X) = A(Q, K, V) = \text{softmax}\left(\frac{QK^T}{\sqrt{d_k}}\right) V \tag{8.3}$$

where $A(X)$ is an $n \times d$ matrix and d is a scaling factor of the dot product attention.

8.4   Multi-head Attention

Multi-head attention performs self-attention multiple times. Instead of inner products, the query, key, and value vectors are multiplied by matrices $W_h^Q q_j$, $W_h^K k_j$, $W_h^V v_j$ for $h = 1, \ldots, m$ and the attention representations:

$$A_h(X) = A_h(Q, K, V) = A_h(W_h^Q Q, W_h^K K, W_h^V V) = \text{softmax}\left(\frac{Q_h K_h^T}{\sqrt{d}}\right) V_h \tag{8.4}$$

are computed for each head $h = 1, \ldots, m$, for each embedded word i. The m multi-head attention representations $A_h(X)$ for $h = 1, \ldots, m$ are concatenated and multiplied:

$$\text{multiheadattn}(X) = [A_1(X), \ldots, A_m(X)] W^o \tag{8.5}$$

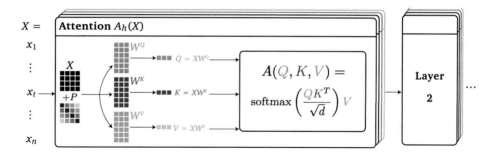

Figure 8.1 Multi-head attention. Given an embedded sequence X of dimensions $n \times d$ and position embedding as input, for each attention head we compute queries Q, keys K, and values V represented by $d \times d$ matrices, which are passed to the multi-head attention layer.

where W^o is an $md \times d$ learned matrix. Multi-head attention is illustrated in Figure 8.1. We first compute the sum of an embedded sequence X of dimensions $n \times d$ and position encoding P as input. Next, for each attention head, we compute queries Q, keys K, and values V represented by $d \times d$ matrices, which are passed to the multi-head attention layer whose output is of dimensions $n \times d$.

8.5 Transformer

Given sentences of embedded words, a Transformer may be used for diverse tasks such as natural language understanding, text generation, and translation of a sentence from one language to another. A Transformer consists of encoder or decoder blocks or both.

8.5.1 Positional Encoding

The position of words is required for computing the attention score. The positions of the words in the sentence are encoded as a position embedding by sine and cosine functions and added to X (Vaswani et al., 2017). Specifically, an $n \times d$ position embedding matrix P is defined by:

$$P_{pos,2i} = \sin\left(\frac{pos}{10,000^{\frac{2i}{d}}}\right), \quad P_{\text{pos},2i+1} = \cos\left(\frac{pos}{10,000^{\frac{2i}{d}}}\right) \tag{8.6}$$

where pos is the position of a word in a sentence, d is the dimension of a word embedding index $i = 1, \dots, d$. Adding P to X allows the model to learn to attend to relative positions.

8.5.2 Encoder

The encoder block takes as input a matrix X of embedded words. The position encoding is added to the embedded words to form the input $X + P$. We then compute queries Q, keys K, and values V, and pass them through a multi-head attention layer whose output is fed to a feed-forward neural network. A block consisting of multi-head attention and feed-forward neural network is repeated multiple times.

8.5.3   Decoder

The output of the encoder is fed into a decoder block, which predicts the translated sentence. The decoder also consists of multiple blocks of multi-head attention, which are fed into feed-forward neural networks and add positional embeddings to the inputs. Both the encoder and decoder may consist of residual connections between blocks and add and norm layers for normalization before the feed-forward neural networks. The output of the decoder is fed through a linear layer followed by a softmax layer. During generation, the decoder predicts new words, whereas during training, the decoder predicts masked words from the input.

8.5.4   Pre-training and Fine-tuning

Pre-training a Transformer is computationally expensive and most often involves vast amounts of unlabeled data. The most common optimization objectives for pre-training language models are (1) masked word prediction, which is predicting a random deleted word in a sentence or predicting the next word; and (2) classifying whether two sentences follow each other or not. This computationally expensive step is usually done once, followed by a relatively fast fine-tuning step. In fine-tuning, the pre-trained model is tuned on a specific dataset and task. Fine-tuning may be performed on a relatively small dataset very efficiently for specific usage. Pre-training followed by fine-tuning is referred to as transfer learning.

8.6   Transformer Models

Transformers may be roughly split into three classes: (1) autoencoding Transformer models that use only an encoder, which is suitable for natural language understanding; (2) auto-regressive Transformer models that use only a decoder, which is suitable for text-generation tasks; and (3) sequence-to-sequence Transformer models that use both an encoder and decoder.

8.6.1   Autoencoding Transformers

Encoder Transformers, also known as autoencoding models, use only an encoder. These models are suitable for natural language understanding tasks such as question answering, sentence classification, and other tasks that require understanding entire sentences. These Transformers include BERT, ALBERT (Lan et al., 2020), DistilBERT (Sanh et al., 2019), and RoBERTa (Liu, Ott, Goyal, Du, Joshi, Chen, Levy, Lewis, Zettlemoyer and Stoyanov, 2019). BERT has been extended and improved in several ways: RoBERTa (Liu, Ott, Goyal, Du, Joshi, Chen, Levy, Lewis, Zettlemoyer and Stoyanov, 2019) improves BERT training and results by fine-tuning hyperparameters; ALBERT (Lan et al., 2020) adds a self-supervised loss to model inter-sequence coherence; and DistilBERT (Sanh et al., 2019) reduces the BERT model size while maintaining performance. BERT is based on the Transformer architecture and uses a mask token for training but not for testing. BERT predicts multiple mask tokens in parallel without modeling direct dependencies between different predictions.

8.6.2   Auto-regressive Transformers

Decoder Transformers, also known as auto-regressive models, use only a decoder. These models are well suited for text generation and include GPT (Radford et al., 2018), GPT-2 (Radford et al., 2019), CTRL (Keskar et al., 2019), Transformer XL (Dai et al., 2019), and XLNet (Yang, Dai, Yang, Carbonell, Salakhutdinov and Le, 2019). A limitation of the Transformer architecture is that it processes the entire sequence at once, which may be a very long sequence of words. The Transformer XL (Dai et al., 2019) splits a long sequence of words into segments and adds a recurrent layer between Transformers, allowing us to process fixed-sized inputs while modeling long-term relationships. The Transformer uses an absolute position embedding, whereas the Transformer XL breaks the sequence into segments and embeds the relative distance between words. XLNet (Yang, Dai, Yang, Carbonell, Salakhutdinov and Le, 2019) is based on the Transformer XL architecture and models the dependencies between multiple predictions by predicting tokens in a random order sequentially, improving performance over BERT across the different natural language processing tasks. GPT is a pre-trained auto-regressive Transformer fine-tuned on multiple natural language processing tasks. GPT-2 (Radford et al., 2019) is trained with 1.5 billion parameters. CTRL (Keskar et al., 2019) is a conditional Transformer-based model providing control over the generated text style and content, trained with 1.63 billion parameters.

8.6.3   Sequence-to-Sequence Transformers

BART (Lewis et al., 2020) and T5 (Raffel et al., 2020) are sequence-to-sequence Transformer models that use both an encoder and decoder. Such models are suitable for translation, summarization, paraphrasing, and question answering that involve generating sentences from input.

8.6.4　GPT-3

In a race to build more powerful Transformer-based language models, the number of model parameters has increased by orders of magnitude. GPT-3 (Brown et al., 2020) is trained with 175 billion parameters and performs well on multiple tasks even without fine-tuning, by zero-shot (without any examples) or few-shot (given a few examples) learning.

Building upon the Megatron-LM model (Shoeybi et al., 2019), trained with 8.3 billion parameters, and the Turing NLG model, trained with 17 billion parameters, Nvidia and Microsoft joined forces to train Megatron-Turing NLG, which is currently one of the largest natural language processing Transformers, with 530 billion parameters. The number of parameters of the largest Transformer models is growing tenfold each year. Transformers will soon reach 100 trillion parameters at this rate, which is a significant milestone since that is roughly the number of connections in a human brain.

8.7　Vision Transformers

In a similar fashion to language models trained by predicting masked words in a sentence or the next word, vision Transformers (ViT) may be trained by predicting a masked pixel in a patch or the next pixel. Vision Transformers have superseded convolutional neural networks (CNNs) in scalability and performance across various applications, including object detection, recognition, and segmentation. Early efforts include the Image Transformer (Parmar et al., 2018), used for image generation. The Vision Transformer (Dosovitskiy et al., 2020) is used for image recognition at scale. It splits an image into non-overlapping patches, embeds the patches, and passes them through a Transformer architecture. In early computer vision, scientists manually designed filters. Next, CNNs learned these filters automatically by backpropagation; however, they required humans to design a suitable architecture. The use of Transformers in computer vision is yet another step forward. The Transformer does not require specific inductive biases in the architecture. Nevertheless, its performance supersedes CNNs, whose architecture is based on a strong inductive bias for processing images.

Various Transformer architectures have been used for object recognition. Beginning with a CNN architecture and replacing part of the layers with Transformer layers results in hybrid architectures such as VT (Wu et al., 2021) and BotNet (Srinivas et al., 2021), whose performance improves upon CNNs. Beginning with a Transformer architecture and introducing inductive biases by local computations, as performed in CNN layers, results in hybrid architectures such as the data-efficient image Transformer (Touvron et al., 2021) (DeiT) and ConViT (d'Ascoli et al., 2021). Hierarchical Transformer architectures reduce computational complexity while maintaining performance. These include the pyramid vision transformer (Wang, Xie, Li, Fan, Song, Liang, Lu, Luo and Shao, 2021), which uses a hierarchical pyramid architecture with non-overlapping patches, and the shifted windows Transformer (Liu, Lin, Cao, Hu, Wei, Zhang, Lin and Guo, 2021), which uses local self-attention.

Detection with Transformer (Carion et al., 2020) (DETR) combines a CNN with an encoder–decoder Transformer architecture, avoiding manually designed object detection components such as sample selection and non-maximum suppression. Deformable DETR (Zhu et al., 2021) improves the computational efficiency of DETR by applying attention to a sparse set of sampled locations. To avoid the collection of a large labeled training set, unsupervised pre-training DETR (Dai et al., 2021) pre-trains a model on random image patches that serve as queries for the decoder.

Video may be treated as a volume consisting of image slices in time. Trajectories may also model the temporal correspondence of physically moving objects in a video. Video Transformer (Patrick et al., 2021) uses self-attention of trajectories for the task of video action recognition.

8.8 Multi-modal Transformers

Rather than modeling language and vision independently, multi-modal Transformers use these modalities together to form multi-modal Transformers with applications in multi-modal search and generation. For example, DALL-E (Ramesh, Pavlov, Goh and Gray, 2021; Ramesh et al., 2022) is a generative model that is trained jointly on both text and images. The model then receives text describing an image as input and generates an image matching the description.

Transformers have been used in a variety of multi-modal settings, including (1) text and images, by models such as VilBERT (Lu et al., 2019), Vl-BERT (Su et al., 2020), LXMERT (Tan and Bansal, 2019), VisualBERT (Li et al., 2020), and Vokenization (Tan and Bansal, 2020); (2) text and video, by models such as VATT (Akbari et al., 2021), VideoBERT (Sun et al., 2019), and video question answering (Kant et al., 2020); and (3) audio and video, such as by a model for learning contextual multi-lingual multi-modal representations (Huang et al., 2021). Sharing parameters across these modalities (Lee et al., 2021) significantly reduces the number of parameters of such multi-modal Transformers.

8.9 Text and Code Transformers

OpenAI Codex (Chen et al., 2021) is a Transformer model trained on text and fine-tuned on code. Codex is used within GitHub-Copilot (OpenAI, 2021) to guide programming by completing and writing code and documentation. Codex is used for solving many university-level math, statistics and other STEM courses (Drori et al., n.d.; Shporer et al., 2022; Tang et al., 2022) by program synthesis and few-shot learning. Question solutions and programs share an underlying tree representation. Codex correctly solves questions by specifying both question and programming contexts, such as which programming packages to load. In addition to generating code that solves problems, the resulting code generates useful plots for understanding the solutions.

8.10 Summary

Transformers, also referred to as foundation models (Bommasani et al., 2021), have become a mainstream architecture in deep learning. Huggingface (Wolf et al., 2020) is a commonly used open-source Transformer platform that consists of multiple models, datasets, and libraries. Transformers have disrupted various fields, including natural language processing, computer vision, audio processing, programming, and education. The number of parameters of Transformers is increasing by an order of magnitude each year and is on track to surpass the number of connections in the human brain. New scalable deep learning architectures such as the Transformer are poised to revolutionize the way machines perceive the world, make decisions (Chen, Lu, Rajeswaran, Lee, Grover, Laskin, Abbeel, Srinivas and Mordatch, 2021), and generate novel output.

Part III

Generative Models

9 Generative Adversarial Networks

9.1 Introduction

Generative adversarial networks (GANs) are an unsupervised generative model used for generating samples that are similar to training examples. They have many applications, including image, video, 3D, trajectory, audio, protein and language synthesis. Common image synthesis applications include image translation, super-resolution, style synthesis, image completion, pose synthesis, image editing, text-to-image synthesis, and medical imaging. Widely used audio synthesis applications include text-to-speech synthesis and music synthesis. In addition to these applications, GANs have also been used for generating images from text, audio from images, and images from audio.

The task of classification maps a set of examples to a label. In contrast, generative models such as GANs map a label to a set of examples. Since there may be many examples with the same label, this generative mapping is stochastic and therefore this generative process involves sampling from a random distribution.

GANs were introduced in 2014 (Goodfellow et al., 2014) as a minimax optimization problem or a zero-sum game in which two agents, a generator and a discriminator, compete with each other. The generator is trained to produce fake examples that fool the discriminator. The generator learns to synthesize samples which are indistinguishable from real data. The generator's synthesized samples serve as negative examples for the discriminator. The discriminator learns to distinguish between the generator's fake synthesized samples and real data. The discriminator penalizes the generator for synthesizing samples which it is able to classify correctly.

The generator and the discriminator are trained alternately. The generator is trained to produce samples that are indistinguishable from real data. The discriminator is trained to distinguish between the generator's fake samples and real data. Generative adversarial networks have been shown to be able to generate high-quality samples in a wide variety of applications.

9.1.1 Progress

The field of GANs has seen exponential growth in research and applications, improving the results of GANs in quality and diversity, while stabilizing GAN

Figure 9.1 Photo-realistic faces synthesized using GANs: the images are of high quality and diverse.

training, and understanding the game-theoretic foundations. From initial low-resolution blurry image results in 2014, GANs have reached a level of photo-realistic synthesis results (Wang, 2019), as shown in Figure 9.1. Given data from a real distribution, the goal of the generator is to synthesize additional samples from the same distribution. Milestones in the development of GANs since their introduction (Goodfellow et al., 2014) include architectures such as deep convolutional generative adversarial networks (DCGAN) (Radford et al., 2015), progressive GAN (Karras et al., 2018), conditional GAN (CGAN) (Isola et al., 2017), cycle-consistent GAN (CycleGAN) (Zhu et al., 2017), single image GAN (Shaham et al., 2019); using the Wasserstein loss (Arjovsky et al., 2017) and the optimistic gradient descent ascent (OGDA) algorithm (Daskalakis et al., 2017) for training GANs. Recent GANs have overcome their initial limitations, including their difficulty in training, and their lack of exploration of the probability space.

9.1.2   Game Theory

Generative adversarial networks are a class of generative models that aim to learn a distribution from training data and then generate new samples from this distribution. The setting is that of two neural networks: a generator network $\mathcal{G}$ and a discriminator network $\mathcal{D}$. The generator is trained to produce samples that are indistinguishable from the training data. The discriminator is trained to distinguish between real and fake samples. The generator and discriminator are trained simultaneously in an adversarial setting, where the generator tries to fool the discriminator by producing realistic samples, while the discriminator tries to distinguish real from fake samples.

The discriminator and generator form two dueling networks with opposing objectives. This unsupervised setting eliminates the need for labels, since the label is whether the sample is real or not. Real data acquired from the real world without any label is abundant. From a game-theoretic viewpoint, we have two neural networks with a minimax objective.

9.1.3 Co-evolution

From a biological viewpoint, GANs are two neural networks that evolve by co-evolution. An example of co-evolution in nature is the evolution of a predator, such as the cheetah, and prey, such as the antelope, that co-evolved for rapid fight and herd flight in an evolutionary arms race. Another example of co-evolution in nature is the long-beaked hummingbird and flowers with long petals, which co-evolved for pollination and feeding.

The cheetah–antelope arms race and the hummingbird–flower arms race are examples of co-evolution in nature, where one species evolves in response to changes in the other species. There have been many studies of co-evolution in nature, and the theory of co-evolution has been very successful in describing how species co-evolve in nature. However, there has been a limitation on the application of the theory of co-evolution in nature to artificial systems because of the lack of co-evolution in the interaction between two neural networks. Generative adversarial networks are two neural networks that evolve by co-evolution, which can be regarded as a generalization of the theory of co-evolution in nature, and can be applied to artificial systems. In other words, GANs are one of the first types of artificial systems in which co-evolution occurs.

In the case of GANs, the two neural networks are called the generator and the discriminator. The generator learns to produce images that are similar to the training data. The discriminator learns to distinguish between real images and fake images produced by the generator. The generator and discriminator are trained together by a joint optimization algorithm.

9.2 Minimax Optimization

A minimax optimization problem or saddle-point problem is defined by:

$$\min_x \max_y f(x, y) \tag{9.1}$$

which is a zero-sum game.

Generative adversarial networks (Goodfellow et al., 2014) as illustrated in

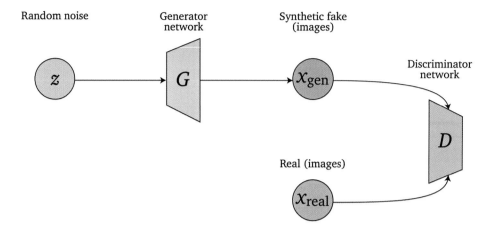

Figure 9.2 Generative adversarial network.

Figure 9.2, were formulated as a minimax optimization problem or a zero-sum game in which two agents, a generator $\mathcal{G}$ and a discriminator $\mathcal{D}$, compete:

$$\min_{\mathcal{G}} \max_{\mathcal{D}} V(\mathcal{G}, \mathcal{D}) = \mathbb{E}_x[\log \mathcal{D}(x)] + \mathbb{E}_z[\log(1 - \mathcal{D}(\mathcal{G}(z)))] \qquad (9.2)$$

The minimax game is a zero-sum game. The discriminator's loss is the generator's gain; the generator's loss is the discriminator's gain. The term $\mathcal{D}(x)$ is the discriminator's estimated probability that real data x is real, and $\mathbb{E}_x$ is the expectation over the real data. The term $\mathcal{G}(z)$ is the output of the generator given random noise z. The term $\mathcal{D}(\mathcal{G}(z))$ is the discriminator's estimated probability that a synthesized sample is real, and $\mathbb{E}_z$ is the expectation over random noise input, that is over the generator's synthesized samples. The goal of the generator is to generate a signal from random noise $z \sim P(z)$ in a way that it will be difficult for the discriminator to distinguish between the generated and real data $x \sim P_{\text{data}}$. The goal of the discriminator is to classify correctly real and generated data. The game between the generator and discriminator is a minimax optimization problem.

Representing the generator $\mathcal{G}$ by a neural network with parameters θ and the discriminator $\mathcal{D}$ by a neural network with parameters ϕ yields:

$$\min_{\theta} \max_{\phi} V(\mathcal{G}_\theta, \mathcal{D}_\phi) = \mathbb{E}_{x \sim P_{\text{data}}}[\log \mathcal{D}_\phi(x)] + \mathbb{E}_{z \sim P_z}[\log(1 - \mathcal{D}_\phi(\mathcal{G}_\theta(z)))] \quad (9.3)$$

$$= \mathbb{E}_{x \sim P_{\text{data}}}[\log \mathcal{D}_\phi(x)] + \mathbb{E}_{x \sim P_\mathcal{G}}[\log(1 - \mathcal{D}_\phi(x))] \qquad (9.4)$$

Since both the generator and discriminator are represented by neural networks the problem is non-convex non-concave (Lin et al., 2020). This formulation as a zero-sum game has been called a saturating GAN (Goodfellow et al., 2014) since initially it did not work due to saturation of gradients which become small and do not converge to a solution. The first term of $\log \mathcal{D}(x)$ is independent of the generator and therefore the generator minimizes the function $\log(1 - \mathcal{D}(\mathcal{G}(z)))$. To fix this saturation problem, a non-saturating GAN formulation was introduced (Goodfellow et al., 2014) which is not a zero-sum game, changing the generator loss to maximize $\log \mathcal{D}(\mathcal{G}(z))$ instead.

The goal of a GAN is to mimic a probability distribution and therefore it uses a loss function that represents the distance between the distribution of the synthesized samples and the distribution of the real data. A GAN has two loss functions, one for the discriminator and the other for the generator, and both are derived from a measure of similarity between the distribution of the synthesized samples $P_{\mathcal{G}}$ and the distribution of the real data P_{data}. The first term in Equation 9.2 depends only on the real data, and therefore training of the generator only involves the second term of Equation 9.2, which depends on the synthesized samples.

9.3   Divergence between Distributions

The relative entropy or Kullback–Leibler (KL) divergence D_{KL} is a measure of how one probability distribution p diverges from another probability distribution q and is defined by:

$$D_{\text{KL}}(q(x)||p(x)) = \int q(x) \log \frac{q(x)}{p(x)} dx \qquad (9.5)$$

which is non-negative and asymmetric. The Jensen–Shannon (JS) divergence D_{JS} is a symmetric smooth version of the KL divergence defined by:

$$D_{\text{JS}}(q||p) = \frac{1}{2} D_{\text{KL}}(q||m) + \frac{1}{2} D_{\text{KL}}(p||m) \qquad (9.6)$$

where $m = \frac{1}{2}(p + q)$. The KL divergence and JS divergence are both special cases of the Bregman divergence. The Bregman divergence is defined by a convex function F and is a measure of distance between two points p and q defined by:

$$\mathcal{D}_F(p,q) = F(p) - F(q) - \langle \nabla F(q), p - q \rangle \qquad (9.7)$$

Each convex function F defines a different divergence. Different divergences are explored with the goals of overcoming the problem of vanishing gradients and improving GAN training stability and diversity. For the special case of $F(p) = p \log(p)$ we get:

$$\begin{aligned} \mathcal{D}_F(p,q) &= p \log(p) - q \log(q) - (\log(q) + 1)(p - q) \\ &= p \log \left(\frac{p}{q} \right) + (q - p) \end{aligned} \qquad (9.8)$$

which is the generalized KL divergence. For the special case of $F(p) = p \log(p) - (p + 1) \log(p + 1)$ we get the JS divergence, which leads to the original GAN formulation (Goodfellow et al., 2014).

9.3.1 Least Squares GAN

The special case of $F = (1 - p)^2$ results in the Pearson χ^2 divergence leading to the least-squares GAN (LS-GAN) formulation (Mao et al., 2017), which uses a least squares loss function for the discriminator:

$$\mathbb{E}_x[(\mathcal{D}(x) - 1)^2] - \mathbb{E}_z[\mathcal{D}(\mathcal{G}(z))^2] \tag{9.9}$$

and generator:

$$\mathbb{E}_z[(\mathcal{D}(\mathcal{G}(z)) - 1)^2] \tag{9.10}$$

providing a smoother loss.

9.3.2 f-GAN

Choosing different convex functions F leads to different GAN formulations, also known as f-GANs (Nowozin et al., 2016).

9.4 Optimal Objective Value

Setting the generator $\mathcal{G}$ to be fixed and optimizing the discriminator by setting the derivative of:

$$\mathcal{L}_{\mathcal{D}}(x) = P_{\text{data}} \log \mathcal{D}(x) + P_{\mathcal{G}} \log(1 - \mathcal{D}(x)) \tag{9.11}$$

to be zero, results in the optimal discriminator $D^\star$:

$$\mathcal{D}^\star(x) = \frac{P_{\text{data}}}{P_{\text{data}} + P_{\mathcal{G}}} \tag{9.12}$$

Plugging the optimal discriminator $D^\star$ into Equation 9.2 results in:

$$\min_{\mathcal{G}} V(G, \mathcal{D}^\star) = 2D_{\text{JS}}(P_{\text{data}} || P_{\mathcal{G}}) - 2\log 2 \tag{9.13}$$

where the JS divergence $D_{\text{JS}}(P_{\text{data}}, P_{\mathcal{G}})$ is:

$$D_{\text{JS}}(P_{\text{data}}, P_{\mathcal{G}}) = \frac{1}{2}(D_{\text{KL}}(P_{\text{data}}, \frac{P_{\text{data}} + P_{\mathcal{G}}}{2}) + D_{\text{KL}}(P_{\mathcal{G}}, \frac{P_{\text{data}} + P_{\mathcal{G}}}{2})) \tag{9.14}$$

Therefore, the optimal value of V is obtained when the distribution of real data is equal to the generator distribution $P_{\text{data}} = P_{\mathcal{G}}$. In this case the discriminator cannot distinguish between real and synthesized data, namely $\mathcal{D}^\star(x) = \frac{1}{2}$, and the JS divergence D_{JS} is zero, optimizing the GAN objective.

9.5 Gradient Descent Ascent

A common algorithm used to solve the minimax optimization problem in Equation 9.1 is gradient descent ascent (GDA), which alternates between gradient descent on x and gradient ascent on y. The minimization variable is updated by gradient descent:

$$x_{t+1} = x_t - \eta_x \nabla_x f(x_t, y_t) \tag{9.15}$$

and the maximization variable is updated by gradient ascent:

$$y_{t+1} = y_t + \eta_y \nabla_y f(x_t, y_t) \tag{9.16}$$

where η_x and η_y are the learning rates.

In our setting we use a stochastic variant of GDA with mini-batches, in which the descent update $\nabla_x f(x_t, y_t)$ for the generator neural network is:

$$\nabla_\theta V(\mathcal{G}_\theta, \mathcal{D}_\phi) = \frac{1}{m} \nabla_\theta \sum_{i=1}^{m} \log(1 - \mathcal{D}_\phi(\mathcal{G}_\theta(z^i))) \tag{9.17}$$

and the ascent update $\nabla_y f(x_t, y_t)$ for the discriminator neural network is:

$$\nabla_\phi V(\mathcal{G}_\theta, \mathcal{D}_\phi) = \frac{1}{m} \nabla_\phi \sum_{i=1}^{m} (\log \mathcal{D}_\phi(x^i) + \log(1 - \mathcal{D}_\phi(\mathcal{G}_\theta(z^i)))) \tag{9.18}$$

If f were convex–concave then playing the game simultaneously or in a sequential order would not matter; however, in our case f is non-convex non-concave and the order matters. Therefore, the updates are performed sequentially in our setting, which is a zero-sum sequential game, also known as a Stackelberg game. In practice the algorithm takes multiple ascent steps, denoted by γ, for each descent step, denoted by γ-GDA.

Unfortunately, GDA may converge to points that are not local minimax or fail to converge to a local minimax. A modification of GDA (Wang, Zhang and Ba, 2020) which partially addresses this issue is:

$$y_{t+1} = y_t + \eta \nabla_y f(x_t, y_t) + \eta H_{yy}^{-1} H_{yx} \nabla_x f(x_t, y_t) \tag{9.19}$$

which converges and only converges to local minimax points, driving the gradient quickly to zero and improving GAN convergence.

9.6 Optimistic Gradient Descent Ascent

When introduced, GANs were implemented using momentum. However, later on the implementations did not use momentum, and using a negative momentum made the saturating GAN work. An algorithm that solves the minimax optimization problem by using negative momentum is optimistic gradient descent ascent; (Daskalakis et al., 2017). This adds negative momentum terms to the gradient updates:

$$x_{t+1} = x_t - \eta_x \nabla_x f(x_t, y_t) - \eta_x (\nabla_x f(x_t, y_t) - \nabla_x f(x_{t-1}, y_{t-1})) \tag{9.20}$$

$$y_{t+1} = y_t + \eta_y \nabla_y f(x_t, y_t) + \eta_y (\nabla_y f(x_t, y_t) - \nabla_y f(x_{t-1}, y_{t-1})) \tag{9.21}$$

Optimistic gradient descent ascent yields better empirical results than GDA, and can be interpreted as an approximation of the proximal point method.

9.7   GAN Training

In the beginning of training of the generator and discriminator, the generator synthesizes samples that are not similar to real data and the discriminator easily classifies the generated samples as fake. As training progresses, the generator improves and synthesizes samples that are able to fool the discriminator into classifying them as real data. When the generator training is successful, the discriminator cannot distinguish between real data and fake samples synthesized by the generator. The generator and discriminator are represented by neural networks and are both trained by backpropagation. The output of the generator serves as input to the discriminator, as shown in Figure 9.2.

9.7.1   Discriminator Training

The discriminator loss serves as a signal to the generator for updating its parameters by backpropagation. The discriminator shown in Figure 9.3 is a classifier that tries to distinguish between real data and samples synthesized by the generator. Training the discriminator uses real data as positive examples and samples synthesized by the generator as negative examples. When the discriminator is trained, the generator is not trained and its parameters are held fixed. The generator synthesizes samples so that the discriminator can train using these generated samples. When the discriminator is training it ignores the generator's loss function and uses only its own loss function, classifying real data and fake samples synthesized by the generator. The discriminator loss penalizes the discriminator for mis-classifying real data as fake and vice versa, and the discriminator weights are updated by backpropagation.

9.7.2   Generator Training

The generator shown in Figure 9.4 learns to synthesize realistic samples by the feedback it receives from the discriminator. The input to the generator is random noise, which it learns to transform to synthesized samples randomly spread across the output distribution. Usually the input random noise is sampled from a lower dimensional space than the output synthesized sample. During generator training the discriminator parameters are held fixed. The discriminator network classifies the synthesized samples and the generator's loss function penalizes the generator if it does not succeed in fooling the discriminator into classifying its synthesized samples as real. During generator training the gradients are back-propagated through both the discriminator network and the generator network.

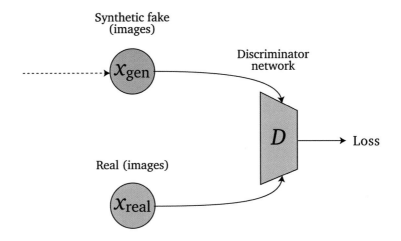

Figure 9.3 GAN discriminator network.

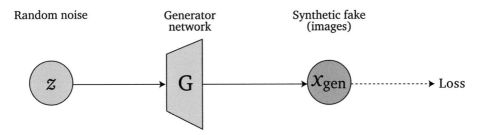

Figure 9.4 GAN generator network.

Even though the discriminator weights are not updated during generator training, the discriminator's fixed weights influence the update of generator parameters.

9.7.3 Alternating Discriminator–Generator Training

Generative adversarial network training alternates between training the discriminator and the generator. The discriminator loss function is usually different from the generator loss function. The discriminator trains for several epochs, then the generator trains for several epochs. This alternating training is repeated. Algorithm 9.1 provides pseudocode for GAN training.

During training, as the generator increases the similarity between the synthesized samples and real data, the discriminator classification accuracy decreases. If the generator training is successful, the discriminator classification accuracy is random. This in turn results in providing uninformative feedback to the discriminator, which illustrates the difficulty of convergence of this saddle-point problem. Solutions to the convergence problem include adding noise to the discriminator's

---

Algorithm 9.1 Alternating GAN training. During training of the discriminator the generator parameters are held fixed and vice versa.

> **for** each epoch $i = 1, \ldots, n$ **do**:
>> Sample mini-batch from real data $x^1, \ldots, x^m \sim P_x$
>> Sample mini-batch from noise $z^1, \ldots, z^m \sim P_z$
>> Take gradient ascent step on discriminator parameters ϕ by Eq. 9.18
>> Take gradient descent step on generator parameters θ by Eq. 9.17

---

input or penalizing the discriminator weights, which are regularization methods that improve GAN convergence.

9.8   GAN Losses

As described, different Bregman divergences and loss functions have been explored with the goals of improving GAN training stability and diversity. Notably, using the Earth Mover's Distance (EMD) in the Wasserstein GAN formulation has had a fundamental contribution to improving GAN training.

9.8.1   Wasserstein GAN

If the real data distribution and generator distribution do not overlap, then the JS divergence is zero, $D_{\mathrm{JS}} = 0$, which occurs even if both distributions are identical but translated. This demonstrates the problem with using the JS divergence for optimizing GANs when distributions have non-overlapping support. Fortunately, this issue has been resolved by using the EMD or Wasserstein-1 distance:

$$W(P, Q) = \min_{\gamma \in \prod(P,Q)} \mathbb{E}_{(x,y) \sim \gamma} \|x - y\| \qquad (9.22)$$

where γ denotes how much mass, or earth, must be moved from x to y in order to transform distribution P into distribution Q, and $\prod(P, Q)$ denotes the set of all disjoint distributions with marginals P and Q. The EMD is the cost of the optimal transport plan and has nicer properties for GAN optimization than the JS divergence. Computing $W(P, Q)$ is intractable since it requires considering all possible combinations of pairs of points between the two distributions, computing the mean distance of all pairs in each combination, and taking the minimum mean distance across all combinations. Fortunately, an alternative is to solve a dual maximization problem that is tractable, which results in the Wasserstein loss.

A GAN uses the minimax loss in which the discriminator outputs a probability in $[0, 1]$ of a sample being real or synthesized. In contrast, a WGAN (Arjovsky et al., 2017) uses a Wasserstein loss formulation for the discriminator, which outputs a real value that is larger for real data than synthesized samples. The WGAN discriminator is called a critic since it does not output values in $[0, 1]$ for performing classification. There is no sigmoid in the final layer of the discriminator, and the range is $[-\infty, \infty]$. The Wasserstein loss function is:

$$\min_{\mathcal{G}} \max_{\mathcal{D}} V(\mathcal{G}, \mathcal{D}) = \mathbb{E}_x[\mathcal{D}(x)] - \mathbb{E}_z[\mathcal{D}(\mathcal{G}(z))] \tag{9.23}$$

where $\mathcal{D}(x)$ is the critic output given real data, $\mathcal{G}(z)$ is the generator output given noise and $\mathcal{D}(\mathcal{G}(z))$ is the output of the critic given synthesized samples. This means that the critic maximizes the difference between its expected output on real data and synthesized samples. The generator loss function is $-\mathbb{E}_{z \sim P(z)}[\mathcal{D}(\mathcal{G}(z))]$, which means that the generator minimizes the negative output of the critic on samples synthesized by the generator.

The Wasserstein loss function is derived from the EMD between the distribution of the real data and the distribution of the synthesized samples. An advantage of using the EMD is a metric between distributions, which handles disjoint distributions without overlapping support. The weights in a WGAN are clipped to within a constant range, and the WGAN avoids vanishing gradients. The Wasserstein loss avoids vanishing gradients even if the critic is optimally trained.

We want the generator to synthesize diverse samples, for example, to synthesize a different sample for each different random input. The generator may learn to synthesize a small set of samples very well, which the discriminator fails on. If the generator repeatedly synthesizes the same samples, the discriminator may learn to reject those samples. However, suppose the discriminator gets stuck in a local minimum and does not find the optimal strategy. The generator may optimize the output that will fail the discriminator in the next generator-training iteration.

If, at each iteration, the generator optimizes for a specific discriminator and the discriminator cannot correctly classify the synthesized samples as fake, the generator will synthesize a small set of samples, not diverse samples, known as mode collapse. The Wasserstein loss trains the critic toward optimality without vanishing gradients. When the critic does not get stuck in local minima, it learns to reject the generator's repeated samples, encouraging the generator to synthesize new samples and diversify the result.

9.8.2 Unrolled GAN

In order to avoid mode collapse and encourage the generator to diversify the synthesized samples and not optimize for a constant discriminator, the generator loss function may be modified to include multiple subsequent discriminators (Metz et al., 2017). There is a classical tradeoff between the approximation quality of the generator loss and the computation time, which is linear in the number of unrolling steps.

9.9   GAN Architectures

9.9.1   Progressive GAN

A coarse-to-fine approach for training allows generating images at increasing resolutions. Progressive GANs (Karras et al., 2018) begin by training the generator and discriminator using low-resolution images and incrementally add layers of higher-resolution images during training. Proceeding from coarse to fine achieves high-resolution results while maintaining training stability.

9.9.2   Deep Convolutional GAN

Deep convolutional GANs are a type of GAN that use convolutional neural networks (CNNs) as the generator and discriminator. In a similar fashion that using CNNs significantly improves classification accuracy over fully connected neural networks, using a CNN as the discriminator network and a deconvolution neural network as the generator, known as a DCGAN (Radford et al., 2015), significantly improves the quality of the synthesized results over a fully connected GAN (Goodfellow et al., 2014). Deep convolutional GANs are capable of generating high-resolution images with realistic textures and have been extended by methods that improve and stabilize GAN training (Salimans et al., 2016).

9.9.3   Semi-Supervised GAN

Instead of having the discriminator be a binary classifier for real or fake samples, in a semi-supervised GAN (SGAN) the discriminator is a multi-class classifier (Salimans et al., 2016; Kumar et al., 2017; Odena et al., 2017; Oliver et al., 2018). The discriminator outputs the likelihood of a sample to be synthesized or real, and if the sample is classified as real then the discriminator outputs the probability of the k classes, estimating to which class the sample belongs. In the semi-supervised setting (Odena, 2016) the SGAN discriminator receives three types of inputs rather than two: fake samples synthesized by the generator; real samples without class labels; and real samples with class labels, thus improving the generated results for specific classes. Training is improved by having the SGAN discriminator trained using two loss functions (Salimans et al., 2016) rather than a single loss function: an unsupervised loss and a supervised loss function.

9.9.4   Conditional GAN

A conditional GAN (Mirza and Osindero, 2014) models the conditional probability distribution $P(x|y)$ by training the generator and discriminator on labeled data. Replacing $\mathcal{D}(x)$ with $\mathcal{D}(x|y)$ and $\mathcal{G}(z)$ with $\mathcal{G}(z|y)$ in Equation 9.2:

$$\min_{\mathcal{G}} \max_{\mathcal{D}} V(\mathcal{G}, \mathcal{D}) = \mathbb{E}_x[\log \mathcal{D}(x|y)] + \mathbb{E}_z[\log(1 - \mathcal{D}(\mathcal{G}(z|y)))] \qquad (9.24)$$

turns a GAN into a conditional GAN. Providing labels allows us to synthesize samples in a specific class or with a specific attribute, providing a level of control over synthesis.

9.9.5 Image-to-Image Translation

Image analogies (Hertzmann et al., 2001) provide a framework for synthesizing images by example. Given a training set of unfiltered and filtered image pairs $A : A'$ and a new unfiltered image B, the output is a filtered image B' such that the analogy $A : A' :: B : B'$ is maintained.

Image-to-image translation also known as Pix2Pix (Isola et al., 2017; Huang et al., 2018; Wang, Liu, Zhu, Tao, Kautz and Catanzaro, 2018; Liu, Huang, Mallya, Karras, Aila, Lehtinen and Kautz, 2019; Park et al., 2019) applies this concept using GANs. An input image is mapped to a synthesized image with different properties. The loss function is a combination of the conditional GAN loss with an additional loss term, which is a pixelwise loss that encourages the generator to match the source image:

$$
\min_{\mathcal{G}} \max_{\mathcal{D}} V(\mathcal{G}, \mathcal{D}) = \mathbb{E}_{x,y}[\log \mathcal{D}(x, y)] + \mathbb{E}_{x,z}[\log(1 - \mathcal{D}(x, \mathcal{G}(x, z)))]
$$
$$
+ \lambda \mathbb{E}_{x,y,z}[\|y - \mathcal{G}(x, z)\|_1] \tag{9.25}
$$

weighted by λ.

9.9.6 Cycle-Consistent GAN

Motivated by style and content separation (Tenenbaum and Freeman, 2000; Drori et al., 2003a), cycle-consistent GAN (Zhu et al., 2017) learns unpaired image-to-image translation using GANs without pixelwise correspondence. The training data are image sets $X \in A$ and $Y \in A'$ from two different domains A and A' without pixelwise correspondence between the images in X and Y. The advantage of this unsupervised approach is that images in correspondence may be expensive to acquire or may not be available altogether.

Cycle-Consistent GAN (CycleGAN) consists of two generators $\mathcal{G}(X) = \hat{Y}$ and $\mathcal{F}(Y) = \hat{X}$ and two discriminators $\mathcal{D}_Y$ and $\mathcal{D}_X$. The generator $\mathcal{G}$ maps a real image X to a synthesized sample $\hat{Y}$ and the discriminator $\mathcal{D}_Y$ compares between them. The generator $\mathcal{F}$ maps a real image Y to a synthesized sample $\hat{X}$ and the discriminator $\mathcal{D}_X$ compares between them. CycleGAN maintains two approximate cycle consistencies. The first cycle consistency $\mathcal{F}(\mathcal{G}(X)) \approx X$ approximately maintains that mapping a real image X to a synthesized image $\hat{Y}$ and back is similar to X, and the second cycle consistency $\mathcal{G}(\mathcal{F}(Y)) \approx Y$ approximately maintains that mapping a real image Y to a synthesized image $\hat{X}$ and back is similar to Y. Consider learning the translation between English and Chinese by applying one generator that translates the sentence from English to Chinese followed by a second generator that translates the result back

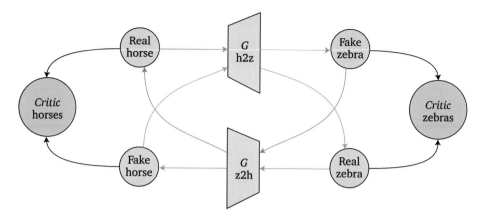

Figure 9.5 CycleGAN for horses and zebras. Generators are shown in green, critics in red, real images in orange, and fake images in gray.

from Chinese to English, while maintaining that the final result is similar to the original English sentence, and vice versa. The discriminators make sure that the generators do not learn the identity function, and synthesize diverse samples.

The overall loss function is defined by (Zhu et al., 2017):

$$\min_{\mathcal{G},\mathcal{F}} \max_{\mathcal{D}_X,\mathcal{D}_Y} \mathcal{L}(\mathcal{G},\mathcal{F},\mathcal{D}_X,\mathcal{D}_Y) = \mathcal{L}_{\mathrm{GAN}}(\mathcal{G},\mathcal{D}_Y,X,Y) + \mathcal{L}_{\mathrm{GAN}}(\mathcal{F},\mathcal{D}_X,Y,X)$$
$$+ \lambda \mathcal{L}_{\mathrm{cyc}}(\mathcal{G},\mathcal{F}) \tag{9.26}$$

where the cycle-consistency loss is defined by:

$$\mathcal{L}_{\mathrm{cyc}}(\mathcal{G},\mathcal{F}) = \mathbb{E}_{x\sim P_X}\left(\|\mathcal{F}(\mathcal{G}(X)) - X\|_1\right) + \mathbb{E}_{Y\sim P_Y}\left(\|\mathcal{G}(\mathcal{F}(Y)) - Y\|_1\right) \tag{9.27}$$

weighted by λ.

For example, consider X to be horse images and Y to be images of zebras. Clearly, there is no pixelwise correspondence between images of horses and zebras in the wild. A CycleGAN for horses and zebras (Zhu et al., 2017) is illustrated in Figure 9.5. One generator maps horses to zebras and the other maps zebras to horses. One discriminator distinguishes between real and fake horses and the other distinguishes between real and fake zebras. One cycle maintains that, given a real horse, a generator synthesizes a fake zebra which the other generator transforms back to a horse matching the original horse. A second cycle maintains that, given a real zebra, a generator synthesizes a fake horse which the other generator transforms back to a zebra matching the original zebra. One critic learns to distinguish between real and fake horses and another critic learns to distinguish between real and fake zebras. StarGAN (Choi et al., 2018) extends CycleGAN to more than two domains.

If the generators $\mathcal{G}$ and $\mathcal{F}$ were invertible mappings $\mathcal{F} = \mathcal{G}^{-1}$ then exact cycle consistencies would be maintained such that $\mathcal{F}(\mathcal{G}(X)) = Y$ and $\mathcal{G}(\mathcal{F}(Y)) = X$. This is achieved by modeling each domain using normalizing flows (Rezende and

Mohamed, 2015), and maintaining exact cycle consistency improves the quality
of the synthesized results (Grover et al., 2020).

9.9.7   Registration GAN

Registration GAN (Kong et al., n.d.) uses a registration network $\mathcal{R}$ after the
generator $\mathcal{G}$, treating the misaligned target images as noisy labels and correcting
the result. A correction loss is defined by:

$$\min_{\mathcal{G},\mathcal{R}} \mathcal{L}_{\text{cor}}(\mathcal{G}, \mathcal{R}) = \mathbb{E}_{x,\tilde{y},z}[\|y - \mathcal{G}(x, z) \circ \mathcal{R}(\mathcal{G}(x, z), \tilde{y})\|_1], \qquad (9.28)$$

where $\circ$ represents resampling and $\mathcal{R}(\mathcal{G}(x, z), \tilde{y})$ is a deformation field that dis-
places each pixel. A smoothness loss on the deformation field is defined by:

$$\min_{\mathcal{R}} \mathcal{L}_{\text{smooth}}(\mathcal{R}) = \mathbb{E}_{x,\tilde{y},z}[\|\nabla \mathcal{R}(\mathcal{G}(x, z), \tilde{y})\|^2] \qquad (9.29)$$

and the total loss is the sum of the GAN, correction and smoothness losses:

$$\min_{\mathcal{G},\mathcal{R}} \max_{\mathcal{D}} \mathcal{L}(\mathcal{G}, \mathcal{R}, \mathcal{D}) = \mathcal{L}_{\text{GAN}}(\mathcal{G}, \mathcal{D}) + \mathcal{L}_{\text{cor}}(\mathcal{G}, \mathcal{R}) + \mathcal{L}_{\text{smooth}}(\mathcal{R}) \qquad (9.30)$$

Registration GAN (RegGAN) outperforms both Pix2Pix on aligned images and
CycleGAN on unpaired images, specifically on medical images where the noise
may be considered as a deformation field.

9.9.8   Self-Attention GAN and BigGAN

Self-attention GAN (Zhang, Goodfellow, Metaxas and Odena, 2019) incorpo-
rates an attention mechanism in both the generator and discriminator networks
to capture long-range spatial dependencies between pixels. Using attention improves the diversity of the synthesized images. Self-attention GAN (SAGAN) is
improved in BigGAN (Brock et al., 2019) by increasing the batch size to improve quality, by using a truncated normal distribution for z during training
which trades off diversity for quality, and by incorporating z into each layer of
the generator for further improving quality.

9.9.9   Composition and Control with GANs

Generative adversarial networks are used for synthesis by sampling a latent variable z passed to generator $\mathcal{G}$ to generate an output x. Until recently, controlling the output synthesized by GANs, for example the pose, illumination and
composition of multiple objects in a scene, has been challenging. Recent work
(Niemeyer and Geiger, 2021) adds control over the synthesized scene by incorporating 3D scene composition into the model. During the forward pass, individual
shape and appearance variables for each object and background are sampled, for
example, sampling the pose for each object, then applying the transformation,
and rendering the scene. During training, objects and their poses are randomly
sampled.

9.9.10   Instance Conditioned GAN

Instance conditioned GAN (Casanova et al., 2021) learns multiple local distributions defined by clusters of data points along with their nearest neighbors. Given an unlabeled dataset of points $x^{(i)}$, their nearest neighbors $\mathcal{N}(i)$ are defined based on the cosine similarity of a set of features $f(x^{(i)})$. A discriminator $\mathcal{D}$ distinguishes between real neighbors $x^{(n)}$ sampled uniformly from $\mathcal{N}(i)$ and generated neighbors. A generator $\mathcal{G}$ synthesizes samples from the distribution $p(x|f(x^{(i)}))$ given Gaussian noise z. The adversarial objective is then defined by:

$$\min_{\mathcal{G}} \max_{\mathcal{D}} \mathbb{E}_{x^{(i)} \sim P_{\text{data}}, x^{(n)} \sim U(\mathcal{N}(i))}[\log \mathcal{D}(x^{(n)}, f(x^{(i)}))]$$
$$+\mathbb{E}_{x^{(i)} \sim P_{\text{data}}, z \sim P_z}[\log(1 - \mathcal{D}(\mathcal{G}(z, f(x^{(i)})), f(x^{(i)})))] \tag{9.31}$$

During training, all data points are used for conditioning the model. The discriminator and generator are conditioned on instance features, and therefore by changing instances the model transfers to unseen datasets. Given labels, Equation 9.31 may be extended to be conditioned on classes. In this case the discriminator and generator are conditioned on class labels and the generator synthesizes samples from the distribution $p(x|f(x^{(i)}), y^{(j)})$. Instance conditioned GAN (IC-GAN) outperforms traditional GANs and conditional GANs, and the trained models transfer well to new unseen datasets without retraining.

9.10   Evaluation

The inception score (IS) and Frechet inception distance (FID) measure the quality of synthesized examples using pre-trained neural network classifiers. The geometry score (Khrulkov and Oseledets, 2018) measures the quality of synthesized examples by comparing the manifold of the synthesized samples with the manifold of the real data. Recent evaluation measures aim to capture both the quality and diversity of synthesized results.

9.10.1   Inception Score

The IS (Salimans et al., 2016) automatically evaluates the quality of images synthesized by the generator by using the pre-trained Inception v3 model (Szegedy et al., 2016) for classification. The probabilities of many synthesized images belonging to each class are used to compute the score based on the conditional label distribution $p(y|x)$ and the marginal label distribution $p(y)$:

$$\text{IS}(\mathcal{G}) = \exp(\mathbb{E}_{x \sim p_\mathcal{G}}[D_{\text{KL}}(p(y|x)||p(y))]) \tag{9.32}$$

A higher IS is better, which corresponds to a larger KL divergence between the distributions.

9.10.2 Frechet Inception Distance

The FID (Heusel et al., 2017) is also based on the Inception v3 modally. The FID uses the feature vectors of the last layer for real and synthesized images to generate multivariate Gaussians that model the real and synthesized distributions. The FID is computed as the difference between these Gaussians measured using the Wasserstein-2 distance by:

$$\text{FID} = \|\mu_{\text{real}} - \mu_{\text{generated}}\|^2 + \text{tr}(\Sigma_{\text{real}} + \Sigma_{\text{generated}} - 2(\Sigma_{\text{real}}\Sigma_{\text{generated}})^{\frac{1}{2}}) \quad (9.33)$$

A lower FID is better, which corresponds to similar real and synthesized distributions.

9.11 Applications

9.11.1 Super Resolution and Restoration

Super-resolution by example (Freeman et al., 2002) increases the resolution of an image given corresponding low-resolution and high-resolution training example pairs. Super Resolution GAN (Ledig et al., 2017) uses a GAN framework for super-resolution. SinGAN (Shaham et al., 2019) uses the self-similarity of image patches within an image for synthesizing versions of an image. Building upon SinGAN, KerGAN (Bell-Kligler et al., 2019) performs blind super resolution without any training examples by utilizing the self-similarity of image patches across scales to learn an image-specific down-sampling kernel used for super-resolution. Generative Facial Prior (GFP) GAN (Wang, Li, Zhang and Shan, 2021) performs blind face restoration using U-Nets and a pre-trained face GAN with excellent results.

9.11.2 Style Synthesis

As described, CycleGAN (Zhu et al., 2017) has been used for style synthesis. StyleGAN (Karras et al., 2019) combines progressive GANs (Karras et al., 2018) with style transfer (Huang and Belongie, 2017) based on CNNs with adaptive normalization layers to disentangle the latent factors controlling image style synthesis. Hyper-LifelongGAN (Zhai et al., 2021) provides a lifelong learning framework for image-conditioned generation. HistoGAN (Afifi et al., 2021) learns to change image colors based on histogram features. ComoGAN (Pizzati et al., 2021) learns non-linear continuous image translation with unsupervised target data using physics-inspired models.

9.11.3 Image Completion

Image completion (Drori et al., 2003b) fills in missing regions of an image. Generative adversarial networks have been used for image completion (Pathak et al.,

2016; Iizuka et al., 2017; Yu et al., 2019; Liu, Wan, Huang, Song, Han and Liao, 2021), face completion (Li, Liu, Yang and Yang, 2017; Yeh et al., 2017), and fashion image completion (Han et al., 2019).

9.11.4   De-raining

Conditional GANs have been applied to realistically remove rain streaks from images with rain (Zhang, Sindagi and Patel, 2019).

9.11.5   Map Synthesis

Generative adversarial networks have been applied to synthesize texture and high-resolution maps without any noticeable artifacts (Frühstück et al., 2019).

9.11.6   Pose Synthesis

Generative adversarial networks have been used for synthesizing humans in arbitrary target poses (Ma et al., 2017).

9.11.7   Face Editing

Generative adversarial networks have been applied for synthesizing faces with varying facial expressions, gender, hair styles and colors, glasses (Liu and Tuzel, 2016; Brock et al., 2017), and ages (Antipov et al., 2017; Zhang, Song and Qi, 2017). PairedCycleGAN (Chang et al., 2018) extends CycleGAN to style control for the application and removal of makeup. GANmut (d'Apolito et al., 2021) learns an interpretable and expressive conditional space of facial emotions rather than conditioning on handcrafted labels. AnycostGANs (Lin et al., 2021) uses adaptive sampling and multi-resolution to achieve interactive face synthesis. A single face image may be sufficient for generating a normalized 3D avatar of a person's head (Luo et al., 2021).

9.11.8   Training Data Generation

Generative adversarial networks have been used for learning to synthesize photorealistic training examples from synthetic eye and hand images (Shrivastava et al., 2017).

9.11.9   Text-to-Image Synthesis

StackGAN (Zhang, Xu, Li, Zhang, Wang, Huang and Metaxas, 2017, 2018) and AttentionalGAN (Xu et al., 2018) receive text as input and synthesize an image described by the text, which works well for specific classes of images. Text-guided diverse image generation and manipulation using a GAN (Xia et al., 2021) maps text and sketches in the latent space of a StyleGAN for controlling generated face images by text.

9.11.10 Medical Imaging

Generative adversarial networks have been applied to a wide range of medical image analysis tasks, including classification, detection, segmentation, de-noising, and reconstruction (Kazeminia et al., 2020). Specifically, CycleGAN has been applied for magnetic resonance to computed tomography (MR-to-CT) synthesis (Wolterink et al., 2017).

9.11.11 Video Synthesis

Generative adversarial networks have been applied for video prediction (Vondrick et al., 2016) using spatio-temporal CNNs that separate moving foreground objects from static backgrounds. Image-to-image transfer has been extended to video-to-video transfer, learning a mapping between a segmentation map and real street video with photorealistic results (Wang, Liu, Zhu, Liu, Tao, Kautz and Catanzaro, 2018). Video portraits (Kim, Carrido, Tewari, Xu, Thies, Niessner, Pérez, Richardt, Zollhöfer and Theobalt, 2018) use GANs to transfer head position and rotation, face expression, eye gaze, and blinking from one person to a portrait video of another person, reanimating a person's face. Self-supervised video GANs (Hyun et al., 2021) represent video as a composition of appearance and motions, synthesizing video with temporal coherence.

9.11.12 Motion Retargeting

CycleGAN has been applied to retarget a given motion to a new cartoon character (Villegas et al., 2018). Image transfer has been extended to video transfer, retargeting the body motion of one person to a new person, achieving videorealistic results (Chan et al., 2019).

9.11.13 3D Synthesis

3D-GANs (Wu et al., 2016) use GANs to synthesize high-quality 3D objects and learn an object representation useful for interpolating between objects and 3D object recognition. Roof-GAN (Qian et al., 2021) learns to generate roof geometry and relations for residential housing. ShapeInversion (Zhang et al., 2021) uses a GAN pre-trained on complete shapes to search for a vector in the latent space that results in a completed shape that reconstructs the partial input. This results in diverse 3D shape completions without using training pairs.

9.11.14   Graph Synthesis

Graphs are the underlying representation of networks with many applications: social networks of friends, the internet of web pages, cellular communication networks of users, financial transaction networks of bank clients, protein-to-protein interaction networks, or neural networks of brains. NetGAN (Bojchevski et al., 2018) synthesizes graphs by learning the distribution of random walks of a given graph dataset, which can then be used for link prediction.

9.11.15   Autonomous Vehicles

Generative adversarial networks have been used in reinforcement learning to learn human driving behaviors from human driving demonstrations (Li, Song and Ermon, 2017) by imitation learning in an unsupervised fashion. SocialGAN combines sequence models and GANs to predict plausible human motion trajectories (Gupta et al., 2018) for accurate prediction and collision avoidance.

9.11.16   Text-to-Speech Synthesis

Generative adversarial networks have been applied to synthesize speech from text, achieving results that are perceptually close to natural speech (Yang, Xie, Chen, Lou, Zhu, Huang and Li, 2017). DriveGAN (Kim et al., 2021) learns to simulate a controllable and dynamic driving environment from video.

9.11.17   Voice Conversion

CycleGAN has been applied to voice conversion (Fang et al., 2018; Kaneko et al., 2019) by modifying a speech signal of one speaker to match that of another speaker.

9.11.18   Music Synthesis

MuseGAN generates long, polyphonic music for multiple instruments (Dong et al., 2018), including pop song phrases with bass, drums, guitar, and piano, taking into account chords, style, melody, and groove. The synthesized music is coherent, with pleasant harmony and unified rhythm. GANSynth (Engel et al., 2019) uses a progressive GAN to synthesize an audio sequence from a latent vector, producing coherent results.

9.11.19   Protein Design

Protein structure determines function; therefore, predicting protein structure and function is important in protein design for drug discovery. Generative adversarial networks have been applied for synthesizing distance matrices between protein atoms (Anand and Huang, 2018) to aid in protein design.

Table 9.1 Summary of discriminator and generator loss functions for different GANs.

GAN	Discriminator loss (maximize)	Generator loss (minimize)
Original	$\mathbb{E}_x[\log \mathcal{D}(x)] + \mathbb{E}_z[\log(1 - \mathcal{D}(\mathcal{G}(z)))]$	$\mathbb{E}_z[\log(1 - \mathcal{D}(\mathcal{G}(z)))]$
Least squares	$\mathbb{E}_x[(\mathcal{D}(x) - 1)^2] - \mathbb{E}_z[\mathcal{D}(\mathcal{G}(z))^2]$	$\mathbb{E}_z[(\mathcal{D}(\mathcal{G}(z)) - 1)^2]$
Wasserstein	$\mathbb{E}_x[\mathcal{D}(x)] - \mathbb{E}_z[\mathcal{D}(\mathcal{G}(z))]$	$-\mathbb{E}_z[\mathcal{D}(\mathcal{G}(z))]$

9.11.20 Natural Language Synthesis

Generative adversarial networks have been applied to natural language. The generator $\mathcal{G}$ generates language and the discriminator $\mathcal{D}$ distinguishes between real text and generated text (Lin, Li, He, Zhang and Sun, 2017; Yu et al., 2017; Fedus et al., 2018; Guo et al., 2018). Computing derivatives through discrete text tokens is a challenge (Caccia et al., 2018), and there is often a trade-off between the quality and the diversity of the generated text.

9.11.21 Cryptography

CycleGAN has been applied to infer simple ciphers given unpaired examples of ciphertext and plaintext (Gomez et al., 2018). The texts were encoded using simple shift or Vigenere ciphers and decoded using CycleGAN in a similar fashion to language translation.

9.12 Software Libraries, Benchmarks, and Visualization

TF-GAN (Shor et al., 2020) is a library for training and evaluating GANs in TensorFlow. TorchGAN (PyTorch, 2021) is a framework for efficient training of GANs based on PyTorch. Compare GAN (Google, 2020) is a library for comparing between GAN architectures, loss functions, and evaluation metrics. GAN Lab (Kahng et al., 2018) is an interactive visualization of GANs available online.

9.13 Summary

This chapter introduces GAN theory, practice, and applications. We present the most significant GAN architectures, loss functions, training algorithms, and applications. Table 9.1 summarizes the discriminator and generator loss functions for different GANs. The roles of the generator and discriminator and the advantages and limitations of different loss functions are important to understand. Issues include mode collapse and vanishing gradients, and various solutions are available. GANs have a broad range of applications with code libraries and benchmarks in the field.

10 Variational Autoencoders

10.1 Introduction

This chapter begins with a review of variational inference (VI) as a fast approximation alternative to Markov chain Monte Carlo (MCMC) methods, solving an optimization problem for approximating the posterior. Variational inference using both the mode-seeking reverse Kullback–Leibler (RKL) divergence and mass-covering forward Kullback–Leibler (FKL) divergence are presented. Reverse KL is covered in detail since it is more reliable and stable than FKL in high dimensions. Variational inference is scaled to stochastic variational inference and generalized to black-box variational inference (BBVI). Amortized VI leads to the variational autoencoder (VAE) framework, which is introduced using deep neural networks and graphical models and used for learning representations and generative modeling. Finally, we explore generative flows, the latent space manifold, and Riemannian geometry of generative models.

10.2 Variational Inference

We begin with observed data x, continuous or discrete, and suppose that the process generating the data involved hidden latent variables z. For example, x may be an image of a face and z a hidden vector describing latent variables such as pose, illumination, gender, or emotion. A probabilistic model is a joint density $p(z, x)$ of the hidden variables z and the observed variables x. Our goal is to estimate the posterior $p(z|x)$ to explain the observed variables x by the hidden variables z, for example, answering the question of what are the hidden latent variables z for a given image x. Inference about the hidden variables is given by the posterior conditional distribution $p(z|x)$ of hidden variables, given observations. By definition:

$$p(z, x) = p(z|x)p(x) = p(x|z)p(z) = p(x, z) \tag{10.1}$$

where $p(z, x)$ is the joint density, $p(z|x)$ the posterior, $p(x)$ the evidence or marginal density, $p(z)$ the prior density, and $p(x|z)$ the likelihood function. We may extend $p(x|z)p(z)$ to multiple layers by:

$$p(x|z_1)p(z_1|z_2), \ldots, p(z_{l-1}|z_l)p(z_l) \tag{10.2}$$

by using deep generative models. For now we will focus on a single layer $p(x|z)p(z)$. Rearranging terms, we get Bayes rule:

$$p(z|x) = \frac{p(x|z)p(z)}{p(x)} \tag{10.3}$$

For most models the denominator $p(x)$ is a high-dimensional intractable integral that requires integrating over an exponential number of terms for z:

$$p(x) = \int p(x|z)p(z)dz \tag{10.4}$$

Therefore, instead of computing $p(z|x)$ the key insight of VI (Jordan et al., 1999; Opper and Saad, 2001; Bishop, 2006; Wainwright and Jordan, 2008; Blei et al., 2017; Kim, Wiseman and Rush, 2018; Zhang, Butepage, Kjellstrom and Mandt, 2018) is to approximate the posterior by a variational distribution $q_\phi(z)$ from a family of distributions Q, defined by variational parameters ϕ such that $q_\phi(z) \in Q$. A choice for Q is the exponential family of distributions. In summary, we choose a parameterized family of distributions Q and find the distribution $q_{\phi^\star}(z) \in Q$ which is closest to $p(z|x)$. Once found, we use this approximation $q_{\phi^\star}(z)$ instead of the true posterior $p(z|x)$, as illustrated in the left side of Figure 10.1.

The posterior $p(z|x)$ is often intractable to compute analytically. For example, if z is a vector of length d, then $p(z|x)$ is a $d \times d$ matrix, and the posterior is a function of the parameters of the model $p(z|x,\theta)$. In machine learning, the parameters θ are often learned from the data x using a learning algorithm. The goal of inference is to estimate the posterior $p(z|x)$ from the data x using a computationally tractable approximation $q(z|x)$. The approximation $q(z|x)$ is called the variational distribution. The variational distribution $q(z|x)$ is defined as the solution to a variational inference problem. The variational inference problem is a mathematical optimization problem of finding the parameters of $q(z|x)$ that minimize the lower bound of a divergence D between the variational distribution $q(z|x)$ and the posterior $p(z|x)$.

Compared with this formulation, methods such as mean-field variational inference (MFVI) (Opper and Saad, 2001; Giordano et al., 2018) and MCMC sampling have several shortcomings. The mean-field method (Parisi, 1988) assumes a full factorization of variables, which is inaccurate. Stochastic variational inference scales MFVI to large datasets (Hoffman et al., 2013). Markov chain Monte Carlo sampling methods (Brooks et al., 2011), such as the Metropolis–Hastings algorithm, may not be scalable to very large datasets and may require manually specifying a proposal distribution.

The f-divergence from a probability distribution $q(z)$ to a probability distribution $p(z)$ is defined by:

$$D_f(q(z)||p(z)) = \int f\left(\frac{q(z)}{p(z)}\right) p(z)dz = \mathbb{E}_p\left[f\left(\frac{q(z)}{p(z)}\right)\right] \tag{10.5}$$

where f is a convex function with $f(1) = 0$. For $f(t) = t\log(t)$ we get the

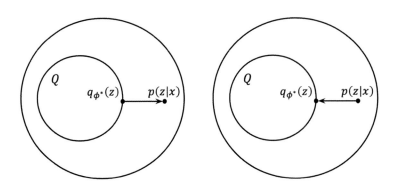

Figure 10.1 Variational inference using RKL (left) and FKL (right) between distributions p and q. In RKL we optimize an approximation $q_{\phi^\star}(z) \in Q$ closest to the posterior $p(z|x)$.

KL divergence. The KL is non-negative $D_{\mathrm{KL}}(p||q) \geq 0$ and is not symmetric $D_{\mathrm{KL}}(q||p) \neq D_{\mathrm{KL}}(p||q)$, hence the KL is not a distance.

The FKL divergence between distributions p and q is defined by:

$$D_{\mathrm{KL}}(p(x)||q(x)) = \int p(x) \log \frac{p(x)}{q(x)} dx \tag{10.6}$$

whereas the RKL divergence is defined by:

$$D_{\mathrm{KL}}(q(x)||p(x)) = \int q(x) \log \frac{q(x)}{p(x)} dx \tag{10.7}$$

The RKL divergence is mode-seeking, whereas the FKL divergence is mass-covering (Jerfel et al., 2021; Zhang et al., 2022). Therefore the RKL is easier to optimize and will be described in detail. Other divergences may be used; for example, the KL divergence is the special case of the α-divergence (Li and Turner, 2016) with $\alpha = 1$, and the special case of the Bregman divergence generated by the entropy function.

10.2.1   Reverse KL

Making the choice of an exponential family and RKL divergence, we minimize the KL divergence between $q(z)$ and $p(z|x)$:

$$\underset{\phi}{\mathrm{minimize}} D_{\mathrm{KL}}(q_\phi(z)||p(z|x)) = \underset{\phi}{\mathrm{minimize}} \int q_\phi(z) \log \frac{q_\phi(z)}{p(z|x)} \tag{10.8}$$

Therefore, when $q_\phi(z)$ is close to zero then $\log \frac{q_\phi(z)}{p(z|x)}$ does not contribute to the integral, ignoring $p(z|x)$. When $q_\phi(z)$ is large and $p(z|x)$ is close to zero there is significant contribution to the integral.

We find the approximate posterior:

$$q_{\phi^\star}(z) = \underset{q_\phi(z)}{\mathrm{argmin}} D_{\mathrm{KL}}(q_\phi(z)||p(z|x)) \tag{10.9}$$

as illustrated on the left side of Figure 10.1, where:

$$D_{\mathrm{KL}}(q_\phi(z)||p(z|x)) = \mathbb{E}_{q_\phi(z)}[\log q_\phi(z)] - \mathbb{E}_{q_\phi(z)}[\log p(z|x)] \tag{10.10}$$

therefore, plugging the RKL into Equation 10.9 we get:

$$q_{\phi^\star}(z) = \underset{q_\phi(z)}{\operatorname{argmin}} \mathbb{E}_{q_\phi(z)}[\log q_\phi(z)] - \mathbb{E}_{q_\phi(z)}[\log p(z|x)] \tag{10.11}$$

and replacing minimization by maximization yields:

$$q_{\phi^\star}(z) = \underset{q_\phi(z)}{\operatorname{argmax}} \mathbb{E}_{q_\phi(z)}[\log p(z|x)] + \mathbb{E}_{q_\phi(z)}[-\log q_\phi(z)] \tag{10.12}$$

which promotes that wherever q_ϕ has high probability, $p(z|x)$ also has high probability, known as mode-seeking.

Specifically, using the definition of the RKL divergence in Equation 10.7 for the variational distribution and posterior we get:

$$D_{\mathrm{KL}}(q(z)||p(z|x)) = \int q(z) \log \frac{q(z)}{p(z|x)} dz \tag{10.13}$$

Unfortunately, the denominator contains the posterior $p(z|x)$, which is the term that we would like to approximate. So how can we get close to the posterior without knowing the posterior? By using Bayes rule, replacing the posterior in Equation 10.13 using Equation 10.1, we get:

$$\int q(z) \log \frac{q(z)}{p(z|x)} dz = \int q(z) \log \frac{q(z)p(x)}{p(z,x)} dz \tag{10.14}$$

Separating the $\log p(x)$ term and replacing the log of the ratio with a difference yields:

$$\int q(z) \log \frac{q(z)p(x)}{p(z,x)} dz = \log p(x) - \int q(z) \log \frac{p(z,x)}{q(z)} dz \tag{10.15}$$

In summary, minimizing the reverse KL divergence between $p(z|x)$ and $q(z)$ is equivalent to minimizing the difference:

$$\log p(x) - \int q(z) \log \frac{p(z,x)}{q(z)} dz \ge 0 \tag{10.16}$$

which is non-negative since the KL divergence is non-negative. Rearranging terms we get:

$$\log p(x) \ge \int q(z) \log \frac{p(z,x)}{q(z)} dz := \mathcal{L} \tag{10.17}$$

The term on the right, denoted by $\mathcal{L}$, is known as the evidence lower bound (ELBO). Therefore, minimizing the KL divergence is equivalent to maximizing the ELBO. We have turned the problem of approximating the posterior $p(z|x)$ into an optimization problem of maximizing the ELBO, which consists of two terms:

$$\mathcal{L} = \mathbb{E}_{q_\phi(z)}[\log p(x,z)] - \mathbb{E}_{q_\phi(z)}[\log q_\phi(z)] \tag{10.18}$$

The term on the left is the expected log likelihood, and the term on the right is the negative entropy. Therefore, when optimizing the ELBO, there is a trade-off between these two terms. The first term places mass on the maximum a-posteriori (MAP) estimate, whereas the second term encourages diffusion, or spreading the variational distribution. In variational inference we maximize the ELBO in Equation 10.18 to find $q_{\phi^*}(z) \in Q$ closest to the posterior $p(z|x)$.

10.2.2   Score Gradient

Now that our objective is to maximize the ELBO, we turn to practical optimization methods. The ELBO is not convex, so we can hope to find a local maximum. We would like to scale up to large data x with many hidden variables z. A practical optimization method which scales to large data is stochastic gradient descent (Robbins and Monro, 1951; Bottou, 2010). Gradient descent optimization is a first-order method which requires computing the gradient. Therefore, our problem is computing the gradient of the ELBO:

$$\nabla_\phi \mathcal{L} = \nabla \mathbb{E}_{q_\phi(z)}[\log p(x, z) - \log q_\phi(z)] \tag{10.19}$$

We would like to compute the gradients of the expectations $\nabla_\phi \mathbb{E}_{q_\phi(z)}[f_\phi(z)]$ of a cost function $f_\phi(z) = \log p(x, z) - \log q_\phi(z)$ by expanding the gradient as:

$$\nabla_\phi \mathbb{E}_{q_\phi(z)}[f_\phi(z)] = \nabla_\phi \int q_\phi(z) f_\phi(z) dz \tag{10.20}$$

By using the chain rule this expands to:

$$\nabla_\phi \int q_\phi(z) f_\phi(z) dz = \int (\nabla_\phi q_\phi(z)) f_\phi(z) + q_\phi(z)(\nabla_\phi f_\phi(z)) dz \tag{10.21}$$

We cannot compute the expectation with respect to $q_\phi(z)$, which involves the unknown term $\nabla_\phi q_\phi(z)$, and therefore we will take Monte Carlo estimates of the gradient by sampling from q and use the score function estimator as described next.

Score Function
The score function is the derivative of the log-likelihood function:

$$\nabla_\phi \log q_\phi(z) = \frac{\nabla_\phi q_\phi(z)}{q_\phi(z)} \tag{10.22}$$

Score Function Estimator
Using Equation 10.20 and multiplying by the identity we get:

$$\nabla_\phi \int q_\phi(z) f_\phi(z) dz = \int \frac{q_\phi(z)}{q_\phi(z)} \nabla_\phi q_\phi(z) f_\phi(z) dz \tag{10.23}$$

and plugging in Equation 10.22 we derive:

$$\int \frac{q_\phi(z)}{q_\phi(z)} \nabla_\phi q_\phi(z) f_\phi(z) dz = \int q_\phi(z) \nabla_\phi \log q_\phi(z) f_\phi(z) dz \tag{10.24}$$

which equals:

$$\int q_\phi(z)\nabla_\phi \log q_\phi(z)f_\phi(z)dz = \mathbb{E}_{q_\phi(z)}[f_\phi(z)\nabla_\phi \log q_\phi(z)] \tag{10.25}$$

In summary, by using the score function, we have passed the gradient through the expectation:

$$\nabla_\phi \mathbb{E}_{q_\phi(z)}[f_\phi(z)] = \mathbb{E}_{q_\phi(z)}[f_\phi(z)\nabla_\phi \log q_\phi(z)] \tag{10.26}$$

Score Gradient

The gradient of the ELBO with respect to the variational distribution $\nabla_\phi \mathcal{L}$ is computed using Equation 10.26 as:

$$\nabla_\phi \mathcal{L} = \mathbb{E}_{q_\phi(z)}[(\log p(x,z) - \log q_\phi(z))\nabla_\phi \log q_\phi(z)] \tag{10.27}$$

Now that the gradient is inside the expectation we can evaluate using Monte Carlo sampling. For stochastic gradient descent we average over samples z_i from $q_\phi(z)$ to get:

$$\nabla_\phi \mathcal{L} = \frac{1}{k}\sum_{i=1}^{k}[(\log p(x,z_i) - \log q_\phi(z_i))\nabla_\phi \log q_\phi(z_i)] \tag{10.28}$$

where $\nabla_\phi \log q_\phi(z_i)$ is the score function. The score gradient works for both discrete and continuous models and a large family of variational distributions and is therefore widely applicable (Ranganath et al., 2014). The problem with the score function gradient is that the noisy gradients have a large variance. For example, if we use Monte Carlo sampling for estimating a mean and there is high variance, we would require many samples for a good estimate of the mean.

10.2.3 Reparameterization Gradient

Distributions can be represented by transformations of other distributions. We therefore express the variational distribution $z \sim q_\phi(z) = \mathcal{N}(\mu,\sigma)$ by a transformation:

$$z = g(\epsilon,\phi) \tag{10.29}$$

where $\epsilon \sim s(\epsilon)$ and get an equivalent way of describing the same distribution:

$$z \sim q_\phi(z) \tag{10.30}$$

For example, instead of $z \sim q_\phi(z) = \mathcal{N}(\mu,\sigma)$ we use:

$$z = \mu + \sigma \odot \epsilon \tag{10.31}$$

where $\epsilon \sim \mathcal{N}(0,1)$ to get the same distribution:

$$z \sim \mathcal{N}(\mu,\sigma) \tag{10.32}$$

Although these are two different ways of describing the same distribution, the advantages of this transformation are that we can (1) express the gradient of the expectation; (2) achieve a lower variance than the score function estimator; and (3) differentiate through the latent variable z to optimize by backpropagation.

We reparameterize $\nabla_\phi \mathbb{E}_{q_\phi(z)}[f_\phi(z)]$, and by a change of variables Equation 10.20 becomes:

$$\nabla_\phi \mathbb{E}_{q_\phi(z)}[f_\phi(z)] = \nabla_\phi \int s(\epsilon) \frac{d\epsilon}{dz} f(g(\epsilon, \phi)) g'(\epsilon, \phi) d\epsilon \qquad (10.33)$$

and:

$$\nabla_\phi \int s(\epsilon) \frac{d\epsilon}{dz} f(g(\epsilon, \phi)) g'(\epsilon, \phi) d\epsilon = \nabla_\phi \mathbb{E}_{s(\epsilon)}[f(g(\phi, \epsilon))] = \mathbb{E}_{s(\epsilon)}[\nabla_\phi f(g(\phi, \epsilon))] \qquad (10.34)$$

where $s(\epsilon)$ is a fixed distribution independent of ϕ, passing the gradient through the expectation:

$$\nabla_\phi \mathbb{E}_{q_\phi(z)}[f_\phi(z)] = \mathbb{E}_{s(\epsilon)}[\nabla_\phi f(g(\phi, \epsilon))] \qquad (10.35)$$

Since the gradient is inside the expectation, we can use Monte Carlo sampling to estimate $\mathbb{E}_{s(\epsilon)}[\nabla_\phi f(g(\phi, \epsilon))]$. The reparameterization method given by Equation 10.35 has a lower variance compared with the score function estimator given in Equation 10.26.

In the case of the ELBO $\mathcal{L}$, the reparameterized gradient (Kingma and Welling, 2014; Rezende et al., 2014) is given by:

$$\nabla_\phi \mathcal{L} = \mathbb{E}_{s(\epsilon)}[\nabla_\phi [\log p(x, z) - \log q_\phi(z)] \nabla_\phi g(\epsilon, \phi)] \qquad (10.36)$$

and rewriting the expectation:

$$\nabla_\phi \mathcal{L} = \frac{1}{k} \sum_{i=1}^{k} \nabla_\phi [\log p(x, g(\epsilon_i, \phi)) - \log q_\phi(g(\epsilon_i, \phi))] \qquad (10.37)$$

provided the entropy term has an analytic derivation and $\log p(x, z)$ and $\log q(z)$ are differentiable with respect to z. Similarly, the reparameterization gradient in Equation 10.36 has a lower variance than the score gradient in Equation 10.27. In addition, we can use auto-differentiation for computing the gradient and reuse different transformations (Kucukelbir et al., 2017). The gradient variance is further reduced by changing the computation graph in automatic differentiation (Roeder et al., 2017). However, a limitation of the reparameterization gradient is that it requires a differentiable model, works only for continuous models (Figurnov et al., 2018) and is computationally more expensive.

10.2.4   Forward KL

The FKL divergence minimizes the KL between $p(z|x)$ and $q_\phi(z)$:

$$\underset{\phi}{\text{minimize}} D_{\text{KL}}(p(z|x) \| q_\phi(z)) = \underset{\phi}{\text{minimize}} \int p(z|x) \log \frac{p(z|x)}{q_\phi(z)} dz \qquad (10.38)$$

If $p(z|x)$ is close to zero then $\log \frac{p(z|x)}{q_\phi(z)}$ does not contribute to the integral and therefore there is no penalty for a large $q_\phi(z)$. We find:

$$q_{\phi^\star}(z) = \underset{q_\phi(z)}{\mathrm{argmin}} D_{\mathrm{KL}}\left(p(z|x)||q_\phi(z)\right) \tag{10.39}$$

as illustrated on the right side of Figure 10.1, where:

$$D_{\mathrm{KL}}(p(z|x)||q_\phi(z)) = \mathbb{E}_{p(z|x)}[\log p(z|x)] - \mathbb{E}_{p(z|x)}[\log q_\phi(z)] \tag{10.40}$$

Since the left term is independent of the parameter ϕ it may be dropped when minimizing for q_ϕ, and turning the objective into maximization results in:

$$q_{\phi^\star}(z) = \underset{q_\phi(z)}{\mathrm{argmin}}\left(-\mathbb{E}_{p(z|x)}[\log q_\phi(z)]\right) = \underset{q_\phi(z)}{\mathrm{argmax}}\,\mathbb{E}_{p(z|x)}[\log q_\phi(z)] \tag{10.41}$$

which promotes that wherever $p(z|x)$ has high probability q_ϕ also has high probability, also known as mass-covering or mean-seeking, which results in q_ϕ covering $p(z|x)$.

10.3 Variational Autoencoder

Instead of optimizing a separate parameter for each example, amortized variational inference (AVI) approximates the posterior across all examples together (Kingma and Welling, 2014; Rezende et al., 2014). Meta-AVI goes a step further and approximates the posterior across models (Choi et al., 2019). Next, we give a formulation of autoencoders, which motivates the AVI algorithm of VAEs.

10.3.1 Autoencoder

As shown in Figure 10.2, an autoencoder is a neural network that performs non-linear principle component analysis (PCA) (Hinton and Salakhutdinov, 2006; Efron and Hastie, 2016). Non-linear PCA extracts useful features from unlabeled data by minimizing:

$$\underset{W^1,W^2}{\mathrm{minimize}} \sum_{i=1}^{m} \|x_i - (W^2)^T f((W^1)^T x_i)\|_2^2 \tag{10.42}$$

where for single-layer networks W^1 and W^2 are matrices that are the network's parameters and f is a pointwise non-linear function. An autoencoder is composed of two neural networks. The first maps an input x by matrix multiplication $(W^1)^T$ and a non-linearity to a low-dimensional variable z, which is a bottleneck, and the second reconstructs the input as $\tilde{x}$ using $(W^2)^T$. When f is the identity this is equivalent to PCA.

The goal of variational inference is to find a distribution q which approximates the posterior $p(z|x)$, and a distribution $p(x)$ which represents the data well. Motivated by autoencoders, we represent q and p using back-to-back neural networks. An encoder network represents q and a decoder network represents

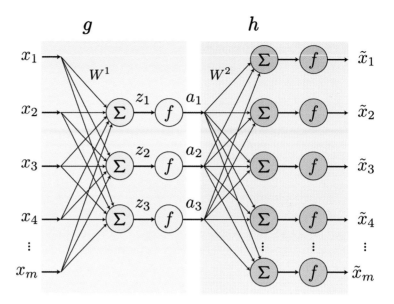

Figure 10.2 Autoencoder. Input x is passed through a low-dimensional bottleneck z and reconstructed to form $\tilde{x}$, minimizing a loss between the input and output. The parameters W^1 of the encoder and W^2 of the decoder are optimized end-to-end.

p. These neural networks are non-linear functions F which are a composition of functions $F(x) = f(f(\ldots f(x)))$, where each individual function f has a linear and non-linear component, and the function F is optimized given a large dataset by stochastic gradient descent (SGD).

10.3.2   Variational Autoencoder

The ELBO is a lower bound on the log-likelihood of the data x given the latent variable z. It is a lower bound because it is not possible to compute the exact log-likelihood of the data x given the latent variable z. We will find the optimal parameters θ^* of the encoder and decoder by maximizing the ELBO. The ELBO can be used to train a generative model and is maximized by SGD. This means that the parameters of the encoder and decoder are updated in each iteration by taking a step in the direction of the gradient of the ELBO with a small learning rate. The ELBO may also be used to train a discriminative model.

The ELBO as defined in Equation 10.17 can be rewritten as:

$$\mathcal{L} = \int q(z) \log p(x|z) dz - \int q(z) \log \frac{p(z)}{q(z)} dz \tag{10.43}$$

which is the lower bound consisting of two terms:

$$\mathcal{L} = \mathbb{E}_{q(z)}[\log p(x|z)] - D_{\mathrm{KL}}(q(z)||p(z)) \tag{10.44}$$

The term $\log p(x|z)$, on the left, is the log-likelihood of the observed data x

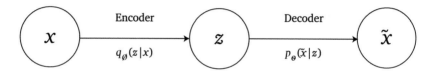

Figure 10.3 Variational autoencoder. The input x is passed through a low-dimensional bottleneck z and reconstructed to form $\tilde{x}$, minimizing a loss between the input and output. The parameters ϕ and θ of the encoder q_ϕ and decoder p_θ deep neural networks are optimized end-to-end by backpropagation.

given the sampled latent variable z. This term measures how well the samples from $q(z)$ explain the data x. The goal of this term is to reconstruct x from z and therefore is called the reconstruction error, representing a decoder which is implemented by a deep neural network. This term measures the likelihood of beginning with data x, encoded by a latent variable z, and decoding it back to the original data x.

The second term, on the right, consists of sampling $z \sim q(z|x)$, representing an encoder which is also implemented by a deep neural network. This term ensures that the explanation of the data does not deviate from the prior beliefs $p(z)$ and is called the regularization term, defined by the KL divergence between q and the prior $p(z)$. This term measures the closeness between the encoder and prior.

The objective function in Equation 10.44 is analogous to the formulation of autoencoders, and therefore gives rise to the VAE. The VAE is a deep learning algorithm, rather than a model, which is used for learning latent representations. The learned representations can be used for applications such as synthesizing examples or interpolation between samples, of different modalities such as images, video, audio, geometry and text.

The VAE algorithm is defined by two back-to-back neural networks as illustrated in Figure 10.3. The first is an encoder neural network which infers a hidden variable z from an observation x. The second is a decoder neural network which reconstructs an observation $\tilde{x}$ from a hidden variable z. The encoder q_ϕ and decoder p_θ are trained end-to-end, optimizing for both the encoder parameters ϕ and decoder parameters θ by backpropagation.

If we assume $q(z|x)$ and $p(x|z)$ are normally distributed then q is represented by:

$$q(z|x) = \mathcal{N}(\mu(x), \sigma(x) \odot \mathcal{I}) \tag{10.45}$$

for deterministic functions $\mu(x)$ and $\sigma(x)$, and p is represented by:

$$p(x|z) = \mathcal{N}(\mu(z), \sigma(z) \odot \mathcal{I}) \tag{10.46}$$

and

$$p(z) = \mathcal{N}(0, \mathcal{I}) \tag{10.47}$$

The variational predictive natural gradient (Tang and Ranganath, 2019) rescales

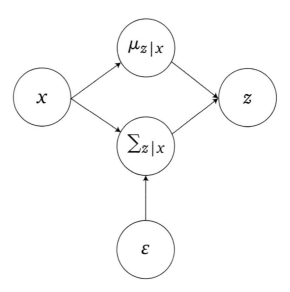

Figure 10.4 Variational encoder. Rather than sampling directly $z \sim \mathcal{N}(\mu, \sigma)$ in the latent space, reparameterization allows for backpropagation through the latent variable $z = \mu + \sigma \odot \epsilon$, which is a sum of the mean μ and covariance. The covariance σ is multiplied by noise $\epsilon \sim \mathcal{N}(0, \mathcal{I})$ sampled from a normal distribution.

the gradient to capture the curvature of variational inference. The correlated VAE (Tang, Liang, Jebara and Ruozzi, 2019) extends the VAE to learn pairwise variational distribution estimations which capture the correlation between data points.

In practice, very good synthesis results for different modalities are achieved using a vector quantized variational autoencoder (VQ-VAE; (van den Oord et al., 2017)) which learns a discrete latent representation. Using an autoregressive decoder or prior with VQ-VAE (De Fauw et al., 2019; Razavi et al., 2019) generates photorealistic high-resolution images (Ravuri and Vinyals, n.d.).

10.4   Generative Flows

This section describes transformations of simple posterior distribution approximations to complex distributions by normalizing flows (Rezende and Mohamed, 2015). We would like to improve our variational approximation $q_\phi(z)$ to the posterior $p(z|x)$. An approach for achieving this goal is to transform a simple density, such as a Gaussian, to a complex density using a sequence of invertible transformations, also known as normalizing flows (Rezende and Mohamed, 2015; Dinh et al., 2017; Kingma and Dhariwal, 2018). Instead of parameterizing a simple distribution directly, a change of variables allows us to define a complex distribution by warping $q(z)$ using an invertible function f. Given a random variable

$z \sim q_\phi(z)$ the log density of $x = f(z)$ is:

$$\log p(x) = \log p(z) - \log \det \left| \frac{\partial f(z)}{\partial z} \right| \tag{10.48}$$

A composition of multiple invertible functions results in a sequence of transformations, called normalizing flows. These transformations may be implemented by neural networks, performing end-to-end optimization of the network parameters. For example, for a planar flow family of transformations:

$$f(z) = z + uh(w^T z + b) \tag{10.49}$$

where h is a smooth differentiable non-linear function, and the log-det Jacobian is computed by:

$$\psi(z) = h'(w^T z + b)w \tag{10.50}$$

and

$$\left| \frac{\partial f}{\partial z} \right| = \left| I + u^T \psi(z) \right| \tag{10.51}$$

If z is a continuous random variable $z(t)$ depending on time t with distribution $p(z(t))$ then for the differential equation $\frac{dz}{dt} = f(z(t), t)$ the change in log probability is:

$$\frac{\partial \log p(z(t))}{\partial t} = -\text{tr} \left(\frac{\partial f}{z(t)} \right) \tag{10.52}$$

and the change in log density is:

$$\log p(z(t_1)) = \log p(z(t_0)) - \int_{t_0}^{t_1} \text{tr} \left(\frac{\partial f}{z(t)} \right) \tag{10.53}$$

also known as continuous normal flows (Chen, Rubanova, Bettencourt and Duvenaud, 2018; Grathwohl et al., 2019).

For the planar flow family of transformations:

$$\frac{dz(t)}{dt} = uh(w^T z(y) + b) \tag{10.54}$$

and

$$\frac{\log p(z(t))}{\partial t} = -u^T \frac{\partial h}{\partial z(t)} \tag{10.55}$$

such that given $p(z(0))$, $p(z(t))$ is sampled and the density evaluated by solving an ordinary differential equation (Chen, Rubanova, Bettencourt and Duvenaud, 2018).

Generative flows have been extended to equivariant normalizing flows (Garcia et al., n.d.), which are normalizing flows that are equivariant to Euclidean symmetries and therefore perform well on particle systems and molecules. Smooth normalizing flows (Köhler et al., n.d.) incorporate forces into normalizing flows and yield smooth functions. These are useful properties for modeling molecular simulations such as simulations of protein backbones represented by torsion angles.

10.5   Denoising Diffusion Probabilistic Model

A denoising diffusion probabilistic model (DDPM) (Sohl-Dickstein et al., 2015; Ho et al., 2020; Dhariwal and Nichol, 2021; Nichol and Dhariwal, 2021), iteratively adds noise to a signal and then reverses the noising process by denoising to generate signals from noise. A DDPM forms a parameterized Markov chain and is trained using variational inference. DDPMs synthesize high-quality images and outperform other generative models (Dhariwal and Nichol, 2021).

10.5.1   Forward Noising Process

Starting with points from a distribution $x_0 \sim q(x_0)$ we iteratively add Gaussian noise to generate a sequence $(x_1, \ldots, x_T)$ consisting of x_t for $t = 1, \ldots, T$. The last element in the sequence, x_T, is approximately isotropic Gaussian noise. The sequence forms a Markov process such that:

$$q(x_t|x_{t-1}) = \mathcal{N}(\sqrt{1 - \beta_t}x_{t-1}, \beta_t I) \tag{10.56}$$

where $\beta_t \in (0, 1)$ is the variance of Gaussian noise. An element in this Markov process may be generated directly from the first element x_0 by:

$$q(x_t|x_0) = \mathcal{N}(\sqrt{\hat{\alpha}_t}x_0, (1 - \hat{\alpha}_t)I) \tag{10.57}$$

where $\alpha_t = 1 - \beta_t$ and $\hat{\alpha}_t = \prod_{j=0}^{t} \alpha_t$ such that:

$$x_t = \sqrt{\hat{\alpha}_t}x_0 + \sqrt{1 - \hat{\alpha}_t}\varepsilon \tag{10.58}$$

for $\varepsilon \sim \mathcal{N}(0, I)$.

10.5.2   Reverse Generation by Sampling

Reversing the noising process requires sampling the posteriors $q(x_{t-1}|x_t)$. The posteriors are Gaussian distributions, however they are unknown since they depend on $q(x_0)$. Therefore we use a neural network to approximate the mean and covariance of the posteriors normal distribution by:

$$p_\theta(x_{t-1}|x_t) = \mathcal{N}(\mu_\theta(x_t, t), \sigma_\theta(x_t, t)) \tag{10.59}$$

Alternatively the mean of the distribution may be derived directly using Bayes' rule by predicting the noise $\varepsilon_\theta(x_t, t)$ (Ho et al., 2020):

$$\mu_\theta(x_t, t) = \frac{1}{\sqrt{x_t}}\left(x_t - \frac{\beta_t}{\sqrt{1 - \hat{\alpha}_t}}\varepsilon_\theta(x_t, t)\right) \tag{10.60}$$

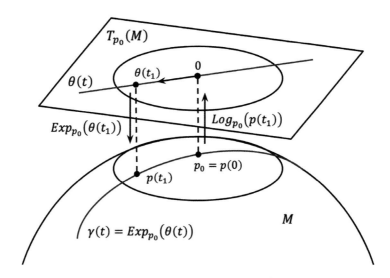

Figure 10.5 Manifold and tangent plane: exponential and logarithm maps between the tangent plane and the manifold. A line in the tangent plane corresponds to a geodesic in the manifold.

10.6   Geometric Variational Inference

This section generalizes variational inference and normalizing flows from Euclidean to Riemannian spaces (Gemici et al., 2016), describing families of distributions that are compatible with a Riemannian geometry and metric (Arvanitidis et al., 2018; Davidson et al., 2018; Holbrook, 2018; Saha et al., 2019). Finally, we consider the geometry of the latent space in variational autoencoders (Chen et al., 2019; Shukla et al., 2018; Wang and Wang, 2019).

We briefly define a Riemannian manifold and metric, geodesic, tangent space, exponential, and logarithm maps (Carmo, 1992; Spivak, 1999; Rahman et al., 2005; O'Neill, 2006; Do Carmo, 2016). A manifold of dimension d has at each $p_0 \in M$ a tangent space $Tp_0(M)$ of dimension d consisting of vectors θ corresponding to derivatives of smooth paths $p(t) \in M$, $t \in [0, 1]$, with $p(0) = p_0$. A Riemannian manifold has a metric on the tangent space. If for tangent vectors θ we adopt a specific coordinate representation θ_i, this quadratic form can be written as $\sum_{ij} g_{ij}(p)\theta_i\theta_j$. Between any two points p_0 and p_1 in the manifold, there is at least one shortest path, having arc length $\ell(p_0, p_1)$. Such a geodesic has an initial position p_0, an initial direction $\frac{\theta}{\|\theta\|_2}$, and an initial speed $\|\theta\|_2$. The procedure of fixing a vector in $\theta \in Tp(M)$ as an initial velocity for a constant-speed geodesic establishes an association between $Tp_0(M)$ and a neighborhood of $p \in M$. This association is one-to-one over a ball of sufficiently small size. The association is formally defined by the exponential map $p_1 = \exp_{p_0}(\theta)$. Within an appropriate neighborhood p_0, the inverse mapping is called the logarithm map and is defined by $\theta = \log_{p_0}(p_1)$, as illustrated in Figure 10.5.

Normalizing flows have been extended from Euclidean space to Riemannian space (Gemici et al., 2016). A simple density on a manifold M is mapped to the tangent space $T_p M$. Normalizing flow transformations are then applied to the mapped density in the tangent space, and the resulting density is mapped back to the manifold.

In VI, several transformation choices of a family of distributions are compatible with a Riemannian geometry (Davidson et al., 2018; Holbrook, 2018; Falorsi et al., 2019; Saha et al., 2019). For example, transforming a distribution by the square root to the positive orthant of the sphere results in the square root density of probability distributions. Probability distributions are then represented by square root densities, and the geodesic distance is defined by the shortest arc length. Again, $p_1 = \exp_{p_0}(\theta)$ maps the tangent space to the sphere, and $\theta = \log_{p_0}(p_1)$ maps the sphere to the tangent space. Densities are represented in the tangent space, and in a similar fashion to normalizing flows, parallel transport is used to map one tangent space to another.

The decoder in the VAE is used for both reconstruction and synthesis, generating new samples x from latent variables z. In the past decade, generating a sequence of samples which smoothly morph or warp graphical objects required meticulously specifying correspondence between landmarks on the objects. In contrast, using the decoder as a generator and interpolating between hidden variables in latent space allows us to perform this transformation without specifying correspondence. A question that arises is whether performing linear interpolation is suitable in the latent space. Interpolation may be performed by walking along a manifold rather than linear interpolation in the latent space. Specifically, the latent space of a VAE can be considered as a Riemannian space (Chen et al., 2019). Using a Riemannian metric rather than a Euclidean metric in the latent space provides better distance estimates (Arvanitidis et al., 2019; Mallasto et al., 2019), which improve interpolation and synthesis results (Shukla et al., 2018), as well as text-generation results (Wang and Wang, 2019), increasing the mutual information between the latent and observed variables.

10.6.1   Moser Flow

Moser Flow (Rozen et al., n.d.) is a continuous normalizing flow on a manifold in which the model density is parameterized by the difference between the prior density and the divergence of a neural network. The divergence operator is simple and local, and this approach avoids solving an ODE during training.

10.6.2   Riemannian Score-Based Generative Models

Riemannian score-based generative models (De Bortoli et al., 2022) extend score-based gradient models to Reimannian manifolds by using the time-reversal of Brownian motion. This approach scales to high dimensions and is applied to a broad range of manifolds.

10.7 Software Libraries

Scalable implementations of VI and VAEs are available as part of Google's TensorFlow Probability library (Dillon et al., 2017) and Uber's Pyro library (Bingham et al., 2019) and for Facebook's PyTorch deep learning platform (Paszke et al., 2017).

10.8 Summary

In this chapter we introduced VI using both RKL and FKL. The extension to BBVI is used in practice for inference on large datasets. Key advantages of Bayesian inference in the deep learning setting are that it generalizes deep learning algorithms by computing posterior approximations and that it enables sequential updates by iteratively setting the prior to be the previous posterior and recomputing the posterior based on new data.

The chapter then covers the VAE algorithm, which consists of an encoder neural network for inference and decoder network for generation, trained end-to-end by backpropagation. We described a way in which the variational approximation of the posterior is improved using a series of invertible transformations, known as normalizing flows, in both discrete and continuous domains. Finally, we explore the latent space manifold and extend variational inference and normalizing flows to manifolds.

Part IV

Reinforcement Learning

11 Reinforcement Learning

11.1 Introduction

Machine learning can be categorized into supervised learning, unsupervised learning and reinforcement learning. In supervised learning we are given input–output pairs; in unsupervised learning we are given only input examples. In reinforcement learning we learn from interaction with an environment to achieve a goal. We have an agent, a learner, that makes decisions under uncertainty. In this setting there is an environment, which is what the agent interacts with. The agent selects actions and the environment responds to those actions with a new state and reward. The agent's goal is to maximize the reward over time, as shown in Figure 11.1. The agent shown on the left of Figure 11.1 which is in a certain state, interacts with the environment, performs an action, receives a reward, and moves to another state. The goal is to learn the value of a state, or the probability of performing an action given a state, or the policy that maps a state to an action. There are many applications of reinforcement learning, including autonomous vehicles, robot control, game playing, portfolio management, and dialogue synthesis. Consider a simple example of the video game Pong. The state is the image of the screen, the actions are the movements up, down, or no movement, and the reward is the game score. In chess, the state is represented by the board configuration; the actions are the possible movements of the game pieces; and the reward is the game outcome of win, lose, or draw.

11.2 Multi-Armed Bandit

Before considering reinforcement learning, we will consider the stateless setting of a multi-armed bandit. Given k slot machines, an action is to pull an arm of one of the machines. Pulling an arm results in a reward, which is a sample drawn from that machine. At each time step t the agent chooses an action a_t among the k actions, and receives a reward r_t. Taking action a is pulling arm i, which gives a reward $r(a)$ with probability p_i. Behind each machine there is a probability distribution, and by pulling an arm we get a sample from that distribution. Our goal is to maximize the total expected return. The value of action a is the expected reward $Q(a) = \mathbb{E}[r_t | a_t = a]$; however, we don't know the

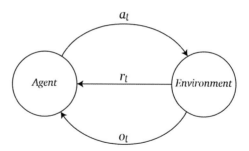

Figure 11.1 Reinforcement learning setting. An agent interacts with an environment by taking actions. The environment transitions the agent to a new state and the agent receives a reward. Next, the agent takes another action and so on. In reinforcement learning the transition function and reward function are unknown to the agent that samples the environment.

action values. We can therefore estimate the value $Q_t(a)$ of action a at time t; for example, by keeping the current mean reward for each action. A greedy action takes the best estimate at time t, exploiting knowledge $a_t = \operatorname{argmax}_a Q_t(a)$, for example by choosing the action with the largest mean reward.

11.2.1   Greedy Approach

Consider the example shown in Figure 11.2, with two possible actions: red or blue (for example, to open a red door or a blue door). If we choose the red door and get a reward of 0, then the value of red is 0. If we then choose the blue door and get a reward of 1, then the value of blue is 1. If we follow a greedy strategy, then since the value of the blue door of 1 is greater than the value of the red door of 0, we will choose blue again. Say we choose blue again and get 3; then if we update our mean for the blue door then the value of the blue door is now 2, which is also greater than the value of the red door which is 0. So we choose the blue door again, and so long as the mean is greater than 0 we will keep on choosing the blue door. However, it could have been the case that the value we received for the red door of 0 was simply bad luck, and that value was sampled from the tail of the distribution behind the red door, whereas the red distribution may yield other high values. However, if we act greedily then a sampled value is deterministically used, and in this case we may continue choosing the blue door indefinitely, without going back to the red door.

11.2.2 ε-greedy Approach

A non-greedy action is exploring. If instead of taking a greedy action we behave greedily most of the time, for example with a small probability ε we choose a random action and with probability $1 - \varepsilon$ we take the greedy action, then we are acting ε-greedy. The ε-greedy approach ensures that once in a while we will

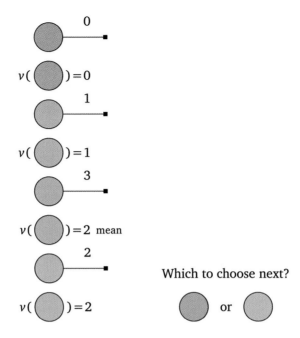

Figure 11.2 Greedy action selection. In the first step the agent chooses red and observes a value of 0. Next, the agent chooses blue and observes a value of 1. Since 1 is greater than 0, the agent chooses blue again and this time observes the value 3, for an average value of 2. The agent will continue selecting blue so long as the mean is greater than 0, even though this result may be due to an unlucky value of 0 observed for red. There is a trade-off between exploiting known knowledge, namely the average values, and exploring.

take a random action; this promotes exploration, and may avoid getting stuck continuously exploiting the known actions. Pseudocode for the ε-greedy approach is shown in Algorithm 11.1.

Algorithm 11.1 ε-greedy.
___
    for each action a **do**:
        $Q(a) = 0$
        $N(a) = 0$ number of times action is chosen
    for each time step **do**:
$$a = \begin{cases} \underset{a}{\operatorname{argmax}} Q(a) & \text{with probability } 1 - \varepsilon \\ \text{random action} & \text{with probability } \varepsilon \end{cases}$$
        $N(a) = N(a) + 1$
        $Q(a) = Q(a) + (r(a) - Q(a))/N(a)$
___

11.2.3   Upper Confidence Bound

We can choose to be optimistic under uncertainty by using both the mean and variance of the reward, taking the action using the upper confidence bound (UCB) criteria (Auer et al., 2002):

$$\operatorname*{argmax}_{a}(\mu(r(a)) + \varepsilon\sigma(r(a))) \tag{11.1}$$

This criteria also appears in Monte Carlo tree search, which is used in Expert Iteration and AlphaZero.

11.3   State Machines

A state machine is defined by a set $\mathcal{S}$ of possible states, an initial state s_0, a set of possible inputs $\mathcal{X}$, a transition function $f : \mathcal{S} \times \mathcal{X} \mapsto \mathcal{S}$ mapping from states and inputs to a state, a set of possible outputs $\mathcal{Y}$ and a mapping $g : \mathcal{S} \mapsto \mathcal{Y}$ from a state to an output. For example, Figure 11.3, shows a state machine with two states denoted by circles $\mathcal{S} = $ standing, moving. The start state in this example $s_0 = $ standing is denoted by two concentric circles. The set of possible inputs $\mathcal{X} = $ slow, fast, and a transition function f is denoted by orange or purple edges from source to target states. The transition function $f(s, x) = s'$ maps each state s and input x to a new state s'. For example $s_1 = f(s_0, \text{fast}) = $ moving.

The states may not be observed directly; for example, they may be sensor measurements or, as shown in the example in Figure 11.4, the state is that there is a lioness in the grass, whereas an observation is only of the occluding grass. The state and observation in this example are different and may result in different outcomes. Formally, define $\mathcal{Y}$ to be the set of possible outputs or observations, and $g : \mathcal{S} \mapsto \mathcal{Y}$ a mapping from a state s to an output or observation y. If the state and observation are the same then g is the identity, and in the example shown in Figure 11.3 we get $y_1 = g(s_1) = s_1 = $ moving. The tuple $(\mathcal{S}, \mathcal{X}, f, \mathcal{Y}, g, s_0)$ defines the state machine. The state machine is applied for each time step t, in which we iteratively compute:

$$\begin{aligned} s_t &= f(s_{t-1}, x_t) \\ y_t &= g(s_t) \end{aligned} \tag{11.2}$$

for $t \geq 1$. Notice that Equation 11.2 defining a state machine is the same as our earlier definition of a recurrent neural network, where the hidden states are replaced with states s_t.

11.4   Markov Processes

In the previous section we considered only actions in a stateless setting. We now consider the state of the agent. In a Markov model, as illustrated in Figure 11.5,

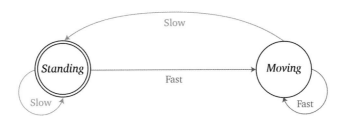

Figure 11.3 State machine with two states $\mathcal{S} = \{standing, moving\}$, a starting state $s_0 = standing$, two inputs $\mathcal{X} = slow, fast$, and a transition function $f : \mathcal{S} \times \mathcal{X} \mapsto \mathcal{S}$ denoted by orange and purple arcs. In this example $f(s_0, slow) = standing$, $f(s_0, fast) = moving$, $f(moving, slow) = standing$, and $f(moving, fast) = moving$.

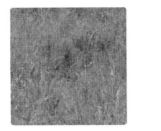 

Figure 11.4 State (right) of a lioness in the grass, compared with an observation (left) of only the grass occluding the lioness.

we make the assumption that state s_2 is only dependent on the previous state s_1, and generally that state s_{t+1} depends only on the previous state s_t.

In a Markov process, as illustrated in Figure 11.6, the probability of a state s_{t+1} is dependent only on the previous state s_t and an action a_t, namely the probability is $p(s_{t+1}|s_t, a_t)$.

Formally, a Markov process is defined by a set of possible states $\mathcal{S}$, a set of possible actions $\mathcal{A}$, and a transition model $T : \mathcal{S} \times \mathcal{A} \times \mathcal{S} \mapsto \mathbb{R}$. An example of a Markov process is illustrated in Figure 11.7. In this example, the set of three possible states of a robot are $\mathcal{S} = \{fallen, standing, moving\}$. For each state, there are two possible actions the robot may take $\mathcal{A} = \{slow, fast\}$ denoted by orange and purple arcs. The transition model defines the probability distribution over the next state given the previous state and action. In this example g is the identity and therefore the output is the state. For example, if the robot is in state fallen and takes a slow action, then with probability $\frac{3}{5}$ the robot will stay fallen and with probability $\frac{2}{5}$ the robot will stand up and be in state standing. If

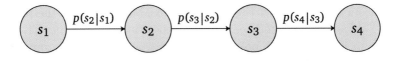

Figure 11.5 In a Markov model state s_{t+1} depends only on the previous state s_t.

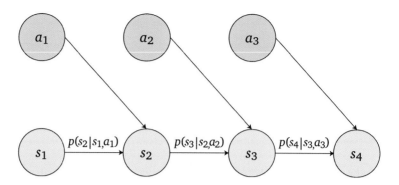

Figure 11.6 In a Markov process the probability of a state s_{t+1} depends only on the previous state s_t and action a_t.

the robot is in state fallen and takes fast action it will stay fallen; therefore the only way for a fallen robot to stand up is by taking a slow action. If the robot is standing and takes a slow action, then it will always, with probability 1, begin to move, transitioning to state moving. If the robot is moving and takes a slow action, it will keep on moving. If the robot is standing and takes a fast action, then with probability $\frac{3}{5}$ it will move, and with probability $\frac{2}{5}$ it will fall. If the robot is moving and takes a fast action, then with probability $\frac{4}{5}$ it will keep on moving and with probability $\frac{1}{5}$ it will fall.

The 3×3 transition matrices $P(s, a, s')$ for slow and fast actions are shown in Equations 11.3 and are completely known. The rows denote states s, the columns denote states s', and the values of the matrix are the transition probabilities. For example, taking a slow action as illustrated by orange arcs, the probability from state fallen to fallen is $\frac{3}{5}$, from fallen to standing is $\frac{2}{5}$ and from fallen to moving there is no arc, which is 0 probability, such that a row of probabilities sums to 1. The entire transition matrices are known, and there is no need to explore in order to find the transition probabilities. In a similar fashion, the transition matrix for taking a fast action is given and known to the robot:

$$P(s, \text{slow}, s') = \begin{bmatrix} \frac{3}{5} & \frac{2}{5} & 0 \\ 0 & 0 & 1 \\ 0 & 0 & 1 \end{bmatrix} \quad P(s, \text{fast}, s') = \begin{bmatrix} 1 & 0 & 0 \\ \frac{2}{5} & 0 & \frac{3}{5} \\ \frac{1}{5} & 0 & \frac{4}{5} \end{bmatrix} \quad (11.3)$$

In a Markov model the probability of a state is conditioned on the previous state, as shown in Figure 11.5. In a Markov process the probability of a state is conditioned both on the previous state and on the action taken, as shown in Figure 11.6. A policy $\pi(a|s)$ maps state to action, and following the policy allows the agent to decide which action to take given the state it is in, as shown in Figure 11.8.

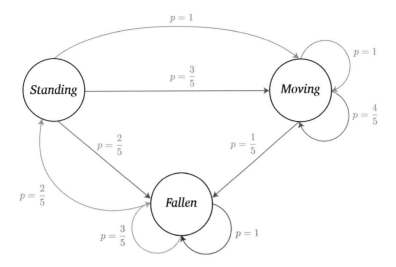

Figure 11.7 A Markov process defined by a set of states $\mathcal{S} = \{\text{Fallen}, \text{Standing}, \text{Moving}\}$ and a set of actions $\mathcal{A} = \{\text{slow}, \text{fast}\}$, with a known transition function $T(s, a, s')$.

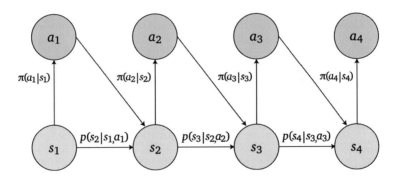

Figure 11.8 In a Markov process the probability of a state is conditioned both on the previous state and on the action taken, and an action may be taken based on a policy π.

11.5 Markov Decision Processes

A Markov decision process (MDP) is defined by a set of possible states S, a set of possible actions $\mathcal{A}$, a transition model $T : \mathcal{S} \times \mathcal{A} \times \mathcal{S} \mapsto \mathbb{R}$, a reward function $R : \mathcal{S} \times \mathcal{A} \mapsto \mathbb{R}$ mapping a state and an action to a real value, and a discount factor γ. Together the tuple $(\mathcal{S}, \mathcal{A}, T, R, \gamma)$ defines an MDP. At every time step t the agent finds itself in state $s \in \mathcal{S}$ and selects an action $a \in \mathcal{A}$. The agent transitions to the next state s' and receives a reward. Next, the agent selects a new action, and so on. The reward $R(s, a)$ is based on state and action. For example, we may define the rewards of our robot to be $R(\text{fallen}, \text{slow}) = 1$, $R(\text{fallen}, \text{fast}) = 0$, $R(\text{standing}, \text{slow}) = 1$, $R(\text{standing}, \text{fast}) = 2$, $R(\text{moving}, \text{slow}) = 1$, and

$R(\text{moving}, \text{fast}) = -1$, regardless of which of the possible arcs happens. The rewards may not necessarily be defined in a deterministic fashion. We may define the rewards to be probabilistic based upon the transition function probabilities as shown in Figure 11.9. For example, instead of having the reward $R(s, a) = R(\text{fallen}, \text{slow}) = 1$ we may define the reward to be dependent on which of the two arcs is taken such that for $T(s, a, s') = p(\text{fallen}, \text{slow}, \text{standing}) = \frac{2}{5}$ the reward is 1 and for $T(s, a, s') = p(\text{fallen}, \text{slow}, \text{fallen}) = \frac{3}{5}$ the reward is -1. The 3×2 matrix R of expected rewards given a state s and action a for the robot example is given by Equation 11.4. The expected reward for state fallen and slow action is $\frac{3}{5} \times (-1) + \frac{2}{5} \times 1 = -\frac{1}{5}$ and the expected reward of state fallen and fast action is 0. In a similar fashion, the expected reward of state standing for slow action is 1 and for fast action is $\frac{4}{5}$, and the expected reward for state moving and slow action is 1 and for a fast action is $\frac{7}{5}$. Considering each row of the reward matrix, we can take the action that maximizes the reward from that state. Therefore, an optimal policy that chooses an action, for a single (myopic) time step, with the maximum reward for each state will choose a fast action from state fallen, receiving an expected reward of 0, a slow action from state standing, receiving an expected reward of 1, and a fast action from state moving, receiving an expected reward of $\frac{7}{5}$. In an MDP both the transition matrices $T(s, a, s')$ and the reward function $R(s, a)$ are known. In contrast, in reinforcement learning the agent does not know T and R and learns them by sampling the environment.

$$R(s, a) = \begin{bmatrix} -\frac{1}{5} & 0 \\ 1 & \frac{4}{5} \\ 1 & \frac{7}{5} \end{bmatrix} \tag{11.4}$$

In summary, in an MDP the transitions are well defined:

$$P(s', r | s, a) = P(s_{t+1} = s', r_{t+1} = r | s_t = s, a_t = a) \tag{11.5}$$

where $\sum_{s'} \sum_r P(s', r | s, a) = 1$ for all (s, a). The expected reward for state–action pairs are:

$$R(s, a) = \mathbb{E}\left[r_{t+1} | s_t = s, a_t = a\right] = \sum_r r \sum_{s'} P(s', r | s, a) \tag{11.6}$$

and the state–transition probabilities are:

$$P(s' | s, a) = P(s_{t+1} = s' | s_t = s, a_t = a) = \sum_r P(s', r | s, a) \tag{11.7}$$

and the expected rewards for state–action–next-state are:

$$R(s, a, s') = \mathbb{E}\left[r_{t+1} | s_t = s, a_t = a, s_{t+1} = s'\right] = \frac{\sum_r r P(s', r | s, a)}{P(s' | s, a)} \tag{11.8}$$

11.5.1   State of Environment and Agent

In the real world the state is more complex since the state and what the agent observes are often not the same. For example, the agent may observe the grass,

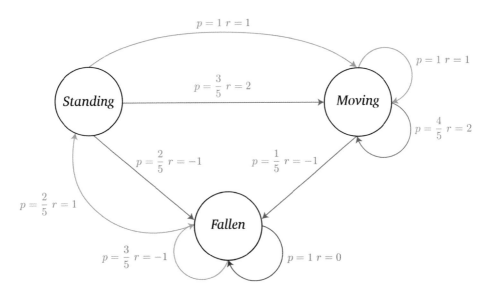

Figure 11.9 Markov decision process defined by a set of states $S = \{\text{Fallen}, \text{Standing}, \text{Moving}\}$ and a set of actions $\mathcal{A} = \{\text{slow}, \text{fast}\}$, with known transition function $T(s, a, s')$ and reward function $R(s, a)$.

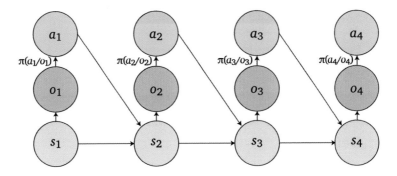

Figure 11.10 The agent action a_t is based on an observation o_t which may be different from the state s_t.

whereas the true state of the environment is that there is a lion hidden in the grass that the agent does not observe and therefore cannot act upon. In the real world the state of the environment s and the observation o are often different. The state of the environment yields an observation and the agent's action is based on the observation rather than the environment state, as shown in Figure 11.10.

For example, in the game Breakout the screen is the observation, whereas the environment is the game console and the state of the environment are the instructions and RAM of the game console, as shown in Figure 11.11. Given sufficient data examples of observations and environment states we may consider performing reverse engineering and infer the environment state from observation.

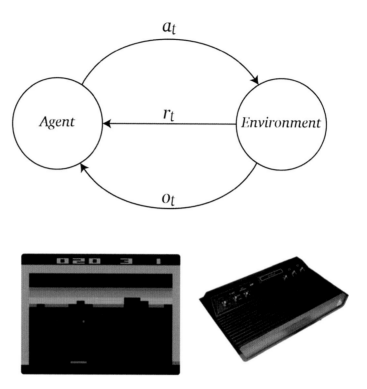

Figure 11.11 In the video game Breakout the agent observes the screen pixels o. The game console is the environment e, and the environment state s^e are the instructions and RAM of the console.

11.6   Definitions

11.6.1   Policy

Next, we define a policy $\pi : \mathcal{S} \mapsto \mathcal{A}$ which is a mapping from state or observation to action. Consider a policy as being similar to a rule book which tells the agent which action to take with a certain probability from each state. For each state s we have a set of possible actions a, and for each of these actions we have a probability of the action given that state. In our robot example, shown in Figure 11.7, we may define four policies: π_A always take a slow action; π_B always take a fast action; π_C if fallen take slow action and otherwise take fast action; and π_D if moving take fast action otherwise take slow action. These four policies may represent four different rule books. A policy does not necessarily need to be deterministic. A policy may be stochastic by adding randomness to the agent actions. For example, the stochastic policy π_E which for all states takes a slow action with probability 0.3 and a fast action with probability 0.7. At each time step t the agent implements the mapping π_t from states to probabilities of

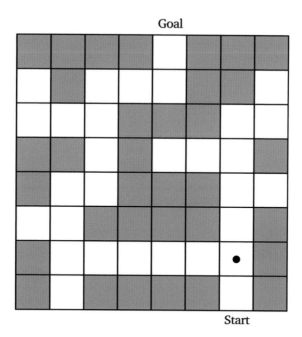

Figure 11.12 Example of the state of an agent in a maze illustrated by a position in the maze denoted by the black dot.

selecting each action:

$$\pi_t(a|s) = P(a_t = a|s_t = s) \tag{11.9}$$

as shown in Figure 11.8.

As a second example of a policy, consider a maze where the state is any position in the maze as shown in Figure 11.12. The agent begins at a state, for example the start state shown on the bottom right of the maze, and has a goal state – shown on the top center of the maze. A policy is a rule book that tells the agent what action to take, with what probability, from each state, as illustrated by the arrows in the maze shown in Figure 11.13. This rule book may be a deterministic policy defined by $a = \pi_t(s)$, as illustrated by a single arrow in each square of the maze, or a stochastic policy with four arrows, one in each direction, in each state of the maze whose lengths denote the probability of moving in each direction given that state $\pi_t(a|s) = P(a_t = a|s_t = s)$. Following the policy shown in Figure 11.13 from any state results in the goal state.

11.6.2 State Action Diagram

Figure 11.14 shows a state–action diagram as a tree. The agent starts from a root node representing state s and takes an action a. The action is selected by the agent based on a policy π mapping state to action. Based on the state–action pair (s, a) represented by a black node, the environment provides the agent with a

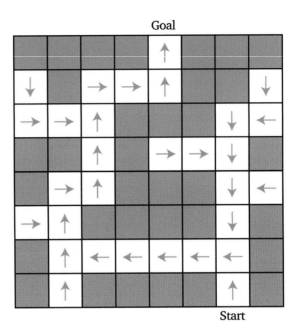

Figure 11.13 Example of a deterministic policy defining movements, from each white square, represented by green arrows. The states are the white squares and the possible actions are $\mathcal{A} = \{\text{up}, \text{down}, \text{left}, \text{right}\}$ arrows. A stochastic policy may define a probability over the actions for each state.

reward r represented by an edge from the black node, and the transition function moves the agent to a new state s' denoted by a leaf node. Nodes representing states are shown in yellow, and nodes representing states and actions are shown in black. The state–action diagram tree represents an episode (s, a, r, s') of the agent. In the first part the agent takes an action, whereas in the second part the transition function or environment provides a reward and moves the agent. This process is repeated from s' for another episode, and so on.

11.6.3   State Value Function

Next we would like to know: What is the value of a policy $\pi : \mathcal{S} \mapsto \mathcal{A}$? This depends on the number of steps we take following the policy. In our robot example shown in Figure 11.9, we may rent the robot for h steps; afterward we do not have access to the robot – we can say the robot will be destroyed after h steps. We call h the horizon, the number of time steps left for the policy to be applied. Define $V_\pi^h(s)$ as the state value function with respect to a policy π with horizon h starting at state s. We can compute $V_\pi^h(s)$ by induction on the number of steps remaining, h. In the base case, there are no steps remaining, $h = 0$; therefore no matter what state the agent is in, the value $V_\pi^0(s) = 0$. Next, the value of a policy π at state s with horizon h is the reward in s plus the next state's expected value

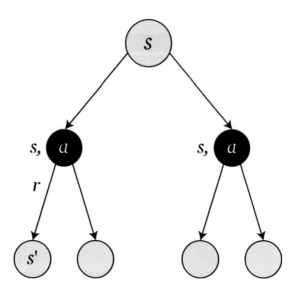

Figure 11.14 State–action diagram tree. The root of the tree represents a state s. The agent takes action a leading to node (s, a). The transition function or environment then gives the agent a reward r and moves the agent to state s' represented by a leaf node.

with horizon $h - 1$. For $h = 1$:

$$V_\pi^1(s) = R(s, \pi(s)) + V_\pi^0(s) = R(s, a) + 0 \tag{11.10}$$

For $h = 2$:

$$V_\pi^2(s) = R(s, \pi(s)) + \sum_{s'} T(s, \pi(s), s')R(s', \pi(s')) \tag{11.11}$$

and for any h:

$$V_\pi^h(s) = R(s, \pi(s)) + \sum_{s'} T(s, \pi(s), s')V_\pi^{h-1}(s') \tag{11.12}$$

which define $V_\pi^h(s)$ recursively as a function of $V_\pi^{h-1}(s')$.

Consider the value of a state $V_\pi(s)$ with respect to a policy π for the maze example shown in Figure 11.15. The goal is to reach the center top state from the start state at the bottom right, and in each step we lose a point. When we are one step away from the goal and we follow the policy shown in Figure 11.13, which says to go up if you are in the state below the goal, then the value of that state is -1. The value V of a state s is always with respect to a policy π. Given a policy, or rule book, as shown in Figure 11.13, we can infer the value of states, as shown in Figure 11.15. On the other hand, given the values of states we can infer a policy. The state value function $V_\pi(s)$ for a policy π measures how good it is for the agent to be in a given state in terms of expected future rewards for an infinite horizon. The value function defined with respect to an agent's policy

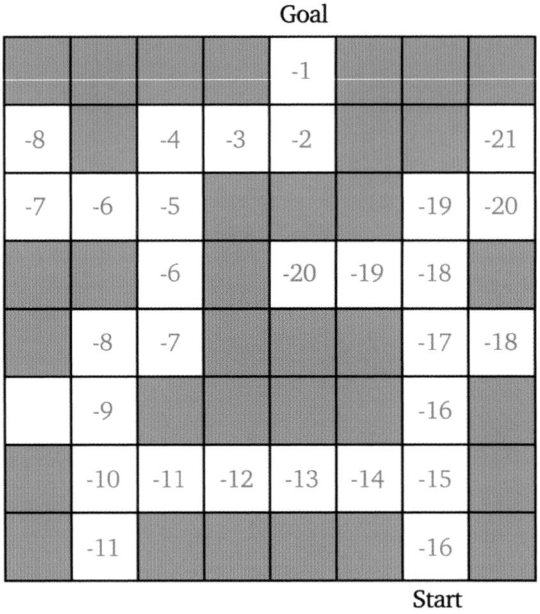

Figure 11.15 Example of a state value function defined on a maze.

π is the expectation over the return:

$$V_\pi(s) = \mathbb{E}_\pi [g_t | s_t = s] = \mathbb{E}_\pi \left[\sum_k \gamma^k r_{t+k+1} | s_t = s \right] \qquad (11.13)$$

and is illustrated in Figure 11.14. This computation involves two steps. In the first step, given a state we consider the set of possible actions. Once we take an action, the second step is that the environment blows us to the next state. We compute the expectation of the return since the policy may be stochastic. We consider the return since we take into account the long-term rewards rather than just the immediate reward. The return is the reward over time discounted by a factor γ. If $\gamma = 0$ then the agent is myopic and takes into account only the immediate reward. If $\gamma = 1$ then the agent is farsighted, taking into account the long-term reward.

In the case of an infinite horizon $h = \infty$ we don't know when the game or robot episodes will be over and may potentially play an infinite number of steps. A problem is that Q^∞ may be infinite, and therefore we cannot select one action over another. One solution is to find a policy that maximizes an infinite horizon discounted value:

$$\mathbb{E} \left[\sum_{t=0}^{\infty} \gamma^t R_t | \pi, s_0 \right] = \mathbb{E} \left[R_0 + \gamma R_1 + \gamma^2 R_2 + \cdots | \pi, s_0 \right] \qquad (11.14)$$

where t denotes the number of steps from the starting state. The expected infinite horizon value of state s under policy π is:

$$
\begin{aligned}
V_\pi(s) &= \mathbb{E}\left[R_0 + \gamma R_1 + \gamma^2 R_2 + \cdots \mid \pi, s_0 = s\right] \\
&= \mathbb{E}\left[R_0 + \gamma(R_1 + \gamma(R_2 + \cdots))\right] \mid \pi, s_0 = s) \\
&= R(s, \pi(s)) + \gamma \sum_{s'} T(s, \pi(s), s') V_\pi(s')
\end{aligned}
$$

where t denotes the number of step from the start, yielding $n = |S|$ linear equations which can be solved.

11.6.4 Action Value Function

Similar to the state value function we can consider the action value function, which extends the mapping to each of the possible actions. We can compute $Q_\pi^h(s, a)$ with respect to a policy π with horizon h for state s and action a in a similar fashion to our iterative computation of $V_\pi^h(s)$. For $h = 0$, $Q_\pi^0(s, a) = 0$. For $h = 1$, $Q_\pi^1(s, a) = R(s, a) + 0$. For $h = 2$:

$$
Q_\pi^2(s, a) = R(s, a) + \sum_{s'} T(s, a, s') \max_{a'} R(s', a') \tag{11.15}
$$

For any h we can use $Q_\pi^{h-1}(s', a')$ to compute $Q_\pi^h(s, a)$:

$$
Q_\pi^h(s, a) = R(s, a) + \sum_{s'} T(s, a, s') \max_{a'} Q_\pi^{h-1}(s', a') \tag{11.16}
$$

For n states $|\mathcal{S}| = n$, m actions $|\mathcal{A}| = m$, and horizon h, computation time of $Q_\pi^h(s, a)$ is $O(nmh)$.

In the maze example shown in Figure 11.16 we have four possible actions: $\mathcal{A} = \{\text{up}, \text{down}, \text{left}, \text{right}\}$ so the action value function $Q_\pi(s, a)$ takes into account both the state s and the action a with respect to a policy π. The action value function $Q_\pi(s, a)$ for policy π is the expected return for s and a under policy π with discount γ:

$$
Q_\pi(s, a) = \mathbb{E}_\pi\left[g_t \mid s_t = s, a_t = a\right] = \mathbb{E}_\pi\left[\sum_k \gamma^k r_{t+k+1} \mid s_t = s, a_t = a\right] \tag{11.17}
$$

The value of taking action a in state s under policy π is the expected return. This expectation is computed by summing the products of the probabilities of each action by their returns, as illustrated in Figure 11.17 in which black nodes represent state–action pairs and yellow nodes represent states.

An example of state value and action value functions for the game of Breakout is shown in Figure 11.18. As the ball moves up toward the bricks the value of the state increases; as the ball moves down toward the paddle the value of the state decreases. The action value function shows the value of the state for each possible action. Given the action value function, we can select the action for which the action value function is maximized.

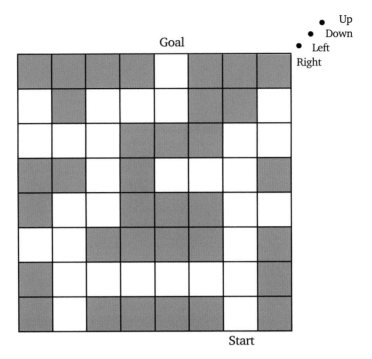

Figure 11.16 Example of an action value function.

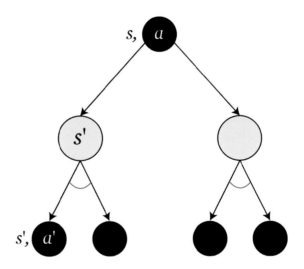

Figure 11.17 Example of an action value state diagram.

The relationship between the state value function $V_\pi(s)$ and the action value function $Q_\pi(s, a)$ is:

$$V_\pi(s) = \sum_a \pi(a|s)Q_\pi(s, a) \tag{11.18}$$

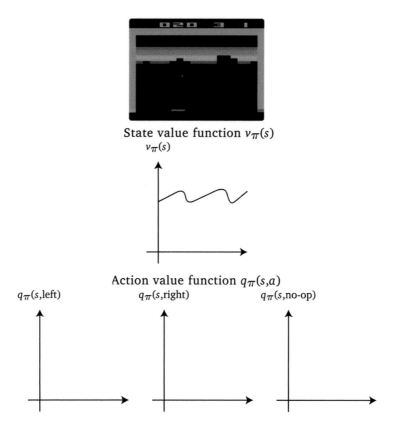

Figure 11.18 State value function $V_\pi(s)$ and action value functions $Q_\pi(s,a)$ for actions $\mathcal{A} = \{\text{left}, \text{right}, \text{no-op}\}$ for the video game Breakout. As the ball gets closer to the brick wall the state value function increases due to the expected reward to be received by hitting the wall, whereas as the ball goes down the state value function decreases due to the possibility of missing the ball.

for all states s.

11.6.5   Reward

In our maze example, the reward shown in Figure 11.19 is -1 for each time step spent in the maze. The return is the sum of rewards $g_t = r_{t+1} + r_{t+2} + \cdots + r_T$. If the agent plays in the maze for a very long time, for many time steps, the agent will accumulate a very large negative reward. Therefore, the reward can be discounted by a discount factor $\gamma \in [0, 1]$ such that:

$$g_t = r_{t+1} + \gamma r_{t+2} + \gamma^2 r_{t+3} + \cdots = \sum_{k=0}^{T-t-1} \gamma^k r_{t+k+1} \tag{11.19}$$

If $\gamma = 0$ then the agent is myopic, maximizing only immediate rewards, and as γ approaches 1 the agent becomes farsighted, considering the long-term horizon.

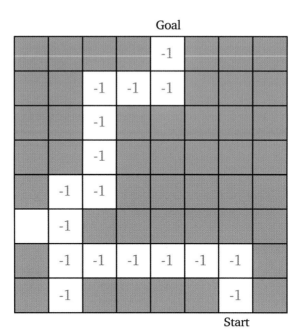

Figure 11.19 Reward for each time step spent in the maze is -1.

The returns at successive time steps are dependent upon on each other. The return at time step t is the next reward plus γ times the return at the next time step $t + 1$, such that for an infinite horizon:

$$g_t = r_{t+1} + \gamma r_{t+2} + \gamma^2 r_{t+3} + \cdots = r_{t+1} + \gamma(r_{t+2} + \gamma r_{t+3} + \cdots) = r_{t+1} + \gamma g_{t+1}$$

(11.20)

which defines a recursive relationship between the return g_t at time step t and the return g_{t+1} at the next time step $t + 1$.

11.6.6   Model

We can build a model for the environment which will help us predict what the environment will do next. If the environment is deterministic then we can form a transition matrix T to predict the next state and a reward matrix R to predict the next reward. A model is optional. Reinforcement learning methods can be classified into model-free methods and model-based methods.

11.6.7   Agent Types

Reinforcement learning methods may be categorized into model-based and model-free methods. Model-based methods learn a model of the environment which is used to predict the value of a given action in a given state. For example, model-based methods may model the transition function and the reward function. Model-based methods may further be divided into methods that are given the model and methods that learn the world model. Model-based reinforcement learning methods that learn the world model begin with a policy and interact with the environment using that policy to yield observations. Next, given the observations, we may build a world model from the known observations, and finally use the world model to train the agent, resulting in an improved policy.

In contrast to model-based approaches, model-free methods either find a policy directly or estimate a value function, for example by Q-learning. Policy-based methods learn a policy that maximizes the expected reward and do not require a model of the environment. Value-based methods learn a value function that estimates the expected reward of taking a given action in a given state. Model-free agents may be based on optimizing only a value function, only a policy, or both. Actor–critic algorithms optimize for both the value function and policy.

Model-free methods are simpler to implement than model-based methods, and are more suitable for real-time applications. However, they are less likely to succeed in complex environments. Model-based methods may be more suitable for complex environments, but require more computational resources.

11.6.8 Problem Types

The planning problem is the case in which the environment is known, such that when we take an action in each state we get a reward. The reinforcement learning problem handles the real world in which the environment is unknown and changes since the agent and others interact with the environment.

There is a classical trade-off between the types of behaviors of an agent: specifically, between exploration in which the agent finds out more about the environment, and exploitation in which the agent uses known information to maximize returns. For example, consider the trade-off between showing a new ad compared with showing the best ad based on previous performance for targeting an audience.

11.6.9 Agent Representation of State

As the agent moves between states by taking an action and receiving a reward, it generates a set of action, state, and reward tuples (a_t, s_t, r_t), called episodes, which together form a history: $h_t = a_1, s_1, r_1, a_2, s_2, r_2, \ldots, a_t, s_t, r_t$. Our reinforcement learning algorithm maps the history h_t to the next action a_{t+1}. If we assume a Markovian property then we may consider the previous state or consider the last episode, otherwise we may consider the entire agent history. Our assumptions about agent state may vary. Consider the example shown in Figure 11.20. In the first interaction with the environment the agent sees green, green, blue, red and receives a reward of 100. In the second interaction with the environment the agent sees red, green, blue, blue and loses 100. In the third

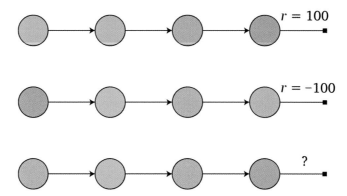

Figure 11.20 Different representations of agent state lead to different predicted rewards. The top row consists of the sequence of the colors green, blue, and red, followed by a reward of 100. The second row consists of 2 blue nodes, 1 green, and 1 red, followed by a reward of -100. In the bottom row, if our representation of state is the sequence of the last three colors we may expect a reward of 100, whereas if our representation of state is the number of appearances of each color regardless of order then we may expect a negative reward of -100. The representation of state may also be different from these two examples, and yield a different reward altogether.

interaction with the environment the agent sees blue, green, blue, red. If we assume a Markov property then we may predict that after the sequence of green, blue, red we may expect a reward of 100. Whereas if we assume that state is modeled by number of reds, greens, and blues, then we may predict that having seen two blues, one green, and one red we will lose 100. This example illustrates that our representation of state results in different predictions.

11.6.10   Bellman Expectation Equation for State Value Function

The expected return starting from s and following policy π satisfies the recursive relationship:

$$V_\pi(s) = \mathbb{E}_\pi\left[g_t | s_t = s\right] \tag{11.21}$$

$$= \mathbb{E}_\pi\left[\sum_k \gamma^k r_{t+k+1} | s_t = s\right] \tag{11.22}$$

$$= \mathbb{E}_\pi\left[r_{t+1} + \gamma \sum_k \gamma^k r_{t+k+2} | s_t = s\right] \tag{11.23}$$

$$= \mathbb{E}_\pi\left[r_{t+1} + \gamma g_{t+1} | s_t = s\right] \tag{11.24}$$

$$= \sum_a \pi(a|s) \sum_{s'} \sum_r P(s', r|s, a)\left(r + \gamma \mathbb{E}_\pi\left[g_{t+1} | s_{t+1} = s'\right]\right) \tag{11.25}$$

$$= \sum_a \pi(a|s) \sum_{s',r} p(s', r|s, a)(r + \gamma V_\pi(s')) \tag{11.26}$$

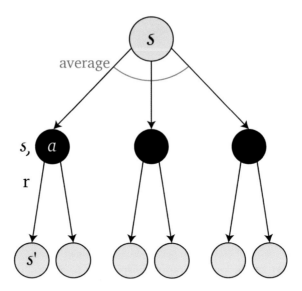

Figure 11.21 Backup diagram corresponding to the Bellman expectation equation for evaluating a state value function V_π. The equation
$V_\pi(s) = \sum_a \pi(a|s) \sum_{s',r} p(s',r|s,a)(r + \gamma V_\pi(s'))$ is linear, and defines a recursive relationship between $V_\pi(s)$ and $V_\pi(s')$. The equation is used for evaluating V_π, and there exists a unique solution. The value of a state s with respect to a policy π is the discounted value of the expected next state with respect to π plus the expected reward. The equation averages over all possibilities, weighing each by its probability to occur.

for all s, called the Bellman equation for V_π which establishes the relationship between the value of a state and values of successor states. The Bellman expectation equation can be used to evaluate $V_\pi(s)$, and defines the relationship between $V_\pi(s)$ and $V_\pi(s')$:

$$V_\pi(s) = \sum_a \pi(a|s) \sum_{s',r} P(s',r|s,a)(r + \gamma V_\pi(s')) \qquad (11.27)$$

which means that the value of a state equals the discounted value of the expected next state with respect to π plus the expected reward. The Bellman expectation equation averages over all possibilities, weighting each by its probability of occurring. The Bellman equation is a linear equation and may be written in vector notation as:

$$V_\pi^{h+1} = r + TV_\pi^h \qquad (11.28)$$

where V_π is the vector of values for each state, r is the reward vector for each state, and T is the transition matrix.

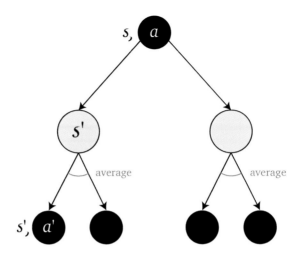

Figure 11.22 Backup diagram corresponding to the Bellman expectation equation for evaluating an action value function Q_π with respect to a given policy π. The equation $Q_\pi(s,a) = \sum_{s',r} p(s',r|s,a)\left(r + \gamma \sum_{a'} \pi(a'|s')Q_\pi(s',a')\right)$ is linear, and defines a recursive relationship between $Q_\pi(s,a)$ and $Q_\pi(s',a')$. Starting at state s and taking action a, the environment moves the agent to state s' where we compute the average over the available actions, and reach the state–action pair (s',a').

11.6.11   Bellman Expectation Equation for Action Value Function

We define $Q_\pi(s,a)$ recursively as a function of $Q_\pi(s',a')$:

$$Q_\pi(s,a) = \mathbb{E}_\pi\left[g_t|s_t = s, a_t = a\right] \tag{11.29}$$

$$= \mathbb{E}_\pi\left[r_{t+1} + \gamma r_{t+2} + \gamma^2 r_{t+3} + \cdots |s,a\right] \tag{11.30}$$

$$= \mathbb{E}_{s',a'}\left[r + \gamma Q_\pi(s',a')|s,a\right] \tag{11.31}$$

$$= \sum_{s'}\sum_{r} P(s',r|s,a)\left(r + \gamma \sum_{a'} \pi(a'|s')Q_\pi(s',a')\right) \tag{11.32}$$

where the first sum denotes where the wind will blow us and the second sum what action we will take. The Bellman expectation equation for action value function is also a linear equation.

11.7   Optimal Policy

Solving a task requires finding the policy that achieves high reward over the long run. We define the optimal policy for MDPs by defining ordering over policies. A policy π is better than or equal to a policy π' if its expected return is greater than or equal to that of π' for all states:

$$\pi \geq \pi' \text{ iff } V_\pi(s) \geq V_{\pi'}(s) \text{ for all } s \tag{11.33}$$

There always exists at least one policy better than or equal to all other policies, which is the optimal policy $\pi^\star$.

11.7.1 Optimal Value Function

The goal of finding an optimal policy is to maximize the expected return, and optimal policies share the same optimal state value function:

$$V_\star(s) = \max_\pi V_\pi(s) = \max_\pi \mathbb{E}_\pi [g_t | s_t = s] \qquad (11.34)$$

for all s. Similarly, optimal policies share the same optimal action value function:

$$Q_\star(s,a) = \max_\pi Q_\pi(s,a) = \max_\pi \mathbb{E}_\pi [g_t | s_t = s, a_t = a] \qquad (11.35)$$

for all s and a.

Given $Q^h(s,a)$ for all states and actions we can compute the optimal finite horizon policy by:

$$\pi_\star^h(s) = \operatorname*{argmax}_a Q^h(s,a) \qquad (11.36)$$

11.7.2 Bellman Optimality Equation for $V_\star$

The Bellman optimality equation for $V_\star$ is that the value of a state under an optimal policy is equal to the expected return for the best action from that state:

$$V_\star(s) = \max_a Q_\pi(s,a) \qquad (11.37)$$

$$= \max_a \mathbb{E}_{\pi^\star} [g_t | s_t = s, a_t = a] \qquad (11.38)$$

$$= \max_a \mathbb{E}_{\pi^\star} \left[\sum_k \gamma^k r_{t+k+1} | s_t = s, a_t = a \right] \qquad (11.39)$$

$$= \max_a \mathbb{E}_{\pi^\star} [r_{t+1} + \gamma g_{t+1} | s_t = s, a_t = a] \qquad (11.40)$$

$$= \max_a \mathbb{E}_{\pi^\star} [r_{t+1} + \gamma V_\star(s_{t+1}) | s_t = s, a_t = a] \qquad (11.41)$$

$$= \max_a \sum_{s',r} P(s',r|s,a)(r + \gamma V_\star(s')) \qquad (11.42)$$

which due to the maximum is a non-linear equation:

$$V_\star(s) = \max_a \sum_{s',r} P(s',r|s,a)(r + \gamma V_\star(s')) \qquad (11.43)$$

with a unique solution independent of π. The computation is illustrated in Figure 11.23. Starting from a state s, we first take the maximum over the actions, $\max_a$; then we are at a state–action pair (s,a) and we take the expectation over where the wind will blow us $\sum_{s',r}$. Compare the non-linear Bellman optimality equation 11.43 that begins with a maximum operation with the linear Bellman

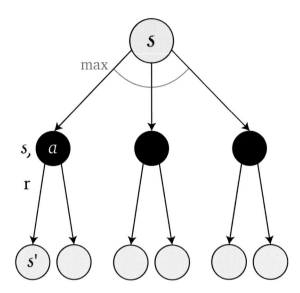

Figure 11.23 Backup diagram corresponding to the Bellman optimality equation for finding the optimal state value function $V_\star$. Starting at state s the agent maximizes over the available actions. From the state–action pair (s, a) we compute the expectation over where the environment takes the agent. The equation $V_\star(s) = \max_a \sum_{s',r} p(s', r|s, a)(r + \gamma V_\star(s'))$ is non-linear due to the maximum operation, and defines a recursive relationship between $V_\star(s)$ and $V_\star(s')$. It has a unique solution that is independent of a policy π.

expectation Equation 11.27 that begins with a summation; the second terms of both equations are the same.

11.7.3   Bellman Optimality Equation for $Q_\star$

Connecting the optimal state value function $V_\star$ to the optimal action value function $Q_\star$:

$$V_\star(s) = \max_a Q_\star(s, a) \tag{11.44}$$

therefore working with Q is convenient.

In a similar fashion, the Bellman optimality equation for $Q_\star$ is:

$$Q_\star(s, a) = \mathbb{E}\left[r_{t+1} + \gamma \max_a Q_\star(s', a')|s, a\right] \tag{11.45}$$

$$= \sum_{s',r} P(s', r|s, a)(r + \gamma \max_a Q_\star(s', a')) \tag{11.46}$$

which is a non-linear equation whose computation is illustrated in Figure 11.24. Starting from a state–action pair (s, a) the environment may take us to a new state s'. Once in the new state s' we maximize over the next actions we can take to reach (s', a').

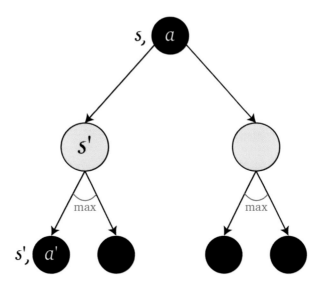

Figure 11.24 Backup diagram corresponding to the Bellman optimality equation for finding the optimal action value function. The equation is non-linear and used for finding $Q_\star$ by defining a recursive relationship between $Q_\star(s, a)$ and $Q_\star(s', a')$. Starting from state and action (s, a) the equation computes the expectation of where the environment will take the agent, and then once in state s' maximizes over the actions the agent can take. Once we compute $Q_\star(s, a) = \sum_{s', r} p(s', r | s, a)(r + \gamma \max_a Q_\star(s', a'))$, the agent can act according to the optimal policy $\pi_\star = \underset{a}{\mathrm{argmax}} Q_\star(s, a)$.

Once we know $Q_\star(s, a)$ we can find the best policy:

$$\pi_\star = \underset{a}{\mathrm{argmax}} Q_\star(s, a) \tag{11.47}$$

Overall, we've seen four Bellman equations: two linear expectation equations (the Bellman expectation equation for state value function $V_\pi(s)$ defined in Equation 11.27 and the Bellman expectation equation for action value function $Q_\pi(s, a)$ defined in Equation 11.29); and two non-linear optimality equations (the Bellman optimality equation for state value function $V_\star(s)$ defined in Equation 11.43 and the Bellman optimality equation for action value function $Q_\star(s, a)$ defined in Equation 11.45).

Next, we can use the Bellman optimality equation to solve the MDP. Consider the example illustrated in Figure 11.9. Applying the Bellman optimality equation we get:

$$V_\star^1(\text{fallen}) = 0 \text{ do nothing or fast action}$$
$$V_\star^1(\text{standing}) = 1 \text{ slow action}$$
$$V_\star^1(\text{moving}) = \frac{7}{5} \text{ fast action}$$

$$V_\star^2(\text{fallen}) = \max\{-\frac{1}{5} + \frac{2}{5} \times 1, 0 + 0\} = \frac{1}{5} \text{ slow action}$$

$$V_\star^2(\text{standing}) = \max\{1 + \frac{7}{5}, \frac{4}{5} + \frac{3}{5} \times \frac{7}{5} + \frac{2}{5} \times 0\} = \frac{12}{5} \text{ slow action}$$

$$V_\star^2(\text{moving}) = \max\{1 + \frac{7}{5}, \frac{7}{5} + \frac{4}{5} \times \frac{7}{5} + \frac{1}{5} \times 0\} = 2.52 \text{ fast action}$$

$$V_\star^3(\text{fallen}) = \max\{-\frac{1}{5} + \frac{2}{5} \times \frac{12}{5} + \frac{3}{5} \times \frac{1}{5}, 0 + 1 \times \frac{1}{5}\} = 0.88 \text{ slow action}$$

$$V_\star^3(\text{standing}) = \max\{1 + 2.52, \frac{4}{5} + \frac{3}{5} \times 2.52 + \frac{2}{5} \times \frac{1}{5}\} = 3.52 \text{ slow action}$$

$$V_\star^3(\text{moving}) = \max\{1 + 2.52, \frac{7}{5} + \frac{4}{5} \times 2.52 + \frac{1}{5} \times \frac{1}{5}\} = 3.52 \text{ slow action}$$

computing the optimal policy given a perfect model by dynamic programming, called planning. Our assumptions are that the environment is an MDP that is known, namely that the state, action, and reward sets are known and finite, and that the dynamics are given by known probability $p(s', r|s, a)$ for all states, actions, and rewards. Unfortunately, in the real world this is rarely useful since we do not know the dynamics or a perfect model of the environment, we do not have sufficient resource to store the entire MDP, and the Markov property may not hold. As a compromise, we will approximately solve the Bellman equation, focusing our efforts on learning to make good decisions at frequent states and putting less effort into learning rare states.

Next, we will use dynamic programming both for the prediction problem of policy evaluation and the control problem of finding the best policy.

11.8   Planning by Dynamic Programming with a Known MDP

11.8.1   Iterative Policy Evaluation

Next, we turn the Bellman expectation equation for state value function into an algorithm for evaluating a policy π, called iterative policy evaluation. We will iteratively approximate V and use Equation 11.27 to update the value of each state. Algorithm 11.2 describes the pseudocode. The inner loop applies the Bellman expectation equation repeatedly until the value of V converges to V_π. Figure 11.25 illustrates the updating of the array storing the state values at each iteration. The algorithm converges both when using two arrays for storing the state values and when updating the state values array in-place.

11.8.2   Policy Iteration

Next, we use the Bellman expectation equation and greedy policy improvement to converge to the optimal policy $\pi_\star$. The policy iteration algorithm has an inner loop of iterative policy evaluation followed by policy improvement. Algorithm 11.3 describes the pseudocode.

Algorithm 11.2 Iterative policy evaluation.

initialize $V(s) = 0$ for each state s
repeat:
$\quad \Delta = 0$
$\quad$**for** each state s **do**:
$\quad\quad v = V(s)$
$\quad\quad V(s) = \sum_a \pi(a|s) \sum_{s',r} P(s', r|s, a)(r + \gamma V(s'))$
$\quad\quad \Delta = \max\{\Delta, \|v - V(s)\|\}$
until $\Delta < \varepsilon$

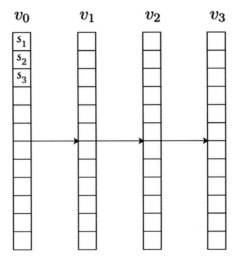

Figure 11.25 Storing iterative updates of the state value function in an array of values for each of the $n = |S|$ states.

11.8.3   Infinite Horizon Value Iteration

Instead of policy iteration we can directly use the Bellman optimality equation to efficiently converge to $Q_\star$. Our update rule is then:

$$Q(s, a) = R(s, a) + \gamma \sum_{s'} T(s, a, s') \max_{a'} Q(s', a') \qquad (11.48)$$

which turns into the value iteration algorithm shown in Algorithm 11.4.

11.9   **Reinforcement Learning**

In the previous section we introduced algorithms for evaluating a policy and finding the optimal policy for a known MDP, given the transition function and reward function, which is also called planning. In this section we introduce algorithms for evaluating a policy and finding the optimal policy for an unknown

---

Algorithm 11.3 Policy iteration.

  initialize $V(s)$ and $\pi(s)$
  repeat:
    policy evaluation
    repeat:
      $\Delta = 0$
      for each state s **do**:
        $v = V(s)$
        $V(s) = \sum_a \pi(a|s) \sum_{s',r} P(s',r|s,a)(r + \gamma V(s'))$
        $\Delta = \max\{\Delta, \|v - V(s)\|\}$
    until $\Delta < \varepsilon$
    policy improvement
    convergence = True
    for each state s **do**:
      $a = \pi(s)$
      $\pi(s) = \operatorname*{argmax}_a \sum_{s',r} P(s',r|s,a)(r + \gamma V(s'))$
      if $a \neq \pi(s)$ **then**:
        convergence = False
  until convergence

Algorithm 11.4 Value iteration.

  initialize $Q(s,a) = 0$ for each state s and action a
  repeat:
    for each state s and action a **do**:
      $q = Q(s,a)$
      $Q(s,a) = R(s,a) + \gamma \sum_{s'} T(s,a,s') \max_{a'} Q(s',a')$
      $\Delta = \max\{\Delta, \|q - Q(s,a)\|\}$
  until $\Delta < \varepsilon$

MDP, without knowing the transition function or reward function in advance, called reinforcement learning. In the real world the MDP is unknown, and yet we would still like to choose the best actions. We do not assume a complete known environment and therefore sample sequences of state, action and reward from actual or simulated interaction with the environment to gain experience. We generate sample transitions not knowing the complete probability distribution of transitions. We will first discuss model-based reinforcement learning and then review two major sampling methods, namely Monte Carlo (MC) sampling and temporal difference (TD) sampling.

Reinforcement learning methods may be divided into model-free and model-based approaches. In turn, model-free approaches may be further divided into (1) value-based or Q-learning methods such as DQN (Mnih et al., 2015); (2) policy-

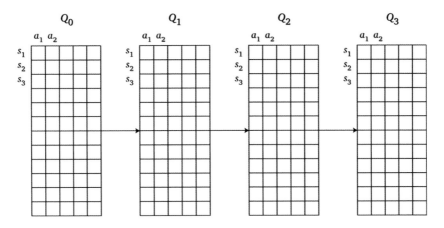

Figure 11.26 Storing iterative updates of the action value function in a 2D array of values for each state and action.

based or policy optimization methods such as A3C (Mnih et al., 2016) and PPO (Schulman et al., 2017); and (3) actor–critic methods such as DDPG (Lillicrap et al., 2016), which are a combination of (1) and (2). Model-based approaches may be divided into methods that are given the model, such as AlphaZero (Silver et al., 2018), and methods that learn the model, such as world models (Ha and Schmidhuber, 2018).

11.9.1   Model-Based Reinforcement Learning

One of the simplest approaches to reinforcement learning is to model the transition and reward based on states, actions, and rewards experienced so far (s, a, r, s') and to use these to model an MDP. A simple model for a transition function is:

$$T(s, a, s') = \frac{N(s, a, s') + 1}{N(s, a) + |\mathcal{S}|} \tag{11.49}$$

where $N(s, a, s')$ counts the number of times the agent was in state s, took action a and moved to state s', and $N(s, a) = \sum_{s'} N(s, a, s')$ counts the number of times the agent was is state s and took action a. The correction by adding 1 to the numerator makes sure we don't estimate the probability to be 0, and adding $|S|$ to the denominator makes sure we don't divide by zero. This correction is only required and significant in the first few samples, and then its effect is diminished. A simple model for the reward function is recording the rewards $R(s, a)$ for state and actions:

$$R(s, a) = \frac{\sum_{(s,a)} r(s, a)}{N(s, a)} \tag{11.50}$$

Next, we can use these empirical estimates of the transition function and reward function to solve the MDP as if T and R were known. A problem with this approach is that it may be infeasible to estimate T or R if the space of states or actions is very large or continuous.

11.9.2   Policy Search

Instead of estimating the transition and reward functions, we can search for a policy directly. We can define a function $f(s, \theta) = p(a|s)$ by a machine learning model with parameters θ to approximate the probability of an action given a state directly. This can be trained by gradient descent for finding the optimal parameters $\theta_\star$. Policy-based methods work well in continuous spaces and for learning stochastic policies, and are described in detail in Chapter 12.

11.9.3   Monte Carlo Sampling

Monte Carlo sampling methods average sample returns and assume the experience is divided into episodes that terminate. Only when an episode completes are the value and policy updated. Sampling is incremental, episode by episode, not step by step. As motivation for incremental updates, consider the incremental computation of the mean. The next mean at step t is the current mean at step $t-1$ plus the update given a new sample x_t. The update is the normalized error between the new sample x_t and the previous mean at step $t-1$:

$$\mu_t = \frac{1}{t} \sum_{i=1}^{t} x_i = \frac{1}{t} \left(\sum_{i=1}^{t-1} x_i + x_t \right) = \frac{1}{t}((t-1)\mu_{t-1} + x_t)$$
$$= \frac{1}{t}(x_t + t\mu_{t-1} - \mu_{t-1}) = \mu_{t-1} + \frac{1}{t}(x_t - \mu_{t-1})$$

Given a policy π our first goal is to learn the state value function V_π. Dynamic programming (DP) computes the value function from the MDP, whereas MC learns the value function from sample returns:

$$V(s_t) = V(s_t) + \alpha(g_t - V(s_t)) \tag{11.51}$$

where g_t is the actual return following time step t, $(g_t - V(s_t))$ is the MC error, and α is a constant step size. In each sample we wait until the end of the episode to determine the increment of $V(s_t)$, as shown in Figure 11.27. Algorithm 11.5 describes the MC prediction pseudocode.

11.9.4   Temporal Difference Sampling

Monte Carlo (MC) TD learning methods use experience to solve the prediction problem. Given experience following policy π, they update estimates of V_π for s_t occurring in that experience. Monte Carlo methods wait until the return is known and use that return as a target for $V(s_t)$. In contrast, TD learning (Sutton, 1988)

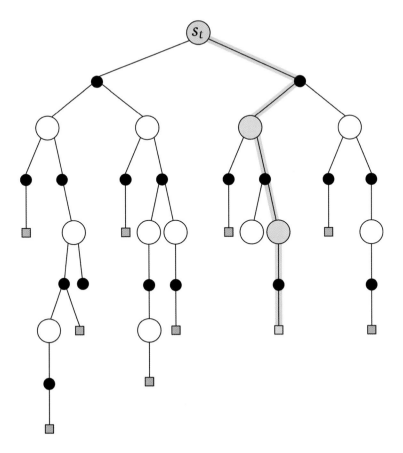

Figure 11.27 Monte Carlo sampling for reinforcement learning. The return is evaluated once an entire path, or rollout, terminates in a leaf node.

waits only until the next time step. At time $t+1$ TD methods form a target and make an update using the observed reward r_{t+1} and the estimate $V(s_{t+1})$:

$$V(s_t) = V(s_t) + \alpha(r_{t+1} + \gamma V(s_{t+1}) - V(s_t)) \tag{11.52}$$

Monte Carlo methods update $V(s_t)$ toward the actual return g_t, as shown in Figure 11.27, whereas TD methods update $V(s_t)$ toward the TD target $r_{t+1} + \gamma V(s_{t+1})$, as shown in Figure 11.28. The difference between the TD target and $V(s_t)$ is called the TD error. Algorithm 11.6 describes the TD prediction pseudocode.

As an example of the difference between MC and TD methods, consider the episodes illustrated in Figure 11.29. Following these samples, the value of red is $\frac{3}{4}$, but what is the value of blue? Here is where MC sampling and TD sampling differ. MC does not exploit the Markov property and therefore according to the MC update rule in Equation 11.51 the value of blue is 0, whereas TD exploits

---

Algorithm 11.5 Monte Carlo prediction.

---

initialize
policy π to be evaluated
$V(s) = 0$ for all s
returns$(s) = \emptyset$ for all states s
repeat:
    Generate episode of π
    for each state s in episode **do**:
        g = return following first occurrence of s
        returns(s) = returns$(s) \cup g$
        $V(s) = \mu(\text{returns}(s))$
until convergence

Algorithm 11.6 Temporal difference prediction.

---

initialize
policy π to be evaluated
$V(s) = 0$ for all s
repeat:
    Generate episode of π
    for each state s in episode **do**:
        a = action given by π for s
        take action a, observe r, s'
        $V(s) = V(s) + \alpha(r + \gamma V(s') - V(s))$
        $s = s'$
until s is terminal

---

the Markov property and according to the TD update rule in Equation 11.52 the value of blue is $\frac{3}{4}$.

Monte Carlo methods use deep sampling until termination, whereas TD methods use shallow sampling. Temporal difference methods with one step look-ahead are called TD(0), and in between TD(0) and MC there exist multiple methods TD(n), depending on the number n of look-ahead steps. We can combine all the n-step returns g_t^n using weights $(1 - \lambda)\lambda^{n-1}$ to form TD(λ) following the update rule:

$$V(s_t) = V(s_t) + \alpha(g_t^\lambda - V(s_t)) \tag{11.53}$$

where $g_t^\lambda = (1 - \lambda) \sum_n \lambda^{n-1} g_t^n$.

11.9.5   *Q*-Learning

Q-learning is a model-free reinforcement learning method that does not model the transitions or reward, and instead directly estimates a value function. In

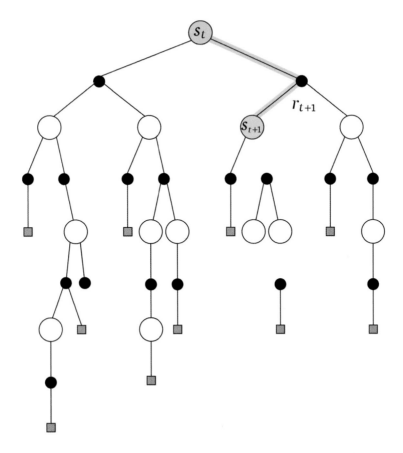

Figure 11.28 Temporal difference sampling for reinforcement learning. A biased estimate of the state value is computed by looking ahead one or more steps, rather than following an episode all the way to termination.

model-based reinforcement learning we estimate T and R, and using value iteration, given T and R we can compute Q by $Q(s, a) = R(s, a) + \gamma \sum_{s'} T(s, a, s')$ $\max_{a'} Q(s', a')$. Next, instead of estimating T and R, we will learn the Q function directly from experience without knowing T or R, known as Q-learning. Q-learning incrementally updates the value function by:

$$Q(s, a) = Q(s, a) - \alpha \left(Q(s, a) - (r + \gamma \max_{a'} Q(s', a')) \right) \tag{11.54}$$

where α is the learning rate, and γ is a discount factor. Instead of just taking the action given by the value function, we use ε-greedy exploration. Therefore, we select a random action with probability ε to promote exploration, and take the action given by the value function otherwise.

   This results in the Q-learning algorithm described in the pseudocode in Algorithm 11.7: Q-learning is an off-policy reinforcement learning method that finds the value function of an optimal policy while using another exploration policy.

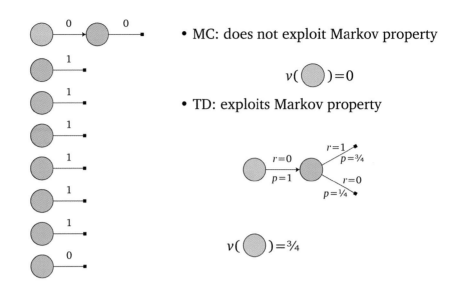

Figure 11.29 Example showing the difference between MC and TD sampling.

Algorithm 11.7 Q-learning.

---

initialize $Q(s, a) = 0$ for all states and actions
select start state $s = s_0$
repeat:

$$a = \begin{cases} \text{select action given } Q \text{ and } s & \text{with probability } 1 - \varepsilon \\ \text{select random action} & \text{with probability } \varepsilon \end{cases}$$

$q = Q(s, a)$
take action a to get reward r and next state s'
$Q(s, a) = Q(s, a) - \alpha \left(Q(s, a) - (r + \gamma \max_{a'} Q(s', a')) \right)$
$\Delta = \max\{\Delta, \|q - Q(s, a)\|\}$
$s = s'$
until $\Delta < \epsilon$

11.9.6   Sarsa

Similar to Q-learning, Sarsa is a model-free reinforcement learning method. In contrast with Q-learning, which is an off-policy method, Sarsa is an on-policy method that estimates a value of a policy while using the policy. Sarsa, as the acronym implies, uses (s, a, r, s', a') tuples to incrementally update the value function by:

$$Q(s, a) = Q(s, a) - \alpha \left(Q(s, a) - (r + \gamma Q(s', a')) \right) \tag{11.55}$$

11.9.7   On-Policy vs. Off-Policy Methods

On-policy methods, such as Sarsa, evaluate or improve the policy that is used to make decisions. They estimate the value of a policy while using it for control. In contrast, off-policy methods, such as Q-learning, evaluate or improve a policy different from that used to generate the data. Off-policy methods separate these two functions into (1) a behavior policy, which is the policy used to generate behavior, and (2) a target policy, which is the policy that is imitated and improved. Off-policy methods follow the behavior policy while improving the target policy, often reusing experience generated from old policies.

11.9.8   Sarsa(λ)

We may use TD updates in Sarsa, and Q-learning, by propagating rewards from states with high rewards to the states that lead to them more efficiently, also known as eligibility traces. The Sarsa(λ) update is defined by:

$$Q(s,a) = Q(s,a) - \alpha N(s,a)\left(Q(s,a) - (r + \gamma Q(s',a'))\right) \tag{11.56}$$

where $N(s,a) = \lambda\gamma N(s,a)$ counts the number of times action a is taken in state s, γ is a discount factor, and the parameter $\lambda \in (0,1)$ controls the rate of decay.

11.10   Maximum Entropy Reinforcement Learning

The objective of reinforcement learning is to find an optimal policy that maximizes return:

$$\pi_\star = \underset{\pi}{\mathrm{argmax}}\,\mathbb{E}_{r\sim\pi}\left[\sum_t R(s_t, a_t)\right] \tag{11.57}$$

The objective of maximum entropy reinforcement learning is to find an optimal policy that maximizes return and conditional action entropy:

$$\pi_\star = \underset{\pi}{\mathrm{argmax}}\,\mathbb{E}_{r\sim\pi}\left[\sum_t R(s_t, a_t) + H_\pi(a_t|s_t)\right] \tag{11.58}$$

where H_π is the entropy of the policy conditional distribution over actions defined by:

$$H_\pi(a_t|s_t) = \mathbb{E}_\pi\left[-\log\pi(a_t|s_t)\right] \tag{11.59}$$

Optimizing this objective promotes both high return and exploration, leading to actions with higher reward that allow taking random actions in the future. Maximum entropy reinforcement learning is more robust to disturbances to the dynamics and rewards (Eysenbach and Levine, 2022) and partial observations. Improving upon this, a maximum–minimum entropy reinforcement learning framework (Han and Sung, 2021) finds an optimal policy that maximizes return while visiting states with low entropy and maximizing their entropy for improving exploration.

11.11   Summary

This chapter begins by defining a stateless multi-armed bandit, presenting the trade-off between exploration and exploitation. Next, we define a state machine, and then define an MDP with known transition and reward functions. Finally, we present reinforcement learning in which the transition and reward functions are unknown and therefore the agent interacts with the environment by sampling the world.

12 Deep Reinforcement Learning

12.1 Introduction

Deep reinforcement learning uses deep neural networks for estimating value functions and policies in reinforcement learning. Deep reinforcement learning has achieved excellent performance on challenging control problems. This success includes virtual environments with large state and action spaces, such as mastering chess, Shogi, and Go (Silver et al., 2018), achieving Grandmaster level in StarCraft II (Vinyals et al., 2019), outracing champion Gran Turismo drivers (Wurman et al., 2022), and real-world changing environments, such as learning quadrupedal locomotion over challenging terrain (Lee et al., 2020), autonomous navigation of stratospheric balloons (Bellemare et al., 2020), and magnetic control of a Tokamak plasma fusion reactor (Degrave et al., 2022).

Chapter 11 presented MDPs and reinforcement learning. A key difference between the two is that when solving MDPs we know the transition function T and reward function R, whereas in reinforcement learning we do not know the transition or reward functions. In reinforcement learning an agent samples the environment; Chapter 11 ends with the Q-learning algorithm, which learns $Q(s, a)$ from experience. In many cases, storing the Q values in a table may be infeasible when the state or action spaces are very large or when they are continuous. For example, the game of Go consists of 10^{170} states. A solution is to approximate the value function or approximate the policy. A deep neural network provides a fast function approximation, allowing efficient interpolation between predicted state values, state–action values, and action probabilities. In deep reinforcement learning we use deep neural networks as fast function approximations for representing the state value function $V(s)$, state–action value function $Q(s, a)$, policy $\pi(a|s)$, or model.

Chapter 5 introduced convolutional neural networks, which classify images, while Chapter 8 described Transformers used in natural language processing and vision. In deep reinforcement learning, instead of predicting image classes we may predict the values of a state or the probabilities of actions $\pi(a|s)$ using a neural network, and based on these probabilities we may take action. The neural network serves as a function approximation. One choice for a non-linear function approximation is a CNN, as shown in Figure 12.1. Given a state s as input, such as an image of pixels, the neural network outputs an approximated value

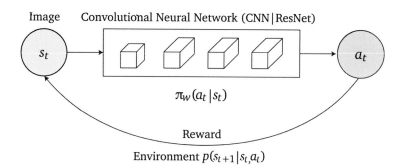

Figure 12.1 Deep reinforcement learning mapping an image state directly to an action using a CNN by evaluating a policy $\pi(a_t|s_t)$.

of the state or an approximated vector of probabilities for each action given the state, and based on these takes an action a. The action a taken by the agent results in the environment responding and sending the agent to state s' with a reward. The CNN may generalize to predict values or action probabilities given an unseen image, or state.

12.2   Function Approximation

Real-world problems often consist of large or continuous state and action spaces. A deep neural network may be used to approximate a state value function $V_\theta(s) \approx V_\pi(s)$, a state–action value function $Q_\theta(s, a) \approx Q_\pi(s, a)$, or to approximate a policy $p_\theta(a|s)$, where θ denotes the network parameters. The neural networks are then optimized by stochastic gradient descent (SGD) as described in Chapter 3.

12.2.1   State Value Function Approximation

Our goal is to find the neural network parameters θ that minimize the mean squared error (MSE) between a value function $V_\pi(s)$ with respect to a policy π such as the optimal policy, and the neural network approximation $V_\theta(s)$:

$$J(\theta) = \frac{1}{2}\mathbb{E}_s\left[(V_\pi(s) - V_\theta(s))^2\right] \tag{12.1}$$

Computing the expectation over states $s \in \mathcal{S}$ results in:

$$J(\theta) = \frac{1}{2|\mathcal{S}|}\sum_{s \in \mathcal{S}}\left((V_\pi(s) - V_\theta(s))^2\right) \tag{12.2}$$

However, since there may be too many states, we may wish to focus on learning states which are visited multiple times. Therefore, under policy π we may spend time $\mu(s)$ in state s and therefore compute the expectation as:

$$J(\theta) = \sum_{s \in \mathcal{S}}\mu(s)\left((V_\pi(s) - V_\theta(s))^2\right) \tag{12.3}$$

where $\sum_{s \in \mathcal{S}} \mu(s) = 1$.

The optimization objective $J(\theta)$ is a differentiable function of the network parameters θ. The gradient of $J(\theta)$ with respect to θ is the vector $\nabla_\theta J(\theta) = \left(\frac{\partial \theta}{\theta_1}, \ldots, \frac{\partial \theta}{\theta_n} \right)^T$ defined by:

$$\nabla_\theta J(\theta) = -\mathbb{E}_s \left[(V_\pi(s) - V_\theta(s)) \nabla_\theta V_\theta(s) \right] \tag{12.4}$$

Optimization by gradient descent involves updating θ in the direction of the negative gradient by:

$$\Delta\theta = \alpha \nabla_\theta J(\theta) = \alpha \mathbb{E}_s \left[(V_\pi(s) - V_\theta(s)) \nabla_\theta V_\theta(s) \right] \tag{12.5}$$

where α is the learning rate, and the optimization starts from an initial guess θ_0. The sequence of parameter values $\{\theta_i\}$:

$$\theta_{i+1} = \theta_i - \alpha \nabla_\theta J(\theta_i) \tag{12.6}$$

where $i = 1, \ldots, n$ are a sequence of monotonically non-increasing values of the objective $J(\theta_0) \geq J(\theta_1) \geq \cdots \geq J(\theta_n)$ that converge toward a local minimum. Using SGD we approximate the gradient using a single random sample at a time such that:

$$\Delta\theta = \alpha \nabla_\theta J(\theta) = \alpha (V_\pi(s) - V_\theta(s)) \nabla_\theta V_\theta(s) \tag{12.7}$$

Since we do not know the ground-truth value function $V_\pi(s)$ we may use an estimate instead, such as the return $g \approx V_\pi(s)$ in Monte Carlo (MC) learning to approximate the value function with respect to π, updating the parameters by:

$$\Delta\theta = \alpha \left(g - V_\theta(s) \right) \nabla_\theta V_\theta(s) \tag{12.8}$$

or use the temporal difference (TD) target $r + \gamma V_\theta(s') \approx V_\pi(s)$ in TD learning, updating the parameters by:

$$\Delta\theta = \alpha \left(r + \gamma V_\theta(s') - V_\theta(s) \right) \nabla_\theta V_\theta(s) \tag{12.9}$$

Since the TD target is a biased sample of the ground-truth value $V_\pi(s)$, we may use the states and targets to form a training set of $\{(s, r + \gamma V_\theta(s))\}$ pairs and then proceed by supervised learning.

12.2.2 Action Value Function Approximation

In action value function approximation the neural network inputs are the states s and actions a and the network parameterized by θ outputs a value $Q_\theta(s, a)$. In a similar fashion to state value function approximation, our objective may be minimizing the MSE between the approximate action value function $Q_\theta(s, a)$ and the action value function $Q_\pi(s, a)$ with respect to a policy π, such as the optimal policy:

$$J(\theta) = \frac{1}{2} \mathbb{E}_{(s,a) \sim \pi} \left[(Q_\pi(s, a) - Q_\theta(s, a))^2 \right] \tag{12.10}$$

where the expectation is over (s, a) pairs from the policy π. The optimization objective $J(\theta)$ is a differentiable function of the network parameters θ. The gradient of $J(\theta)$ with respect to θ is the vector $\nabla_\theta J(\theta) = (\frac{\partial J}{\theta_1}, \ldots, \frac{\partial J}{\theta_n})^T$ defined by:

$$\nabla_\theta J(\theta) = -\mathbb{E}_{(s,a)\sim\pi} \left[(Q_\pi(s, a) - Q_\theta(s, a)) \nabla_\theta Q_\theta(s, a) \right] \tag{12.11}$$

Optimization by gradient descent involves updating θ in the direction of the negative gradient by:

$$\Delta\theta = -\alpha \nabla_\theta J(\theta) = \alpha (Q_\pi(s, a) - Q_\theta(s, a)) \nabla_\theta Q_\theta(s, a) \tag{12.12}$$

Since again we don't know the true action value function Q_π we may use an estimate instead based on the return $g \approx Q_\pi(s_t, a_t)$ in MC learning:

$$\Delta\theta = \alpha \left(g - Q_\theta(s, a) \right) \nabla_\theta Q_\theta(s, a) \tag{12.13}$$

or use the TD target $r + \gamma Q_\theta(s', a') - Q_\theta(s, a) \approx Q_\pi(s, a)$ in TD learning, updating the parameters by:

$$\Delta\theta = \alpha \left(r + \gamma Q_\theta(s', a') - Q_\theta(s, a) \right) \nabla_\theta Q_\theta(s, a) \tag{12.14}$$

Challenges of function approximation in the reinforcement learning setting include that (1) the agent's experience is not independent and identically distributed (IID); (2) the agent's policy affects the future data it will sample; and (3) the environment may change. In addition, methods that use function approximation along with bootstrapping and off-policy learning may not converge. Next, we describe deep reinforcement learning methods that attempt to overcome these challenges.

We will describe model-free approaches which may be divided into (1) value-based or Q-learning methods such as NFQ (Riedmiller, 2005) and DQN (Mnih et al., 2015); (2) policy-based or policy optimization methods such as PPO (Schulman et al., 2017); and (3) actor–critic methods such as DDPG (Lillicrap et al., 2016), which are a combination of (1) and (2).

12.3   Value-Based Methods

Value-based methods for deep reinforcement learning approximate the state value function or the action value function using a neural network.

12.3.1   Experience Replay

In supervised learning the training examples may be sampled independently from an underlying distribution. In contrast, in reinforcement learning the states, actions, and rewards that an agent learns from experience in successive time steps are correlated in time. A solution to this problem, known as experience replay, is to use a replay buffer that stores previous states, actions, and rewards, specifically storing tuples of (s, a, r, s'), and then sample from the replay buffer when updating the Q values. Using a replay buffer may avoid catastrophic forgetting of the state and action spaces. Each experience tuple may be used for updating the network weights multiple times, which is an efficient use of the data. Random uniform sampling from the replay buffer reduces variance and the temporal correlations between episodes.

12.3.2 Neural Fitted Q-Iteration

In action value function approximation we minimized the MSE loss between the approximate action value function $Q_\theta(s, a)$ and the action value function $Q_\pi(s, a)$ with respect to a policy π. Q-learning converges to $Q_\star$ using a table lookup. Therefore we will minimize the MSE loss between the approximate action value function $Q_\theta(s, a)$ and the optimal action value function $Q_\star(s, a)$ by minimizing the loss:

$$J(\theta) = \frac{1}{2}\mathbb{E}_{(s,a)\sim\pi}\left[(Q_\star(s, a) - Q_\theta(s, a))^2\right] \tag{12.15}$$

Again, optimization by gradient descent involves updating θ in the direction of the negative gradient by:

$$\Delta\theta = \alpha(Q_\star(s, a) - Q_\theta(s, a))\nabla_\theta Q_\theta(s, a) \tag{12.16}$$

Since we don't know the optimal action value function we may approximate $Q_\star(s, a)$ by:

$$r + \gamma\max_{a'} Q_\theta(s', a') \approx Q_\star(s, a) \tag{12.17}$$

updating the network parameters by:

$$\Delta\theta = \alpha\left(r + \gamma\max_{a'} Q_\theta(s', a') - Q_\theta(s, a)\right)\nabla_\theta Q_\theta(s, a) \tag{12.18}$$

Just using a neural network to approximate the action value function in Q-learning may diverge since there are correlations between the samples and the target is non-stationary. Therefore, to remove the correlations between samples we may generate a dataset from the agent's experience. Neural fitted Q-iteration (NFQ; (Riedmiller, 2005)) and Batch-Q (Ernst et al., 2005) methods store batches of data in a buffer $\mathcal{D}$ and use supervised learning with a neural network to learn the action value function.

This results in the neural fitted Q-iteration pseudocode described in Algorithm 12.1.

12.3.3 Deep Q-Network

Deep Q-Network (DQN) (Mnih et al., 2015) builds upon fitted Q-learning by incorporating a replay buffer and a second target neural network, as described next.

Algorithm 12.1 Neural fitted Q-iteration (NFQ).

---

initialize $\mathcal{D} = \emptyset$ empty replay buffer
Q_θ network parameters θ with random values
select start state $s = s_0$
repeat:
   for k steps **do**:
      run ε-greedy policy based on Q_θ network
      collect transitions (s, a, r, s') into $\mathcal{D}^+$
   $\mathcal{D} = \mathcal{D} \cup \mathcal{D}^+$
   create supervised training set $\mathcal{S} = \{(x^{(i)}, y^{(i)})\}$
   for each $(s, a, r, s') \in \mathcal{D}$ **do**:
      $x^{(i)} = (s, a)$
      $y^{(i)} = r + \gamma \max_{a'} Q_\theta(s', a')$
   retrain Q network by supervised learning on $\mathcal{S}$

12.3.4   Target Network

In NFQ we set $y^{(i)} = r + \gamma \max_{a'} Q_\theta(s', a')$, whereas in DQN we set $y^{(i)} = r + \gamma \max_{a'} Q_{\theta^-}(s', a')$, where θ^- are parameters of a target network. At each iteration, DQN minimizes the MSE loss:

$$\mathcal{L}(\theta_i) = \mathbb{E}_{(s,a,r,s') \sim \mathcal{D}_i} \left[(y^{(i)} - Q_{\theta_i}(s, a))^2 \right] \tag{12.19}$$

$$= \mathbb{E}_{(s,a,r,s') \sim \mathcal{D}_i} \left[(r + \gamma \max_{a'} Q_{\theta^-}(s', a') - Q_{\theta_i}(s, a))^2 \right] \tag{12.20}$$

The parameters θ^- of the target network $Q_{\theta^-}(s', a')$ are frozen for multiple steps while the parameters θ_i of the online network $Q_{\theta_i}(s, a)$ are updated by SGD:

$$\nabla_{\theta_i} \mathcal{L}(\theta_i) = \mathbb{E}_{(s,a,r,s') \sim \mathcal{D}_i} \left[(y^{(i)} - Q_{\theta_i}(s, a)) \nabla_{\theta_i} Q_{\theta_i}(s, a) \right] \tag{12.21}$$

$$= \mathbb{E}_{(s,a,r,s') \sim \mathcal{D}_i} \left[(r + \gamma \max_{a'} Q_{\theta^-}(s', a') - Q_{\theta_i}(s, a)) \nabla_{\theta_i} Q_{\theta_i}(s, a) \right] \tag{12.22}$$

12.3.5   Algorithm

Deep Q-Network uses experience replay and a target network. States and rewards are generated by the environment and therefore the algorithm is model-free. The states and rewards are generated by an ε-greedy behavior policy that is different from the online policy learned and therefore the algorithm is off-policy. The DQN algorithm is described in pseudocode in Algorithm 12.2.

12.3.6   Prioritized Replay

Instead of sampling from the replay buffer uniformly, prioritized experience replay (Schaul et al., 2016) samples important transitions more frequently, which

---

Algorithm 12.2 Deep Q-network (DQN).

---

initialize $\mathcal{D} = \emptyset$ empty replay buffer
online Q_θ network with parameters θ with random values
target Q_{θ^-} network with parameters $\theta^- = \theta$
start state $s = s_0$
repeat:
    for each episode **do**:
        run ε-greedy policy based on Q_θ network
        collect transitions (s, a, r, s') into $\mathcal{D}$
    $q = Q_\theta(s, a)$
    take action a to get reward r and next state s'
    $Q_\theta(s, a) = Q_\theta(s, a) + \alpha \left(r + \gamma \max_{a'} Q_{\theta^-}(s', a') - Q_\theta(s, a) \right)$
    $\Delta = \max\{\Delta, \|q - Q_\theta(s, a)\|\}$
    $s = s'$
    update $\theta^- = \theta$ every number of episodes

---

results in more efficient learning. We store the experiences in a priority queue by their DQN error $|r + \gamma \max_{a'} Q_{\theta^-}(s', a') - Q_\theta(s, a)|$ and prioritize samples by $\frac{p_i^\alpha}{\sum_j p_j^\alpha}$ where p_i is proportional to the DQN error, and α controls the amount of prioritization such that setting $\alpha = 0$ results in no prioritization.

12.3.7 Double DQN

A problem with DQN is that the maximum operator uses the same values for both selecting and evaluating an action, which may result in a higher value. For example, given a state with ground truth $Q_\star(s, a) = 0$ the estimates of $Q(s, a)$ may be positive or negative such that $Q\left(s, \operatorname*{argmax}_a Q(s, a)\right) > 0$ whereas $Q_\star\left(s, \operatorname*{argmax}_a Q_\star(s, a)\right) = 0$. A solution, called double DQN (Van Hasselt et al., n.d.), replaces the DQN target:

$$y^{(i)} = r + \gamma \max_{a'} Q_{\theta^-}(s', a') \tag{12.23}$$

with:

$$y^{(i)} = r + \gamma Q_{\theta^-}\left(s', \operatorname*{argmax}_{a'} Q_{\theta_i}(s', a')\right) \tag{12.24}$$

such that the current Q-network with parameters θ_i are used to select actions whereas the previous Q-network with parameters θ^- are used to evaluate actions.

12.3.8 Dueling Networks

Dueling network architectures for deep reinforcement learning (Wang et al., 2016) use two separate neural networks. One network approximates the state value function $V(s)$, and a second network approximates the state–action advantage function $A_\pi(s, a)$. The advantage function is the difference between the state–action value function and state value function:

$$A_\pi(s, a) = Q_\pi(s, a) - V_\pi(s), \tag{12.25}$$

The advantage function is a relative measure of the importance of each action, comparing each action to the average action of the policy. The expectation of the advantage function over all actions is zero $\mathbb{E}_{a \sim \pi(s)}[A_\pi(s, a)] = 0$.

12.4   Policy-Based Methods

Stochastic policy functions may output a distribution over a discrete set of actions, or may be continuous such that $a \sim \mathcal{N}(\mu_\theta(s), \sigma_\theta^2(s))$. Policy-based methods work well in continuous spaces for learning stochastic policies.

An agent that interacts with the environment generates a trajectory τ of state, action and reward episodes $\tau = s_0, a_0, r_0, \ldots, s_t, a_t, r_t$. The return $g(\tau)$ of a trajectory τ is the discounted sum of rewards $g(\tau) = \sum_t \gamma^t r_t$. The goal or objective of policy-based methods $J(\pi_\theta)$ is to find a policy π_θ parameterized by θ that maximizes the expected return over all trajectories $\tau \sim \pi_\theta$ sampled from the policy. The objective $J(\pi_\theta)$ is defined by:

$$J(\pi_\theta) = \mathbb{E}_{\tau \sim \pi_\theta}[g(\tau)] = \mathbb{E}_{\tau \sim \pi_\theta}\left[\sum_t \gamma^t r_t\right] \tag{12.26}$$

and taking the maximum over θ results in:

$$\max_\theta J(\pi_\theta) = \max_\theta \mathbb{E}_{\tau \sim \pi_\theta}\left[\sum_t \gamma^t r_t\right] \tag{12.27}$$

We maximize $J(\pi_\theta)$ by gradient ascent on the policy parameters θ, updating the parameters by:

$$\theta = \theta + \alpha \nabla_\theta J(\pi_\theta) \tag{12.28}$$

where α is a learning rate and $\nabla_\theta J(\pi_\theta)$ is the policy gradient.

The expectation with respect to the trajectory τ of the return $g(\tau)$ is:

$$J(\pi_\theta) = \mathbb{E}_{\tau \sim \pi_\theta}[g(\tau)] = \sum_\tau p(\tau|\theta)g(\tau) \tag{12.29}$$

where $p(\tau|\theta)$ is the probability of a trajectory when following policy π parameterized by θ:

$$p(\tau|\theta) = \prod_t p(s_{t+1}|s_t, a_t)\pi_\theta(a_t|s_t) \tag{12.30}$$

and our goal is to compute the gradient of the expectation with respect to the parameters θ:

$$\nabla_\theta J(\pi_\theta) = \nabla_\theta \mathbb{E}_{\tau \sim \pi_\theta}[g(\tau)] \tag{12.31}$$

We assume that $p(\tau|\theta)$ is a differentiable probability density function that we may sample from.

12.4.1 Policy Gradient

By definition of expectation, taking the gradient of Equation 12.26, and then bringing in the gradient, the policy gradient is:

$$\nabla_\theta J(\pi_\theta) = \nabla_\theta \mathbb{E}_{\tau \sim \pi_\theta}[g(\tau)] = \nabla_\theta \int_\tau g(\tau)p(\tau|\theta)\, d\tau = \int_\tau \nabla_\theta g(\tau)p(\tau|\theta)\, d\tau \quad (12.32)$$

Using the chain rule we get:

$$\nabla_\theta J(\pi_\theta) = \int_\tau \nabla_\theta g(\tau)p(\tau|\theta)\, d\tau = \int_\tau \left(g(\tau)\nabla_\theta p(\tau|\theta) + p(\tau|\theta)\nabla_\theta g(\tau)\right) d\tau,$$
$$(12.33)$$

and setting $\nabla_\theta g(\tau) = 0$, and then multiplying by $\frac{p(\tau|\theta)}{p(\tau|\theta)}$ results in:

$$\nabla_\theta J(\pi_\theta) = \int_\tau g(\tau)\nabla_\theta p(\tau|\theta)\, d\tau = \int_\tau g(\tau)p(\tau|\theta)\frac{\nabla_\theta p(\tau|\theta)}{p(\tau|\theta)}\, d\tau \quad (12.34)$$

Since $\log(x)' = \frac{1}{x}$, we replace $\nabla_\theta \log p(\tau|\theta) = \frac{\nabla_\theta p(\tau|\theta)}{p(\tau|\theta)}$, and then by the definition of expectation we get:

$$\nabla_\theta J(\pi_\theta) = \int_\tau g(\tau)p(\tau|\theta)\nabla_\theta \log p(\tau|\theta)\, d\tau = \mathbb{E}_{\tau \sim \pi_\theta}\left[g(\tau)\nabla_\theta \log p(\tau|\theta)\right] \quad (12.35)$$

The probability $p(\tau|\theta)$ of a trajectory τ given parameters θ may be represented using the policy $\pi_\theta(a|s)$ and the transition probabilities of the environment $p(s'|s,a)$. In state s the agent takes an action a with probability based on the policy, and then the environment transitions the agent to state s' based on the state s and the agent's action a, and this process continues over all time steps; therefore:

$$p(\tau|\theta) = \prod_t p(s_{t+1}|s_t, a_t)\pi_\theta(a_t|s_t), \quad (12.36)$$

where the product is over time steps. Taking the logarithm allows us to turn the product into a sum:

$$\log p(\tau|\theta) = \sum_t \left(\log p(s_{t+1}|s_t, a_t) + \log \pi_\theta(a_t|s_t)\right) \quad (12.37)$$

Taking the gradient with respect to θ and noticing that the environment transition probabilities are independent of θ results in:

$$\nabla_\theta \log p(\tau|\theta) = \nabla_\theta \sum_t (\log p(s'|s, a) + \log \pi_\theta(a|s)) = \nabla_\theta \sum_t \log \pi_\theta(a|s) \quad (12.38)$$

Now, plugging Equation 12.38 into Equation 12.35 and then bringing the return $g(\tau)$ into the sum results in the expectation:

$$\nabla_\theta J(\pi_\theta) = \mathbb{E}_{\tau \sim \pi_\theta}\left[g(\tau)\nabla_\theta \log p(\tau|\theta)\right] = \mathbb{E}_{\tau \sim \pi_\theta}\left[\sum_t g_t(\tau)\nabla_\theta \log \pi_\theta(a_t|s_t)\right]$$
$$(12.39)$$

which is a differentiable function and may be estimated by a sample mean.

12.4.2   REINFORCE

The REINFORCE algorithm estimates the policy gradient numerically by MC sampling, using random samples to approximate the policy gradient. For each episode we sample a new trajectory τ. Next, for each time step t we compute the return g_t, and sum the policy gradients over all time steps to get $\nabla_\theta J(\pi_\theta)$. The contribution of each time step to the policy gradient is the return g_t times the score $\nabla_\theta \log \pi_\theta(a_t|s_t)$ which both depend on the current policy π_θ, and therefore REINFORCE is an on-policy algorithm. Finally, we update the network parameters θ using the policy gradient $\nabla_\theta J(\pi_\theta)$. The REINFORCE pseudocode is described in Algorithm 12.3.

Algorithm 12.3 REINFORCE.

    initialize learning rate α, parameters θ of policy network π_θ

    repeat for each episode:

        sample trajectory $\tau = s_0, a_0, r_0, \ldots, s_T, a_T, r_T$ following π_θ

        $\nabla_\theta J(\pi_\theta) = 0$

        for each time step $t = 0, \ldots, T$ **do**:

            $g_t(\tau) = \sum_{i=t}^{T} \gamma^{i-t} r_t$

            update policy gradient $\nabla_\theta J(\pi_\theta) = \nabla_\theta J(\pi_\theta) + g_t(\tau) \nabla_\theta \log \pi_\theta(a_t|s_t)$

        update policy parameters $\theta = \theta + \alpha \nabla_\theta J(\pi_\theta)$

12.4.3   Subtracting a Baseline

The estimate of the gradient, given by:

$$\hat{g} = \frac{1}{n} \sum_{i=1}^{n} \nabla_\theta \log p_\theta(\tau^{(i)}) g(\tau) \tag{12.40}$$

accurately approximates the true gradient for many samples $i = 1, \ldots, n$. To reduce the variance we may subtract a baseline b from the return such that:

$$\hat{g} = \frac{1}{n} \sum_{i=1}^{n} \nabla_\theta \log p_\theta(\tau^{(i)})(g(\tau) - b) \tag{12.41}$$

$$= \frac{1}{n} \sum_{i=1}^{n} \nabla_\theta \log p_\theta\left(\tau^{(i)}\right) g(\tau) - \frac{1}{n} \sum_{i=1}^{n} \nabla_\theta \log p_\theta(\tau^{(i)}) b \tag{12.42}$$

where the expectation of the term on the right is zero:

$$\sum_\tau p_\theta(\tau)\nabla_\theta \log p_\theta(\tau)b = \sum_\tau p_\theta(\tau)\frac{\nabla_\theta p_\theta(\tau)}{p_\theta(\tau)}b \qquad (12.43)$$

$$= b\sum_\tau \nabla_\theta p_\theta(\tau) = b\nabla_\theta \sum_\tau p_\theta(\tau) = 0 \qquad (12.44)$$

The baseline may be a constant $b = \mathbb{E}[g(\tau)]$, dependent on time $b_t = \sum_{i=1}^n g_t^i$, or a function of state $b(s) = V_\pi(s)$.

12.5 Actor–Critic Methods

Actor–critic methods combine policy-based methods with value-based methods by using both the policy gradient and value function. The actor is a policy network π_θ with parameters θ mapping states to action probabilities. The critic is a value network $V_\phi(s)$ or $Q_\phi(s, a)$ or $A_\phi(s, a)$ with parameters ϕ approximating a state value function or action value function or advantage function. Putting these two networks back-to-back, the critic provides a loss function for the actor and the gradients backpropagate from the critic to the actor.

In the policy-based REINFORCE algorithm we estimated the policy gradient $\nabla_\theta J(\pi_\theta)$ by randomly sampling one trajectory at a time. This trajectory results in a return that may be significantly different from returns of other trajectories and therefore the policy gradient has high variance. We may use value function approximation to reduce this variance. Specifically, in REINFORCE we estimate the policy gradient by:

$$\nabla_\theta J(\pi_\theta) = \mathbb{E}_{\tau \sim \pi_\theta}\left[\sum_t g_t(\tau)\nabla_\theta \log \pi_\theta(a_t|s_t)\right] \qquad (12.45)$$

To reduce variance we may replace the return $g(\tau)$ times the score $\nabla_\theta \log \pi_\theta(a_t|s_t)$, with a value function approximation $Q_\phi(s, a)$ times the score, which results in the Q-value actor–critic algorithm. Alternatively, we may use the estimate $V_\phi(s)$ as a baseline computing the action advantage function $A(s, a) = g(\tau) - V_\phi(s)$.

The actor–critic pseudocode is shown in Algorithm 12.4. We first initialize the policy parameters θ and critic parameters ϕ. Next, we repeatedly perform the following steps: (1) sample trajectory $\tau = \{s_t, a_t\}_t$ using the current policy π_θ; (2) fit a value function $V_\phi(s)$ using MC or TD learning and update critic parameters ϕ; (3) compute the action advantage function $A_\phi(s_t, a_t) = g_t - V_\phi(s_t)$; (4) approximate the policy gradient $\nabla_\theta J(\pi_\theta)$; and (5) update the policy parameters θ.

Algorithm 12.4 Actor–critic.

initialize learning rate α, actor policy parameters θ and critic parameters ϕ
for each episode **do**:
    sample trajectory $\tau = s_0, a_0, r_0, \ldots, s_T, a_T, r_T$ following π_θ
    fit value function $V_\phi(s)$ using MC or TD learning
    update critic parameters ϕ
    compute action advantage function $A_\phi(s_t, a_t)$
    approximate policy gradient $\nabla_\theta J(\pi_\theta)$
    update policy parameters $\theta = \theta + \alpha \nabla_\theta J(\pi_\theta)$
=0

12.5.1   Advantage Actor–Critic

Advantage actor–critic (A2C) methods (Mnih et al., 2016) estimate the policy gradient based on an approximation of the advantage function:

$$\nabla_\theta J(\pi_\theta) = \mathbb{E}_{\tau \sim \pi_\theta} \left[\sum_t \nabla_\theta \log \pi_\theta(a_t|s_t) \gamma^{t-1} A_\phi(s_t, a_t) \right] \tag{12.46}$$

where the advantage function is defined by:

$$A_\phi(s, a) = \mathbb{E}_{r,s'} \left[r + \gamma V_{\pi_\theta}(s') - V_{\pi_\theta}(s) \right] \tag{12.47}$$

The critic estimates $(r + \gamma V_{\pi_\theta}(s') - V_{\pi_\theta}(s))$ by the TD error $(r + \gamma V_\phi(s') - V_\phi(s))$ where V_ϕ is an estimate of the value function V_{π_θ}, and the gradient of the actor (Schulman et al., 2016) is estimated by:

$$\nabla_\theta J(\pi_\theta) = \mathbb{E}_{\tau \sim \pi_\theta} \left[\sum_t \nabla_\theta \log \pi_\theta(a_t|s_t) \gamma^{t-1} (r + \gamma V_\phi(s_{t+1}) - V_\phi(s_t)) \right] \tag{12.48}$$

by rolling out trajectories. Generalized advantage estimation (GAE) approximates the advantage by:

$$A_\theta(s, a) = \mathbb{E} \left[\sum_t (\lambda\gamma)^{t-1} (r_t + \gamma V_\phi(s_{t+1}) - V_\phi(s_t)) \right] \tag{12.49}$$

where λ trades-off bias and variance.

12.5.2   Asynchronous Advantage Actor–Critic

In order for neural network training to be stable, the gradient updates should not be correlated, which is why experience replay is used in DQN. An alternative that does not use a replay buffer is to parallelize the experiences using multiple threads, and therefore not be limited to off-policy methods and able to use data from the current policy to improve the policy. Asynchronous advantage actor–critic (A3C) (Mnih et al., 2016) explores different parts of the environment using multiple agents that contribute experiences in parallel. The agents may be trained using diverse policy gradient methods and may use diverse exploration values of ε. In A3C, each agent is reset to a global network which may have diverse policies or critics. Next, the agents interact with the environment, computing the value, policy loss, and gradients. Finally, the agents update the global network with the gradients, and the process is repeated. The gradient updates may be performed asynchronously, or applied synchronously by averaging the gradients from all agents and updating the global network parameters.

12.5.3 Importance Sampling

Given a function $f(x)$, computing the expectation $\mathbb{E}_{p(x)}[f(x)]$ from a distribution P may be difficult, and therefore importance sampling allows sampling from a different distribution Q:

$$\mathbb{E}_{P(x)}[f(x)] = \mathbb{E}_{Q(x)}\left[\frac{P(x)}{Q(x)}f(x)\right] \tag{12.50}$$

and reweighting the samples.

Importance sampling may be used to estimate the expected return of a stochastic policy by turning:

$$J(\pi_\theta) = \mathbb{E}_{\tau \sim \pi_\theta}[P(\tau|\theta)r(\tau)] \tag{12.51}$$

into a surrogate loss:

$$J(\pi_\theta) = \mathbb{E}_{\tau \sim \pi_{\theta'}}\left[\frac{P(\tau|\theta')}{P(\tau|\theta)}r(\tau)\right] \tag{12.52}$$

such that the gradient is:

$$\nabla_\theta J(\pi_\theta) = \mathbb{E}_{\tau \sim \pi_{\theta'}}\left[\frac{\nabla_{\theta'} P(\tau|\theta')}{P(\tau|\theta)}r(\tau)\right] \tag{12.53}$$

which allows collecting data from an old policy parameterized by θ and computing the direction in which the new policy parameterized by θ' should be improved. For $\theta' = \theta$ this reduces to policy gradient.

12.5.4 Surrogate Loss

Policy gradient reinforcement learning algorithms rely on updating a policy by modifying its parameters. If this modification results in a poor policy then this will result in poor samples from that policy so that altogether the reinforcement learning algorithm may become stuck with poor policies and subsequent samples. To overcome this problem we may add a constraint to the reinforcement learning objective that encourages the policy to improve while avoiding deteriorating performance. Trust region policy optimization (TRPO) and proximal policy optimization (PPO) add a constraint to the optimization objective, encouraging consecutive policies to improve monotonically. These algorithms differ in the implementation of this constraint: TRPO implements a second-order constraint, whereas PPO implements a simpler first-order constraint.

12.5.5   Natural Policy Gradient

In reinforcement learning the dataset collected depends on the policy and when using neural networks depends on the network parameters. Therefore, when optimizing policy-based methods, choosing a step size for updating the policy parameters is key. If the step size is too large then that will result in a bad policy, which in turn will result in collecting bad data under that policy from which the agent may not recover. If the step size is too small then that will result in not using the experience efficiently.

Taking gradient steps in the parameter space θ of a policy network π_θ is defined by:

$$\Delta\theta = \theta' - \theta = \alpha\nabla_\theta J(\pi_\theta) \tag{12.54}$$

Using the first-order Taylor expansion of the objective $J(\pi_{\theta'}) \approx J(\pi_\theta) + \nabla_\theta J(\pi_\theta)^T \Delta\theta$ we may constrain the gradient step using the term dependent on θ' by a threshold ε on the ℓ_2 norm of $\Delta\theta$:

$$\underset{\theta'}{\text{maximize}}\nabla_\theta J(\pi_\theta)^T \Delta\theta \quad \text{s.t.} \quad \frac{1}{2}\Delta\theta^T I\Delta\theta = \|\Delta\theta\|_2^2 \le \varepsilon \tag{12.55}$$

which has an analytic solution:

$$\Delta\theta = \sqrt{2\varepsilon}\frac{\nabla_\theta J(\pi_\theta)}{\|\nabla_\theta J(\pi_\theta)\|} \tag{12.56}$$

Directly constraining $\Delta\theta$ does not consider the corresponding distance in the policy space between $\pi_{\theta'}$ and π_θ. Therefore, we may constrain the distribution over policy trajectories based on the Kullback–Leibler (KL) divergence between the old distribution π_θ and new distribution $\pi_{\theta'}$ such that $D_{\mathrm{KL}}(\pi_\theta\|\pi_{\theta'}) \le \varepsilon$. The natural policy gradient (NPG) constrains the objective function to be subject to $\mathbb{E}\left[D_{\mathrm{KL}}(\pi_\theta(\cdot|s_t)\|\pi_{\theta'}(\cdot|s_t)\right] \le \varepsilon$. Computing the second-order Taylor expansion of the KL results in the objective:

$$\underset{\theta'}{\text{maximize}}\nabla_\theta J(\pi_\theta)^T \Delta\theta \quad \text{s.t.} \quad \frac{1}{2}\Delta\theta^T F_\theta\Delta\theta \le \varepsilon \tag{12.57}$$

where F_θ is the Fisher information matrix (Kakade, 2001), defined as:

$$F_\theta = \mathbb{E}_{\tau\sim\pi_\theta}\left[\nabla\log p(\tau|\theta)\nabla\log p(\tau|\theta)^T\right] \tag{12.58}$$

and has an analytic solution:

$$\Delta\theta = F_\theta^{-1}\nabla_\theta J(\pi_\theta)\sqrt{\frac{2\varepsilon}{\nabla_\theta J(\pi_\theta)^T F_\theta^{-1}\nabla_\theta J(\pi_\theta)}} \tag{12.59}$$

which results in the natural gradient (Amari, 1998) g_N such that $\Delta\theta = \alpha g_N$ and $\nabla_\theta J(\pi_\theta)$ and F_θ may be approximated by sampling trajectories using conjugate gradient descent (Kakade, 2001).

12.5.6 Trust Region Policy Optimization

The policy gradient approach uses a step size and gradient to update the policy parameters, which is a first-order approximation. In contrast, TRPO (Schulman et al., 2015) is a second-order method that uses the conjugate gradient to avoid computing the inverse of the Hessian. In supervised learning, using a step size which is too large may be corrected for in following iterations; however, in reinforcement learning it may result in a bad policy that will result in poor data collection and will be difficult to recover from. Therefore, selecting a good step size is important in policy gradient approaches. Using line search for selecting an optimal step size would require performing multiple rollouts for different step sizes, which is computationally expensive. Instead, we use the NPG approach to constrain the surrogate loss by the KL divergence between the new and old policy, which results in a second-order method:

$$\theta_\star = \underset{\theta}{\arg\max} \mathcal{L}(\pi_\theta, \pi_{\theta'}) \quad \text{s.t.} \quad D_{\text{KL}}(P(\tau; \theta) \| P(\tau; \theta')) \leq \varepsilon \tag{12.60}$$

where:

$$\mathcal{L}(\pi_\theta, \pi_{\theta'}) = \mathbb{E}\left[\frac{\pi_{\theta'}(a|s)}{\pi_\theta(a|s)} A_\theta(s, a)\right] \tag{12.61}$$

Plugging in

$$P(\tau; \theta) = P(s_0) \prod_t \pi_\theta(a_t|s_t) P(s_{t+1}|s_t, a_t) \tag{12.62}$$

to the KL divergence:

$$D_{\text{KL}}(P(\tau; \theta) \| P(\tau; \theta')) = \sum_\tau P(\tau; \theta) \log \frac{P(\tau; \theta')}{P(\tau; \theta)} \tag{12.63}$$

we get:

$$D_{\text{KL}}(P(\tau; \theta) \| P(\tau; \theta_t)) = \sum_\tau P(\tau; \theta) \log \frac{P(s_0) \prod_t \pi_{\theta'}(a_t|s_t) P(s_{t+1}|s_t, a_t)}{P(s_0) \prod_t \pi_\theta(a_t|s_t) P(s_{t+1}|s_t, a_t)} \tag{12.64}$$

and canceling out the dynamics yields:

$$D_{\text{KL}}(P(\tau; \theta) \| P(\tau; \theta')) = \sum_\tau P(\tau; \theta) \log \frac{\prod_t \pi_{\theta'}(a_t|s_t)}{\prod_t \pi_\theta(a_t|s_t)} \tag{12.65}$$

and sampling from the new policy:

$$D_{\text{KL}}(P(\tau; \theta) \| P(\tau; \theta')) \approx \frac{1}{n} \sum_{(a,s) \sim \pi_{\theta'}} \log \frac{\pi_{\theta'}(a|s)}{\pi_\theta(a|s)} \tag{12.66}$$

resulting in the constrained optimization or surrogate objective:

$$\underset{\theta}{\text{maximize}} \mathbb{E}\left[\frac{\pi_{\theta'}(a|s)}{\pi_\theta(a|s)} A_\theta(a, s)\right] \quad \text{s.t.} \quad \mathbb{E}\left[D_{\text{KL}}(\pi_\theta(\cdot|s) \| \pi_{\theta'}(\cdot|s))\right] \leq \varepsilon \tag{12.67}$$

A high-level TRPO pseudocode is described in Algorithm 12.5.

Algorithm 12.5 Trust region policy optimization.

---

initialize learning rate α, parameters θ of policy network π_θ
for each episode **do**:
    sample trajectory $\tau = s_0, a_0, r_0, \ldots, s_T, a_T, r_T$ following π_θ
    estimate advantage function at all time steps
    compute policy gradient g
    use conjugate gradient to compute $F^{-1}g$
    F is the Fisher information matrix
    perform line search on the surrogate loss and KL constraint

---

12.5.7   Proximal Policy Optimization

Trust region policy optimization requires solving a second-order optimization problem. Proximal policy optimization (Schulman et al., 2017) is based on TRPO; however, it is a first-order method that avoids computing the Hessian matrix or line search by clipping the surrogate objective. It clips the TRPO surrogate objective in Equation 12.67 around $1 \pm \delta$ and takes the minimum of the original and clipped objectives resulting in the PPO surrogate objective:

$$\underset{\theta}{\text{maximize}} \mathbb{E}\left[\min\left(\frac{\pi_{\theta'}(a|s)}{\pi_\theta(a|s)} A_\theta(s,a), \text{clip}\left(\frac{\pi_{\theta'}(a|s)}{\pi_\theta(a|s)}, 1-\delta, 1+\delta\right) A_\theta(s,a)\right)\right]$$

$$(12.68)$$

$$\text{s.t.} \quad \mathbb{E}\left[D_{\text{KL}}(\pi_\theta(\cdot|s)\|\pi_{\theta'}(\cdot|s))\right] \le \varepsilon \qquad (12.69)$$

A high-level PPO pseudocode is described in Algorithm 12.6.

Algorithm 12.6 Proximal policy optimization.

---

initialize policy π_θ parameters θ
for each episode **do**:
    run old policy π_θ
    compute advantage estimates A_θ
    optimize surrogate objective in Eq. 12.68 with respect to θ
    update policy parameters

12.5.8   Deep Deterministic Policy Gradient

Deep deterministic policy gradient (DDPG) Lillicrap et al. (2016) may be used in continuous action spaces and combines DQN with REINFORCE. It uses an action value critic $Q_\phi(s,a)$ parameterized by ϕ and a deterministic policy $\pi_\theta(s)$ parameterized by θ. In a similar fashion to actor–critic methods, we perform gradient descent to minimize the loss function with respect to the parameters ϕ of the critic and gradient ascent to find the parameters θ that maximize the actor objective. The critic loss is defined by:

$$\mathcal{L}(\phi) = \frac{1}{2}\mathbb{E}_{(s,a,r,s')}\left[(r + \gamma Q_\phi(s', \pi_\theta(s')) - Q_\phi(s,a))^2\right] \tag{12.70}$$

and the gradient as:

$$\nabla_\phi \mathcal{L}(\phi) = \mathbb{E}_{(s,a,r,s')}\left[(r + \gamma Q_\phi(s', \pi_\theta(s')) - Q_\phi(s,a))\right.$$
$$\left.(\gamma \nabla_\phi Q_\phi(s', \pi_\theta(s')) - \nabla_\phi Q_\phi(s,a))\right) \tag{12.71}$$

The actor loss is defined by:

$$J(\theta) = \mathbb{E}_s[Q_\phi(s, \pi_\theta(s))] \tag{12.72}$$

In practice DDPG uses experience replay to improve stability and adding Gaussian noise to the actions of the policy π_θ improves exploration. The DDPG pseudocode is described in Algorithm 12.7.

Algorithm 12.7 Deep deterministic policy gradient.

---

initialize policy parameters θ of an actor π_θ and action value parameters ϕ of a critic network Q_ϕ
for each episode **do**:
  given initial state s
  for each time step **do**:
    select action a according to policy network $\pi_\theta(a|s)$
    execute action a and observe reward r and next state s'
    store tuple (s, a, r, s') in buffer $\mathcal{D} = \mathcal{D} \cup (s, a, r, s')$
    sample mini-batch of tuples from buffer $(s^i, a^i, r^i, s'^i) \in \mathcal{D}$
    update critic by minimizing loss in Eq. 12.70 over sampled tuples
    update actor policy using sampled policy gradients
    update actor and critic network parameters

12.6 Model-Based Reinforcement Learning

Model-based reinforcement learning approaches may be divided into methods that are given the model, such as AlphaZero (Silver et al., 2018), and methods that learn the model, such as world models (Ha and Schmidhuber, 2018).

12.6.1 Monte Carlo Tree Search

Search trees have been used in board games such as chess (Arenz, 2012). A key problem with these search algorithms is that their branching factor grows exponentially with the number of units or pieces in the game. A simple forward search has exponential time complexity of $O((|\mathcal{S}||\mathcal{A}|)^d)$ for a state set $\mathcal{S}$, action set $\mathcal{A}$ and tree depth d. The set of states may be reduced by sampling a subset of states, though still has an exponential time complexity. Branch-and-bound uses a lower bound on the value function and an upper bound on the action value function to prune branches of the search tree, though still has an exponential time complexity in the worst case. In contrast, Monte Carlo tree search (MCTS) runs simulations from a given state and therefore has time complexity of $O(nd)$, where n is the number of simulations and d the tree depth.

The MCTS algorithm selects actions based on the upper confidence bound (UCB):

$$Q(s,a) + c\sqrt{\frac{\log N(s)}{N(s,a)}} \tag{12.73}$$

where $Q(s,a)$ is the action value function, c is an exploration constant, $N(s,a)$ is the number of action–state pairs, and $N(s) = \sum_a N(s,a)$ is the number of state visits.

Algorithm 12.8 Monte Carlo tree search.

---

initialize start state s, action value function $Q(s,a)$, number of state visits $N(s)$, number of state–action pairs $N(s,a)$
for each simulation **do**:
    sample trajectory τ following π
    update policy parameters $\theta = \theta + \alpha \nabla_\theta J(\pi_\theta)$

12.6.2   Expert Iteration and AlphaZero

Model-based reinforcement learning (Feinberg et al., 2018) has given rise to expert iteration (Anthony et al., 2017), which iterates between dual policies of a deep neural network and MCTS, applied to the game of Hex, followed by AlphaZero (Silver et al., 2017, 2018), which adds self-play, applied to chess, Shogi, and Go. The MCTS hyperparameters are tuned using Bayesian optimization (Chen, Huang, Wang, Antonoglou, Schrittwieser, Silver and de Freitas, 2018). Initially devised for two-player competitive board games such as Hex, Go, chess, and Shogi, expert iteration and AlphaZero have been extended to single-player games using a sequence model for automatic machine learning (Drori, Krishnamurthy, Rampin, Lourenco, One, Cho, Silva and Freire, 2018) in a system called AlphaD3M, which automatically synthesizes solution machine learning pipelines for a given dataset and task. The single-player extension has been used for solving the Rubik's Cube (McAleer et al., 2018) using a training set generated by scrambling the solution. These methods have also been generalized to continuous domains (Moerland et al., 2018) for control with applications in robotics and self-driving cars for good sequential decision-making.

Expert iteration, or AlphaZero, uses a neural network to output a policy approximation $\pi_\theta(a|s)$ and state value function $V_\phi(s)$ approximation for guiding

MCTS. Originally, two separate networks were used, which were merged into a single network $f_\theta(s)$ that receives a state representation as input s and computes a vector of probabilities $p_\theta = P(a|s)$ over all valid actions a and state values $V_{\theta(s)}$ over states s. AlphaZero learns these action probabilities and estimated values from games of self-play, which guide the search in future games. The parameters θ are updated by SGD on the following loss function:

$$\mathcal{L}(\theta) = -\pi \log p + (V - e)^2 + \alpha \|\theta\|^2 \tag{12.74}$$

maximizing cross entropy between policy vector p and search probabilities π, minimizing the MSE between predicted performance v and actual evaluation e, and regularizing the network parameters θ to avoid overfitting. AlphaZero uses MCTS which is a stochastic search using a UCB update rule of the action value function:

$$U(s, a) = Q(s, a) + cP(a|s)\frac{\sqrt{N(s)}}{1 + N(s, a)} \tag{12.75}$$

where $Q(s, a)$ is the expected reward for action a from state s, $N(s, a)$ is the number of times action a was taken from state s, $P(a|s)$ is the estimate of the neural network for the probability of taking action a from state s and c is a constant that determines the amount of exploration. At each step of the simulation, we find the action a and state s which maximize $U(s, a)$ and add the new state to the tree, if it does not exist, with the neural network estimates $P(a|s), V(s)$, or call the search recursively. Finally, the search terminates and action is taken.

12.6.3   World Models

World models (Ha and Schmidhuber, 2018) are an example of model-based reinforcement learning in which the model is not given. A world model is a neural game simulator that uses a variational autoencoder (VAE) and recurrent neural network (RNN) to take action in an environment. The VAE is trained on images from the environment, learning a low-dimension latent representation z of state s. The RNN is trained on the VAE latent vectors z_t through time, predicting $p(z_{t+1}|a_t, z_t, h_t)$. The latent vector z_t and RNN hidden vector h_t are fed into a neural network controller that outputs an action that affects the environment, resulting in a new image or state s_t that is fed back to the VAE. Since the world model also predicts the next latent space vector it may be used to synthesize images of the environment, creating a neural simulation of the environment. The world model may then be trained within that simulation; however, the agent needs to sample new data from the environment by exploration in order to learn new regions of the state and action spaces.

12.7   Imitation Learning

Rather than learning from rewards, imitation learning learns from example demonstrations provided by an expert. Behavioral cloning uses supervised learning to find parameters θ of a policy π_θ by computing the maximum log-likelihood:

$$\theta_\star = \underset{\theta}{\mathrm{argmax}} \sum_{(s,a)\in\mathcal{D}} \log \pi_\theta(a|s) \tag{12.76}$$

where $\mathcal{D}$ are expert demonstrations and the policy π_θ may be a neural network. A limitation of behavioral cloning is that it performs poorly near boundary states that are not well represented by the demonstrations, and once encountered may not recover from cascading errors.

Dataset aggregation (DAgger) (Ross et al., 2011) aims to solve the problem of cascading errors by augmenting the data with expert action labels of policy rollouts. DAgger iteratively aggregates additional correctly labeled data and retrains the policy. Stochastic mixing iterative learning (SMILe) (Ross and Bagnell, 2010) trains a new policy only on the augmented data and then mixes the new policy with the previous policies by having the agent act according to each new policy π_i with probability $p(p-1)^i$.

Generative adversarial imitation learning (GAIL) (Ho and Ermon, 2016) uses state and action examples $(s, a) \sim \mathcal{P}_{\mathrm{real}}$ from expert demonstrations as real samples for a discriminator in a GAN setting, as described in Chapter 9. The generator learns a policy $\pi_\theta(a|s)$ by generating actions from states, and these $(a, \pi_\theta(s))$ pairs are input to a discriminator. The discriminator's $\mathcal{D}_\phi$ goal is to distinguish between expert demonstration pairs $(s, a) \sim \mathcal{P}_{\mathrm{real}}$ and pairs synthesized by the generator $(s, \pi_\theta(s))$. The generator may learn a policy, such as TRPO, using the discriminator's feedback as a reward.

Inverse reinforcement learning explicitly derives a reward function from a set of expert demonstrations and uses that reward to learn an optimal policy. Maximum entropy inverse reinforcement learning (Ziebart et al., 2008) prefers a distribution over policy trajectories τ of the form:

$$P_\theta(\tau) = \frac{\exp\left(R_\theta(\tau)\right)}{\sum_\tau \exp\left(R_\theta(\tau)\right)} \tag{12.77}$$

where θ are the parameters of the reward function $R_\theta(\tau)$ and $P_\theta(\tau)$ is the probability of a trajectory τ. In a similar fashion to Equation 12.76 we may find the best parameter $\theta_\star$ by computing the maximum log-likelihood:

$$\theta_\star = \underset{\theta}{\mathrm{argmax}} \left(\sum_{\tau\in\mathcal{D}} \log P_\theta(\tau)\right) \tag{12.78}$$

where $\mathcal{D}$ is a set of expert demonstrations.

12.8 Exploration

Chapter 11 described ε-greedy, which is a simple approach that promotes exploration by taking a random action with probability ε and the greedy action with probability $1 - \varepsilon$. We may also promote exploration using only greedy actions by modifying the transition function and reward instead. In the model-based reinforcement learning method presented in Chapter 11 the transition function and reward are modeled based on the number of visited state–action pairs $N(s, a)$ and the number of visited (s, a, s') tuples $N(s, a,' s)$. To promote exploration of unknown parts of state space we may modify the transition function and reward by preferring states and actions that have not been highly explored (Brafman and Tennenholtz, 2002). The modified transition function $T(s, a, s')$ sets the next state s' to be the current state s if $N(s, a) < k$, and $\frac{N(s,a,s')+1}{N(s,a)+|S|}$ otherwise. Similarly, the modified reward $R(s, a)$ is set to a maximum value $R_{\max}$ if $N(s, a) < k$, and $\frac{\sum_{(s,a)} r(s,a)}{N(s,a)}$ otherwise.

12.8.1 Sparse Rewards

Environments with sparse rewards, such as the video games Montezuma's Revenge and Pitfall, posed a challenge to reinforcement learning. Early deep reinforcement learning methods such as DQN perform no better than random on these games. Go-Explore (Ecoffet et al., 2019) and First Return, then Explore (Ecoffet et al., 2021) are reinforcement learning algorithms that perform at super-human level on these sparse reward game environments as well as real-world pick-and-place tasks. Rather than adding randomness to a fraction of the actions using ε-greedy or by sampling from a stochastic policy, Go-Explore (1) stores promising states in a buffer, (2) first returns to these states and then (3) explores the environment.

12.9 Summary

This chapter covers deep reinforcement learning starting from function approximation. Deep model-free and policy-based methods are described in detail, followed by their combination resulting in actor–critic methods. Deep model-based methods that are given the model, including MCTS and AlphaZero, as well as world models that learn the model, are presented. Imitation learning learns a policy from expert demonstrations rather than from an explicit reward. Finally, we discuss methods that promote exploration and recent methods that work well in environments with sparse rewards.

Part V

Applications

13 Applications

13.1 Introduction

This chapter covers a dozen state-of-the-art applications of deep learning in a broad range of domains: autonomous vehicles, climate change and climate monitoring, computer vision, audio processing, voice swapping, music synthesis, natural language processing, automated machine learning, learning-to-learn courses, protein structure prediction and docking, combinatorial optimization, computational fluid dynamics, and plasma physics. Each deep learning application is briefly described, along with a visualization or system architecture.

13.2 Autonomous Vehicles

With the rise in self-driving cars, building systems that translate to high on-road performance is key to achieving deployable systems. End-to-end models have been used to predict steering commands using raw pixels from a front camera alone (Bojarski et al., 2016). The authors argue that such a system optimizes overall performance instead of optimizing human-selected intermediate criteria like lane detection, which does not necessarily guarantee overall performance. Other systems try to use a 360-degree view and a route planner as part of the inputs. These incorporate more information than simply a front camera view. This is closely related to the broader field of perception and the mental mapping of a route that a human inherently perceives. These are especially useful in complex driving scenarios like intersections and city environments (Hecker et al., 2018). Map information along with passenger comfort measures have also been shown to improve accuracy (Hecker et al., 2020). Related works have shown the power of neural memory networks to capture temporal information (Fernando et al., 2017), moving away from the paradigm of mapping a single frame to action and instead incorporating long-term dependencies, which are crucial in self-driving.

Rather than predicting a vehicle's trajectory directly, many systems first construct mid-level representations of the environment. These systems may rely on LiDAR (light detection and ranging) and ultrasonic sensors in addition to image data. Typical tasks include object detection for objects relevant to driving, such as pedestrians, traffic lights, and other vehicles, semantic segmentation to delineate the boundaries of the road as opposed to the sidewalk and other areas, and scene reconstruction, to generate 3D scenes given the input data (Shafiee et al., 2020). These representations are then used as input for predicting driving actions.

A multi-modal multi-task approach (Yang et al., 2018) was introduced to address the inherent relationship between a speed and steering angle prediction. They note that a human driver does not independently make decisions for each of these tasks. For example, to navigate an imminent obstacle, a human driver would choose a different steering angle depending on their current speed. A multi-task system addresses the inherent interconnectedness of predicting both of these actions. Another approach (Luo et al., 2018), tried to jointly reason about 3D detection, tracking, and forecasting, given data captured by a 3D sensor from a bird's eye view representation of the 3D world. Using this joint representation makes the model more robust to problems such as occlusion and sparse data.

ChauffeurNet (Bansal et al., 2018) uses imitation learning to learn driving patterns from 30 million examples. To augment the dataset, they introduce perturbations that may result in undesirable events like collisions, and they incorporate additional losses into their training loss to penalize these undesirable events. This leads to a more robust model. Rather than predicting speed and steering wheel angle directly, ChauffeurNet predicts trajectories, then uses a mid-level controller to translate the trajectories to vehicle-specific actions. This provides a system that can be used more generally in autonomous vehicles of various makes.

Several works study the trajectory prediction of all agents within an environment. Multiple futures prediction (Tang and Salakhutdinov, 2019) performs planning via computing a conditional probability density over the trajectories of other agents. Multiple future predictions for the agent under consideration and other agents are essential in considering the various possibilities at a given instant in time. Multi-head attention-based probabilistic vehicle trajectory prediction (Kim et al., 2020) also goes about multiple future predictions, using multi-head attention to attend to particular futures of specific agents more than the rest.

Predicting the trajectory of a vehicle in a multi-agent environment is a challenging and critical task for developing safe autonomous vehicles. State-of-the-art models rely on a representation of the environment from direct, low-level input from sensors on the vehicle or a mid-level representation of the scene, which is commonly a map annotated with agent positions. These approaches rely on a model to encode either camera data in the low-level case or annotated maps in the mid-level case. We show an example of both types of representations in Figure 13.1. As depicted in the top-left, mid-level representations are used to predict candidate trajectories, as shown in the top-right. Low-level representations such as camera data shown in the bottom-left can be used end-to-end to predict steering angles, as illustrated in the bottom right. To encode these input representations, rather than training a model from scratch, state-of-the-art

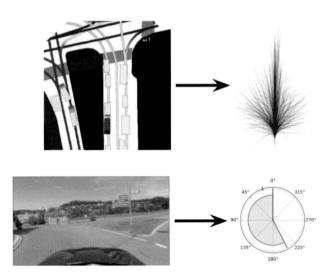

Figure 13.1 An example of input and output representations for mid-level (top) and low-level (bottom) representations. The mid-level input representation is an annotated map of the scene (top-left) in the top row, with boxes representing agent positions and colors representing semantic categories. The output (top-right) is a probability distribution over candidate trajectories. In the bottom row, a low-level representation uses the vehicle's front-facing camera image as input (bottom-left). It predicts the future steering wheel angle (bottom-right) and vehicle speed.

models rely on transfer learning with a model pre-trained on a supervised task (Messaoud et al., 2021; Phan-Minh et al., 2020), such as ImageNet classification. We perform an ablation study comparing transfer learning of supervised and semi-supervised models while keeping all other factors equal and showing that semi-supervised models perform better than supervised models for low-level and mid-level representations.

13.3   Climate Change and Climate Monitoring

13.3.1   Predicting Ocean Biogeochemistry

Ship-based ocean measurements, like those collected by the Global Ocean Ship-Based Hydrographic Investigations Program (GO-SHIP), as shown in Figure 13.2, provide valuable insight into ocean carbon uptake, biological processes, circulation, and climate variability. However, research cruises are expensive, sparse, and often seasonally biased due to weather conditions. The Biogeochemical-Argo (BGC-Argo) program aims to become the first globally comprehensive sensing array for ocean ecosystems and biogeochemistry. However, profiling floats are limited in the number of sensors they can support (Chai et al., 2020). Developing models that accurately predict additional features, such as nutrient ratios,

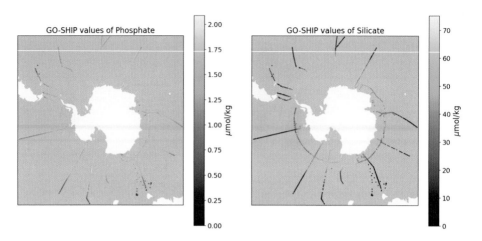

Figure 13.2 Transect locations of GO-SHIP oceanographic cruises in the Southern Ocean, between 03/08/2001-05/02/2019. Latitude $45 - 90°$ S, Longitude: $-180 - 180°$ E, with surface ($P < 10$ dbar) values of phosphate (left) and silicate (right) in μmol kg^{-1}.

from limited sensor data will broaden the applicability of BGC-Argo floats and allow us to better monitor and understand changes to the Earth's climate.

Previous work demonstrates the utility of applying machine learning to cruise and float data to estimate values of global N_2 fixation (Tang, Li and Cassar, 2019), particulate organic carbon (Sauzède et al., 2020), alkalinity, pH, and nitrate (Carter et al., 2018). Using Bayesian neural networks (Bittig et al., 2018) allows accounting for uncertainties around predicted values to estimate nutrient concentrations. Regression methods have also been applied for examining interannual variability in primary productivity (D'Alelio et al., 2020).

We draw on these methods to develop neural networks trained on cruise data to predict phosphate and silicate, essential nutrients controlling ocean productivity and biodiversity (Weber and Deutsch, 2010). This is important because these nutrients regulate biological processes that remove carbon from the surface ocean at an annual rate roughly equivalent to anthropogenic carbon emissions. The Southern Ocean is selected for developing and testing these models as it is an important global carbon sink and has the most extensive BGC-Argo float coverage at this time (Gruber et al., 2019).

We use GO-SHIP data (Carbon Hydrographic Data Office, 2021) in our training set to train our models. The dataset includes 42, 412 data points from Southern Ocean cruises for 2001–2019. We use GO-SHIP data for latitude, longitude, pressure, temperature, salinity, oxygen, and nitrate to predict phosphate and silicate. We restrict our data to latitudes below $45°$ S, remove rows with missing data and follow the World Ocean Circulation Experiment Hydrographic Program standards, and use quality control flags to down-select our data. We standardize the pressure, temperature, salinity, oxygen, and nitrate features. The position latitude and longitude data are projected to the WGS 84/Antarctic Polar Stereographic coordinate reference system. We do not include time dependency (month) because the initial evaluation of our linear regression indicates the low importance of seasonal variability in predicting silicate and phosphate variation. We randomly shuffle the feature-encoded data into a 9:1 ratio of training to test size and train our model using 10-fold cross-validation with mean squared error (MSE) loss. We select the model with the lowest validation loss to evaluate the testing error for both phosphate and silicate. To evaluate uncertainty when predicting silicate and phosphate from our data, we train (1) a one-layer feedforward, fully connected neural network with linear activation (equivalent computation to linear regression); and (2) a two-layer feed-forward, fully connected neural network with 64 hidden units, ReLU activation, and $p = 0.2$ dropout probability. We estimate uncertainty by sampling using dropout (Kendall and Gal, 2017), training the network using dropout, and then testing each example by running multiple forward passes with dropout weights.

We evaluate our network's performance by comparing our model's results of phosphate and silicate to the values predicted from an Earth system model (ESM). We use the Institut Pierre Simon Laplace Climate Model 5 (IPSL-CM5) (Climate Modeling Center, 2021) model results from a 10-year historical model run initialized in 2000 and a 30-year projection initialized in 2005. We take the monthly averaged surface values (59,088) of temperature, salinity, oxygen, nitrate, phosphate, and silicate at each location over the historical and predicted span of 35 years (2000–2035), apply our network model to these surface values (assuming surface pressure $= 5$ dbar), and compare our model results to the IPSL-CM5 values of phosphate and silicate. Next, we apply our network to test data from BGC-Argo float profiles in the Southern Ocean equipped with dissolved oxygen and nitrate sensors. There are 175 floats in the period 2000–2020, measuring 16,710 profiles that meet these criteria, and we only use data points where all input features are measured. We apply our network to 181,329 data points and run 100 dropout iterations to generate standard deviations for our estimates.

The results from our linear regression analysis revealed a more significant uncertainty in our estimated phosphate values than our silicate values. Additionally, the uncertainty of our silicate results is more uniform over our test data range. In contrast, the phosphate results have more significant uncertainty at lower values and lower uncertainty at higher ones. The uncertainties in our phosphate and silicate estimates are reduced with our two-layer neural network. The MSE also decreases substantially for phosphate (MSE linear: 0.019, MSE NN: 0.0031) and silicate (MSE linear: 240, MSE NN: 50). The most significant uncertainties for phosphate are at lower values, and for silicate, the most significant uncertainties are at higher silicate values. This could result from the differences in the distribution of these compounds in the water column. Phosphate has a more significant variance in the upper water column (where phosphate values are lowest) and lower variance at depth. In contrast, the variance of silicate is more uniform throughout the water column.

Neural networks for ESM data: We compared the ESM output values of phosphate and silicate to our neural network predicted values of phosphate and silicate from the ESM features. Our neural network under-predicts phosphate values across the Southern Ocean and under-predicts silicate values away from the Antarctic continent compared to the ESM values. However, our neural network is able to capture the spatial variations for both surface phosphate and silicate. These results suggest that our neural network model is able to capture processes modeled by the ESM. However, there are still discrepancies between these two model types. Based on these results, we believe our neural network has a high enough performance to apply to BGC-Argo data to estimate phosphate and silicate values from actual observations.

Neural networks for BGC-Argo data: Our neural network applied to BGC-Argo data predicts similar spatial patterns of phosphate and silicate to those measured by GO-SHIP and modeled by the ESM. However, a few float trajectories have noticeably different values from other floats in the region. While this could be due to local biogeochemical processes, it is likely due to sensor noise or drifts missed during quality control. The uncertainties estimated for phosphate are generally low and uniform throughout the region. In contrast, the uncertainty estimates for silicate present similar spatial patterns as the mean value estimates, with high uncertainties near the continent. This suggests a systematic error close to the continent, which could be attributed to ice dynamics causing higher variability in our features. These results suggest a relationship between latitude and silicate distributions.

Our neural network models are generally successful, demonstrating high potential for progress in this application. However, our proof-of-concept implementation leaves areas for improvement. We plan to improve our models by: (1) including a temporal component and using a spatial-temporal graph neural network (GNN) representation; (2) preserving the spatial relationships within the training data using a GNN; and (3) training the models on a subset of shallower GO-SHIP data to better compare our model output to the surface model results from the ESM.

13.3.2   Predicting Atlantic Multidecadal Variability

The Atlantic Multidecadal Variability (AMV, also known as the Atlantic Multidecadal Oscillation) is a basin-wide fluctuation of sea-surface temperatures (SST) in the North Atlantic with a periodicity of approximately 60–70 years. The AMV has broad societal impacts. The positive phase of AMV, for example, is associated with anomalously warm summers in northern Europe and hot, dry summers in southern Europe (Gao et al., 2019), and increased hurricane activity (Zhang and Delworth, 2006). These impacts highlight the importance of predicting extreme AMV states.

The AMV Index measures the state of AMV (Figure 13.3, bottom-right panel, solid black line), calculated by averaging SST anomalies over the entire North Atlantic basin. The maximum warming characterizes the spatial pattern of SST associated with a positive AMV phase in the subpolar North Atlantic and a secondary maximum in the tropical Atlantic with minimum warming (or slightly cooling) in between.

Notwithstanding the value of reliable prediction of AMV, progress in predicting AMV at decadal and longer timescales has been limited. Previous efforts have used computationally expensive numerical climate models to perform seasonal to multi-year predictions with lead times of up to 10 years. The subpolar region in the North Atlantic is one of the most predictable regions globally. It has been associated with the predictability of weather and climate in Europe and North America for up to 10 years. An outstanding question is whether such predictability can be extended to prediction lead times longer than ten years, particularly in a changing climate.

Our objective is to predict these extreme states of the AMV using various oceanic and atmospheric fields as predictors. This is formulated as a classification problem, where years above and below one standard deviation of the AMV index correspond to extremely warm and cold states. In this work, we use multiple machine learning models to explore the predictability of AMV up to 25 years in advance.

Machine learning techniques have been successfully applied to predict climate variability, especially the El Niño-Southern Oscillation (ENSO), an interannual mode of variability (each cycle is about 3–7 years) in the tropical Pacific Ocean. Several studies have used convolutional neural networks (CNNs) to predict ENSO 12–16 months ahead using various features (e.g. SST, ocean heat content, sea surface height; (Ham et al., 2019; Pal et al., 2020; Yan et al., 2020). This outperformed the typical 10-month lead time ENSO forecast with state-of-the-art, fully coupled dynamic models (Ham et al., 2019).

However, little work has been done to predict decadal and longer modes of variability, such as the AMV using ML. The biggest challenge is the lack of data. Widespread observational records for many variables are only available after the 1980s, limiting both the temporal extent and pool of predictors that may be used for training. For interannual modes such as ENSO, current observations can be easily partitioned into ample training and testing datasets with multiple ENSO cycles in each subset of data. However, a single AMV cycle requires 60–70 years, making it nearly impossible to train and test a neural network on observational data alone.

To remedy the lack of observational data for the AMV, we used the Community Earth System Model version 1.1 Large Ensemble Simulations.[1] This is a fully coupled global climate model that includes the best of current knowledge of physics and has shown good performance in simulating the periodicity and

----

[1] See https://ncar.github.io/cesm-lens-aws

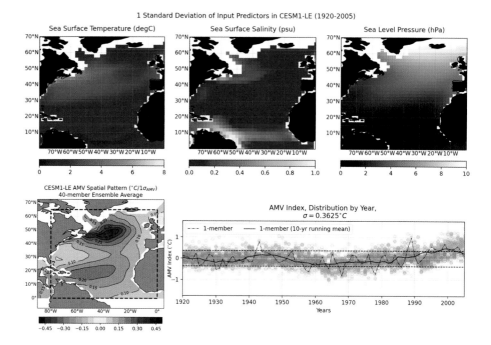

Figure 13.3 Variability of input predictors, which include SST, sea surface salinity, and sea-level pressure. The prediction objectives (lower right) are strongly positive (red) and negative (blue) AMV states outside one standard deviation of the AMV index (dashed black line). The AMV spatial pattern from the CESM simulation reasonably captures the enhanced warming at subpolar and tropical latitudes.

large-scale patterns of the AMV, comparable with observations (Wang et al., 2015). There are 40 ensemble runs, each between 1920 and 2005. The individual runs are slightly perturbed in their initial conditions and thus treated as 40 parallel worlds. The variability of the ocean and atmospheric dynamics in each run represents intrinsic natural variability in the climate system that we aim to predict and provides a diverse subsampling of AMV behavior.

Our objective is to train machine learning models to predict the AMV state (AMV+, AMV−, neutral). Each model is given two-dimensional maps of SST, sea surface salinity (SSS), and sea-level pressure (SLP) and is trained to predict the AMV state at a given lead time ahead, from 0-year (AMV at the current year) to 25-year lead (AMV 25 years into the future). We train models to make predictions every three years. This results in nine models for each architecture, each specialized in predicting AMV at a particular lead time. The procedure is repeated ten times for each lead time to account for sensitivity to the initialization of model weights and randomness during the training and testing process.

To quantify the success of each model, we define prediction skill as the accuracy of correct predictions for each AMV state. We compare the performance of the models against a persistence forecast, which is a standard baseline in the discipline. The persistence forecast is formulated so that the current state is used to predict the target state. The accuracy of this prediction method is evaluated for each lead time in the dataset. This study used a CNN residual neural network (specifically ResNet50), AutoML, and FractalDB.

13.3.3   Predicting Wildfire Growth

According to projections, the warmer, drier conditions caused in part by climate change will result in longer, more severe fire seasons as time goes on (Halofsky et al., 2020). When taken together, the direct and indirect costs of wildfires in the United States account for hundreds of billions of dollars in losses each year, with the state of California alone suffering some \$100 billion in costs after the 2017 fire season (Roman et al., 2020). Since the early 2000s, machine learning has been applied in a variety of wildfire applications (Jain et al., 2020). Of particular interest is predicting how quickly and in which direction wildfires grow within the ignition. With early detection of wildfires pivotal to fire response efforts and the inherent unpredictability of wildfire movements, predicting the behavior of a wildfire within the first few hours of ignition provides first responders with invaluable information (Sahin and Ince, 2009).

To this end, we compare the performance of baseline models in predicting the growth of wildfire fronts up to 30 hours after ignition using a dataset of simulated wildfires. Leveraging OpenAI's Codex model, we synthesize model variants from the baseline models, tune hyperparameters, and ensemble the human expert model variants and the Codex model variants. Among the human baseline models, a many-to-many convolutional long short-term memory (LSTM) model performs best. Our results demonstrate the power of leveraging program synthesis to generate variations of wildfire behavior prediction models automatically.

Within the subfield of fire behavior, researchers have predicted fire growth on various scales. At a high level, fire behavior has been formulated as a classification problem (Markuzon and Kolitz, 2009) using Bayesian networks, k-nearest neighbors, and random forests on satellite data to predict the future size of an incipient fire as a binary value. Several works have attempted to predict fire spread at the pixel level on a more granular scale. Convolutional LSTMs (ConvLSTMs; (Burge et al., 2020)) yield more accurate predictions than CNNs (Hodges and Lattimer, 2019). Convolutional LSTMs model the transient dynamics in the wildfire data. Reinforcement learning has been used for modeling forest wildfire dynamics from satellite images (Ganapathi Subramanian and Crowley, 2018). The relationships between forest fires and weather conditions from long-term observations have also been explored (Koutsias et al., 2013). In this work, we demonstrate a decrease in performance due to distribution shift when training on simulated data and testing on real-world data. Next, we compare a CNN, CNN-LSTM, and a ConvLSTM on a more complex dataset of simulated fires. Among these baseline models, ConvLSTM performs best. Finally, we demonstrate that a synthesized model outperforms these baselines.

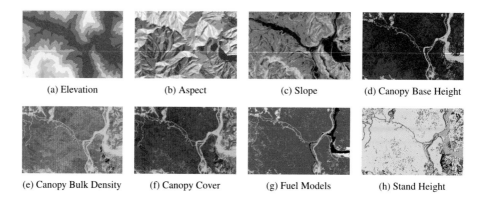

(a) Elevation (b) Aspect (c) Slope (d) Canopy Base Height

(e) Canopy Bulk Density (f) Canopy Cover (g) Fuel Models (h) Stand Height

Figure 13.4 Examples of input channels used in the FARSITE wildfire simulator. The domain in this figure is the Eel River area in California. These environmental features and FARSITE burn maps are used as input for our models.

The data used in this work is the output of the FARSITE wildfire simulator (Hodges and Lattimer, 2019), which is a burn map simulation of the fire growth. The FARSITE simulator uses images of topography, vegetation, precipitation, and wind as inputs. Sample simulator inputs are shown in Figure 13.4. The simulator uses Finney's method (Finney, 1998) of crown fire calculation to simulate the fire growth. Our training and testing set consists of 2,500 FARSITE simulations of randomly selected 50×50 km regions in the state of California with resolutions of 0.03 km of realistic landscape and vegetation and varying moisture content and wind. Each fire is simulated up to 48 hours with output burn maps at 1 km resolution (50×50 arrays) extracted every 6 hours. In addition to these burn maps, the input to our models also included 12 relevant down-sampled environmental variables, also represented by 50×50 arrays: a fuel model; 1-, 10-, and 100-hour moistures; live herbaceous and woody moistures; canopy cover, top height, and base height; east–west and north–south winds; and elevation. We note that we split the dataset such that we train on 1,804 images and test on 290 images for all models.

13.4 Computer Vision

13.4.1 Kinship Verification

The ability to recognize kinship between faces based only on images contributes to applications such as social media, forensics, reuniting families, and genealogy. However, these fields each possess unique datasets that are highly varied in terms of image quality, lighting conditions, pose, facial expression, and viewing angle, making creating an image-processing algorithm that works in general quite challenging. To address these issues, an annual automatic kinship recognition challenge *Recognizing Families in the Wild* (RFIW) releases a sizeable

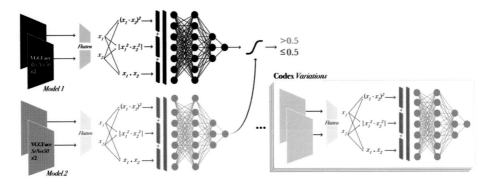

Figure 13.5 Kinship verification deep learning architecture: Multiple deep Siamese networks are used. A pair of images for verification are fed through a pre-trained convolutional backbone (He et al., 2016a; Hu et al., 2018). The backbones project the images into a latent feature space which are flattened and then combined by feature fusion (Yu et al., 2020). The result of the feature fusion is fed through a fully connected network in which the final layer is a single binary classification predicting kin or non-kin. Multiple Siamese networks written by both human experts and OpenAI Codex are ensembled.

multi-task dataset to aid the development of modern data-driven approaches for solving these critical visual kin-based problems (Robinson et al., 2016, 2021).

Deep learning models have been developed for kinship verification, which entails the binary classification of two pictures' relationships as kin or non-kin. The architecture shown in Figure 13.11 uses a variety of models written by both human experts and automatically by OpenAI Codex (Chen et al., 2021). The models are then ensembled to predict the confidence that a pair of face images are kin. Each model utilizes a Siamese convolutional backbone with pre-trained weights to encode one-dimensional embeddings of each image. Embeddings are combined by feature fusion (He et al., 2016a; Hu et al., 2018; Yu et al., 2020), and the fused encoding is fed through a series of fully connected layers in order to make a prediction. The network predictions of many models are ensembled before applying a threshold to obtain a binary classification.

13.4.2   Image-to-3D

Three-dimensional model construction from 2D images of objects is an active research area (Fu et al., 2021; Kniaz et al., 2020; Yu and Oh, 2022). Algorithms exist (Lim et al., 2013) for modeling the fine-pose of objects within captured 2D images and matching them to a set of 3D models. Generative adversarial network (GAN)-based approaches (Pan et al., 2021; Hu et al., 2021) for 3D reconstruction demonstrate high-quality outputs and have recently been extended to allow control over the output. Other approaches (Girdhar et al., 2016) develop vector representations of 3D objects that are predictable from 2D images and methods

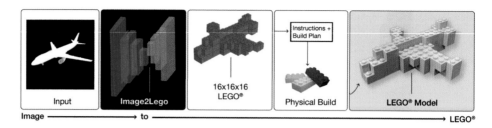

Figure 13.6 Our method takes an image as input and produces a voxelized 3D model, which is then converted to a LEGO® brick set. From the provided pieces and instructions, the LEGO® model can then be built in the real world; example shown at the right.

for automatic generation of 3D models through octree-based pruning (Stigeborn, 2018).

13.4.3 Image2LEGO®

For decades, LEGO® bricks have been a staple of entertainment for children and adults alike, offering the ability to construct anything one can imagine from simple building blocks. However, for all but the most exceptional LEGO® engineers, dreams quickly outgrow skills, and constructing the complex images around them becomes too great a challenge. LEGO® bricks have been assembled into intricate and fantastical structures in many cases, and simplifying constructing the more complex designs is essential to maintaining appeal for amateur builders and attracting a new generation of LEGO® enthusiasts. To make these creative possibilities accessible to all, we developed an end-to-end approach for producing LEGO®-type brick 3D models directly from 2D images. Our work has three sequential components: it (1) converts a 2D image to a latent representation; (2) decodes the latent representation to a 3D voxel model; and (3) applies an algorithm to transform the voxelized model to 3D LEGO® bricks. Our work represents the first complete approach that allows users to generate real LEGO® sets from 2D images in a single pipeline. A basic high-level demonstration of the entire Image2LEGO® pipeline is presented in Figure 13.6. A photograph of an airplane is converted to a 3D LEGO® model, and the corresponding instructions and brick parts list are used to construct a physical LEGO® airplane build. We tackle the issues specific to constructing high-resolution real 3D LEGO® models, such as color and hollow structures. We present a pipeline that combines creating a 3D model from a 2D image with an algorithm for mapping this 3D model to a set of LEGO®-compatible bricks to provide this new Image2LEGO® application and evaluate by examples and analysis to show how and when this pipeline works.

We focus on our novel approach for multi-class object-image-to-Lego construction. However, the same approach is extended to other creative applications by leveraging previous image-to-model work. For instance, generating LEGO® models from pictures of one's face is already an application of interest. However, current work is limited to the generation of 2D LEGO® mosaics from images, generated by the commercial product called LEGO® Mosaic Maker (Lego, 2020). However, we extend the Image2LEGO® pipeline to include the pre-trained Volumetric Regression Network (VRN) for single-image 3D reconstruction of faces (Jackson et al., 2017). In contrast to the 2D mosaic, our approach generates a 3D LEGO® face from a single 2D image. Moreover, other learned tools may be appended to the base pipeline to develop more innovative tools. For instance, by prepending the VRN with a sketch-to-face model (Chen et al., 2020), we develop a tool that directly converts an imagined drawing into a LEGO® model, offering nearly limitless creative possibilities. We demonstrate another extension, where we apply the Image2LEGO® pipeline with DALL-E (Ramesh, Pavlov, Goh, Gray, Voss, Radford, Chen and Sutskever, 2021; Ramesh et al., 2022) outputs to create a tool that automatically converts captions to LEGO® models.

The challenge of converting voxelized 3D models into LEGO® designs has been previously explored. Real-time conversion of surface meshes to voxels to LEGOs® (Silva et al., 2009) and methods for high-detail LEGO® representations of triangle mesh boundaries (Lambrecht, 2006) have been demonstrated. A gap has remained between 3D model generation from images and LEGO® generation from 3D models. Our work aims to bridge this gap by developing a complete Image2LEGO® pipeline, allowing anyone to create custom LEGO® models from 2D images.

The problem of LEGO® generation from images adds a goal to 3D model generation, namely that it is essential to have flexibility in the output resolution. Additionally, the latent space should have some flexibility to generate unseen structures from new input images. The former helps provide users with LEGO® designs of different scales and resolutions, to achieve better varying levels of difficulty, availability of material resources, and cognitive effort. For instance, small renditions of an object may be helpful as fine elements in a greater scene, while larger renditions may serve as independent LEGO® models. The latter feature of a generalizable latent space allows users to generate new LEGO® sets associated with newly captured images. This work represents the first effort to combine these approaches, using an octree-structured autoencoder in the image-to-model pipeline. We evaluate its ability to perform this task on new images in several examples.

13.4.4 Imaging through Scattering Media

In biological imaging, tissues act as scattering media that induce aberration and background noise in the captured image, where the true object is faded out. Retrieving the hidden object from the image thus becomes a challenging inverse problem in computational optics. Normally, the random scattering media properties are unknown and are difficult to characterize fully. Traditional techniques formulate this problem as an optimization based on a transmission matrix or forward operator, with a regularization term derived from the object prior knowledge: $\hat{x} = \underset{x}{\arg\min} \|y - Ax\|^2 + \lambda\Phi(x)$, where x is the unknown object with $\hat{x}$ being its estimation, and y is the observed image, A the forward matrix, and a regularization function $\Phi(x)$ with a weighting parameter λ. However, many practical imaging instances arise when such formulations and methods fail. The nonlinearity in the forward imaging process, especially under heavy light scattering conditions, means that learning from examples is an ideal solution due to the ability to handle nonlinearities.

Real-world applications of imaging through scattering media include (1) imaging through tissue with visible light, which allows for non-invasive sensing inside the body without exposure to excess radiation while potentially allowing for better functional imaging than standards today such as MRI; (2) privacy-preserving use cases, such as human–computer interaction systems, where the agent must observe the characteristics of the human, but the image of them is obscured to preserve their privacy. Thus, the agent is able to capture essential information without capturing identifying information; (3) sensing through dense fog for autonomous navigation (driving, flight, etc.) allows for safe movement in inclement weather; and (4) underwater imaging, where turbulence and particulate matter obscure the line of sight.

Instead of solving for data fidelity and regularizer by optimization, learning-based methods alternatively model the forward operator and regularizer simultaneously through known objects and images through random media. The first implementation of this approach (Horisaki et al., 2016) used support vector regression learning and successfully learned to reconstruct face objects. However, the fully connected two-layer architecture fails to effectively generalize from trained face objects to other non-facial object classes. A better network architecture is necessary for more generalizable learning and accurate performance. A U-Net was first proposed for biomedical image segmentation (Ronneberger et al., 2015). The skip-connection in the U-Net architecture enables its superiority in extracting image features over other CNN architectures.

Such a U-Net model has been applied to this problem (Li, Deng, Lee, Sinha and Barbastathis, 2018), taking a speckle pattern as input and using an encoder–decoder structure to generate high-resolution images. In order to account for the data sparsity that often accompanies computational imaging, the negative Pearson correlation coefficient (NPCC) is used (Li, Deng, Lee, Sinha and Barbastathis, 2018) rather than cross entropy as the neural network loss function. The resulting network, called IDiffNet, adapts to different scattering media for sparse inputs, with the NPCC used to learn sparsity as a strong prior in the ground-truth values. While IDifNet works well on training and testing data from the same database and distribution, it does not generalize well among different databases and suffers from overfitting (Li, Deng, Lee, Sinha and Barbastathis, 2018).

Similarly, a U-Net is used (Li, Xue and Tian, 2018) to map speckle patterns to two output images – the predicted object and background – for a set of different diffusers. Instead of implementing computational imagining as an inverse problem, recent work learns the statistical properties of speckle intensity patterns in a way that generalizes to various scattering media. Data augmentation may be used to increase the training set size, for example, by simulation (Wang, Wang, Wang, Li and Situ, 2019). In this work, we use a new experimental setup, using a digital micromirror device (DMD) instead of a spatial light modulator (SLM) as the pixelwise intensity object, resulting in speckles of 10 micrometers instead of 16 micrometers, as seen in previous work (Li, Xue and Tian, 2018). When testing on speckles from previously unseen objects through unseen diffusers (types of scattering media), neural networks trained on image sets with multiple diffusers perform better than ones trained on a single diffuser (Li, Xue and Tian, 2018).

An experimental setup is illustrated in Figure 13.7. Light from a laser source is first collimated and then illuminates onto a DMD (DLP LightCrafter 6500, pixel size 7.6 micrometers). The DMD, placed at a certain angle relative to the illumination beam, acts as a pixelwise intensity object. After modulation by the DMD, the beam passes through a thin glass diffuser (Thorlabs, 220 grits, DG10-220) and is scattered. A two-lens telescope imaging system then relays the resulting image onto a camera (FLIR, Grasshopper 3, pixel size 3.45 micrometers).

A two-channel network splits each input image into two tensors, one for the object and another for the background. A U-Net considers a single channel outputted through a sigmoid activation layer. This produces a clear reconstruction. Each convolutional layer is replaced with a dense block. The U-Net model is separated into an encoder and decoder. The encoder uses five layers, each consisting of 2D Convolution-ReLU-Dense Blocks followed by max-pooling, to reduce the lateral size of the image while increasing the number of tensors in the channel dimension. The convolutional kernel is size 3×3, and the dense kernel is 5×5. The decoder uses a similar series of operations joined by upsampling and concatenation in the channel dimension with the corresponding encoder layer. This re-expands the lateral image size and results in the number of channel-dimension tensors being one output image.

Each dense block consists of several subsequent convolutional blocks. This convolutional block series is repeated four times during encoding, while decoding has this series repeated only three times. The basic structure of a convolutional block consists of batch normalization, ReLU, convolutional layer, and conditional dropout with a probability of 0.5. The resulting feature maps from these subsequent convolutional blocks are concatenated in the channel dimension. The upsampling function consists of three layers: nearest-neighbor up-sampling, 2D convolution, and ReLU. The upsampling is used in the decoding part of the network, which is iteratively followed by concatenation with the previous dense block outputs in the channel dimension.

The network is trained using stochastic gradient descent (SGD) with momentum. During training, the batch is forward-propagated through the model, the

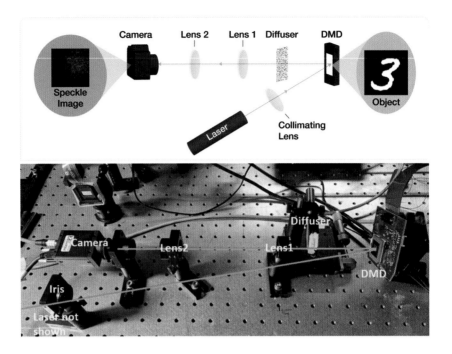

Figure 13.7 Experimental setup of the scattering media imaging system. Top: schematic of the optical configuration, with an example of a speckle pattern (right) that is mapped to the corresponding ground truth object (left). Bottom: the physical configuration corresponding to the schematic diagram.

loss is computed and backpropagated, the tracked gradients for the modules are zeroed, and the step function is applied to the optimizer. During evaluation, the model is validated using previously unseen validation data. The training loss and validation loss are computed for each epoch. Commonly used loss functions including MSE and mean absolute error (MAE) do not promote sparsity since they assume the underlying signals follow Gaussian and Laplace statistics, respectively. Considering the high sparsity in the MNIST database, we consider two more appropriate candidates for the loss function: the negative Pearson correlation coefficient (NPCC) and average binary cross entropy (BCE):

$$L_{\text{NPCC}} = -\frac{\sum_i (x - \tilde{x})(p - \tilde{p})}{\sqrt{\sum_i (x - \tilde{x})^2}\sqrt{\sum_i (p - \tilde{p})^2}} \tag{13.1}$$

$$L_{\text{BCE}} = -\frac{1}{2N} \sum_i (x \log(p) + (1 - x) \log(1 - p)) \tag{13.2}$$

where $\tilde{x}$ and $\tilde{p}$ are the average ground truth x and network output p, and i indexes each of the N pixels of the image.

13.4.5   Contrastive Language-Image Pre-training

Contrastive language-image pre-training (CLIP) (Radford et al., 2021) uses 400 million text–image pairs collected from the web to train a pair of encoders: one for text and another for images. CLIP is trained using a contrastive loss, encouraging the model to map similar images to similar text and different images to different text. A new image is first embedded, and then the model is used to find the most similar embedded text, performing zero-shot classification. The CLIP model is used in downstream tasks such as image captioning, image retrieval, and zero-shot classification.

13.5   Speech and Audio Processing

13.5.1   Audio Reverb Impulse Response Synthesis

Artificial Reverberation

Historically, recording studios built reverberant chambers with speakers and microphones to apply reverb to prerecorded audio directly within a physical space (Rettinger, 1957). Reverberation circuits, first proposed in the 1960s, use a network of filters and delay lines to mimic a reverberant space (Schroeder and Logan, 1961). Later, digital algorithmic approaches applied numerical methods to simulate similar effects. Conversely, convolution reverb relies on audio recordings of a space's response to a broadband stimulus, typically a noise burst or sine sweep. This results in a digital replica of a space's reverberant characteristics, which can then be applied to any audio signal (Anderegg et al., 2004).

Convolutional neural networks have been used for estimating late-reverberation statistics from images (Kon and Koike, 2019, 2020), though not to model the complete audio impulse response (IR) from an image. This work is based on the finding that experienced acoustic engineers readily estimate a space's IR or reverberant characteristics from an image (Kon and Koike, 2018). Room geometry has also been estimated from 360-degree images of four specific rooms (Remaggi et al., 2019) and used to create virtual acoustic environments that are compared with ground-truth recordings, though again, IRs are not directly synthesized from the images. A related line of work synthesizes spatial audio based on visual information (Li, Langlois and Zheng, 2018; Gao and Grauman, 2019; Kim et al., 2019). Prior work exists on the synthesis of IRs using RNNs (Sali and Lerch, 2020), autoencoders (Steinmetz, 2018), and GANs: IR-GAN (Ratnarajah et al., 2021) uses parameters from real-world IRs to generate new synthetic IRs, whereas our work synthesizes an audio IR directly from an image.

Recent work has shown that GANs are amenable to audio generation and can result in more globally coherent outputs (Donahue et al., 2018). GANSynth (Engel et al., 2019) generates an audio sequence in parallel via a progressive GAN architecture, allowing faster than real-time synthesis and higher efficiency than the autoregressive WaveNet (Oord et al., 2016) architecture. Unlike WaveNet, which uses time-distributed latent coding, GANSynth synthesizes an entire audio segment from a single latent vector. Given our need for a global structure, we create a fixed-length representation of our input and adapt our generator model from this approach.

Measured IRs have been approximated with shaped noise (Lee et al., 2010; Bryan, 2020). While room IRs exhibit statistical regularities (Traer and McDermott, 2016) that can be modeled stochastically, the domain of this modeling is time and frequency limited (Badeau, 2019) and may not reflect all characteristics of real-world recorded IRs. Simulating reverb with ray tracing is possible but prohibitively expensive for typical applications (Schissler and Manocha, 2016). By directly approximating measured audio IRs at the spectrogram level, our outputs are immediately applicable to tasks such as convolution reverb, which applies the reverberant characteristics of the IR to another audio signal.

Between visual and auditory domains, conditional GANs have been used for translating between images and audio samples of people playing instruments (Chen et al., 2017). The model employs a conditional GAN with an image encoder that takes images as input and produces spectrograms. A similar overall design, with an encoder, generator, and conditional discriminator (Mentzer et al., n.d.) has been applied to obtain state-of-the-art results on image compression, among many other applications. The generator and discriminator are deep convolutional networks based on the GANSynth (Engel et al., 2019) model (non-progressive variant), with modifications to suit our dataset, dimensions, and training procedure.

The encoder module combines image feature extraction with depth estimation to produce latent vectors from two-dimensional images of scenes. For depth estimation, we use the pre-trained Monodepth2 network (Godard et al., 2019), a monocular depth-estimation encoder–decoder network that produces a one-channel depth map corresponding to our input image. The main feature extractor is a ResNet50 (He et al., 2016a) pre-trained on Places365 (Zhou et al., n.d.), which takes a four-channel representation of our scene including the depth channel ($4 \times 224 \times 224$). We add randomly initialized weights to accommodate the additional input channel for the depth map. Since we are fine-tuning the entire network, albeit, at a low learning rate, we expect it will learn the relevant features during optimization. The architecture's components are shown in Figure 13.8.

13.5.2   Voice Swapping

Deep learning systems allow two speakers to swap their voices from any two unpaired sentences such that the result is indistinguishable from authentic voices and is performed in real-time on a laptop. Each of the two speakers pronounces any unpaired single short sentences into a microphone. The system plays the original voice recordings, then swaps the speakers' voices, playing the words pronounced by the first speaker with the second speaker's voice and vice-versa.

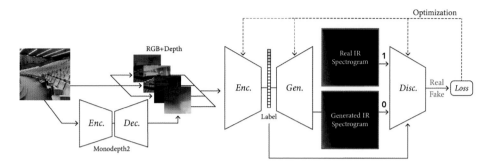

Figure 13.8 Image2Reverb deep learning system architecture. The system consists of an autoencoder and GAN networks. Left: An input image is converted into four channels: red, green, blue, and depth. The depth map is estimated by Monodepth2, a pre-trained encoder–decoder network. Right: The model employs a conditional GAN. An image feature encoder is given the RGB and depth images and produces part of the generator's latent vector, which is then concatenated with noise. The discriminator applies the image latent vector label at an intermediate stage via concatenation to make a conditional real/fake prediction, calculating loss and optimizing the encoder, generator, and discriminator.

The two input voices are processed in two distinct ways; one to extract the text of each speech and one to learn each speaker's unique voice profile. The text from speaker A's speech is extracted using state-of-the-art pre-trained voice-to-text models. Next, the audio from speaker B is passed through an encoder, which derives an embedding that describes speaker B's distinctive features. Next, we use the text extracted from speaker A and the embeddings of speaker B to synthesize the Mel spectrogram, which is fed into a vocoder to generate the final audio of speaker A's sentence with speaker B's voice. The exact process is mirrored with speakers' roles swapped. Our implementation leverages pre-trained neural networks – an encoder, synthesizer, and vocoder models – for a realistic real-time performance.

13.5.3 Explainable Musical Phrase Completion

Music is a multi-modal medium, having both rich spectro-temporal and symbolic representations and tactile and motor experiences. Thanks to this multi-modality, neuroscientists have observed that learning a new musical instrument has a profound impact on our cognitive ability (Zatorre et al., 2007). Music can be synthesized and completed using multiple modalities, most naturally using the audio spectrogram (Drori et al., 2004). While music consists of multiple note streams (Huang, Cooijmans, Roberts, Courville and Eck, 2017), this work uses a language model. We demonstrate the completion of partial musical sequences by deep neural networks, conditioned on the surrounding context, using explainable edit operations of insertion, deletion, and replacement of musical notes and shifting attention between notes. Related work, such as MidiNet (Yang, Chou and

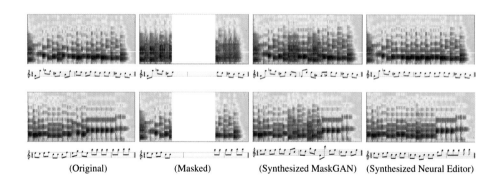

(Original)   (Masked)   (Synthesized MaskGAN)   (Synthesized Neural Editor)

Figure 13.9 Sample of musical phrases: (a) Spectrogram of original musical phrase with corresponding notes below; (b) musical phrase with missing time segment; (c) result of MaskGAN completion; and, (d) result of Neural Editor completion.

Yang, 2017), demonstrates a compelling ability to generate music using a conditional GAN. DeepBach uses a graphical model which successfully produces polyphonic rhythmic outputs using pseudo-Gibbs sampling (Hadjeres et al., 2017). Our approach of using Neural Editor (Guu et al., 2018) for music is unique in that it is explainable by design.

We collected 3,428 classical music compositions by eight of the top classical composers from a large digital music repository (Smythe, 2018). We tokenized the main instrument of each song to generate simple monophonic musical phrases. We split the dataset into 95% training and 5% test sets, using the same sets for the Neural Editor and MaskGAN models. We masked out the middle notes of equal length from the held-out test data, which we completed and synthesized by our models.

Figure 13.9 shows a sample of results of musical phrase completion using the MaskGAN and Neural Editor. The odd rows show spectrograms, and the even rows show their corresponding notes. Column (a) shows the input spectrogram, (b) shows the spectrogram of the music with missing notes, (c) shows the spectrogram completed by MaskGAN, and (d) shows the spectrogram completed by Neural Editor.

The Neural Editor model generates vector representations for discrete musical note tokens. The middle phrase of the note sequence is masked and is completed by our model. These masked vectors serve as inputs to a bi-directional LSTM model, where edit vectors apply various operations to musical notes: insert, delete, replace, move left, move right. The output is a novel synthesized musical sequence, and we train the model by maximizing the marginal likelihood. MaskGAN (Fedus et al., 2018) takes a unique approach to conditional sequence generation. When using MaskGAN to generate new notes to complete the masked out portion of a musical sequence, rather than being only autoregressive, MaskGAN conditions its output on the entire context.

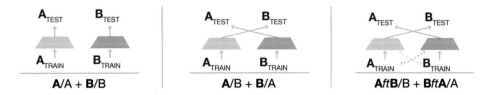

Figure 13.10 Our experimental setup. For a given pair of datasets (**A** and **B**), we perform three sets of train/test combinations. We train and test within the same distribution (**A**/A and **B**/B), between distributions (**A**/B and **B**/A), and between distributions with target fine-tuning (**A**ft**B**/B and **B**ft**A**/A).

13.6   Natural Language Processing

13.6.1   Quantifying and Alleviating Distribution Shifts in Foundation Models on Review Classification

The impact of distribution shifts on the accuracy of review classification when using Transformer models is significant. Consider the task of classifying customer reviews as fake or real based only on the review text. The extent of the drop in accuracy when the model tries to predict labels for distributions other than the one it was trained on is significant, not only because of the dearth of labeled datasets but also to gain insight into the information encoded by the Transformer embeddings and what steps may be taken to make their decisions more robust to possible shifts. The extent of the degradation in accuracy depends primarily on the independent variable across which the shift is created. We use the available metadata to narrow down four independent variables that give us balanced training and testing dataset splits while differing with the chosen variable. We train and test across all four permutations of splits for each of these. The distribution shifts investigated are: (1) *Industry Type* – hotel and restaurant reviews; (2) *Time* – old (pre-2014) and new (post-2014) reviews; (3) *Product Type* – Japanese and Italian restaurant reviews; and (4) *Sentiment* – positive and negative reviews.

Since one of our goals is to gain insights into Transformer model selection for tasks that require robustness across distribution shifts, we use three popular constructs for Transformers: encoder-only BERT (bidirectional encoder representations from Transformers) models, an encoder and decoder T5 model, and the Jurassic-I model with few-shot training. Subsequently, to address the problem of accuracy degradation due to distribution shifts, we suggest and report results from our solution of first training on the known distribution, then freezing weights for all but the final layer in the model, and fine-tuning weights for this final layer with a much smaller subset of the new distribution (100–300 review text samples compared to the previous 10,000 samples) to allow the model a chance at using the generalizable patterns it saw in the first distribution, while also enabling it to create distribution-specific insights for the new distribution.

Detecting fake reviews is a well-known task, the economic implications of which have been analyzed thoroughly in previous work (He et al., 2020), but with the growth of the industry for hiring and selling fake reviews, detecting fake reviews at scale has become a trade of its own and one particularly suited for the use of natural language processing (Ren and Ji, 2017). We build on the same motivation by combining this natural language processing task of review classification with methodology partly based on existing work outside of natural language processing (Koh et al., 2021) that sets up structures for analyzing implications of distribution shifts and creating insights for model selection and red flags in model training. Moreover, the architecture for our BERT instances is inspired by previous work (Kennedy et al., 2019) that created BERT models for review datasets. We build on previous work by using a richer dataset, testing three sizes of BERT, a T5 model, and then, most importantly, investigating and interpreting the performance of these models on distribution shifts. We also take inspiration from two notable works (Sun et al., 2017; Arjovsky et al., 2019) to suggest and report results from a solution of fine-tuning the model based on a small subset of the distribution-shifted data.

We use the methodology shown in Figure 13.10, which is partly based on previous work (Koh et al., 2021) on distribution shifts. (1) We begin by standardizing the review texts to make them compliant with the pre-trained Transformer models' expected input, ensuring all steps are applied to any other source's review texts. (2) We fine-tune our pre-trained Transformer models, evaluating the performance of the models on an out-of-sample test set in the same distribution to ascertain how well the model does when it sees reviews similar to the ones it was trained on. This gives us baseline benchmarks (upper bounds) to assess our distribution shift metrics. We make sure to achieve state-of-the-art performance in this problem space by employing Transformer models that were previously shown to be most successful with the task. (3) For each of the distribution shifts above, we train and test within the same distribution (e.g., train and test both on pre-2014 reviews), as well as train and test across the distribution shifts (e.g., train on pre-2014 reviews and test on post-2014 reviews). We do so for all the different permutations for these shifts – employing BERT (three size instances), T5, and Jurassic-I (with few-shot learning). (4) Lastly, we use the created models that were trained on one distribution, freeze the weights for all but the last layer, and fine-tune this layer based on a small subset of 100–300 review text samples from the new distribution. We do this for each split that was explored in the previous step, employing only the BERT and T5 instances to report this method as a solution to the degradation.

We use two labeled datasets: the first is for restaurant reviews from Yelp (Rayana and Akoglu, 2015) and the second is for hotel reviews (Ott et al., 2013), which combines internet sources like Expedia, Hotels.com, Orbitz, Priceline, and Tri-pAdvisor. Both datasets have the review text, fake/actual labels, and metadata. The metadata was used to find the independent variables along which we could split the data to create distribution shifts. Since our goal is to look at the general-

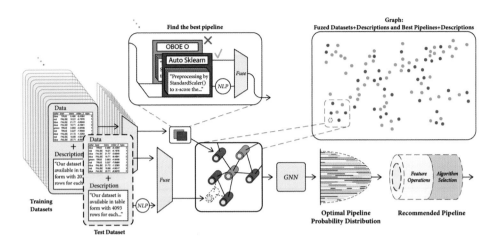

Figure 13.11 Overview of our method. We leverage dataset descriptions and other AutoML methods to provide zero-shot ML pipeline selection.

izability of the models, we create and their translations to a different distribution (e.g., from various sources), we decided to limit our input features to standardized review text only. We chose these datasets to work in conjunction because they are both collections of consumer reviews but are different in that the customers are restaurant clients in one and hotel clients in the other. We found these datasets to be common enough to cross validate transfer learning and, at the same time, different enough to create an interesting distribution shift.

13.7 Automated Machine Learning

A data scientist facing a challenging new supervised learning task does not generally invent a new algorithm. Instead, they consider what they know about the dataset and which algorithms have worked well for similar datasets. Automated machine learning (AutoML) seeks to automate such tasks, enabling the widespread and accessible use of machine learning by non-experts. A significant challenge in the field is to develop fast, efficient algorithms to accelerate machine learning applications (Kokiopoulou et al., 2019).

This work develops automated solutions that exploit human expertise to learn which datasets are similar and which algorithms perform best. We use a transformer-based language model (Vaswani et al., 2017) to process text descriptions of datasets and algorithms and a feature extractor (BYU-DML, 2019) to represent the data itself. Our approach fuses each of these representations, representing each dataset as a node in a graph of datasets. We train our model on other existing AutoML system solutions, specifically: AutoSklearn (Feurer et al., 2015) and OBOE (Yang, Akimoto, Kim and Udell, 2019). By leveraging these existing systems and openly accessible datasets, we achieve state-of-the-art results using multiple approaches across various classification problems.

To predict a machine learning pipeline, a simple idea is to use a pipeline that performed well on the same task and similar datasets; however, what constitutes a similar dataset? The success of an AutoML system often hinges on this question. Different frameworks have different answers: for example, AutoSklearn (Feurer et al., 2015) computes a set of meta-features, that is, features describing the data features, for each dataset, while OBOE (Yang, Akimoto, Kim and Udell, 2019) uses the performance of a few fast, informative models to compute latent features. More generally, for any supervised learning task, one can view the recommended algorithms generated by any AutoML system as a vector describing that task. This work is the first to use the information that a human would check first: a summary description of the dataset and algorithms, written in free text. These dataset features induce a metric structure on the space of datasets. Under an ideal metric, a model that performs well on one dataset would also perform well on nearby datasets. The methods we develop in this work show how to learn such a metric using the recommendations of an AutoML framework together with the dataset description. We provide a new zero-shot AutoML method that predicts accurate machine learning pipelines for an unseen dataset and classification task in real-time.

Bringing techniques from natural language processing to AutoML, we specifically use a large-scale Transformer model to extract information from the description of both the datasets and algorithms. This allows us to access large amounts of relevant information that existing AutoML systems are typically not privy to. These embeddings of dataset and pipeline descriptions are fused with data meta-features to build a graph where each dataset is a single node. This graph is then the input to a GNN.

Our real-time AutoML method predicts a pipeline with good performance within milliseconds given a new dataset. The running time of this predicted pipeline is typically up to one second, mainly for hyperparameter tuning. The accuracy of our method is competitive with state-of-the-art AutoML methods that are given minutes, thus, reducing computation time by orders of magnitude while improving performance.

Generally, GNNs are used for three main tasks: (1) node prediction, (2) link prediction, and (3) sub-graph or entire graph property prediction. In this work, we use a GNN for node prediction, predicting the best machine learning pipeline for an unseen dataset. Specifically, we use a graph attention network (GAT) (Veličković et al., 2018) with neighborhood aggregation, in which an attention function adaptively controls the contribution of neighbors. An advantage of using a GNN in our use case is that data, metadata, and algorithm information are shared between datasets (graph nodes) by messages passed between the graph nodes. In addition, GNNs generalize well to new unknown datasets using their aggregated weights learned during training, which are shared with the test dataset during testing. Beyond just a single new dataset, GNNs can generalize further to an entirely new set of datasets.

Solutions from existing AutoML systems are used to train a new AutoML model. Our flexible architecture can be extended to use pipeline recommendations from other AutoML systems to improve performance further. AutoML is an emerging field of machine learning with the potential to transform the practice of data science by automatically choosing a model to fit the data best. Several comprehensive surveys of the field are available (He et al., 2021; Zöller and Huber, 2021). The most straightforward approach to AutoML considers each dataset in isolation and asks how to choose the best hyperparameter settings for a given algorithm. While the most popular method is still grid search, other more efficient approaches include Bayesian optimization (Snoek et al., 2012) and random search (Solis and Wets, 1981). Recommender systems learn, often exhaustively, which algorithms and hyperparameter settings perform best for a training set of datasets and use this information to select better algorithms on a test set without exhaustive search. This approach reduces the time required to find a good model. An example is OBOE (Yang, Akimoto, Kim and Udell, 2019) and TensorOBOE (Yang et al., 2020), which fit a low-rank model to learn the low-dimensional representations for the models or pipelines and datasets that best predict the cross-validated errors, among all bilinear models. To find promising models for a new dataset, OBOE runs a set of fast but informative algorithms on the new dataset. It uses their cross-validated errors to infer the feature vector for the new dataset. A related approach (Fusi et al., 2018) using probabilistic matrix factorization powers Microsoft Azure's AutoML service (Mukunthu, 2019). Auto-tuned models (Swearingen et al., 2017) represent the search space as a tree with nodes being algorithms or hyperparameters and searches for the best branch using a multi-armed bandit. AlphaD3M (Drori, Krishnamurthy, Rampin, Lourenco, One, Cho, Silva and Freire, 2018; Drori et al., 2019) formulates AutoML as a single-player game. The system uses reinforcement learning with self-play and a pre-trained model, which generalizes from many different datasets and similar tasks. TPOT (Olson and Moore, 2016) and Autostacker (Chen, Wu, Mo, Chattopadhyay and Lipson, 2018) use genetic programming to choose both hyperparameter settings and the topology of a machine learning pipeline. TPOT represents pipelines as trees, whereas Autostacker represents them as layers.

AutoSklearn (Feurer et al., 2015) chooses a model for a new dataset by first computing data meta-features to find nearest-neighbor datasets. The best-performing methods on the neighbors are refined by Bayesian optimization and used to form an ensemble. End-to-end learning of machine learning pipelines can be performed using differentiable primitives (Milutinovic et al., 2017) forming a directed acyclic graph. One major factor in the performance of an AutoML system is the base set of algorithms it can use to compose more complex pipelines. For a fair comparison, in our numerical experiments, we compare our proposed methods only to other AutoML systems that use Scikit-learn (Pedregosa et al., 2011) primitives.

13.8   Education

13.8.1   Learning-to-Learn STEM Courses

Can a machine learn university-level STEM courses? The answer is a resounding yes (Drori et al., n.d.; Tang et al., 2022). There is a common misconception that neural networks cannot solve STEM courses at a university level (Choi, 2021). Recent progress in solving machine learning problems (Tran et al., 2021) uses Transformers pre-trained on code, and GNNs achieve super-human performance. However, those systems handle only numeric outputs, take a week of curation and training for one specific course, overfit the course, and do not scale up to multiple courses.

We automatically solve, explain, and generate university-level course problems from multiple STEM courses (at MIT, Harvard, and Columbia) for the first time. We curate a new dataset of course questions and answers across a dozen departments: Aeronautics and Astronautics, Chemical Engineering, Chemistry, Computer Science, Economics, Electrical Engineering, Materials Science, Mathematics, Mechanical Engineering, Nuclear Science, Physics, and Statistics. The courses, their departments, and their universities are shown in Table 13.1.

In order to test the quality of our machine-generated questions, we generate new questions and use them in a Columbia University course, and perform A/B tests demonstrating that these machine-generated questions are indistinguishable from human-written questions and that machine-generated explanations are as useful as human-written explanations, again for the first time. Our approach consists of the following steps: (1) given course questions, we automatically generate programs by program synthesis and few-shot learning using a Transformer model, OpenAI Codex (Chen et al., 2021), pre-trained on text and fine-tuned on code; (2) execute the programs to obtain and evaluate the answers; (3) automatically explain the correct solutions using Codex; (4) automatically generate new questions that are qualitatively indistinguishable from human-written questions. Our approach handles multiple output modalities, including numbers, text, and visual outputs. We verify that we do not overfit by solving an entirely new course not available online. This work is a significant step forward in applying machine learning to education, automating a considerable part of the work involved in teaching. Our approach allows the personalization of questions based on difficulty level and student backgrounds. It is the first scalable solution, scaling up to a broad range of courses across the schools of engineering and science.

The generative aspect of OpenAI's Codex also gives us the ability to generate new questions appropriate for developing new course content. We introduce these newly generated questions into a Columbia University course and demonstrate by an A/B test that the quality of these questions is on par with human-written questions, again for the first time.

This work is a significant step forward in applying machine learning to education, automating a considerable part of the work involved in teaching. Our

Table 13.1 University STEM courses: we curate, solve, explain, and generate new questions for each course.

ID	Uni.	Department	Course	Number
1	MIT	Aeronautics and Astronautics	Unified Engineering 1-4	16.01-4
2	MIT	Aeronautics and Astronautics	Estimation & Control of Aerospace Systems	16.30
3	MIT	Aeronautics and Astronautics	Intro to Propulsion Systems	16.50
4	MIT	Materials Science & Eng.	Fundamentals of Materials Science	3.012
5	MIT	Materials Science & Eng.	Math for Materials Scientists & Engineers	3.016
6	MIT	Materials Science & Eng.	Introduction to Solid-State Chemistry	3.091
7	MIT	Chemical Engineering	Chemical and Biological Reaction Eng.	10.37
8	MIT	Chemistry	Principles of Chemical Science	5.111
9	MIT	IDSS	Statistical Thinking & Data Analysis	IDS.013(J)
10	MIT	EECS	Signal Processing	6.003
11	MIT	EECS	Introduction to Machine Learning	6.036
12	MIT	EECS	Mathematics for Computer Science	6.042
13	MIT	Physics	Introduction to Astronomy	8.282
14	MIT	Nuclear Science & Engineering	Intro to Nuclear Eng. & Ionizing Radiation	22.01
15	MIT	Economics	Principles of Microeconomics	14.01
16	MIT	Mechanical Engineering	Hydrodynamics	2.016
17	MIT	Mechanical Engineering	Nonlinear Dynamics I: Chaos	2.050J
18	MIT	Mechanical Engineering	Information & Entropy	2.110J
19	MIT	Mechanical Engineering	Marine Power and Propulsion	2.611
20	MIT	Mathematics	Single Variable Calculus	18.01
21	MIT	Mathematics	Multi-variable Calculus	18.02
22	MIT	Mathematics	Differential Equations	18.03
23	MIT	Mathematics	Introduction to Probability and Statistics	18.05
24	MIT	Mathematics	Linear Algebra	18.06
25	MIT	Mathematics	Theory of Numbers	18.781
26	Harvard	Statistics	Probability	STATS110
27	Columbia	Computer Science	Computational Linear Algebra	COMS3251

approach allows the personalization of questions based on difficulty level and student backgrounds and scales up to multiple courses across a broad range of STEM topics.

As a first example, we solve MIT's Linear Algebra 18.06 and Columbia University's Computational Linear Algebra COMS3251 courses with perfect accuracy by interactive program synthesis. This surprisingly strong result is achieved by turning the course questions into programming tasks and then running the programs to produce the correct answers. We use OpenAI Codex with zero-shot learning to synthesize code from questions without providing any examples in the prompts. We quantify the difference between the original question text and the transformed question text that yields a correct answer. Since none of the COMS3251 questions are available online, the model is not overfitting. We interactively work with Codex to produce both the correct result and visually good plots, as shown in Figure 13.12. We place the question in context by augmenting the question with definitions and information required for solving the question, then rephrase and simplify.

Finally, we automatically generate new questions given a few sample questions that may be used as new course content.

As a second example, we solve university-level probability and statistics ques-

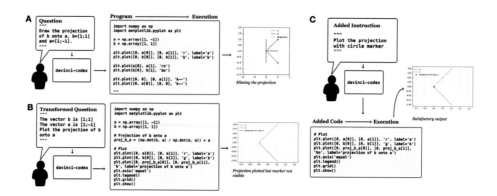

Figure 13.12 Interactive workflow: (a) We begin with the original question. Codex generates a program, which is executed. The result is missing the projection. (b) We transform the question, and Codex generates a program again to get the correct answer, though the zero projection vector does not appear on the plot. (c) An additional task to plot the projection vector with a marker so that it is visible results in Codex generating modified code which is executed to yield a correct answer and visually pleasing result.

tions by program synthesis using OpenAI's Codex. We transform course problems from MIT's 18.05 Introduction to Probability and Statistics and Harvard's STAT110 Probability into programming tasks. We then execute the generated code to get a solution. Since these course questions are grounded in probability, we often aim to have Codex generate probabilistic programs that simulate many probabilistic dependencies to compute its solution. Our approach requires prompt engineering to transform the question from its original form to an explicit, tractable form that results in a correct program and solution. To estimate the amount of work needed to translate an original question into its tractable form, we measure the similarity between original and transformed questions. Our work is the first to introduce a new dataset of university-level probability and statistics problems and solve these problems in a scalable fashion using the program synthesis capabilities of large language models.

This work is a significant step forward in solving quantitative math problems and opens the door for solving many university-level STEM courses by machine.

13.9   Proteomics

13.9.1   Protein Structure Prediction

Proteins are necessary for various functions within cells, including transport, antibodies, enzymes, and catalysis. They are polymer chains of amino acid residues whose sequences dictate stable spatial conformations, with particular torsion angles between successive monomers. The amino acid residues must fold into proper configurations to perform their functions. The sequence space of proteins is vast, with 20 possible residues per position, and evolution has been sampling it over billions of years. Thus, current proteins are highly diverse in sequences, structures, and functions. The high-throughput acquisition of DNA sequences, and therefore the ubiquity of known protein sequences, stands in contrast to the limited availability of 3D structures, which are more functionally relevant. From a physics standpoint, the process of protein folding is a search for the minimum energy conformation that happens in nature paradoxically fast (Levinthal, 1969). Unfortunately, explicitly computing the energy of a protein conformation and its surrounding water molecules is highly complex.

Inferring local *secondary structure* (Drori, Dwivedi, Shrestha, Wan, Wang, He, Mazza, Krogh-Freeman, Leggas, Sandridge et al., 2018) consists of linear annotation of structural elements along the sequence (Kabsch and Sander, 1983). Inferring *tertiary structure* consists of resolving the 3D atom coordinates of proteins. When highly similar sequences are available with known structures, this homology can be used for modeling. PSP was recently tackled by first predicting contact points between amino acids and then leveraging the contact map to infer structure. A primary contact indicator between a pair of amino acids is their tendency to have correlated and compensatory mutations during evolution. The availability of large-scale data on DNA, and therefore protein sequences, allows detection of such co-evolutionary constraints from sets of sequences that are homologous to a protein of interest. Registering such contacting pairs in a matrix facilitates a framework for their probabilistic prediction. This contact map matrix can be generalized to register distances between amino acids (Xu, 2019).

Machine learning approaches garnered recent success in PSP (Anand and Huang, 2018; AlQuraishi, 2019) and its sub-problems (Wang, Cao, Zhang and Qi, 2018). These leverage available repositories of tertiary structure (Berman et al., 2000) and its curated compilations (Orengo et al., 1997) as training data for models that predict structure from sequence. Specifically, the recent biannual critical assessment of PSP methods (Moult et al., 2018) featured multiple such methods. Most prominently, a ResNet-based architecture (Jumper et al., 2021) has achieved impressive results in the CASP evaluation settings, based on representing protein structures both by their distance matrices as well as their torsion angles. In this work, we design a novel representation of biologically relevant input data and construct a processing flow for PSP, as shown in Figure 13.13. Our method leverages advances in deep sequence models and proposes a method to learn transformations of amino acids and their auxiliary information. The method operates in three stages by (1) predicting backbone atom distance matrices and torsion angles; (2) recovering backbone atom 3D coordinates; and (3) reconstructing the full atom protein by optimization.

We demonstrate state-of-art protein structure prediction results using deep learning models to predict backbone atom distance matrices and torsion angles, recover backbone atom 3D coordinates and reconstruct the full atom protein

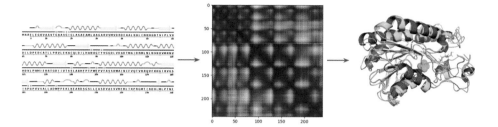

Figure 13.13 Our method operates by (1) predicting backbone atom distance matrices and torsion angles; (2) recovering backbone atom 3D coordinates; and (3) reconstructing the full atom protein by optimization

by optimization. We present a gold standard dataset of around 75,000 proteins, which we call the CUProtein dataset, which is easy to use in developing deep learning models for PSP. Next, we demonstrate competitive results with the winning teams on CASP13 and a comparison with AlphaFold (A7D) (Jumper et al., 2021) with results mostly superseding the winning teams on CASP12. This work explores encoded representation for sequences of amino acids alongside their auxiliary information. We offer full access to data, models, and code, which removes entry barriers for investigators and makes publicly available the methods for this critical application domain.

We address two problems: (1) predicting backbone distance matrices and torsion angles of backbone atoms from amino acid sequences, Q8 secondary structure, PSSMs, and co-evolutionary multiple sequence alignment; and (2) reconstruction of all-atom coordinates from the predicted distance matrices and torsion angles.

We begin with a one-hot representation of each amino acid and secondary structure sequence, and real-valued PSSMs and MSA covariance matrices. These are passed through *embedding layers* and then onto an encoder–decoder architecture. To leverage sequence homology, we compute the covariance matrix of the MSA features by embedding the homology information along a k-dimensional vector to form a 3-tensor and contract the tensor A_{ijk} along with the k-dimensional embedding, which is then passed as input to the encoder: $\Sigma = A_{ji}^k A_{ijk}$.

We use encoder–decoder models with a bottleneck to train prediction models. The encoder f receives as input the aggregation A (by concatenation) of the embeddings e_i of each input x_i, and two separate decoders g_1 and g_2 that output distance matrices and torsion angles for $i \in \{1, \ldots, 4\}$: $g_j \left(f \left(\underset{x_i \in \mathcal{X}}{\mathrm{Agg}} (e_i(x_i)) \right) \right)$. In addition, we also use a model that consists of separate encoders f_i for each embedded input $e_i(x_i)$, which are aggregated by concatenation after encoding, and separate decoders g_1 and g_2 for torsion angles and backbone distance matrices: $g_j \left(\underset{x_i \in \mathcal{X}}{\mathrm{Agg}} (f_i(e_i(x_1))) \right)$. Using a separate encoder model involves a more significant number of trainable parameters. Our models differ in the use of embeddings for the input, their models, and loss functions.

Building on techniques commonly used in natural language processing, our models use embeddings and a sequence of bidirectional gated recurrent units (GRUs) and LSTMs with skip connections. They include batch normalization, dropout, and dense layers. We experimented with various loss functions, including MAE, MSE, Frobenius norm, and distance logarithm, to handle the dynamic range of distances. We have also implemented distance matrix prediction using conditional GANs and variational autoencoders (VAEs) for protein subsequences to learn the loss function.

Once backbone distance matrices and torsion angle are predicted, we address two reconstruction sub-problems: (1) reconstructing the protein backbone coordinates from their distance matrices, and (2) reconstructing the full atom protein coordinates from the C_α or C_β coordinates and torsion angles.

We employ three different techniques for reconstructing the 3D coordinates X between backbone atoms of a protein from the predicted matrix of their pairwise distances (Dokmanic et al., 2015). Given a predicted distance matrix $\hat{D}$, our goal is to recover 3D coordinates $\hat{X}$ of n points. We notice that $D(X)$ depends only on the Gram matrix $X^T X$:

$$D(X) = \mathbf{1}\text{diag}(X^T X)^T - 2X^T X + \text{diag}(X^T X)\mathbf{1}^T \tag{13.3}$$

Multi-dimensional scaling (MDS):

$$\underset{\hat{X}}{\text{minimize}} D(\hat{X}) - \hat{D}F^2 \tag{13.4}$$

Semi-definite programming (SDP) and relaxation (SDR):

$$\underset{G}{\text{minimize}} K(G) - \hat{D}F^2 \quad \text{s.t.} \quad G \in C \tag{13.5}$$

where $K(G) = \mathbf{1}\text{diag}(G)^T - 2G + \text{diag}(G)\mathbf{1}^T$ operates on the Gram matrix G.

Alternating direction method of multipliers (ADMM) (Anand and Huang, 2018):

$$\underset{G,Z,\eta}{\text{minimize}} \quad \lambda\eta 1 + \frac{1}{2}\left(\sum_{i,j=1}^{n}(G_{ii} + G_{jj} - 2G_{ij} + \eta_{ij} - \hat{D}_{ij}^2)\right)^2$$

$$+ 1\{Z \in S_+^n\} \quad \text{s.t.} \quad G - Z = 0$$

We have found multi-dimensional scaling to be the fastest and most robust method of the three, without depending on algorithm hyperparameters, which is most suitable for our purposes.

We assign plausible coordinates to the rest of the protein's atoms given backbone coordinates. We begin with an initial guess or prediction for ϕ and ψ torsion angles. We maintain a look-up table of mean ϕ, ψ values for each combination of two consecutive α torsions and three α-angles (the angles defined by three consecutive atoms). Using these values and the C_α positions we generate an initial model. A series of energy minimization simulations then relax this model under an energy function that includes: standard bonded terms (bond, angle, plane and out-of-plane), knowledge-based Ramachandran and pairwise terms, torsion constraints on the ϕ and ψ angles, and tether constraints on the C_α position. The latter term reduces the perturbations of the initial high forces. Finally, we add side-chains using a rotamer library, and remove clashes by a series of energy minimization simulations. We develop a very similar method for reconstructing the full-atom protein from C_β atom distance matrices.

We have compared our predictions on CASP12 and CASP13 (Abriata et al., 2019) test targets. Deep learning methods were widely used only starting from CASP13. AlphaFold was introduced starting from CASP13. The use of deep learning methods in CASP13, due to the availability of DL programming frameworks, significantly improved performance over CASP12. A representative comparison between the winning CASP12 and CASP13 competition models, AlphaFold models for CASP13 for which A7D submitted predictions to CASP, and our models shows results of RMSD around 2 Angstrom on test targets, which is considered accurate in CASP. Our results supersede the winning teams of CASP12 compared with each best team for each protein, highlighting the improvement using deep learning methods. Our approach is on par with the winning teams in CASP13, compared with the winning team for each protein, highlighting that our method is state-of-the-art. We measure the sequence-independent RMSD, consistent with the CASP evaluation reports, and match the deposited structures and our predictions. CASP competitors such as AlphaFold provide predictions for selected proteins. Overall, our performance on CASP is highly competitive. Training our models on a cloud instance takes two days using GPUs. Prediction of backbone distance matrices and torsion angles takes a few seconds per protein, and reconstruction of full-atom proteins from distance matrices and torsion angles takes a few minutes per protein, depending on protein length. Limitations of this work are: (1) we only handle single-domain proteins and not complexes with multiple chains; (2) PSSM and MSA data for several of the CASP targets are limited to a subsequence of the full length protein; and (3) we do not use available methods for detecting and reconstructing beta-sheets.

13.9.2   Protein Docking

Modeling protein–protein interactions is a primary challenge for elucidating the mechanisms behind biology's most fundamental processes. Recent advances in machine learning for protein folding have established the foundation for predicting protein–protein interactions through co-folding. A generalized folding pipeline operates directly on structures for end-to-end protein docking, eliminating the need for costly sequence alignments. Euclidean-equivariant networks for inferring pairwise three-dimensional matching between pairs of proteins, and geometric models for iterative construction and refinement of complexes significantly reduce the computational cost and inference time for protein docking, reaching metrics on par with state-of-the-art classical methods.

13.10   Combinatorial Optimization

A core and essential area in computer science and operations research is the domain of graph algorithms and combinatorial optimization. The literature is rich in both exact (slow) and heuristic (fast) algorithms (Golden et al., 1980); however, each algorithm is designed afresh for each new problem with careful attention by an expert to the problem structure. Approximation algorithms for NP-hard problems provide only worst-case guarantees (Williamson and Shmoys, 2011), and are not usually linear time, and hence not scalable. Our motivation is to learn new heuristic algorithms for these problems that require an evaluation oracle for the problem as input and return a good solution in a pre-specified time budget. Concretely, we target combinatorial and graph problems in increasing order of complexity, from polynomial problems such as minimum spanning tree (MST), and shortest paths (SSP), to NP-hard problems such as the traveling salesman problem (TSP) and the vehicle routing problem (VRP).

The aptitude of deep learning systems for solving combinatorial optimization problems has been demonstrated across a wide range of applications in the past several years (Dai et al., 2017; Bengio et al., 2021). Two recent surveys of reinforcement learning methods (Mazyavkina et al., 2021) and machine learning methods (Vesselinova et al., 2020) for combinatorial optimization over graphs with applications have become available during the time of this writing. The power of GNNs (Xu et al., 2019) and the algorithmic alignment between GNNs and combinatorial algorithms have recently been studied (Xu et al., 2020). Graph neural networks trained using specific aggregation functions emulate specific algorithms: for example, a GNN aligns well (Xu et al., 2020) with the Bellman–Ford algorithm for shortest paths.

Our work is motivated by recent theoretical and empirical results in reinforcement learning and GNNs. Graph neural network training is equivalent to a dynamic programming algorithm (Xu et al., 2020), hence GNNs by themselves can be used to mimic algorithms with polynomial time complexity. Reinforcement learning methods with GNNs can be used to find approximate solutions to NP-hard combinatorial optimization problems (Dai et al., 2017; Bengio et al., 2021; Kool et al., 2019).

Combinatorial optimization problems may be solved by exact methods, approximation algorithms, or heuristics. Machine learning approaches for combinatorial optimization have mainly used supervised or reinforcement learning. Our approach is unsupervised and is based on reinforcement learning. We require neither output labels nor knowing the optimal solutions, and our method improves by self-play. Reinforcement learning methods can be divided into model-free and model-based methods. In turn, model-free methods can be divided into Q-learning and policy optimization methods (OpenAI, 2020). Model-based methods have two flavors: methods in which the model is given, such as expert iteration (Anthony et al., 2017) or AlphaZero (Silver et al., 2017), and methods that learn the model, such as World Models (Ha and Schmidhuber, 2018) or

MuZero (Schrittwieser et al., 2019). AlphaZero has been generalized to many games (Cazenave et al., 2020), both multiplayer and single-player (Drori, Krishnamurthy, Rampin, Lourenco, One, Cho, Silva and Freire, 2018). This work views algorithms on graphs as single-player games and learns graph algorithms. The supplementary material includes a comprehensive list of supervised and reinforcement learning methods used for combinatorial optimization of NP-hard problems and classification of all previous work by problem, method, and type. This work provides a general framework for model-free reinforcement learning using a GNN representation that elegantly adapts to different problem classes by changing an objective or reward and using the line graph.

Our approach generalizes well from examples on small graphs, where even exhaustive search is easy, to larger graphs; and the architecture works equally well when trained on polynomial problems such as MST and on NP-hard problems such as TSP, though training time is significantly larger for hard problems. We explore the limits of these algorithms as well: For what kinds of problem classes, problem instances, and time budgets do they outperform classical approximation algorithms?

For all graph problems, our approximation running time is linear $O(n + m)$ in the number of nodes n and edges m, both in theory and in practice. For MST and SSP our running time is linear $O(m)$ in the number of edges. For TSP and VRP our running time is linear $O(n)$ in the number of nodes. The TSP approximation algorithms and heuristics have runtimes that grow at least quadratically in the graph size.

On random Euclidean graphs with 100 nodes, our method is 1–3 orders of magnitude faster and delivers a comparable optimality gap, Moreover, this speedup improves as the graph size increases. S2V-DQN (Dai et al., 2017), another reinforcement learning method, builds a 10-nearest-neighbor graph, and also has quadratic runtime complexity; on these graphs, our method runs 52 times faster and obtains a lower (better) optimality gap, the ratio between a method's reward and the optimal reward. GPN (Ma et al., 2020) has runtime complexity $O(n \log n)$ with a more significant optimality gap and does not generalize as well nor easily extend to other problems.

The running time for solving MST using Prim's algorithm is $O(m \log m)$ and the running time for solving SSP using Dijkstra's algorithm is $O(n \log n + m)$. For MST, running our method on larger graphs (for longer times) results in optimality gaps close to 1, converging to an optimal solution.

Generalization on graphs. (1) From small to large random graphs: For MST, we generalize from small to large graphs accurately. For TSP, we generalize from small to larger graphs with median tour lengths (and optimality gaps) better than other methods. (2) Between different types of random graphs: For MST, we generalize accurately between different types of random graphs. (3) From random to real-world graphs: For TSP, we generalize from random graphs to real-world graphs better than other methods.

A unified framework for solving any combinatorial optimization problem over

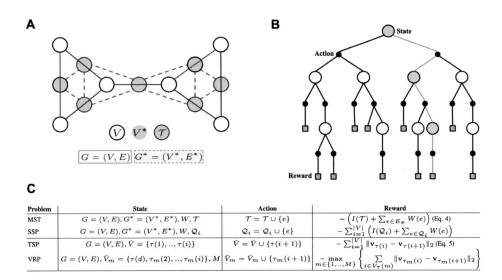

Problem	State	Action	Reward
MST	$G = (V, E), G^* = (V^*, E^*), W, \mathcal{T}$	$\mathcal{T} = \mathcal{T} \cup \{e\}$	$-\left(I(\mathcal{T}) + \sum_{e \in E_\pi} W(e) \right)$ (Eq. 4)
SSP	$G = (V, E), G^* = (V^*, E^*), W, \mathcal{Q}_i$	$\mathcal{Q}_i = \mathcal{Q}_i \cup \{e\}$	$-\sum_{i=1}^{|V|} \left(I(\mathcal{Q}_i) + \sum_{e \in \mathcal{Q}_i} W(e) \right)$
TSP	$G = (V, E), \hat{V} = \{\tau(1), .., \tau(i)\}$	$\hat{V} = \hat{V} \cup \{\tau(i+1)\}$	$-\sum_{i=1}^{|V|} \|v_{\tau(i)} - v_{\tau(i+1)}\|_2$ (Eq. 5)
VRP	$G = (V, E), \hat{V}_m = \{\tau(d), \tau_m(2), .., \tau_m(i)\}, M$	$\hat{V}_m = \hat{V}_m \cup \{\tau_m(i+1)\}$	$-\max_{m \in \{1,..,M\}} \left\{ \sum_{i \in V_\tau(m)} \|v_{\tau_m(i)} - v_{\tau_m(i+1)}\|_2 \right\}$

Figure 13.14 Our unified framework. (a) The primal graph (white nodes and solid edges) and its edge-to-vertex line graph (gray nodes and dashed edges). Two nodes in the line graph are connected if the corresponding edges in the primal graph share a node. Notice that while the number of primal edges (7) is equal to the number of dual nodes (7), the number of dual edges (10) is not necessarily equal to the number of primal nodes (6). (b) Combinatorial optimization as a single-player game defined by states, actions, and rewards. Traversing a path (green) from the root to a leaf node (pink square) corresponds to a solution for a problem. White nodes represent states and black nodes represent actions. From each state, there may be many possible actions (more than the two illustrated here) representing the possible nodes or edges in the problem graph. The leaf nodes represent rewards or costs, such as the sum of weights in MST or length of the tour in TSP. (c) Graph algorithms for polynomial problems MST and SSP, and NP-hard problems TSP and VRP formulated as single-player games by reinforcement learning using states, actions, and rewards. For MST, the state includes the graph, line graph, weights, and selected edges $\mathcal{T}$ (red).

graphs: (a) We model problems that involve both actions on nodes and edges by using the edge-to-vertex *line graph*. Figure 13.14a shows an example of a primal graph and its line graph. (b) We model graph algorithms as a single-player game as shown in Figure 13.14b. (c) We learn different problems by changing the objective or reward function, as shown in Figure 13.14c.

Given a graph $\mathcal{G} = (V, E, W)$, $V = \{1, \ldots, n\}$ is the set of vertices (nodes), E is the set of edges and W is the set of edge weights. For edges e_{ij} between nodes i and j in an undirected graph, $w_{ij} = w_{ji}$. $|V|$ and $|E|$ represent the number of vertices and edges in the graph. Given a node i, $\mathcal{N}(i)$ denotes the set of its neighboring nodes. Given a primal graph $\mathcal{G} = (V, E, W)$, the edge-to-vertex dual or *line graph*, $\mathcal{G}^* = (V^*, E^*, W^*)$, is defined so each edge in the primal graph corresponds to a node in the line graph: $V^* = E$. Two nodes in the line graph are connected if the corresponding edges in the primal graph share a node. Edge weights in the primal graph become node weights W^* in the line graph. Figure 13.14a illustrates the relationship between the primal and line graphs.

We learn MST and SSP by training and running on five different types of random graphs: Erdős–Rényi (ER) (Erdös and Rényi, 2011), Barabási–Albert (Albert and Barabási, 2002), stochastic block model (Holland et al., 1983), Watts–Strogatz (Watts and Strogatz, 1998), and random regular (Steger and Wormald, 1999; Kim and Vu, 2003). We learn TSP and VRP by training and running on complete graphs with different numbers of random nodes drawn uniformly from $[0, 1]^2$. For MST and SSP, edge weights are chosen uniformly between 0 and 1 for pairs of nodes that are connected. For TSP and VRP, these weights are the distances between the nodes. We also test our models on real-world graphs (Reinelt, 2020).

13.10.1   Problems over Graphs

Given a connected and undirected graph $\mathcal{G} = (V, E, W)$, the MST problem is to find a tree $\mathcal{T} = (V_{\mathcal{T}}, E_{\mathcal{T}})$ with $V_{\mathcal{T}} = V$, $E_{\mathcal{T}} \subset E$ minimizing the sum of the edge weights $W_{\mathcal{T}} \subset W$. Algorithms for MST problems include Boruvka's (Nešetřil et al., 2001), Prim's (Prim, 1957) and Kruskal's (Kruskal, 1956) algorithms; all are greedy algorithms with time complexity $O(|E| \log |V|)$.

We consider the SSP problem with non-negative edge weights. Given a connected and directed graph $\mathcal{G} = (V, E, W)$ and a source vertex, the SSP problem is to find the shortest paths from the source to all other vertices. For the SSP problem with non-negative weights, Dijkstra's algorithm (Dijkstra, 1959) complexity is $O(|V| \log |V| + |E|)$ using a heap. For the general single-source shortest paths problem, Bellman–Ford (Bang-Jensen and Gutin, 2000) runs in $O(|V||E|)$. In addition, the Floyd–Warshall algorithm (Cormen et al., 1990) solves the SSP problem between all pairs of nodes with cubic time complexity $O(|V|^3)$.

Given a graph $\mathcal{G} = (V, E, W)$, let V represent a list of cities and W represent the distances between each pair of cities. The goal of the TSP is to find the shortest tour that visits each city once and returns to the starting city. The TSP is an NP-hard problem. Approximation algorithms and heuristics include LKH (Lin and Kernighan, 1973), Christofides (Christofides, 1976), 2-opt (Lin, 1965; Aarts and Lenstra, 2003), farthest insertion and nearest neighbor (Rosenkrantz et al., 1977). Concorde (Applegate et al., 2006) is an exact TSP solver. Gurobi (Achterberg, 2019) is a general integer programming solver that can also be used to find an exact TSP solution.

Given M vehicles and a graph $\mathcal{G} = (V, E)$ with $|V|$ cities, the goal of the VRP is to find optimal routes for the vehicles. Each vehicle $m \in \{1, \dots, M\}$ starts from the same depot node, visits a subset $V(m)$ of cities and returns to the depot node. The routes of different vehicles do not intersect except at the depot; together, the vehicles visit all cities. The optimal routes minimize the longest tour length of any single route. The TSP is a special case of VRP for one vehicle.

13.10.2   Learning Graph Algorithms as Single-Player Games

We represent the problem space as a search tree. The leaves of the search tree represent all (possibly exponentially many) possible solutions to the problem. A search traverses this tree, choosing a path guided by a neural network as shown in Figure 13.14b. The initial state, represented by the root node, may be the empty set, random, or other initial states. Each path from the root to a leaf consists of moving between nodes (states) along edges (taking actions), reaching a leaf node (reward). Actions may include adding or removing a node or edge. The reward (or cost) may be the solution's value; for example, a sum of weights or length of tour. For each problem, Figure 13.14c defines the states, actions, and rewards within our framework. We show that the single-player formulation extends our framework to other combinatorial optimization problems on graphs.

When the predictions of our neural network capture the global structure of the problem, this mechanism is very efficient. On the other hand, even if the network makes poor predictions for a particular problem, the search will still find the solution if run for a sufficiently long (possibly exponential) time. The network is retrained using the results of the evaluation oracle on the leaf nodes reached by the search to improve its predictions. In the context of perfect information games, a similar mechanism converges asymptotically to the optimal policy (Sun et al., 2018).

13.11   Physics

13.11.1   Pedestrian Wind Estimation in Urban Environments

The field of fluid dynamics deals with enormous amounts of data from field measurements and experiments to more extensive full-flow field data generated from computational fluid dynamics (CFD) simulations (Brunton et al., 2020). This wealth of data, coupled with advances in computing architectures and progress in machine learning in the last decade, has led to an interest in applying deep neural networks for rapidly approximating CFD. Applications of deep neural networks to fluid dynamics include physics model augmentation with uncertainty quantification, accuracy prediction improvements, and surrogate modeling for enabling design exploration (Nathan Kutz, 2017; Duraisamy et al., 2019). Convolutional neural networks have been particularly explored for the latter due to their capacity to represent non-linear input and output functions while extracting spatial relationships, and GANs as well due to their additional ability to learn without explicitly defining a loss function. A number of implementations have been successful at reducing the computational expense of velocity fluid flow approximations with a minor error compromise (Guo et al., 2016; Farimani et al., 2017). In contrast to other deep neural network applications such as image and speech recognition, a major challenge in fluid dynamics is the strict requirement for fluid flow fields quantification to be precise, generalizable and interpretable

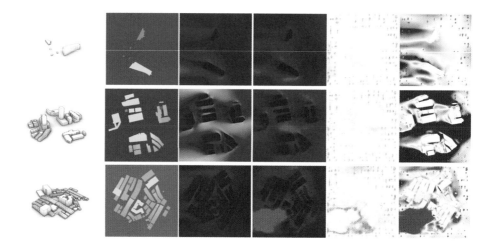

Figure 13.15 Testing set sample generator predictions, uncertainties, and absolute errors. A sample of model predictions for select urban patches is shown and their associated uncertainties and the absolute error. Visual inspection of the results shows the model's capacity to identify zones of impact created by wind obstructions in an urban scene. It also shows its limited capacity to capture the scale of impact for high wind factor zones. Other artifacts include inconsistent color patches in portions of the image and grainy noise.

(Brunton et al., 2020). The computational expense of CFD simulations additionally makes it largely unfeasible to repeat experiments and expand datasets. Thus, the finite amount of training data, coupled with distinct feature representation and accuracy requirements across fluid domain disciplines, motivates the development of application-specific deep learning models. Figure 13.15 shows a sample of model predictions, uncertainties, and absolute errors.

13.11.2   Fusion Plasma

The analysis of turbulent flows is a significant area in fusion plasma physics. Current theoretical models quantify the degree of turbulence based on the evolution of specific plasma density structures, called blobs. In this work, we track these blobs' shape and position in high-frequency video data obtained from gas puff imaging (GPI) diagnostics. We compare various tracking approaches and find that an optical flow method is appropriate for these applications. We train on synthetic data and test on both synthetic and real data. As a result, our model effectively tracks blob structures on both synthetic and real experimental GPI data, showing its prospect as a powerful tool to estimate blob statistics linked with edge turbulence of the tokamak plasma.

In tokamak fusion reactors, plasmas are magnetically confined to produce energy from nuclear fusion. In order to maximize the rate of fusion, it is vital to maintain confinement as long as possible. The quality of this confinement is

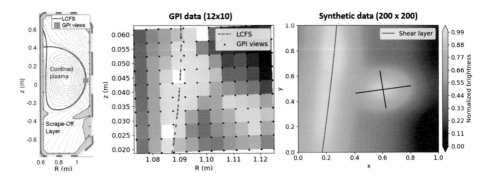

Figure 13.16 (left) Cross-section of a plasma in tokamak reactor, TCV, with the locations GPI views on the last closed flux surface (LCFS). (center) Snapshot of real GPI data capturing a blob passing by the LCFS. Here, empty spots correspond to dead GPI views. The brightness level is color-coded, low as blue and high as yellow. (right) Snapshot of synthetic data capturing a blob passing by the LCFS. The blob is represented with a Gaussian ellipse with a major and minor axis marked by perpendicular black lines.

closely related to the turbulence at the edge region of the plasma core (Figure 13.16a). Current theoretical models can quantify the degree of turbulence from the evolution of specific structures ("blobs") within the plasma density field. This is an evolving area of research. Different models require the analysis of different "blob statistics" that can be derived from image data (e.g. blob velocity, size, and intermittency). For example, the fluctuations in the plasma can be described by a stochastic model as a superposition of uncorrelated Lorentzian pulses, which is parameterized by the intermittency of blobs (Garcia et al., 2016; Garcia and Theodorsen, 2017). Furthermore, the radial velocity and the size of blobs can be used to determine the theoretical regime, predicting dependencies for the radial velocity of blobs on plasma parameters (Myra et al., 2006). Comparing various approaches for tracking, we find that optical flow based on deep learning accurately tracks the position of blobs in low-resolution (12×10 pixel), high-frequency (2 MHz) video data obtained from GPI diagnostics (Zweben et al., 2017). Gass puff imaging is an edge diagnostic tool that measures the spatially resolved fluctuations of brightness which can be used as a proxy for plasma density measurements. Figure 13.16b shows a snapshot of the GPI data that captures a blob passing by the plasma edge (i.e., the last closed flux surface, or LCFS) and moving radially out.

13.12 Summary

We have covered a dozen novel applications of deep learning, demonstrating system architectures and representative results. These include breakthrough applications in deep learning for protein structure prediction, climate science, autonomous driving, combinatorial optimization, vision, audio and language, and education. While humans are generalists, many deep learning applications are specialists. However, deep learning systems are not limited to specialized domains, as demonstrated by the application of learning-to-learn in many STEM courses using a single foundation model trained on both text and code.

Appendix A: Matrix Calculus

Matrix calculus defines the partial derivatives of a function with respect to variables and is used in gradient computations for backpropagation and optimization. We will write the derivative of a scalar with respect to a column vector as a column vector, adopting the denominator layout commonly used in machine learning. In contrast, in numerator layout the dimensions are transposed.

A.1 Gradient Computations for Backpropagation

We define the gradients of a scalar with respect to a vector or a matrix. This is useful for computing the gradient of a loss function with respect to activations, pre-activations, or weights. The dimension of the gradient in these cases is the dimension of the denominator. Next, we define the gradient of a vector with respect to another vector which results in the Hessian matrix. Finally, we define the gradient of a matrix with respect to a scalar.

A.1.1 Scalar by Vector

The gradient of a scalar y with respect to an $n \times 1$-dimensional column vector x is defined by the $n \times 1$-dimensional column vector:

$$\frac{\partial y}{\partial x} = \begin{bmatrix} \frac{\partial y}{\partial x_1} \\ \vdots \\ \frac{\partial y}{\partial x_n} \end{bmatrix} \tag{A.1}$$

For example, the gradient of the loss $\mathcal{L}$ with respect to the $n \times 1$ weight vector w is the $n \times 1$-dimensional gradient $\frac{\partial \mathcal{L}}{\partial w}$.

A.1.2 Scalar by Matrix

The gradient of a scalar y with respect to the $m \times n$-dimensional matrix X is defined by the $m \times n$-dimensional matrix:

$$\frac{\partial y}{\partial X} = \begin{bmatrix} \frac{\partial y}{\partial x_{11}} & \cdots & \frac{\partial y}{\partial x_{1n}} \\ \vdots & \vdots & \\ \frac{\partial y}{\partial x_{m1}} & \cdots & \frac{\partial y}{\partial x_{mn}} \end{bmatrix} \tag{A.2}$$

For example, the gradient of the loss function $\mathcal{L}$, which is a scalar, with respect to an $m \times n$ weight matrix W is the $m \times n$-dimensional gradient $\frac{\partial \mathcal{L}}{\partial W}$.

A.1.3   Vector by Vector

The gradient of the $m \times 1$-dimensional vector y with respect to the $n \times 1$-dimensional vector x is defined by the $m \times n$-dimensional matrix:

$$\frac{\partial y}{\partial x} = \begin{bmatrix} \frac{\partial y_1}{\partial x_1} & \cdots & \frac{\partial y_1}{\partial x_n} \\ \vdots & \vdots & \\ \frac{\partial y_m}{\partial x_1} & \cdots & \frac{\partial y_m}{\partial x_n} \end{bmatrix} \tag{A.3}$$

For example, the gradient of the $n \times 1$ activation vector a with respect to the $n \times 1$ pre-activation vector z is an $n \times n$-dimensional gradient $\frac{\partial a}{\partial z}$.

A.1.4   Matrix by Scalar

The derivative of an $m \times n$-dimensional matrix Y with respect to a scalar x is the $m \times n$-dimensional matrix:

$$\frac{\partial Y}{\partial x} = \begin{bmatrix} \frac{\partial y_{11}}{\partial x} & \cdots & \frac{\partial y_{1n}}{\partial x} \\ \vdots & \vdots & \\ \frac{\partial y_{m1}}{\partial x} & \cdots & \frac{\partial y_{mn}}{\partial x} \end{bmatrix} \tag{A.4}$$

A.2   Gradient Computations for Optimization

We define the gradient of a dot product of vectors with respect to a vector used in optimization and the gradient of a quadratic form with respect to a vector, which is useful for quasi-Newton method computations.

A.2.1   Dot Product by Vector

The gradient of the dot product $a^T x$ of the $1 \times n$ vector a^T with the $n \times 1$ vector x with respect to the vector x is the $n \times 1$ vector:

$$\frac{\partial a^T x}{\partial x} = a \tag{A.5}$$

since $\frac{\partial a^T x}{\partial x_i} = a_i$ for all $i = 1, \ldots, n$. The gradient of the dot product of vectors $a^T b$ with respect to another vector x is:

$$\frac{\partial a^T b}{\partial x} = \frac{\partial a}{\partial x} b + \frac{\partial b}{\partial x} a \tag{A.6}$$

A.2.2   Quadratic Form by Vector

The gradient of the quadratic form $x^T A x$ with respect to an $n \times 1$-dimensional vector x is the $n \times 1$-dimensional vector:

$$\frac{\partial x^T A x}{\partial x} = (A + A^T) x \tag{A.7}$$

since $\frac{\partial x^T A x}{\partial x_i} = \sum_{j=1}^{n} x_j (a_{ij} + a_{ji})$ for all $i = 1, \ldots, n$. The second-order derivative with respect to x is therefore $A + A^T$. If A is a symmetric matrix then $A + A^T = 2A$. These equations are used for deriving quasi-Newton optimization methods.

Appendix B: Scientific Writing and Reviewing Best Practices

Communicating deep learning methods and results is essential for successful research in academia and industry. This Appendix describes writing and reviewing best practices.

B.1 Writing Best Practices

Good writing requires rewriting, and therefore, it often helps to start writing early, write a draft, take breaks, and return to the manuscript while iterating the process. Once we have a draft version of the text, we may improve it by omitting needless words (Strunk Jr. and White, 2007), specifically: Omitting subjective words that are often unnecessary and may even be misleading, omitting unnecessary phrases, simplifying the text, using active voice, and using parallel constructions.

B.1.1 Introduction

A research paper usually begins with an abstract followed by three sections: introduction, methods, and results, and ends with a discussion or conclusions. An abstract may consist of the opening sentences from paragraphs of each text part. It is essential to place the key contributions upfront in an abstract, explaining them clearly to the reader. Introductory paragraphs may begin with the main point or an example and then expand. The introduction usually moves from a general description to specific details, whereas the discussion moves from the specific to the general big picture. The introduction may describe a research problem, explaining why it is essential to the reader. A related-work section may be part of the introduction and describes previous work, other solutions to the same problem, or similar approaches previously applied to other problems. The related work may explain the limitations of previous work and then describe the contribution of the work presented.

B.1.2 Methods

Methods sections describe the proposed solution, the dataset, and the evaluation metrics. The proposed solution should be described in detail, including the architecture, the training process, and the hyperparameters. The dataset should be described in detail, including the number of samples, the number of classes, the number of features, and the distribution of the classes. The evaluation metrics should be described in detail, for example, the number of folds, the number of repetitions, and the number of samples per fold.

B.1.3 Figures and Tables

Figures should display information, and following a guiding principle of "less is more" may produce good graphics (Tufte, 1985). Readers first skim the figures of a manuscript and the first sentence of each paragraph. Therefore, the figures and their captions should be self-contained. Captions may be lengthy, explaining what to pay attention to. Tables may compare different approaches and the present method.

B.1.4 Results

In the results section, it is essential not to over-sell the work and deliver a correct message regarding the performance of the methods while clearly explaining the scope and limitations of the work.

B.1.5 Abbreviations and Notation

Writing a book chapter or book requires consistent notation and text style throughout the manuscript. Once a version of the text is ready, copy editing and proofreading best practice is to prepare a style sheet of abbreviations, spelling, hyphenation, capitalization, and text style so that the manuscript is consistent. An example of parts of the style sheet prepared for this book is:

- Spelling: US (not UK) spelling, spell out and capitalize Equation (not Eq.) when referring to a numbered equation, okay to use Eq. in an algorithm.
- Hyphens: Hyphenated as an adjective: long-term, long-range, high-quality, multi-XX, pre-XX; hyphenated as an adjective and noun: image-to-image, video-to-video, etc., trade-off, mini-batch, saddle-point(s), non-linear; not hyphenated: pseudocode, overfit, overfitting, underfit, underfitting, hyperparameter, pointwise, piecewise, stepwise, elementwise, cross validation (two words).
- Capitalization and text style: the internet is lowercased unless starting a sentence. Always capitalize Transformer(s), Swish, TensorFlow, and PyTorch. Use "quasi-Newton" not "Quasi-Newton" or "Quasi Newton."

B.2 Reviewing Best Practices

Reviewing scientific work begins by reading the paper or work and listing the strengths and weaknesses, optionally classifying them into minor and major strengths and weaknesses. The reviewer may mark everything they would like to comment on, including typos, missing references, observations, etc. A typical conference paper review takes around 2–4 hours.

The reviewer should briefly describe the report. The reviewer should address whether the exposition and presentation are clear and suggest how they could be improved. Next, the reviewer should check if the references are adequate and list any additional references that are missing. The review may involve going through the implementation code or evaluating whether the work may be reproduced based on the paper. The reviewer should verify that the paper discusses all the essential details and clearly states the work's scope and limitations.

B.2.1   Ranking

After reading the paper and optionally going through the supplementary material, the reviewer scores the report. This includes explaining the score by discussing strengths and weaknesses. The ranking should be based on scientific merit rather than personal opinion. The review may include suggestions for improvement.

B.2.2   Rebuttal

A rebuttal is part of the review process. The authors' goal in the rebuttal is to clarify and improve the evaluation. The goal of both the authors and the reviewers is to help understand what can be improved, have a discussion, and clear up any misunderstandings.

In summary, a good review process is not only fair and rigorous. It also respects the time and effort the authors put into the work and, therefore, should be kind.

References

Aarts, E. and Lenstra, J. K. (2003), *Local Search in Combinatorial Optimization*, Princeton University Press.

Abadi, M., Barham, P., Chen, J., Chen, Z. *et al.* (2016), "Tensorflow: A system for large-scale machine learning", in *Proceedings of the 12th USENIX Symposium on Operating Systems Design and Implementation*, pp. 265–283.

Abriata, L. A., Tamò, G. E., and Dal Peraro, M. (2019), "A further leap of improvement in tertiary structure prediction in CASP13 prompts new routes for future assessments", *Proteins: Structure, Function, and Bioinformatics* **87**(12), 1100–1112.

Achterberg, T. (2019), "Gurobi solver", www.gurobi.com/pdfs/benchmarks.pdf.

Afifi, M., Brubaker, M. A., and Brown, M. S. (2021), "HistoGAN: Controlling colors of GAN-generated and real images via color histograms", in *Proceedings of the IEEE/CVF Conference on Computer Vision and Pattern Recognition (CVPR)*, pp. 7941–7950.

Akbari, H., Yuan, L., Qian, R., Chuang, W.-H. *et al.* (2021), "VATT: Transformers for multimodal self-supervised learning from raw video, audio and text", in *Proceedings of Advances in Neural Information Processing Systems (NeurIPS)*.

Albert, R. and Barabási, A.-L. (2002), "Statistical mechanics of complex networks", *Reviews of Modern Physics* **74**(1), 47.

AlQuraishi, M. (2019), "ProteinNet: A standardized data set for machine learning of protein structure", *BMC Bioinformatics* **20**(1), 311.

Amari, S.-I. (1998), "Natural gradient works efficiently in learning", *Neural Computation* **10**(2), 251–276.

Anand, N. and Huang, P. (2018), "Generative modeling for protein structures", in *Proceedings of Advances in Neural Information Processing Systems (NeurIPS)*, pp. 7494–7505.

Anderegg, R., Felber, N., Fichtner, W., and Franke, U. (2004), "Implementation of high-order convolution algorithms with low latency on silicon chips", in *Audio Engineering Society Convention*, number 117.

Anthony, T., Tian, Z., and Barber, D. (2017), "Thinking fast and slow with deep learning and tree search", in *Proceedings of Advances in Neural Information Processing Systems (NeurIPS)*, pp. 5360–5370.

Antipov, G., Baccouche, M., and Dugelay, J.-L. (2017), "Face aging with conditional generative adversarial networks", in *Proceedings of the IEEE International Conference on Image Processing (ICIP)*, pp. 2089–2093.

Applegate, D., Bixby, R., Chvatal, V., and Cook, W. (2006), "Concorde TSP Solver", Computer program.

Arenz, O. (2012), Monte Carlo Chess, Master's thesis, Technische Universitaet Darmstadt.

Arjovsky, M., Bottou, L., Gulrajani, I., and Lopez-Paz, D. (2019), "Invariant risk minimization", *arXiv preprint arXiv:1907.02893*.

Arjovsky, M., Chintala, S., and Bottou, L. (2017), "Wasserstein generative adversarial networks", in *Proceedings of the International Conference on Machine Learning (ICML)*, pp. 214–223.

Arvanitidis, G., Hansen, L. K., and Hauberg, S. (2018), "Latent space oddity: On the curvature of deep generative models", in *Proceedings of the International Conference on Learning Representations (ICLR)*.

Arvanitidis, G., Hauberg, S., Hennig, P., and Schober, M. (2019), "Fast and robust shortest paths on manifolds learned from data", in *Proceedings of the International Conference on Artificial Intelligence and Statistics (AISTATS)*.

Auer, P., Cesa-Bianchi, N., and Fischer, P. (2002), "Finite-time analysis of the multiarmed bandit problem", *Machine Learning* **47**(2–3), 235–256.

Badeau, R. (2019), "Common mathematical framework for stochastic reverberation models", *Journal of the Acoustical Society of America* **145**(4), 2733–2745.

Bahdanau, D., Cho, K., and Bengio, Y. (2015), "Neural machine translation by jointly learning to align and translate", in *Proceedings of the International Conference on Learning Representations (ICLR)*.

Bang-Jensen, J. and Gutin, G. (2000), "Section 2.3. 4: The Bellman–Ford–Moore algorithm", in *Digraphs: Theory, Algorithms and Applications*, Springer.

Bansal, M., Krizhevsky, A., and Ogale, A. (2018), "ChauffeurNet: Learning to drive by imitating the best and synthesizing the worst", *arXiv preprint arXiv:1812.03079*.

Battaglia, P., Pascanu, R., Lai, M., Rezende, D. J., et al. (2016), "Interaction networks for learning about objects, relations and physics", in *Proceedings of Advances in Neural Information Processing Systems (NeurIPS)*, pp. 4502–4510.

Baydin, A. G., Cornish, R., Rubio, D. M., Schmidt, M., and Wood, F. (2018), "Online learning rate adaptation with hypergradient descent", in *Proceedings of the International Conference on Learning Representations (ICLR)*.

Behrmann, J., Grathwohl, W., Chen, R. T., Duvenaud, D., and Jacobsen, J.-H. (2019), "Invertible residual networks", in *Proceedings of the International Conference on Machine Learning (ICML)*, pp. 573–582.

Belkin, M., Hsu, D., Ma, S., and Mandal, S. (2019), "Reconciling modern machine-learning practice and the classical bias–variance trade-off", *Proceedings of the National Academy of Sciences* **116**(32), 15849–15854.

Bell-Kligler, S., Shocher, A., and Irani, M. (2019), "Blind super-resolution kernel estimation using an internal-GAN", in *Proceedings of Advances in Neural Information Processing Systems (NeurIPS)*, pp. 284–293.

Bellemare, M. G., Candido, S., Castro, P. S., Gong, J. *et al.* (2020), "Autonomous navigation of stratospheric balloons using reinforcement learning", *Nature* **588**(7836), 77–82.

Bellman, R. E., Kagiwada, H. H., and Kalaba, R. E. (1965), "Wengert's numerical method for partial derivatives, orbit determination and quasilinearization", *Communications of the ACM* **8**(4), 231–232.

Bengio, Y., Ducharme, R., Vincent, P., and Jauvin, C. (2003), "A neural probabilistic language model", *Journal of Machine Learning Research* **3**, 1137–1155.

Bengio, Y., Lodi, A., and Prouvost, A. (2021), "Machine learning for combinatorial optimization: A methodological tour d'horizon", *European Journal of Operational Research* **290**(2), 405–421.

Bentivogli, L., Clark, P., Dagan, I., and Giampiccolo, D. (2009), "The Fifth PASCAL Recognizing Textual Entailment Challenge", in *Proceedings of the Text Analysis Conference*.

Berman, H. M., Westbrook, J., Feng, Z., Gilliland, G. *et al.* (2000), "The protein data bank", *Nucleic Acids Research* **28**(1), 235–242.

Bingham, E., Chen, J. P., Jankowiak, M., Obermeyer, F. *et al.* (2019), "Pyro: Deep universal probabilistic programming", *Journal of Machine Learning Research* **20**, 1–6.

Bishop, C. M. (2006), *Pattern Recognition and Machine Learning*, Springer.

Bittig, H. C., Steinhoff, T., Claustre, H., Fiedler, B. *et al.* (2018), "An alternative to static climatologies: Robust estimation of open ocean CO_2 variables and nutrient concentrations from T, S, and O2 data using Bayesian neural networks", *Frontiers in Marine Science* **5**, 328.

Blei, D. M., Kucukelbir, A., and McAuliffe, J. D. (2017), "Variational inference: A review for statisticians", *Journal of the American Statistical Association* **112**(518), 859–877.

Bojarski, M., Del Testa, D., Dworakowski, D., Firner, B. *et al.* (2016), "End to end learning for self-driving cars", *arXiv preprint arXiv:1604.07316*.

Bojchevski, A., Shchur, O., Zügner, D., and Günnemann, S. (2018), "NetGAN: Generating graphs via random walks", in *Proceedings of the International Conference on Machine Learning (ICML)*, pp. 609–618.

Bommasani, R., Hudson, D. A., Adeli, E., Altman, R. *et al.* (2021), "On the opportunities and risks of foundation models", *arXiv preprint arXiv:2108.07258*.

Böttcher, A. and Grudsky, S. M. (2005), *Spectral Properties of Banded Toeplitz Matrices*, Vol. 96, SIAM.

Bottou, L. (2010), "Large-scale machine learning with stochastic gradient descent", in *Proceedings of the International Conference on Computational Statistics (COMPSTAT)*, pp. 177–186.

Brafman, R. I. and Tennenholtz, M. (2002), "R-MAX: A general polynomial time algorithm for near-optimal reinforcement learning", *Journal of Machine Learning Research* **3**, 213–231.

Brock, A., Donahue, J., and Simonyan, K. (2019), "Large scale GAN training for high fidelity natural image synthesis", in *Proceedings of the International Conference on Learning Representations (ICLR)*.

Brock, A., Lim, T., Ritchie, J. M., and Weston, N. (2017), "Neural photo editing with introspective adversarial networks", in *Proceedings of the International Conference on Learning Representations (ICLR)*.

Brooks, S., Gelman, A., Jones, G., and Meng, X.-L. (2011), *Handbook of Markov Chain Monte Carlo*, CRC Press.

Brown, T. B., Mann, B., Ryder, N., Subbiah, M. *et al.* (2020), "Language models are few-shot learners", in *Proceedings of Advances in Neural Information Processing Systems (NeurIPS)*.

Brunton, S. L., Noack, B. R., and Koumoutsakos, P. (2020), "Machine learning for fluid mechanics", *Annual Review of Fluid Mechanics* **52**, 477–508.

Bryan, N. J. (2020), "Impulse response data augmentation and deep neural networks for blind room acoustic parameter estimation", in *Proceedings of the IEEE International Conference on Acoustics, Speech and Signal Processing (ICASSP)*, pp. 1–5.

Burge, J., Bonanni, M., Ihme, M., and Hu, L. (2020), "Convolutional LSTM neural networks for modeling wildland fire dynamics", *arXiv preprint arXiv:2012.06679*.

BYU-DML (2019), "BYU's Python library of useable tools for metalearning", github.com/byu-dml/metalearn/tree/develop/metalearn/metafeatures.

Caccia, M., Caccia, L., Fedus, W., Larochelle, H. *et al.* (2018), "Language GANs falling short", in *Proceedings of the International Conference on Learning Representations (ICLR)*.

Carbon Hydrographic Data Office (2021), "GO-SHIP data", cchdo.ucsd.edu.

Carion, N., Massa, F., Synnaeve, G., Usunier, N. *et al.* (2020), "End-to-end object detection with transformers", in *Proceedings of the European Conference on Computer Vision (ECCV)*, pp. 213–229.

Carmo, M. P. d. (1992), *Riemannian Geometry*, Birkhäuser.

Carter, B., Feely, R., Williams, N., Dickson, A. *et al.* (2018), "Updated methods for global locally interpolated estimation of alkalinity, pH, and nitrate", *Limnology and Oceanography: Methods* **16**(2), 119–131.

Casanova, A., Careil, M., Verbeek, J., Drozdzal, M., and Romero, A. (2021), "Instance-conditioned GAN", in *Proceedings of Advances in Neural Information Processing Systems (NeurIPS)*.

Cazenave, T., Chen, Y.-C., Chen, G.-W., Chen, S.-Y. *et al.* (2020), "Polygames: Improved zero learning", *ICGA Journal* **42**(4), 244–256.

Cer, D., Diab, M., Agirre, E., Lopez-Gazpio, I., and Specia, L. (2017), "SemEval-2017 task 1: Semantic textual similarity multilingual and cross-lingual focused evaluation", in *International Workshop on Semantic Evaluation*.

Chai, F., Johnson, K. S., Claustre, H., Xing, X. *et al.* (2020), "Monitoring ocean biogeochemistry with autonomous platforms", *Nature Reviews Earth & Environment* **1**(6), 315–326.

Chan, C., Ginosar, S., Zhou, T., and Efros, A. A. (2019), "Everybody dance now", in *Proceedings of the IEEE/CVF International Conference on Computer Vision (ICCV)*, pp. 5933–5942.

Chang, H., Lu, J., Yu, F., and Finkelstein, A. (2018), "PairedcycleGAN: Asymmetric style transfer for applying and removing makeup", in *Proceedings of the IEEE Conference on Computer Vision and Pattern Recognition (CVPR)*, pp. 40–48.

Chang, M. B., Ullman, T., Torralba, A., and Tenenbaum, J. B. (2017), "A compositional object-based approach to learning physical dynamics", in *Proceedings of the International Conference on Learning Representations (ICLR)*.

Chen, B., Wu, H., Mo, W., Chattopadhyay, I., and Lipson, H. (2018), "Autostacker: A compositional evolutionary learning system", *The Genetic and Evolutionary Computation Conference (GECCO)*.

Chen, L., Lu, K., Rajeswaran, A., Lee, K. *et al.* (2021), "Decision transformer: Reinforcement learning via sequence modeling", *arXiv preprint arXiv:2106.01345*.

Chen, L., Srivastava, S., Duan, Z., and Xu, C. (2017), "Deep cross-modal audio-visual generation", in *Proceedings of the Thematic Workshops of ACM Multimedia*, pp. 349–357.

Chen, M. et al. (2021), "Evaluating large language models trained on code", *arXiv preprint 2107.03374*.

Chen, N., Ferroni, F., Klushyn, A., Paraschos, A. *et al.* (2019), "Fast approximate geodesics for deep generative models", in *International Conference on Artificial Neural Networks (ICANN)*, pp. 554–566.

Chen, S.-Y., Su, W., Gao, L., Xia, S., and Fu, H. (2020), "DeepFaceDrawing: Deep generation of face images from sketches", *ACM Transactions on Graphics (Proceedings of ACM SIGGRAPH 2020)* **39**(4), 72:1–72:16.

Chen, T. Q., Rubanova, Y., Bettencourt, J., and Duvenaud, D. K. (2018), "Neural ordinary differential equations", in *Proceedings of Advances in Neural Information Processing Systems (NeurIPS)*, pp. 6571–6583.

Chen, Y., Huang, A., Wang, Z., Antonoglou, I. *et al.* (2018), "Bayesian optimization in AlphaGo", *arXiv preprint arXiv:1812.06855*.

Chen, Z., Zhang, H., Zhang, X., and Zhao, L. (2018), "Quora question pairs", www.kaggle.com/c/quora-question-pairs.

Cho, K., Van Merriënboer, B., Gulcehre, C., Bahdanau, D. *et al.* (2014), "Learning phrase representations using RNN encoder-decoder for statistical machine translation", in *Proceedings of the Conference on Empirical Methods in Natural Language Processing (EMNLP)*.

Choi, C. Q. (2021), "7 revealing ways AIs fail: Neural networks can be disastrously brittle, forgetful, and surprisingly bad at math", *IEEE Spectrum* **58**(10), 42–47.

Choi, K., Wu, M., Goodman, N., and Ermon, S. (2019), "Meta-amortized variational inference and learning", in *Proceedings of the International Conference on Learning Representations (ICLR)*.

Choi, Y., Choi, M., Kim, M., Ha, J.-W. *et al.* (2018), "StarGAN: Unified generative adversarial networks for multi-domain image-to-image translation", in *Proceedings of the IEEE Conference on Computer Vision and Pattern Recognition (CVPR)*, pp. 8789–8797.

Chollet, F. (2015), "Keras", github.com/fchollet/keras.

Christofides, N. (1976), Worst-case analysis of a new heuristic for the travelling salesman problem, Technical report, Carnegie-Mellon University Pittsburgh PA Management Sciences Research Group.

Cichy, R. M., Khosla, A., Pantazis, D., Torralba, A., and Oliva, A. (2016), "Comparison of deep neural networks to spatio-temporal cortical dynamics of human visual object recognition reveals hierarchical correspondence", *Scientific Reports* **6**(1), 1–13.

Climate Modeling Center (2021), "Institut Pierre Simon Laplace Climate Model 5 (IPSL-CM5)", cmc.ipsl.fr/international-projects/cmip5/.

Cormen, T. H., Leiserson, C. E., Rivest, R. L., and Stein, C. (1990), *Introduction to Algorithms*, MIT Press.

Dai, H., Khalil, E., Zhang, Y., Dilkina, B., and Song, L. (2017), "Learning combinatorial optimization algorithms over graphs", in *Proceedings of Advances in Neural Information Processing Systems (NeurIPS)*, pp. 6348–6358.

Dai, Z., Cai, B., Lin, Y., and Chen, J. (2021), "Up-DETR: Unsupervised pre-training for object detection with transformers", in *Proceedings of the IEEE/CVF Conference on Computer Vision and Pattern Recognition (CVPR)*, pp. 1601–1610.

Dai, Z., Yang, Z., Yang, Y., Cohen, W. W. *et al.* (2019), "Transformer-XL: Attentive language models beyond a fixed-length context".

d'Apolito, S., Paudel, D. P., Huang, Z., Romero, A., and Van Gool, L. (2021), "Ganmut: Learning interpretable conditional space for gamut of emotions", in *Proceedings of the IEEE/CVF Conference on Computer Vision and Pattern Recognition (CVPR)*, pp. 568–577.

d'Ascoli, S., Touvron, H., Leavitt, M., Morcos, A. *et al.* (2021), "ConViT: Improving vision transformers with soft convolutional inductive biases", in *Proceedings of the International Conference on Machine Learning (ICML)*.

Daskalakis, C., Ilyas, A., Syrgkanis, V., and Zeng, H. (2017), "Training GANs with optimism", *arXiv preprint arXiv:1711.00141*.

Davidon, W. C. (1991), "Variable metric method for minimization", *SIAM Journal on Optimization* **1**(1), 1–17.

Davidson, T. R., Falorsi, L., De Cao, N., Kipf, T., and Tomczak, J. M. (2018), "Hyperspherical variational auto-encoders", in *Proceedings of the Conference on Uncertainty in Artificial Intelligence Conference (UAI)*.

De Bortoli, V., Mathieu, E., Hutchinson, M., Thornton, J. *et al.* (2022), "Riemannian score-based generative modeling", *arXiv preprint arXiv:2202.02763*.

De Fauw, J., Dieleman, S., and Simonyan, K. (2019), "Hierarchical autoregressive image models with auxiliary decoders", *arXiv preprint arXiv:1903.04933*.

Degrave, J., Felici, F., Buchli, J., Neunert, M. *et al.* (2022), "Magnetic control of tokamak plasmas through deep reinforcement learning", *Nature* **602**(7897), 414–419.

Devlin, J., Chang, M.-W., Lee, K., and Toutanova, K. (2019), "BERT: Pre-training of deep bidirectional transformers for language understanding", in *Proceedings of the North American Chapter of the Association for Computational Linguistics: Human Language Technologies (NAACL)*, pp. 4171–4186.

Dhariwal, P. and Nichol, A. (2021), "Diffusion models beat GANs on image synthesis", in *Proceedings of Advances in Neural Information Processing Systems (NeurIPS)*.

Dijkstra, E. W. (1959), "A note on two problems in connexion with graphs", *Numerische Mathematik* **1**(1), 269–271.

Dillon, J. V., Langmore, I., Tran, D., Brevdo, E. *et al.* (2017), "TensorFlow distributions", *arXiv preprint arXiv:1711.10604*.

Dinh, L., Sohl-Dickstein, J., and Bengio, S. (2017), "Density estimation using real NVP", in *Proceedings of the International Conference on Learning Representations (ICLR)*.

Do Carmo, M. P. (2016), *Differential Geometry of Curves and Surfaces*, 2nd edn, Courier Dover Publications.

Dokmanic, I., Parhizkar, R., Ranieri, J., and Vetterli, M. (2015), "Euclidean distance matrices: Essential theory, algorithms, and applications", *IEEE Signal Processing Magazine* **32**(6), 12–30.

Dolan, W. B. and Brockett, C. (2005), "Automatically constructing a corpus of sentential paraphrases", in *International Workshop on Paraphrasing*.

Donahue, C., McAuley, J., and Puckette, M. (2018), "Adversarial audio synthesis", in *International Conference on Learning Representations (ICLR)*.

Dong, H.-W., Hsiao, W.-Y., Yang, L.-C., and Yang, Y.-H. (2018), "MuseGAN: Multi-track sequential generative adversarial networks for symbolic music generation and accompaniment", in *Proceedings of Thirty-Second AAAI Conference on Artificial Intelligence*.

Dosovitskiy, A., Beyer, L., Kolesnikov, A., Weissenborn, D. *et al.* (2020), "An image is worth 16x16 words: Transformers for image recognition at scale", in *Proceedings of the International Conference on Learning Representations (ICLR)*.

Dozat, T. (2016), "Incorporating Nesterov momentum into Adam", in *Proceedings of the International Conference on Learning Representations (ICLR)*.

Drori, I., Cohen-Or, D., and Yeshurun, H. (2003a), "Example-based style synthesis", in *Proceedings of the IEEE/CVF Conference on Computer Vision and Pattern Recognition (CVPR)*, Vol. 2, pp. II–143.

Drori, I., Cohen-Or, D., and Yeshurun, H. (2003b), "Fragment-based image completion", in *ACM Transactions on Graphics (TOG)*, Vol. 22, pp. 303–312.

Drori, I., Dwivedi, I., Shrestha, P., Wan, J. *et al.* (2018), "High quality prediction of protein q8 secondary structure by diverse neural network architectures", *NeurIPS Workshop on Machine Learning for Molecules and Materials.*

Drori, I., Fishbach, A., and Yeshurun, Y. (2004), "Spectral sound gap filling", in *Proceedings of the International Conference on Pattern Recognition (ICPR).*

Drori, I., Krishnamurthy, Y., Rampin, R., Lourenco, R. *et al.* (2018), "AlphaD3M: Machine learning pipeline synthesis", in *ICML International Workshop on Automated Machine Learning.*

Drori, I., Krishnamurthy, Y., Rampin, R., Lourenco, R. *et al.* (2019), "Automatic machine learning by pipeline synthesis using model-based reinforcement learning and a grammar", in *ICML International Workshop on Automated Machine Learning.*

Drori, I., Zhang, S., Shuttleworth, R., Tang, L. *et al.* (n.d.), "A neural network solves, explains, and generates university math problems by program synthesis and few-shot learning at human level", *Submitted.*

Duchi, J., Hazan, E., and Singer, Y. (2011), "Adaptive subgradient methods for online learning and stochastic optimization", *Journal of Machine Learning Research* **12**, 2121–2159.

Duraisamy, K., Iaccarino, G., and Xiao, H. (2019), "Turbulence modeling in the age of data", *Annual Review of Fluid Mechanics* **51**, 357–377.

Duvenaud, D. K., Maclaurin, D., Iparraguirre, J., Bombarell, R. *et al.* (2015), "Convolutional networks on graphs for learning molecular fingerprints", in *Proceedings of Advances in Neural Information Processing Systems (NeurIPS)*, pp. 2224–2232.

D'Alelio, D., Rampone, S., Cusano, L. M., Morfino, V. *et al.* (2020), "Machine learning identifies a strong association between warming and reduced primary productivity in an oligotrophic ocean gyre", *Scientific Reports* **10**(1), 1–12.

Ecoffet, A., Huizinga, J., Lehman, J., Stanley, K. O., and Clune, J. (2019), "Go-Explore: A new approach for hard-exploration problems", *arXiv preprint arXiv:1901.10995.*

Ecoffet, A., Huizinga, J., Lehman, J., Stanley, K. O., and Clune, J. (2021), "First return, then explore", *Nature* **590**(7847), 580–586.

Efron, B. and Hastie, T. (2016), *Computer Age Statistical Inference*, Cambridge University Press.

Engel, J., Agrawal, K. K., Chen, S., Gulrajani, I. *et al.* (2019), "GANSynth: Adversarial neural audio synthesis", in *Proceedings of the International Conference on Learning Representations (ICLR).*

Erdös, P. and Rényi, A. (2011), On the evolution of random graphs, *in* The structure and dynamics of networks, Princeton University Press, pp. 38–82.

Ernst, D., Geurts, P., and Wehenkel, L. (2005), "Tree-based batch mode reinforcement learning", *Journal of Machine Learning Research* **6**, 503–556.

Eysenbach, B. and Levine, S. (2022), "Maximum entropy RL (provably) solves some robust RL problems", in *Proceedings of the International Conference on Learning Representations (ICLR).*

Falorsi, L., de Haan, P., Davidson, T. R., and Forré, P. (2019), "Reparameterizing distributions on Lie groups", in *Proceedings of Machine Learning Research (PMLR)*, pp. 3244–3253.

Fang, F., Yamagishi, J., Echizen, I., and Lorenzo-Trueba, J. (2018), "High-quality nonparallel voice conversion based on cycle-consistent adversarial network", in *Proceedings of the IEEE International Conference on Acoustics, Speech and Signal Processing (ICASSP)*, pp. 5279–5283.

Farimani, A. B., Gomes, J., and Pande, V. S. (2017), "Deep learning the physics of transport phenomena", *arXiv preprint arXiv:1709.02432*.

Fedus, W., Goodfellow, I., and Dai, A. M. (2018), "MaskGAN: Better text generation via filling in the_", in *Proceedings of the International Conference on Learning Representation (ICLR)*.

Feinberg, V., Wan, A., Stoica, I., Jordan, M. I. *et al.* (2018), "Model-based value estimation for efficient model-free reinforcement learning", *arXiv preprint arXiv:1803.00101*.

Felleman, D. J. and Van Essen, D. C. (1991), "Distributed hierarchical processing in the primate cerebral cortex", *Cerebral Cortex* **1**(1), 1–47.

Fernando, T., Denman, S., Sridharan, S., and Fookes, C. (2017), "Going deeper: Autonomous steering with neural memory networks", in *Proceedings of the IEEE/CVF International Conference on Computer Vision Workshops*, pp. 214–221.

Feurer, M., Klein, A., Eggensperger, K., Springenberg, J. *et al.* (2015), "Efficient and robust automated machine learning", in *Proceedings of Advances in Neural Information Processing Systems (NeurIPS)*, pp. 2962–2970.

Fey, M. and Lenssen, J. E. (2019), "Fast graph representation learning with Py-Torch Geometric", in *Proceedings of the International Conference on Learning Representations (ICLR)*.

Figurnov, M., Mohamed, S., and Mnih, A. (2018), "Implicit reparameterization gradients", in *Proceedings of Advances in Neural Information Processing Systems (NeurIPS)*, pp. 441–452.

Finney, M. A. (1998), *FARSITE: Fire Area Simulator–model development and evaluation*, number 4, US Department of Agriculture, Forest Service, Rocky Mountain Research Station.

Fletcher, R. and Powell, M. J. (1963), "A rapidly convergent descent method for minimization", *The Computer Journal* **6**(2), 163–168.

Freeman, W. T., Jones, T. R., and Pasztor, E. C. (2002), "Example-based super-resolution", *IEEE Computer Graphics and Applications* pp. 56–65.

Frühstück, A., Alhashim, I., and Wonka, P. (2019), "TileGAN: Synthesis of large-scale non-homogeneous textures", *ACM Transactions on Graphics (TOG)* **38**(4), 1–11.

Fu, K., Peng, J., He, Q., and Zhang, H. (2021), "Single image 3D object reconstruction based on deep learning: A review", *Multimedia Tools and Applications* **80**, 463–498.

Fukushima, K. (1988), "Neocognitron: A hierarchical neural network capable of visual pattern recognition", *Neural Networks* **1**(2), 119–130.

Fusi, N., Sheth, R., and Elibol, M. (2018), "Probabilistic matrix factorization for automated machine learning", in *Proceedings of Advances in Neural Information Processing Systems (NeurIPS)*, pp. 3348–3357.

Ganapathi Subramanian, S. and Crowley, M. (2018), "Using spatial reinforcement learning to build forest wildfire dynamics models from satellite images", *Frontiers in ICT* **5**, 6.

Gao, M., Yang, J., Gong, D., Shi, P. *et al.* (2019), "Footprints of Atlantic multidecadal oscillation in the low-frequency variation of extreme high temperature in the northern hemisphere", *Journal of Climate* **32**(3), 791–802.

Gao, R. and Grauman, K. (2019), "2.5D visual sound", in *Proceedings of the IEEE/CVF Conference on Computer Vision and Pattern Recognition (CVPR)*, pp. 324–333.

Garcia, O. E., Kube, R., Theodorsen, A., and Pécseli, H. L. (2016), "Stochastic modelling of intermittent fluctuations in the scrape-off layer: Correlations, distributions, level crossings, and moment estimation", *Physics of Plasmas* **23**(5), 052308.

Garcia, O. E. and Theodorsen, A. (2017), "Power law spectra and intermittent fluctuations due to uncorrelated Lorentzian pulses", *Physics of Plasmas* **24**(2), 020704.

Garcia, V. and Bruna, J. (2018), "Few-shot learning with graph neural networks", in *Proceedings of the International Conference on Learning Representations (ICLR)*.

Garcia, V., Hoogeboom, E., Fuchs, F., Posner, I., and Welling, M. (n.d.), "E(n) equivariant normalizing flows", in *Proceedings of Advances in Neural Information Processing Systems (NeurIPS)*.

Gemici, M. C., Rezende, D., and Mohamed, S. (2016), "Normalizing flows on Riemannian manifolds", in *Proceedings of the NeurIPS Bayesian Deep Learning Workshop*.

Gilmer, J., Schoenholz, S. S., Riley, P. F., Vinyals, O., and Dahl, G. E. (2017), "Neural message passing for quantum chemistry", in *Proceedings of the International Conference on Machine Learning (ICML)*, pp. 1263–1272.

Giordano, R., Broderick, T., and Jordan, M. I. (2018), "Covariances, robustness, and variational Bayes", *Journal of Machine Learning Research* **19**(1), 1981–2029.

Girdhar, R., Fouhey, D. F., Rodriguez, M., and Gupta, A. (2016), "Learning a predictable and generative vector representation for objects", in *European Conference on Computer Vision*, pp. 484–499.

Glorot, X. and Bengio, Y. (2010), "Understanding the difficulty of training deep feedforward neural networks", in *Proceedings of the Thirteenth International Conference on Artificial Intelligence and Statistics (AISTATS)*, pp. 249–256.

Godard, C., Mac Aodha, O., Firman, M., and Brostow, G. J. (2019), "Digging into self-supervised monocular depth prediction", in *Proceedings of the IEEE/CVF International Conference on Computer Vision (ICCV)*.

Golden, B., Bodin, L., Doyle, T., and W, S. J. (1980), "Approximate traveling salesman algorithms", *Operations Research* **28**(3,part-II), 694–711.

Gomez, A. N., Huang, S., Zhang, I., Li, B. M. *et al.* (2018), "Unsupervised cipher cracking using discrete GANs", in *Proceedings of the International Conference on Learning Representations (ICLR)*.

Goodfellow, I., Pouget-Abadie, J., Mirza, M., Xu, B. *et al.* (2014), "Generative adversarial nets", in *Proceedings of Advances in Neural Information Processing Systems (NeurIPS)*, pp. 2672–2680.

Google (2020), "Compare GAN library", github.com/google/compare_gan.

Grathwohl, W., Chen, R. T., Bettencourt, J., Sutskever, I., and Duvenaud, D. (2019), "FFJORD: Free-form continuous dynamics for scalable reversible generative models", in *Proceedings of the International Conference on Learning Representations (ICLR)*.

Grover, A., Chute, C., Shu, R., Cao, Z., and Ermon, S. (2020), "AlignFlow: Cycle consistent learning from multiple domains via normalizing flows", in *Proceedings of the AAAI Conference on Artificial Intelligence*, Vol. 34, pp. 4028–4035.

Grover, A. and Leskovec, J. (2016), "Node2Vec: Scalable feature learning for networks", in *Proceedings of the 22nd ACM SIGKDD International Conference on Knowledge Discovery and Data Mining*, pp. 855–864.

Gruber, N., Landschützer, P., and Lovenduski, N. S. (2019), "The variable Southern Ocean carbon sink", *Annual Review of Marine Science* **11**, 159–186.

Guo, J., Lu, S., Cai, H., Zhang, W. *et al.* (2018), "Long text generation via adversarial training with leaked information", in *Proceedings of the Thirty-Second AAAI Conference on Artificial Intelligence*.

Guo, X., Li, W., and Iorio, F. (2016), "Convolutional neural networks for steady flow approximation", in *Proceedings of the 22nd ACM SIGKDD International Conference on Knowledge Discovery and Data Mining*, pp. 481–490.

Gupta, A., Johnson, J., Fei-Fei, L., Savarese, S., and Alahi, A. (2018), "Social-GAN: Socially acceptable trajectories with generative adversarial networks", in *Proceedings of the IEEE/CVF Conference on Computer Vision and Pattern Recognition (CVPR)*, pp. 2255–2264.

Guu, K., Hashimoto, T. B., Oren, Y., and Liang, P. (2018), "Generating sentences by editing prototypes", *Transactions of the Association for Computational Linguistics* **6**, 437–450.

Ha, D. and Schmidhuber, J. (2018), "World models", in *Proceedings of Advances in Neural Information Processing Systems (NeurIPS)*.

Hadjeres, G., Pachet, F., and Nielsen, F. (2017), "DeepBach: A steerable model for Bach chorales generation", in *Proceedings of the International Conference on Machine Learning (ICML)*.

Halofsky, J., Peterson, D., and Harvey, B. (2020), "Changing wildfire, changing forests: The effects of climate change on fire regimes and vegetation in the Pacific Northwest, USA", *Fire Ecology* **16**(4).

Ham, Y.-G., Kim, J.-H., and Luo, J.-J. (2019), "Deep learning for multi-year ENSO forecasts", *Nature* **573**(7775), 568–572.

Hamilton, W., Ying, Z., and Leskovec, J. (2017), "Inductive representation learning on large graphs", in *Proceedings of Advances in Neural Information Processing Systems (NeurIPS)*, pp. 1024–1034.

Han, S. and Sung, Y. (2021), "A max–min entropy framework for reinforcement learning", in *Proceedings of Advances in Neural Information Processing Systems (NeurIPS)*.

Han, X., Wu, Z., Huang, W., Scott, M. R., and Davis, L. S. (2019), "FiNet: Compatible and diverse fashion image inpainting", in *Proceedings of the IEEE/CVF International Conference on Computer Vision (ICCV)*, pp. 4481–4491.

Hansen, N. (2006), *The CMA evolution strategy: A comparing review*, Springer, pp. 75–102.

He, K., Zhang, X., Ren, S., and Sun, J. (2016*a*), "Deep residual learning for image recognition", in *Proceedings of the IEEE/CVF Conference on Computer Vision and Pattern Recognition (CVPR)*, pp. 770–778.

He, K., Zhang, X., Ren, S., and Sun, J. (2016*b*), "Identity mappings in deep residual networks", in *Proceedings of the European Conference on Computer Vision (ECCV)*, pp. 630–645.

He, S., Hollenbeck, B., and Proserpio, D. (2020), "The market for fake reviews", *Marketing Science*.

He, X., Zhao, K., and Chu, X. (2021), "AutoML: A survey of the state-of-the-art", *Knowledge-Based Systems* **212**.

Hecker, S., Dai, D., Liniger, A., Hahner, M., and Van Gool, L. (2020), "Learning accurate and human-like driving using semantic maps and attention", in *IEEE/RSJ International Conference on Intelligent Robots and Systems (IROS)*, pp. 2346–2353.

Hecker, S., Dai, D., and Van Gool, L. (2018), "End-to-end learning of driving models with surround-view cameras and route planners", in *Proceedings of the European Conference on Computer Vision (ECCV)*, pp. 435–453.

Hertzmann, A., Jacobs, C. E., Oliver, N., Curless, B., and Salesin, D. H. (2001), "Image analogies", in *Proceedings of ACM SIGGRAPH Conference on Computer Graphics and Interactive Techniques*, pp. 327–340.

Heusel, M., Ramsauer, H., Unterthiner, T., Nessler, B., and Hochreiter, S. (2017), "GANs trained by a two time-scale update rule converge to a local Nash equilibrium", in *Proceedings of Advances in Neural Information Processing Systems (NeurIPS)*, pp. 6626–6637.

Hinton, G. E. and Salakhutdinov, R. R. (2006), "Reducing the dimensionality of data with neural networks", *Science* **313**(5786), 504–507.

Ho, J. and Ermon, S. (2016), "Generative adversarial imitation learning", in *Proceedings of Advances in Neural Information Processing Systems (NeurIPS)*.

Ho, J., Jain, A., and Abbeel, P. (2020), "Denoising diffusion probabilistic models", in *Proceedings of Advances in Neural Information Processing Systems (NeurIPS)*, pp. 6840–6851.

Hochreiter, S. and Schmidhuber, J. (1997), "Long short-term memory", *Neural Computation* **9**(8), 1735–1780.

Hodges, J. and Lattimer, B. (2019), "Wildland fire spread modeling using convolutional neural networks", *Springer Fire Technology* **55**, 2115–2142.

Hoffman, M. D., Blei, D. M., Wang, C., and Paisley, J. (2013), "Stochastic variational inference", *Journal of Machine Learning Research* **14**(1), 1303–1347.

Holbrook, A. (2018), Geometric Bayes, PhD thesis, UC Irvine.

Holland, P. W., Laskey, K. B., and Leinhardt, S. (1983), "Stochastic blockmodels: First steps", *Social Networks* **5**(2), 109–137.

Horisaki, R., Takagi, R., and Tanida, J. (2016), "Learning-based imaging through scattering media", *Optics Express* **24**(13), 13738–13743.

Howard, A., Zhu, M., Chen, B., Kalenichenko, D. *et al.* (2017), "MobileNets: Efficient convolutional neural networks for mobile vision applications", *arXiv preprint arXiv:1704.04861*.

Hu, J., Shen, L., and Sun, G. (2018), "Squeeze-and-excitation networks", in *Proceedings of the IEEE Conference on Computer Vision and Pattern Recognition (CVPR)*, pp. 7132–7141.

Hu, T., Wang, L., Xu, X., Liu, S., and Jia, J. (2021), "Self-supervised 3D mesh reconstruction from single images", in *Proceedings of the IEEE/CVF Conference on Computer Vision and Pattern Recognition (CVPR)*, pp. 6002–6011.

Huang, C.-Z. A., Cooijmans, T., Roberts, A., Courville, A., and Eck, D. (2017), "Counterpoint by convolution", in *Proceedings of the 18th International Society for Music Information Retrieval Conference (ISMIR)*.

Huang, G., Liu, Z., van der Maaten, L., and Weinberger, K. Q. (2017), "Densely connected convolutional networks", in *Proceedings of the IEEE/CVF Conference on Computer Vision and Pattern Recognition (CVPR)*, pp. 4700–4708.

Huang, P.-Y., Patrick, M., Hu, J., Neubig, G. *et al.* (2021), "Multilingual multimodal pre-training for zero-shot cross-lingual transfer of vision-language models", in *Proceedings of the Annual Conference of the North American Chapter of the Association for Computational Linguistics (NAACL)*, pp. 2443–2459.

Huang, X. and Belongie, S. (2017), "Arbitrary style transfer in real-time with adaptive instance normalization", in *Proceedings of the IEEE/CVF International Conference on Computer Vision (ICCV)*, pp. 1501–1510.

Huang, X., Liu, M.-Y., Belongie, S., and Kautz, J. (2018), "Multimodal unsupervised image-to-image translation", in *Proceedings of the European Conference on Computer Vision (ECCV)*, pp. 172–189.

Hubel, D. H. and Wiesel, T. N. (1968), "Receptive fields and functional architecture of monkey striate cortex", *Journal of Physiology* **195**(1), 215–243.

Hyun, S., Kim, J., and Heo, J.-P. (2021), "Self-supervised video GANs: Learning for appearance consistency and motion coherency", in *Proceedings of the IEEE/CVF Conference on Computer Vision and Pattern Recognition (CVPR)*, pp. 10826–10835.

Iizuka, S., Simo-Serra, E., and Ishikawa, H. (2017), "Globally and locally consistent image completion", *ACM Transactions on Graphics (ToG)* **36**(4), 107.

Ioffe, S. and Szegedy, C. (2015), "Batch normalization: Accelerating deep network training by reducing internal covariate shift", in *Proceedings of the International Conference on Machine Learning (ICML)*.

Isola, P., Zhu, J.-Y., Zhou, T., and Efros, A. A. (2017), "Image-to-image translation with conditional adversarial networks", in *Proceedings of the IEEE/CVF Conference on Computer Vision and Pattern Recognition (CVPR)*, pp. 1125–1134.

Izmailov, P., Podoprikhin, D., Garipov, T., Vetrov, D., and Wilson, A. G. (2018), "Averaging weights leads to wider optima and better generalization", in *Proceedings of the Conference on Uncertainty in Artificial Intelligence (UAI)*.

Jackson, A. S., Bulat, A., Argyriou, V., and Tzimiropoulos, G. (2017), "Large pose 3D face reconstruction from a single image via direct volumetric CNN regression", in *Proceedings of the IEEE/CVF International Conference on Computer Vision*.

Jain, P., Coogan, S. C., Subramanian, S. G., Crowley, M. *et al.* (2020), "A review of machine learning applications in wildfire science and management", *Environmental Reviews* **28**(4), 478–505.

Jerfel, G., Wang, S., Wong-Fannjiang, C., Heller, K. A. *et al.* (2021), "Variational refinement for importance sampling using the forward Kullback–Leibler divergence", in *Proceedings of the Conference on Uncertainty in Artificial Intelligence (UAI)*, pp. 1819–1829.

Jin, W., Barzilay, R., and Jaakkola, T. (2018), "Junction tree variational autoencoder for molecular graph generation", *arXiv preprint arXiv:1802.04364*.

Jordan, M. I., Ghahramani, Z., Jaakkola, T. S., and Saul, L. K. (1999), "An introduction to variational methods for graphical models", *Machine Learning* **37**(2), 183–233.

Jozefowicz, R., Zaremba, W., and Sutskever, I. (2015), "An empirical exploration of recurrent network architectures", in *Proceedings of International Conference on Machine Learning*, pp. 2342–2350.

Jumper, J., Evans, R., Pritzel, A., Green, T. *et al.* (2021), "Highly accurate protein structure prediction with AlphaFold", *Nature* **596**(7873), 583–589.

Kabsch, W. and Sander, C. (1983), "Dictionary of protein secondary structure: Pattern recognition of hydrogen-bonded and geometrical features", *Biopolymers: Original Research on Biomolecules* **22**(12), 2577–2637.

Kahng, M., Thorat, N., Chau, D. H. P., Viégas, F. B., and Wattenberg, M. (2018), "GAN Lab: Understanding complex deep generative models using interactive visual experimentation", *IEEE Transactions on Visualization and Computer Graphics* **25**(1), 1–11.

Kakade, S. M. (2001), "A natural policy gradient", in *Proceedings of Advances in Neural Information Processing Systems (NeurIPS)*.

Kaneko, T., Kameoka, H., Tanaka, K., and Hojo, N. (2019), "CycleGAN-VC2: Improved CycleGAN-based non-parallel voice conversion", in *Proceedings of the IEEE International Conference on Acoustics, Speech and Signal Processing (ICASSP)*, pp. 6820–6824.

Kant, Y., Batra, D., Anderson, P., Schwing, A. *et al.* (2020), "Spatially aware multimodal transformers for textVQA", in *Proceedings of the European Conference on Computer Vision (ECCV)*, pp. 715–732.

Karras, T., Aila, T., Laine, S., and Lehtinen, J. (2018), "Progressive growing of GANs for improved quality, stability, and variation", in *Proceedings of the International Conference on Learning Representations (ICLR)*.

Karras, T., Laine, S., and Aila, T. (2019), "A style-based generator architecture for generative adversarial networks", in *Proceedings of the IEEE/CVF Conference on Computer Vision and Pattern Recognition (CVPR)*, pp. 4401–4410.

Kazeminia, S., Baur, C., Kuijper, A., van Ginneken, B. *et al.* (2020), "GANs for medical image analysis", *Artificial Intelligence in Medicine* **109**.

Kendall, A. and Gal, Y. (2017), "What uncertainties do we need in Bayesian deep learning for computer vision?", in *Proceedings of Advances in Neural Information Processing Systems (NeurIPS)*, Vol. 30.

Kennedy, S., Walsh, N., Sloka, K., Foster, J., and McCarren, A. (2019), "Fact or factitious? Contextualized opinion spam detection", *Proceedings of the Annual Meeting of the Association for Computational Linguistics: Student Research Workshop* pp. 344–350.

Keskar, N. S., McCann, B., Varshney, L. R., Xiong, C., and Socher, R. (2019), "CTRL: A conditional transformer language model for controllable generation", *arXiv preprint arXiv:1909.05858*.

Khrulkov, V. and Oseledets, I. (2018), "Geometry score: A method for comparing generative adversarial networks", in *Proceedings of the International Conference on Machine Learning (ICML)*.

Kim, H., Carrido, P., Tewari, A., Xu, W. *et al.* (2018), "Deep video portraits", *ACM Transactions on Graphics (TOG)* **37**(4), 163.

Kim, H., Kim, D., Kim, G., Cho, J., and Huh, K. (2020), "Multi-head attention based probabilistic vehicle trajectory prediction", in *IEEE Intelligent Vehicles Symposium (IV)*, pp. 1720–1725.

Kim, H., Remaggi, L., Jackson, P. J. B., and Hilton, A. (2019), "Immersive spatial audio reproduction for VR/AR using room acoustic modelling from 360° images", in *Proceedings of the IEEE Conference on Virtual Reality and 3D User Interfaces (VR)*, pp. 120–126.

Kim, J. H. and Vu, V. H. (2003), "Generating random regular graphs", in *Proceedings of the Annual ACM Symposium on Theory of Computing (STOC)*, pp. 213–222.

Kim, S. W., Philion, J., Torralba, A., and Fidler, S. (2021), "DriveGAN: Towards a controllable high-quality neural simulation", in *Proceedings of the IEEE/CVF Conference on Computer Vision and Pattern Recognition (CVPR)*, pp. 5820–5829.

Kim, Y., Wiseman, S., and Rush, A. M. (2018), "A tutorial on deep latent variable models of natural language", *arXiv preprint arXiv:1812.06834*.

Kingma, D. P. and Ba, J. (2014), "Adam: A method for stochastic optimization", in *Proceedings of the International Conference on Learning Representations (ICLR)*.

Kingma, D. P. and Dhariwal, P. (2018), "Glow: Generative flow with invertible 1x1 convolutions", in *Proceedings of Advances in Neural Information Processing Systems (NeurIPS)*, pp. 10215–10224.

Kingma, D. P. and Welling, M. (2014), "Auto-encoding variational Bayes", in *Proceedings of the International Conference on Learning Representations (ICLR)*.

Kipf, T. N. and Welling, M. (2017), "Semi-supervised classification with graph convolutional networks", in *Proceedings of the International Conference on Learning Representations (ICLR)*.

Kiros, R., Zhu, Y., Salakhutdinov, R. R., Zemel, R. *et al.* (2015), "Skip-thought vectors", in *Proceedings of Advances in Neural Information Processing Systems (NeurIPS)*, pp. 3294–3302.

Kniaz, V. V., Knyaz, V. A., Remondino, F., Bordodymov, A., and Moshkantsev, P. (2020), "Image-to-voxel model translation for 3D scene reconstruction and segmentation", in *Proceedings of the European Conference on Computer Vision (ECCV)*, pp. 105–124.

Koh, P. W., Sagawa, S., Marklund, H., Xie, S. M. *et al.* (2021), "Wilds: A benchmark of in-the-wild distribution shifts", in *Proceedings of the International Conference on Machine Learning (ICML)*, pp. 5637–5664.

Köhler, J., Krämer, A., and Noé, F. (n.d.), "Smooth normalizing flows", in *Proceedings of Advances in Neural Information Processing Systems (NeurIPS)*.

Kokiopoulou, E., Hauth, A., Sbaiz, L., Gesmundo, A. *et al.* (2019), "Fast task-aware architecture inference", *arXiv preprint arXiv:1902.05781*.

Kon, H. and Koike, H. (2018), "Deep neural networks for cross-modal estimations of acoustic reverberation characteristics from two-dimensional images", in *Audio Engineering Society*, number 144.

Kon, H. and Koike, H. (2019), "Estimation of late reverberation characteristics from a single two-dimensional environmental image using convolutional neural networks", *Journal of the Audio Engineering Society* **67**, 540–548.

Kon, H. and Koike, H. (2020), "An auditory scaling method for reverb synthesis from a single two-dimensional image", *Acoustical Science and Technology* **41**(4), 675–685.

Kong, L., Lian, C., Huang, D., Li, Z. *et al.* (n.d.), "Breaking the dilemma of medical image-to-image translation", in *Proceedings of Advances in Neural Information Processing Systems (NeurIPS)*.

Kool, W., van Hoof, H., and Welling, M. (2019), "Attention, learn to solve routing problems!", in *Proceedings of the International Conference on Learning Representations (ICLR)*.

Koutsias, N., Xanthopoulos, G., Founda, D., Xystrakis, F. *et al.* (2013), "On the relationships between forest fires and weather conditions in Greece from long-term national observations (1894–2010)", *International Journal of Wildland Fire* **22**, 493–507.

Krizhevsky, A., Sutskever, I., and Hinton, G. E. (2012), "ImageNet classification with deep convolutional neural networks", in *Proceedings of Advances in Neural Information Processing Systems (NeurIPS)*, pp. 1097–1105.

Kruskal, J. B. (1956), "On the shortest spanning subtree of a graph and the traveling salesman problem", *Proceedings of the American Mathematical Society* **7**(1), 48–50.

Kucukelbir, A., Tran, D., Ranganath, R., Gelman, A., and Blei, D. M. (2017), "Automatic differentiation variational inference", *Journal of Machine Learning Research* **18**(1), 430–474.

Kumar, A., Sattigeri, P., and Fletcher, T. (2017), "Semi-supervised learning with GANs: Manifold invariance with improved inference", in *Proceedings of Advances in Neural Information Processing Systems (NeurIPS)*, pp. 5534–5544.

Lambrecht, B. (2006), "Voxelization of boundary representations using oriented LEGO® plates", code.google.com/archive/p/lsculpt/.

Lan, Z., Chen, M., Goodman, S., Gimpel, K. *et al.* (2020), "Albert: A lite BERT for self-supervised learning of language representations", in *Proceedings of the International Conference on Learning Representations (ICLR)*.

Le, Q. and Mikolov, T. (2014), "Distributed representations of sentences and documents", in *Proceedings of the International Conference on Machine Learning (ICML)*, pp. 1188–1196.

LeCun, Y., Kavukcuoglu, K., and Farabet, C. (2010), "Convolutional networks and applications in vision", in *Proceedings of the IEEE International Symposium on Circuits and Systems*, pp. 253–256.

Ledig, C., Theis, L., Huszár, F., Caballero, J. *et al.* (2017), "Photo-realistic single image super-resolution using a generative adversarial network", in *Proceedings of the IEEE Conference on Computer Vision and Pattern Recognition (CVPR)*, pp. 4681–4690.

Lee, J., Hwangbo, J., Wellhausen, L., Koltun, V., and Hutter, M. (2020), "Learning quadrupedal locomotion over challenging terrain", *Science Robotics* **5**(47).

Lee, K. S., Bryan, N. J., and Abel, J. S. (2010), "Approximating measured reverberation using a hybrid fixed/switched convolution structure", in *Proceedings of the 13th International Conference on Digital Audio Effects (DAFX)*.

Lee, S., Yu, Y., Kim, G., Breuel, T. *et al.* (2021), "Parameter efficient multimodal transformers for video representation learning", in *Proceedings of the International Conference on Learning Representations (ICLR)*.

Lego (2020), "Lego Mosaic Maker", www.lego.com/en-us/product/mosaic-maker-40179.

Levinthal, C. (1969), "How to fold graciously", in *Proceedings of a meeting held at Allerton House*, pp. 22–24.

Lewis, M., Liu, Y., Goyal, N., Ghazvininejad, M. *et al.* (2020), "BART: Denoising sequence-to-sequence pre-training for natural language generation, translation, and comprehension", *Proceedings of the Annual Meeting of the Association for Computational Linguistics (ACL)* pp. 7871–7880.

Li, D., Langlois, T. R., and Zheng, C. (2018), "Scene-aware audio for 360 videos", *ACM Transactions on Graphics (TOG)* **37**(4), 1–12.

Li, L., Yatskar, M., Yin, D., Hsieh, C.-J., and Chang, K.-W. (2020), "Visual-BERT: A simple and performant baseline for vision and language", *Proceedings of the Annual Meeting of the Association for Computational Linguistics (ACL)*.

Li, S., Deng, M., Lee, J., Sinha, A., and Barbastathis, G. (2018), "Imaging through glass diffusers using densely connected convolutional networks", *Optica* **5**(7), 803–813.

Li, Y., Choi, D., Chung, J., Kushman, N. *et al.* (2022), "Competition-level code generation with AlphaCode", *arXiv preprint arXiv:2203.07814*.

Li, Y., Liu, S., Yang, J., and Yang, M.-H. (2017), "Generative face completion", in *Proceedings of the IEEE/CVF Conference on Computer Vision and Pattern Recognition (CVPR)*, pp. 3911–3919.

Li, Y., Song, J., and Ermon, S. (2017), "Infogail: Interpretable imitation learning from visual demonstrations", in *Proceedings of Advances in Neural Information Processing Systems (NeurIPS)*, pp. 3812–3822.

Li, Y., Tarlow, D., Brockschmidt, M., and Zemel, R. (2016), "Gated graph sequence neural networks", in *Proceedings of the International Conference on Learning Representations (ICLR)*.

Li, Y. and Turner, R. E. (2016), "Rényi divergence variational inference", in *Proceedings of Advances in Neural Information Processing Systems (NeurIPS)*, pp. 1073–1081.

Li, Y., Xue, Y., and Tian, L. (2018), "Deep speckle correlation: A deep learning approach toward scalable imaging through scattering media", *Optica* **5**(10), 1181–1190.

Lillicrap, T. P., Hunt, J. J., Pritzel, A., Heess, N. *et al.* (2016), "Continuous control with deep reinforcement learning", in *Proceedings of the International Conference on Learning Representations (ICLR)*.

Lim, J. J., Pirsiavash, H., and Torralba, A. (2013), "Parsing IKEA objects: Fine pose estimation", in *Proceedings of the IEEE/CVF International Conference on Computer Vision (ICCV)*, pp. 2992–2999.

Lin, J., Zhang, R., Ganz, F., Han, S., and Zhu, J.-Y. (2021), "Anycost GANs for interactive image synthesis and editing", in *Proceedings of the IEEE/CVF Conference on Computer Vision and Pattern Recognition (CVPR)*, pp. 14986–14996.

Lin, K., Li, D., He, X., Zhang, Z., and Sun, M.-T. (2017), "Adversarial ranking for language generation", in *Proceedings of Advances in Neural Information Processing Systems (NeurIPS)*, pp. 3155–3165.

Lin, S. (1965), "Computer solutions of the traveling salesman problem", *Bell System Technical Journal* **44**(10), 2245–2269.

Lin, S. and Kernighan, B. W. (1973), "An effective heuristic algorithm for the traveling-salesman problem", *Operations Research* **21**(2), 498–516.

Lin, T., Jin, C., and Jordan, M. I. (2020), "On gradient descent ascent for nonconvex-concave minimax problems", in *Proceeding of the International Conference on Machine Learning (ICML)*, pp. 6083–6093.

Lin, Z., Feng, M., Santos, C. N. d., Yu, M. *et al.* (2017), "A structured self-attentive sentence embedding", in *Proceedings of the International Conference on Learning Representations (ICLR)*.

Liu, B., Hu, W., Zitnik, M., and Leskovec, J. (2020), "Open Graph Benchmark", ogb.stanford.edu.

Liu, D. C. and Nocedal, J. (1989), "On the limited memory BFGS method for large scale optimization", *Mathematical Programming* **45**(1-3), 503–528.

Liu, H., Wan, Z., Huang, W., Song, Y. *et al.* (2021), "PD-GAN: Probabilistic diverse GAN for image inpainting", in *Proceedings of the IEEE/CVF Conference on Computer Vision and Pattern Recognition (CVPR)*, pp. 9371–9381.

Liu, M.-Y., Huang, X., Mallya, A., Karras, T. *et al.* (2019), "Few-shot unsupervised image-to-image translation", in *Proceedings of the IEEE/CVF International Conference on Computer Vision (ICCV)*.

Liu, M.-Y. and Tuzel, O. (2016), "Coupled generative adversarial networks", in *Proceedings of Advances in Neural Information Processing Systems (NeurIPS)*, pp. 469–477.

Liu, Y., Ott, M., Goyal, N., Du, J. *et al.* (2019), "RoBERTa: A robustly optimized BERT pretraining approach", *arXiv preprint arXiv:1907.11692*.

Liu, Z., Lin, Y., Cao, Y., Hu, H. *et al.* (2021), "Swin Transformer: Hierarchical vision transformer using shifted windows", *Proceedings of the IEEE/CVF International Conference on Computer Vision (ICCV)*.

Lu, J., Batra, D., Parikh, D., and Lee, S. (2019), "ViLBERT: Pretraining task-agnostic visiolinguistic representations for vision-and-language tasks", in *Proceedings of Advances in Neural Information Processing Systems (NeurIPS)*.

Luo, H., Nagano, K., Kung, H.-W., Xu, Q. *et al.* (2021), "Normalized avatar synthesis using StyleGAN and perceptual refinement", in *Proceedings of the IEEE/CVF Conference on Computer Vision and Pattern Recognition (CVPR)*, pp. 11662–11672.

Luo, W., Yang, B., and Urtasun, R. (2018), "Fast and furious: Real time end-to-end 3d detection, tracking and motion forecasting with a single convolutional net", in *Proceedings of the IEEE/CVF Conference on Computer Vision and Pattern Recognition (CVPR)*, pp. 3569–3577.

Luong, M.-T., Pham, H., and Manning, C. D. (2015), "Effective approaches to attention-based neural machine translation", in *Proceedings of the Conference on Empirical Methods in Natural Language Processing (EMNLP)*, pp. 1412–1421.

Ma, L., Jia, X., Sun, Q., Schiele, B. *et al.* (2017), "Pose guided person image generation", in *Proceedings of Advances in Neural Information Processing Systems (NeurIPS)*, pp. 406–416.

Ma, N., Zhang, X., Zheng, H.-T., and Sun, J. (2018), "Shufflenet v2: Practical guidelines for efficient CNN architecture design", in *Proceedings of the European Conference on Computer Vision (ECCV)*, pp. 116–131.

Ma, Q., Ge, S., He, D., Thaker, D., and Drori, I. (2020), "Combinatorial optimization by graph pointer networks and hierarchical reinforcement learning", *AAAI Workshop on Deep Learning on Graphs: Methodologies and Applications*.

Mallasto, A., Hauberg, S., and Feragen, A. (2019), "Probabilistic Riemannian submanifold learning with wrapped Gaussian process latent variable models", in *Proceedings of the International Conference on Artificial Intelligence and Statistics (AISTATS)*.

Mao, X., Li, Q., Xie, H., Lau, R. Y. *et al.* (2017), "Least squares generative adversarial networks", in *Proceedings of the IEEE/CVF International Conference on Computer Vision (ICCV)*, pp. 2794–2802.

Markuzon, N. and Kolitz, S. (2009), "Data driven approach to estimating fire danger from satellite images and weather information", *IEEE Applied Imagery Pattern Recognition Workshop* pp. 1–7.

Mazyavkina, N., Sviridov, S., Ivanov, S., and Burnaev, E. (2021), "Reinforcement learning for combinatorial optimization: A survey", *Computers & Operations Research* **134**.

McAleer, S., Agostinelli, F., Shmakov, A., and Baldi, P. (2018), "Solving the Rubik's Cube with approximate policy iteration", *Proceedings of the International Conference on Learning Representations (ICLR)*.

Mentzer, F., Toderici, G. D., Tschannen, M., and Agustsson, E. (n.d.), "High-fidelity generative image compression", in *Proceedings of Advances in Neural Information Processing Systems (NeurIPS)*.

Messaoud, K., Deo, N., Trivedi, M. M., and Nashashibi, F. (2021), "Trajectory prediction for autonomous driving based on multi-head attention with joint agent-map representation", in *IEEE Intelligent Vehicles Symposium (IV)*, pp. 165–170.

Metz, L., Poole, B., Pfau, D., and Sohl-Dickstein, J. (2017), "Unrolled generative adversarial networks (2016)", in *Proceedings of the International Conference on Learning Representations (ICLR)*.

Mikolov, T., Chen, K., Corrado, G., and Dean, J. (2013), "Efficient estimation of word representations in vector space", in *Proceedings of the International Conference on Learning Representations Workshop*.

Mikolov, T., Sutskever, I., Chen, K., Corrado, G. S., and Dean, J. (2013), "Distributed representations of words and phrases and their compositionality", in *Proceedings of Advances in Neural Information Processing Systems (NeurIPS)*, pp. 3111–3119.

Milutinovic, M., Baydin, A. G., Zinkov, R., Harvey, W. *et al.* (2017), "End-to-end training of differentiable pipelines across machine learning frameworks", in *NIPS Workshop on Autodiff*.

Mirza, M. and Osindero, S. (2014), "Conditional generative adversarial nets", *NIPS Deep Learning and Representation Learning Workshop*.

Mnih, V., Badia, A. P., Mirza, M., Graves, A. *et al.* (2016), "Asynchronous methods for deep reinforcement learning", in *Proceedings of the International Conference on Machine Learning (ICML)*, pp. 1928–1937.

Mnih, V., Kavukcuoglu, K., Silver, D., Rusu, A. A. *et al.* (2015), "Human-level control through deep reinforcement learning", *Nature* **518**(7540), 529–533.

Moerland, T. M., Broekens, J., Plaat, A., and Jonker, C. M. (2018), "A0C: Alpha Zero in continuous action space", *arXiv preprint arXiv:1805.09613*.

Monti, F., Boscaini, D., Masci, J., Rodola, E. *et al.* (2017), "Geometric deep learning on graphs and manifolds using mixture model CNNs", in *Proceedings of the IEEE Conference on Computer Vision and Pattern Recognition (CVPR)*, pp. 5115–5124.

Morgenstern, L. and Ortiz, C. (2015), "The Winograd schema challenge: Evaluating progress in commonsense reasoning", in *Proceedings of the Twenty-Seventh IAAI Conference*.

Moult, J., Fidelis, K., Kryshtafovych, A., Schwede, T., and Birkbeck, M. T. (2018), "13th Community Wide Experiment on the Critical Assessment of Techniques for Protein Structure Prediction", predictioncenter.org/casp13/index.cgi.

Mukunthu, D. (2019), "Announcing automated ML capability in Azure Machine Learning", azure.microsoft.com.

Myra, J. R., D'Ippolito, D. A., Stotler, D. P., Zweben, S. J. *et al.* (2006), "Blob birth and transport in the tokamak edge plasma: Analysis of imaging data", *Physics of Plasmas* **13**(9), 092509.

Nadaraya, E. A. (1964), "On estimating regression", *Theory of Probability & Its Applications* **9**(1), 141–142.

Nathan Kutz, J. (2017), "Deep learning in fluid dynamics", *Fluid Mechanics* **814**, 1–4.

Nešetřil, J., Milková, E., and Nešetřilová, H. (2001), "Otakar borvka on minimum spanning tree problem translation of both the 1926 papers, comments, history", *Discrete Mathematics* **233**(1-3), 3–36.

Nichol, A. Q. and Dhariwal, P. (2021), "Improved denoising diffusion probabilistic models", in *Proceedings of International Conference on Machine Learning (ICML)*, pp. 8162–8171.

Niemeyer, M. and Geiger, A. (2021), "Giraffe: Representing scenes as compositional generative neural feature fields", in *Proceedings of the IEEE/CVF Conference on Computer Vision and Pattern Recognition (CVPR)*, pp. 11453–11464.

Nowozin, S., Cseke, B., and Tomioka, R. (2016), "f-GAN: Training generative neural samplers using variational divergence minimization", in *Proceedings of Advances in Neural Information Processing Systems (NeurIPS)*, pp. 271–279.

Odena, A. (2016), "Semi-supervised learning with generative adversarial networks", *arXiv preprint arXiv:1606.01583*.

Odena, A., Olah, C., and Shlens, J. (2017), "Conditional image synthesis with auxiliary classifier GANs", in *Proceedings of the International Conference on Machine Learning (ICML)*, Vol. 70, pp. 2642–2651.

Oliver, A., Odena, A., Raffel, C. A., Cubuk, E. D., and Goodfellow, I. (2018), "Realistic evaluation of deep semi-supervised learning algorithms", in *Proceedings of Advances in Neural Information Processing Systems (NeurIPS)*, pp. 3235–3246.

Olson, R. S. and Moore, J. H. (2016), "TPOT: A tree-based pipeline optimization tool for automating machine learning", in *Proceeding of the Workshop on Automatic Machine Learning*, pp. 66–74.

O'Neill, B. (2006), *Elementary Differential Geometry*, Elsevier.

Oord, A. v. d., Dieleman, S., Zen, H., Simonyan, K. *et al.* (2016), "WaveNet: A generative model for raw audio", in *Proceedings of the ISCA Workshop on Speech Synthesis*, p. 125.

OpenAI (2020), "Spinning Up in Deep RL", spinningup.openai.com.

OpenAI (2021), "GitHub Co-Pilot", copilot.github.com.

Opper, M. and Saad, D. (2001), *Advanced Mean Field Methods: Theory and Practice*, MIT Press.

Orengo, C. A., Michie, A. D., Jones, S., Jones, D. T. *et al.* (1997), "CATH: A hierarchic classification of protein domain structures", *Structure* **5**(8), 1093–1109.

Ott, M., Cardie, C., and Hancock, J. T. (2013), "Negative deceptive opinion spam", in *Proceedings of the Conference of the North American Chapter of the Association for Computational Linguistics: Human Language Technologies (NAACL)*, pp. 497–501.

Pal, M., Maity, R., Ratnam, J., Nonaka, M., and Behera, S. K. (2020), "Long-lead prediction of ENSO Modoki index using machine learning algorithms", *Scientific Reports* **10**(1), 1–13.

Pan, X., Dai, B., Liu, Z., Loy, C. C., and Luo, P. (2021), "Do 2D GANs know 3D shape? Unsupervised 3D shape reconstruction from 2D image GANs", in *Proceedings of the International Conference on Learning Representations (ICLR)*.

Parisi, G. (1988), *Statistical Field Theory*, Addison-Wesley.

Park, T., Liu, M.-Y., Wang, T.-C., and Zhu, J.-Y. (2019), "Semantic image synthesis with spatially-adaptive normalization", in *Proceedings of the IEEE Conference on Computer Vision and Pattern Recognition (CVPR)*, pp. 2337–2346.

Parmar, N., Vaswani, A., Uszkoreit, J., Kaiser, L. *et al.* (2018), "Image transformer", in *Proceedings of the International Conference on Machine Learning (ICML)*, pp. 4055–4064.

Paszke, A., Gross, S., Chintala, S., Chanan, G. *et al.* (2017), "Automatic differentiation in PyTorch", in *Proceedings of NIPS Workshop on Autodiff.*

Pathak, D., Krahenbuhl, P., Donahue, J., Darrell, T., and Efros, A. A. (2016), "Context encoders: Feature learning by inpainting", in *Proceedings of the IEEE conference on Computer Vision and Pattern Recognition (CVPR)*, pp. 2536–2544.

Patrick, M., Campbell, D., Asano, Y. M., Metze, I. M. F. *et al.* (2021), "Keeping your eye on the ball: Trajectory attention in video transformers", in *Proceedings of Advances in Neural Information Processing Systems (NeurIPS)*.

Pedregosa, F., Varoquaux, G., Gramfort, A., Michel, V. *et al.* (2011), "Scikit-learn: Machine learning in Python", *Journal of Machine Learning Research* **12**, 2825–2830.

Perozzi, B., Al-Rfou, R., and Skiena, S. (2014), "Deepwalk: Online learning of social representations", in *Proceedings of the 20th ACM SIGKDD International Conference on Knowledge Discovery and Data Mining*, pp. 701–710.

Peters, M. E., Neumann, M., Iyyer, M., Gardner, M. *et al.* (2018), "Deep contextualized word representations", *Annual Conference of the North American Chapter of the Association for Computational Linguistics*.

Phan-Minh, T., Grigore, E. C., Boulton, F. A., Beijbom, O., and Wolff, E. M. (2020), "CoverNet: Multimodal behavior prediction using trajectory sets", in *Proceedings of the IEEE/CVF Conference on Computer Vision and Pattern Recognition (CVPR)*, pp. 14074–14083.

Pizzati, F., Cerri, P., and de Charette, R. (2021), "CoMoGAN: Continuous model-guided image-to-image translation", in *Proceedings of the IEEE/CVF Conference on Computer Vision and Pattern Recognition (CVPR)*, pp. 14288–14298.

Pope, A. P., Ide, J. S., Mićović, D., Diaz, H. *et al.* (2021), "Hierarchical reinforcement learning for air-to-air combat", in *Proceedings of the International Conference on Unmanned Aircraft Systems (ICUAS)*, pp. 275–284.

Prim, R. C. (1957), "Shortest connection networks and some generalizations", *Bell System Technical Journal* **36**(6), 1389–1401.

PyTorch (2021), "TorchGAN library", github.com/torchgan/torchgan.

Qian, Y., Zhang, H., and Furukawa, Y. (2021), "Roof-GAN: Learning to generate roof geometry and relations for residential houses", in *Proceedings of the IEEE/CVF Conference on Computer Vision and Pattern Recognition (CVPR)*, pp. 2796–2805.

Radford, A., Kim, J. W., Hallacy, C., Ramesh, A. *et al.* (2021), "Learning transferable visual models from natural language supervision", in *Proceedings of International Conference on Machine Learning (ICML)*, pp. 8748–8763.

Radford, A., Metz, L., and Chintala, S. (2015), "Unsupervised representation learning with deep convolutional generative adversarial networks", *arXiv preprint arXiv:1511.06434*.

Radford, A., Narasimhan, K., Salimans, T., and Sutskever, I. (2018),

"Improving language understanding by generative pre-training", openai.com/blog/language-unsupervised.

Radford, A., Wu, J., Child, R., Luan, D. *et al.* (2019), "Language models are unsupervised multitask learners", *OpenAI Blog* **1**(8).

Raffel, C., Shazeer, N., Roberts, A., Lee, K. *et al.* (2020), "Exploring the limits of transfer learning with a unified text-to-text transformer", *Journal of Machine Learning Research* **21**, 1–67.

Rahman, I. U., Drori, I., Stodden, V. C., Donoho, D. L., and Schröder, P. (2005), "Multiscale representations for manifold-valued data", *Multiscale Modeling & Simulation* **4**(4), 1201–1232.

Rajpurkar, P., Zhang, J., Lopyrev, K., and Liang, P. (2016), "SQuAD: 100,000+ questions for machine comprehension of text", in *Proceedings of the Conference on Empirical Methods in Natural Language Processing (EMNLP)*.

Ramachandran, P., Zoph, B., and Le, Q. V. (2017), "Searching for activation functions", *arXiv preprint arXiv:1710.05941*.

Ramesh, A., Dhariwal, P., Nichol, A., Chu, C., and Chen, M. (2022), "Hierarchical text-conditional image generation with CLIP latents", *arXiv preprint arXiv:2204.06125*.

Ramesh, A., Pavlov, M., Goh, G., and Gray, S. (2021), "DALL·E: Creating images from text", openai.com/blog/dall-e.

Ramesh, A., Pavlov, M., Goh, G., Gray, S. *et al.* (2021), "Zero-shot text-to-image generation", *Proceedings of the International Conference on Machine Learning (ICML)* pp. 8821–8831.

Ranganath, R., Gerrish, S., and Blei, D. (2014), "Black box variational inference", in *Proceedings of the International Conference on Artificial Intelligence and Statistics (AISTATS)*, pp. 814–822.

Ratnarajah, A., Tang, Z., and Manocha, D. (2021), "IR-GAN: Room impulse response generator for speech augmentation", in *Proceedings of Interspeech*, pp. 286–290.

Ravuri, S. and Vinyals, O. (n.d.), "Classification accuracy score for conditional generative models", *Proceedings of Advances in Neural Information Processing Systems*.

Rayana, S. and Akoglu, L. (2015), "Collective opinion spam detection: Bridging review networks and metadata", in *Proceedings of the 21th ACM SIGKDD International Conference on Knowledge Discovery and Data Mining*, pp. 985–994.

Razavi, A., van den Oord, A., and Vinyals, O. (2019), "Generating diverse high-resolution images with VQ-VAE", in *Proceedings of the International Conference on Learning Representations Workshop*.

Reddi, S. J., Kale, S., and Kumar, S. (2018), "On the convergence of Adam and beyond", in *Proceedings of the International Conference on Learning Representations (ICLR)*.

Reinelt, G. (2020), "TSPLIB: Library of sample instances for the TSP".

Remaggi, L., Kim, H., Jackson, P. J., and Hilton, A. (2019), "Reproducing real world acoustics in virtual reality using spherical cameras", in *Proceedings of the AES International Conference on Immersive and Interactive Audio*.

Ren, Y. and Ji, D. (2017), "Neural networks for deceptive opinion spam detection: An empirical study", *Information Sciences* **385**, 213–224.

Rettinger, M. (1957), "Reverberation chambers for broadcasting and recording studios", *Journal of the Audio Engineering Society* **5**(1), 18–22.

Rezende, D. J. and Mohamed, S. (2015), "Variational inference with normalizing flows", in *Proceedings of the International Conference on Machine Learning (ICML)*.

Rezende, D. J., Mohamed, S., and Wierstra, D. (2014), "Stochastic backpropagation and approximate inference in deep generative models", in *Proceedings of the International Conference on Machine Learning (ICML)*.

Riedmiller, M. (2005), "Neural fitted Q iteration–first experiences with a data efficient neural reinforcement learning method", in *Proceedings of the European Conference on Machine Learning (ECML)*, pp. 317–328.

Robbins, H. and Monro, S. (1951), "A stochastic approximation method", *Annals of Mathematical Statistics* **22**(3), 400–407.

Robinson, J. P., Shao, M., and Fu, Y. (2021), "Survey on the analysis and modeling of visual kinship: A decade in the making", *IEEE Transactions on Pattern Analysis and Machine Intelligence*.

Robinson, J., Shao, M., Wu, Y., and Fu, Y. (2016), "Families in the wild (FIW): Large-scale kinship image database and benchmarks", in *Proceedings of the ACM on Multimedia Conference*.

Roeder, G., Wu, Y., and Duvenaud, D. K. (2017), "Sticking the landing: Simple, lower-variance gradient estimators for variational inference", in *Proceedings of Advances in Neural Information Processing Systems (NeurIPS)*, pp. 6925–6934.

Roman, J., Verzoni, A., and Sutherland, S. (2020), "Greetings from the 2020 wildfire season: Five undeniable truths from a pivotal year in the world's growing struggle with wildfire", www.nfpa.org/News-and-Research/Publications-and-media/NFPA-Journal/2020/November-December-2020/Features/Wildfire.

Ronneberger, O., Fischer, P., and Brox, T. (2015), "U-Net: Convolutional networks for biomedical image segmentation", in *Proceedings of the International Conference on Medical Image Computing and Computer-Assisted Intervention (MICCAI)*, pp. 234–241.

Rosenkrantz, D. J., Stearns, R. E., and Lewis, II, P. M. (1977), "An analysis of several heuristics for the traveling salesman problem", *SIAM Journal on Computing* **6**(3), 563–581.

Ross, S. and Bagnell, D. (2010), "Efficient reductions for imitation learning", in *Proceedings of the thirteenth International Conference on Artificial Intelligence and Statistics (AISTATS)*, pp. 661–668.

Ross, S., Gordon, G., and Bagnell, D. (2011), "A reduction of imitation learning and structured prediction to no-regret online learning", in *Proceedings of the fourteenth International Conference on Artificial Intelligence and Statistics (AISTATS)*, pp. 627–635.

Rozen, N., Grover, A., Nickel, M., and Lipman, Y. (n.d.), "Moser Flow: Divergence-based generative modeling on manifolds", *Proceedings of Advances in Neural Information Processing Systems (NeurIPS)*.

Rumelhart, D. E., Hinton, G. E., and Williams, R. J. (1986), "Learning representations by back-propagating errors", *Nature* **323**(6088), 533.

Saha, A., Bharath, K., and Kurtek, S. (2019), "A geometric variational approach to Bayesian inference", *Journal of the American Statistical Association* **115**, 822–835.

Sahin, Y. G. and Ince, T. (2009), "Early forest fire detection using radio-acoustic sounding system", *Sensors* **9**(3), 1485–1498.

Sali, K. and Lerch, A. (2020), "Generating impulse responses using recurrent neural networks", 109ecc9c-0e76-482f-90c5-fe6cd93cf581.filesusr.com/ugd/4a27c6$_f$a8281568425494e8ca16133fe724c6e.pdf.

Salimans, T., Goodfellow, I., Zaremba, W., Cheung, V. *et al.* (2016), "Improved techniques for training GANs", in *Proceedings of Advances in Neural Information Processing Systems (NeurIPS)*, pp. 2234–2242.

Salimans, T., Ho, J., Chen, X., Sidor, S., and Sutskever, I. (2017), "Evolution strategies as a scalable alternative to reinforcement learning", *arXiv preprint arXiv:1703.03864*.

Sanchez-Gonzalez, A., Heess, N., Springenberg, J. T., Merel, J. *et al.* (2018), "Graph networks as learnable physics engines for inference and control", in *Proceedings of the International Conference on Machine Learning (ICML)*.

Sang, E. F. and Meulder, F. D. (2003), "Introduction to the CoNLL-2003 shared task: Language-independent named entity recognition", in *Proceedings of the Conference on Natural Language Learning at HLT-NAACL*.

Sanh, V., Debut, L., Chaumond, J., and Wolf, T. (2019), "DistilBERT, a distilled version of BERT: Smaller, faster, cheaper and lighter", *arXiv preprint arXiv:1910.01108*.

Santoro, A., Raposo, D., Barrett, D. G., Malinowski, M. *et al.* (2017), "A simple neural network module for relational reasoning", in *Proceedings of Advances in Neural Information Processing Systems (NeurIPS)*, pp. 4967–4976.

Santurkar, S., Tsipras, D., Ilyas, A., and Madry, A. (2018), "How does batch normalization help optimization?", in *Proceedings of Advances in Neural Information Processing Systems (NeurIPS)*, pp. 2483–2493.

Sauzède, R., Johnson, J. E., Claustre, H., Camps-Valls, G., and Ruescas, A. (2020), "Estimation of oceanic particulate organic carbon with machine learning", *ISPRS Annals of the Photogrammetry, Remote Sensing and Spatial Information Sciences* **2**, 949–956.

Schaul, T., Quan, J., Antonoglou, I., and Silver, D. (2016), "Prioritized experience replay", in *Proceedings of the International Conference on Learning Representations (ICLR)*.

Schissler, C. and Manocha, D. (2016), "Interactive sound propagation and rendering for large multi-source scenes", *ACM Transactions on Graphics (TOG)* **36**(4), 1.

Schrittwieser, J., Antonoglou, I., Hubert, T., Simonyan, K. *et al.* (2019), "Mastering Atari, Go, chess and Shogi by planning with a learned model", *arXiv preprint arXiv:1911.08265*.

Schroeder, M. R. and Logan, B. F. (1961), ""Colorless" artificial reverberation", *IRE Transactions on Audio* (6), 209–214.

Schulman, J., Levine, S., Abbeel, P., Jordan, M., and Moritz, P. (2015), "Trust region policy optimization", in *Proceedings of the International Conference on Machine Learning (ICML)*, pp. 1889–1897.

Schulman, J., Moritz, P., Levine, S., Jordan, M., and Abbeel, P. (2016), "High-dimensional continuous control using generalized advantage estimation", in *Proceedings of the International Conference on Learning Representations (ICLR)*.

Schulman, J., Wolski, F., Dhariwal, P., Radford, A., and Klimov, O. (2017), "Proximal policy optimization algorithms", *arXiv preprint arXiv:1707.06347*.

Shafiee, M. J., Jeddi, A., Nazemi, A., Fieguth, P., and Wong, A. (2020), "Deep neural network perception models and robust autonomous driving systems: Practical solutions for mitigation and improvement", *IEEE Signal Processing Magazine* **38**(1), 22–30.

Shaham, T. R., Dekel, T., and Michaeli, T. (2019), "SinGAN: Learning a generative model from a single natural image", in *Proceedings of the IEEE/CVF International Conference on Computer Vision (ICCV)*, pp. 4570–4580.

Shoeybi, M., Patwary, M., Puri, R., LeGresley, P. *et al.* (2019), "Megatron-LM: Training multi-billion parameter language models using GPU model parallelism", *arXiv preprint arXiv:1909.08053*.

Shor, J., Sarna, A., Drori, Y., and Westbrook, D. (2020), "TensorFlow GAN library", github.com/tensorflow/gan.

Shporer, A., Tran, S., Singh, N., Kates, B. *et al.* (2022), "Learning methods for solving Astronomy course problems".

Shrivastava, A., Pfister, T., Tuzel, O., Susskind, J. *et al.* (2017), "Learning from simulated and unsupervised images through adversarial training", in *Proceedings of the IEEE/CVF Conference on Computer Vision and Pattern Recognition (CVPR)*, pp. 2107–2116.

Shukla, A., Uppal, S., Bhagat, S., Anand, S., and Turaga, P. (2018), "Geometry of deep generative models for disentangled representations", in *Proceedings of the Indian Conference on Computer Vision, Graphics and Image Processing*, pp. 1–8.

Silva, L. F., Pamplona, V. F., and Comba, J. L. (2009), "Legolizer: A real-time system for modeling and rendering lego representations of boundary models", in *Proceedings of the Brazilian Symposium on Computer Graphics and Image Processing*, pp. 17–23.

Silver, D., Huang, A., Maddison, C. J., Guez, A. *et al.* (2016), "Mastering the game of Go with deep neural networks and tree search", *Nature* **529**(7587), 484–489.

Silver, D., Hubert, T., Schrittwieser, J., Antonoglou, I. *et al.* (2017), "Mastering chess and Shogi by self-play with a general reinforcement learning algorithm", *arXiv preprint arXiv:1712.01815.*

Silver, D., Hubert, T., Schrittwieser, J., Antonoglou, I. *et al.* (2018), "A general reinforcement learning algorithm that masters chess, Shogi, and Go through self-play", *Science* **362**(6419), 1140–1144.

Simonyan, K. and Zisserman, A. (2014), "Very deep convolutional networks for large-scale image recognition", *arXiv preprint arXiv:1409.1556.*

Smilkov, D. and Carter, S. (n.d.), "Tensorflow playground", playground.tensorflow.org.

Smythe, T. (2018), "Kunst der Fuge site: Classical music in MIDI files", www.kunstderfuge.com.

Snoek, J., Larochelle, H., and Adams, R. P. (2012), "Practical Bayesian optimization of machine learning algorithms", in *Proceedings of Advances in Neural Information Processing Systems (NeurIPS)*, pp. 2951–2959.

Socher, R., Perelygin, A., Wu, J., Chuang, J. *et al.* (2013), "Recursive deep models for semantic compositionality over a sentiment treebank", in *Proceedings of the Conference on Empirical Methods in Natural Language Processing (EMNLP)*, pp. 1631–1642.

Sohl-Dickstein, J., Weiss, E., Maheswaranathan, N., and Ganguli, S. (2015), "Deep unsupervised learning using nonequilibrium thermodynamics", in *Proceedings of International Conference on Machine Learning (ICML)*, pp. 2256–2265.

Solis, F. J. and Wets, R. J.-B. (1981), "Minimization by random search techniques", *Mathematics of Operations Research* **6**(1), 19–30.

Spivak, M. D. (1999), *A Comprehensive Introduction to Differential Geometry*, 3rd edn, Publish or Perish.

Srinivas, A., Lin, T.-Y., Parmar, N., Shlens, J. *et al.* (2021), "Bottleneck transformers for visual recognition", in *Proceedings of the IEEE/CVF Conference on Computer Vision and Pattern Recognition (CVPR)*, pp. 16519–16529.

Srivastava, N., Hinton, G., Krizhevsky, A., Sutskever, I., and Salakhutdinov, R. (2014), "Dropout: A simple way to prevent neural networks from overfitting", *Journal of Machine Learning Research* **15**(1), 1929–1958.

Steger, A. and Wormald, N. C. (1999), "Generating random regular graphs quickly", *Combinatorics, Probability and Computing* **8**(4), 377–396.

Steinmetz, C. (2018), "NeuralReverberator", www.christiansteinmetz.com/projects-blog/neuralreverberator.

Stigeborn, P. (2018), "Generating 3D-objects using neural networks".

Strunk Jr., W. and White, E. B. (2007), *The Elements of Style Illustrated*, Penguin.

Su, W., Zhu, X., Cao, Y., Li, B. *et al.* (2020), "Vl-BERT: Pre-training of generic visual-linguistic representations", in *Proceedings of the International Conference on Learning Representations (ICLR)*.

Sun, B., Feng, J., and Saenko, K. (2017), Correlation alignment for unsupervised domain adaptation, *in* G. Csurka, ed., Domain Adaptation in Computer Vision Applications, pp. 153–171.

Sun, C., Myers, A., Vondrick, C., Murphy, K., and Schmid, C. (2019), "VideoBERT: A joint model for video and language representation learning", in *Proceedings of the IEEE/CVF International Conference on Computer Vision (ICCV)*, pp. 7464–7473.

Sun, W., Gordon, G. J., Boots, B., and Bagnell, J. (2018), "Dual policy iteration", in *Proceedings of Advances in Neural Information Processing Systems (NeurIPS)*, pp. 7059–7069.

Sutskever, I., Martens, J., Dahl, G., and Hinton, G. (2013), "On the importance of initialization and momentum in deep learning", in *Proceedings of the International Conference on Machine Learning (ICML)*, pp. 1139–1147.

Sutskever, I., Vinyals, O., and Le, Q. V. (2014), "Sequence to sequence learning with neural networks", in *Proceedings of Advances in Neural Information Processing Systems (NeurIPS)*, pp. 3104–3112.

Sutton, R. S. (1988), "Learning to predict by the methods of temporal differences", *Machine Learning* **3**(1), 9–44.

Swearingen, T., Drevo, W., Cyphers, B., Cuesta-Infante, A. *et al.* (2017), "ATM: A distributed, collaborative, scalable system for automated machine learning", in *Proceedings of the IEEE International Conference on Big Data*.

Szegedy, C., Liu, W., Jia, Y., Sermanet, P. *et al.* (2015), "Going deeper with convolutions", in *Proceedings of the IEEE/CVF Conference on Computer Vision and Pattern Recognition (CVPR)*.

Szegedy, C., Vanhoucke, V., Ioffe, S., Shlens, J., and Wojna, Z. (2016), "Rethinking the inception architecture for computer vision", in *Proceedings of the IEEE/CVF Conference on Computer Vision and Pattern Recognition (CVPR)*, pp. 2818–2826.

Tan, H. and Bansal, M. (2019), "LXMERT: Learning cross-modality encoder representations from transformers", in *Proceedings of the Conference on Empirical Methods in Natural Language Processing (EMNLP)*.

Tan, H. and Bansal, M. (2020), "Vokenization: Improving language understanding with contextualized, visual-grounded supervision", in *Proceedings of the Conference on Empirical Methods in Natural Language Processing (EMNLP)*.

Tang, C. and Salakhutdinov, R. R. (2019), "Multiple futures prediction", in *Proceedings of Advances in Neural Information Processing Systems (NeurIPS)*, pp. 15424–15434.

Tang, D., Liang, D., Jebara, T., and Ruozzi, N. (2019), "Correlated variational autoencoders", in *Proceedings of the International Conference on Machine Learning (ICML)*.

Tang, D. and Ranganath, R. (2019), "The variational predictive natural gradient", in *Proceedings of the International Conference on Machine Learning (ICML)*.

Tang, J., Qu, M., Wang, M., Zhang, M. *et al.* (2015), "Line: Large-scale information network embedding", in *Proceedings of the 24th International Conference on World Wide Web (WWW)*, pp. 1067–1077.

Tang, L., Ke, E., Feng, B., Austin, D. *et al.* (2022), "Solving Probability and Statistics problems by probabilistic program synthesis at human level and predicting solvability", in *Proceedings of the International Conference on Artificial Intelligence in Education*.

Tang, W., Li, Z., and Cassar, N. (2019), "Machine learning estimates of global marine nitrogen fixation", *Journal of Geophysical Research: Biogeosciences* **124**(3), 717–730.

Tenenbaum, J. B. and Freeman, W. T. (2000), "Separating style and content with bilinear models", *Neural Computation* **12**(6), 1247–1283.

Tieleman, T. and Hinton, G. (2012), "RMSProp", Coursera lecture.

Touvron, H., Cord, M., Douze, M., Massa, F. *et al.* (2021), "Training data-efficient image transformers & distillation through attention", in *Proceedings of the International Conference on Machine Learning (ICML)*, pp. 10347–10357.

Traer, J. and McDermott, J. H. (2016), "Statistics of natural reverberation enable perceptual separation of sound and space", *Proceedings of the National Academy of Sciences* **113**(48), E7856–E7865.

Tran, S., Krishna, P., Pakuwal, I., Kafle, P. *et al.* (2021), "Solving machine learning problems", *Proceedings of the Asian Conference on Machine Learning (ACML)*.

Tufte, E. R. (1985), "The visual display of quantitative information", *Journal for Healthcare Quality (JHQ)* **7**(3), 15.

van den Oord, A., Vinyals, O., and Koray, K. (2017), "Neural discrete representation learning", in *Proceedings of Advances in Neural Information Processing Systems (NeurIPS)*, pp. 6306–6315.

Van Hasselt, H., Guez, A., and Silver, D. (n.d.), "Deep reinforcement learning with double Q-learning", in *Proceedings of the AAAI conference on artificial intelligence*.

Van Steenkiste, S., Chang, M., Greff, K., and Schmidhuber, J. (2018), "Relational neural expectation maximization: Unsupervised discovery of objects and their interactions", in *Proceedings of the International Conference on Learning Representations (ICLR)*.

Vaswani, A., Shazeer, N., Parmar, N., Uszkoreit, J. *et al.* (2017), "Attention is all you need", in *Proceedings of Advances in Neural Information Processing Systems (NeurIPS)*, pp. 5998–6008.

Veličković, P., Cucurull, G., Casanova, A., Romero, A. *et al.* (2018), "Graph attention networks", in *Proceedings of the International Conference on Learning Representations (ICLR)*.

Vesselinova, N., Steinert, R., Perez-Ramirez, D. F., and Boman, M. (2020), "Learning combinatorial optimization on graphs: A survey with applications to networking", *IEEE Access* **8**, 120388–120416.

Villegas, R., Yang, J., Ceylan, D., and Lee, H. (2018), "Neural kinematic networks for unsupervised motion retargetting", in *Proceedings of the IEEE/CVF Conference on Computer Vision and Pattern Recognition (CVPR)*, pp. 8639–8648.

Vinyals, O., Babuschkin, I., Czarnecki, W. M., Mathieu, M. *et al.* (2019), "Grandmaster level in StarCraft II using multi-agent reinforcement learning", *Nature* **575**(7782), 350–354.

Vondrick, C., Pirsiavash, H., and Torralba, A. (2016), "Generating videos with scene dynamics", in *Proceedings of Advances in Neural Information Processing Systems (NeurIPS)*, pp. 613–621.

Wainwright, M. J. and Jordan, M. I. (2008), "Graphical models, exponential families, and variational inference", *Foundations and Trends in Machine Learning* **1**(1–2), 1–305.

Wang, A., Singh, A., Michael, J., Hill, F. *et al.* (2019), "GLUE: A multi-task benchmark and analysis platform for natural language understanding", in *Proceedings of the International Conference on Learning Representations (ICLR)*.

Wang, F., Wang, H., Wang, H., Li, G., and Situ, G. (2019), "Learning from simulation: An end-to-end deep-learning approach for computational ghost imaging", *Optics Express* **27**(18), 25560–25572.

Wang, J., Cao, H., Zhang, J. Z., and Qi, Y. (2018), "Computational protein design with deep learning neural networks", *Scientific Reports* **8**(1), 6349.

Wang, J., Zhang, Y., Tang, K., Wu, J., and Xiong, Z. (2019), "AlphaStock: A buying-winners-and-selling-losers investment strategy using interpretable deep reinforcement attention networks", in *Proceedings of the ACM SIGKDD International Conference on Knowledge Discovery and Data Mining*, pp. 1900–1908.

Wang, M., Yu, L., Gan, Q., Zhaoogle, J. *et al.* (2020), "Deep Graph Library", www.dgl.ai.

Wang, P. (2019), "Imagined by a GAN", www.thispersondoesnotexist.com.

Wang, P. Z. and Wang, W. Y. (2019), "Riemannian normalizing flow on variational Wasserstein autoencoder for text modeling", in *Proceedings of the Conference of the North American Chapter of the Association for Computational Linguistics: Human Language Technologies*, pp. 284–294.

Wang, T.-C., Liu, M.-Y., Zhu, J.-Y., Liu, G. *et al.* (2018), "Video-to-video synthesis", in *Proceedings of Advances in Neural Information Processing Systems (NeurIPS)*.

Wang, T.-C., Liu, M.-Y., Zhu, J.-Y., Tao, A. *et al.* (2018), "High-resolution image synthesis and semantic manipulation with conditional GANs", in *Proceedings of the IEEE Conference on Computer Vision and Pattern Recognition (CVPR)*, pp. 8798–8807.

Wang, W., Xie, E., Li, X., Fan, D.-P. *et al.* (2021), "Pyramid vision transformer: A versatile backbone for dense prediction without convolutions", *Proceedings of the IEEE/CVF International Conference on Computer Vision (ICCV)*.

Wang, X., Li, Y., Zhang, H., and Shan, Y. (2021), "Towards real-world blind face restoration with generative facial prior", in *Proceedings of the IEEE/CVF Conference on Computer Vision and Pattern Recognition (CVPR)*, pp. 9168–9178.

Wang, Y., Sun, Y., Liu, Z., Sarma, S. E. *et al.* (2019), "Dynamic graph CNN for learning on point clouds", *ACM Transactions on Graphics (TOG)* **38**(5), 1–12.

Wang, Y., Zhang, G., and Ba, J. (2020), "On solving minimax optimization locally: A follow-the-ridge approach", in *Proceedings of the International Conference on Learning Representations (ICLR)*.

Wang, Z., Li, Y., Liu, B., and Liu, J. (2015), "Global climate internal variability in a 2000-year control simulation with community earth system model (CESM)", *Chinese Geographical Science* **25**(3), 263–273.

Wang, Z., Schaul, T., Hessel, M., Hasselt, H. *et al.* (2016), "Dueling network architectures for deep reinforcement learning", in *Proceedings of the International Conference on Machine Learning (ICML)*, pp. 1995–2003.

Warstadt, A., Singh, A., and Bowman, S. R. (2019), "Neural network acceptability judgments", *Transactions of the Association for Computational Linguistics* **7**, 625–641.

Watson, G. S. (1964), "Smooth regression analysis", *Sankhyā: The Indian Journal of Statistics, Series A* **26**(4), 359–372.

Watters, N., Zoran, D., Weber, T., Battaglia, P. *et al.* (2017), "Visual interaction networks: Learning a physics simulator from video", in *Proceedings of Advances in Neural Information Processing Systems (NeurIPS)*, pp. 4539–4547.

Watts, D. J. and Strogatz, S. H. (1998), "Collective dynamics of small-world networks", *Nature* **393**(6684), 440.

Weber, T. S. and Deutsch, C. (2010), "Ocean nutrient ratios governed by plankton biogeography", *Nature* **467**(7315), 550–554.

Wengert, R. E. (1964), "A simple automatic derivative evaluation program", *Communications of the ACM* **7**(8).

Williams, A., Nangia, N., and Bowman, S. R. (2018), "A broad-coverage challenge corpus for sentence understanding through inference", *Proceedings of the North American Chapter of the Association for Computational Linguistics (NAACL)*.

Williamson, D. P. and Shmoys, D. B. (2011), *The Design of Approximation Algorithms*, Cambridge University Press.

Wilson, A. C., Roelofs, R., Stern, M., Srebro, N., and Recht, B. (2017), "The marginal value of adaptive gradient methods in machine learning", in *Proceedings of Advances in Neural Information Processing Systems (NeurIPS)*, pp. 4148–4158.

Wolf, T., Debut, L., Sanh, V., Chaumond, J. *et al.* (2020), "Huggingface's transformers: State-of-the-art natural language processing", in *Proceedings of the Conference on Empirical Methods in Natural Language Processing (EMNLP)*.

Wolterink, J. M., Dinkla, A. M., Savenije, M. H., Seevinck, P. R. *et al.* (2017), "Deep MR to CT synthesis using unpaired data", in *International Workshop on Simulation and Synthesis in Medical Imaging*, pp. 14–23.

Wu, B., Xu, C., Dai, X., Wan, A. *et al.* (2021), "Visual Transformers: Where do Transformers really belong in vision models?", in *Proceedings of the IEEE/CVF International Conference on Computer Vision (CVPR)*, pp. 599–609.

Wu, F., Zhang, T., Souza Jr, A. H. d., Fifty, C. *et al.* (2019), "Simplifying graph convolutional networks", in *Proceedings of the International Conference on Machine Learning (ICML)*.

Wu, J., Zhang, C., Xue, T., Freeman, B., and Tenenbaum, J. (2016), "Learning a probabilistic latent space of object shapes via 3D generative-adversarial modeling", in *Proceedings of Advances in Neural Information Processing Systems (NeurIPS)*, pp. 82–90.

Wurman, P. R., Barrett, S., Kawamoto, K., MacGlashan, J. *et al.* (2022), "Outracing champion Gran Turismo drivers with deep reinforcement learning", *Nature* **602**(7896), 223–228.

Xia, W., Yang, Y., Xue, J.-H., and Wu, B. (2021), "TediGAN: Text-guided diverse face image generation and manipulation", in *Proceedings of the IEEE/CVF Conference on Computer Vision and Pattern Recognition (CVPR)*, pp. 2256–2265.

Xu, J. (2019), "Distance-based protein folding powered by deep learning", *Proceedings of the National Academy of Sciences* **116**(34), 16856–16865.

Xu, K., Hu, W., Leskovec, J., and Jegelka, S. (2019), "How powerful are graph neural networks?", in *Proceedings of the International Conference on Learning Representations (ICLR)*.

Xu, K., Li, J., Zhang, M., Du, S. S. *et al.* (2020), "What can neural networks reason about?", in *Proceedings of the International Conference on Learning Representations (ICLR)*.

Xu, T., Zhang, P., Huang, Q., Zhang, H. *et al.* (2018), "AttnGAN: Fine-grained text to image generation with attentional generative adversarial networks", in *Proceedings of the IEEE Conference on Computer Vision and Pattern Recognition (CVPR)*, pp. 1316–1324.

Yan, J., Mu, L., Wang, L., Ranjan, R., and Zomaya, A. Y. (2020), "Temporal convolutional networks for the advance prediction of ENSO", *Scientific Reports* **10**(1), 1–15.

Yang, C., Akimoto, Y., Kim, D. W., and Udell, M. (2019), "OBOE: Collaborative filtering for AutoML model selection", in *Proceedings of the ACM SIGKDD Conference on Knowledge Discovery and Data Mining*, pp. 1173–1183.

Yang, C., Wu, Z., Fan, J., and Udell, M. (2020), "AutoML pipeline selection: Efficiently navigating the combinatorial space", in *Proceedings of the ACM SIGKDD Conference on Knowledge Discovery and Data Mining*.

Yang, L.-C., Chou, S.-Y., and Yang, Y.-H. (2017), "MidiNet: A convolutional generative adversarial network for symbolic-domain music generation", in *Proceedings of the 18th International Society for Music Information Retrieval Conference (ISMIR)*.

Yang, S., Xie, L., Chen, X., Lou, X. *et al.* (2017), "Statistical parametric speech synthesis using generative adversarial networks under a multi-task learning framework", in *IEEE Automatic Speech Recognition and Understanding Workshop (ASRU)*, pp. 685–691.

Yang, Z., Dai, Z., Yang, Y., Carbonell, J. *et al.* (2019), "XLNet: Generalized autoregressive pretraining for language understanding", *Proceedings of Advances in Neural Information Processing Systems (NeurIPS)*.

Yang, Z., Zhang, Y., Yu, J., Cai, J., and Luo, J. (2018), "End-to-end multimodal multi-task vehicle control for self-driving cars with visual perceptions", in *Proceedings of the 24th International Conference on Pattern Recognition (ICPR)*, pp. 2289–2294.

Yeh, R. A., Chen, C., Yian Lim, T., Schwing, A. G. *et al.* (2017), "Semantic image inpainting with deep generative models", in *Proceedings of the IEEE Conference on Computer Vision and Pattern Recognition (CVPR)*, pp. 5485–5493.

Yu, H. and Oh, J. (2022), "Anytime 3D object reconstruction using multi-modal variational autoencoder", *IEEE Robotics and Automation Letters*.

Yu, J., Li, M., Hao, X., and Xie, G. (2020), "Deep fusion siamese network for automatic kinship verification", in *Proceedings of the IEEE International Conference on Automatic Face and Gesture Recognition (FG)*, pp. 892–899.

Yu, J., Lin, Z., Yang, J., Shen, X. *et al.* (2019), "Free-form image inpainting with gated convolution", in *Proceedings of the IEEE/CVF International Conference on Computer Vision (ICCV)*, pp. 4471–4480.

Yu, L., Zhang, W., Wang, J., and Yu, Y. (2017), "SeqGAN: Sequence generative adversarial nets with policy gradient", in *Proceedings of the Thirty-First AAAI Conference on Artificial Intelligence*.

Zaheer, M., Reddi, S., Sachan, D., Kale, S., and Kumar, S. (2018), "Adaptive methods for nonconvex optimization", in *Proceedings of Advances in Neural Information Processing Systems (NeurIPS)*, pp. 9815–9825.

Zatorre, R. J., Chen, J. L., and Penhune, V. B. (2007), "When the brain plays music: Auditory–motor interactions in music perception and production", *Nature Neuroscience* **8**(7), 547–558.

Zeiler, M. D. (2012), "AdaDelta: An adaptive learning rate method", *arXiv preprint arXiv:1212.5701*.

Zellers, R., Bisk, Y., Schwartz, R., and Choi, Y. (2018), "SWAG: A large-scale adversarial dataset for grounded commonsense inference", in *Proceedings of the Conference on Empirical Methods in Natural Language Processing (EMNLP)*.

Zhai, M., Chen, L., and Mori, G. (2021), "Hyper-LifelongGAN: Scalable lifelong learning for image conditioned generation", in *Proceedings of the IEEE/CVF Conference on Computer Vision and Pattern Recognition (CVPR)*, pp. 2246–2255.

Zhang, C., Butepage, J., Kjellstrom, H., and Mandt, S. (2018), "Advances in variational inference", *IEEE Transactions on Pattern Analysis and Machine Intelligence* **41**(8), 2008–2026.

Zhang, H., Goodfellow, I., Metaxas, D., and Odena, A. (2019), "Self-attention generative adversarial networks", in *Proceedings of the International Conference on Machine Learning (ICML)*.

Zhang, H., Sindagi, V., and Patel, V. M. (2019), "Image de-raining using a conditional generative adversarial network", *IEEE Transactions on Circuits and Systems for Video Technology*.

Zhang, H., Xu, T., Li, H., Zhang, S. *et al.* (2017), "StackGAN: Text to photo-realistic image synthesis with stacked generative adversarial networks", in *Proceedings of the IEEE/CVF International Conference on Computer Vision (ICCV)*, pp. 5907–5915.

Zhang, H., Xu, T., Li, H., Zhang, S. *et al.* (2018), "StackGAN++: Realistic image synthesis with stacked generative adversarial networks", *IEEE Transactions on Pattern Analysis and Machine Intelligence* **41**(8), 1947–1962.

Zhang, J., Chen, X., Cai, Z., Pan, L. *et al.* (2021), "Unsupervised 3d shape completion through GAN inversion", in *Proceedings of the IEEE/CVF Conference on Computer Vision and Pattern Recognition (CVPR)*, pp. 1768–1777.

Zhang, L., Naesseth, C. A., and Blei, D. M. (2022), "Transport score climbing: Variational inference using forward KL and adaptive neural transport", *arXiv preprint arXiv:2202.01841*.

Zhang, R. and Delworth, T. L. (2006), "Impact of Atlantic multidecadal oscillations on India/Sahel rainfall and Atlantic hurricanes", *Geophysical Research Letters* **33**(17).

Zhang, X., Zhou, X., Lin, M., and Sun, J. (2018), "ShuffleNet: An extremely efficient convolutional neural network for mobile devices", in *Proceedings of the IEEE/CVF Conference on Computer Vision and Pattern Recognition (CVPR)*, pp. 6848–6856.

Zhang, Z., Song, Y., and Qi, H. (2017), "Age progression/regression by conditional adversarial autoencoder", in *Proceedings of the IEEE/CVF Conference on Computer Vision and Pattern Recognition (CVPR)*, pp. 5810–5818.

Zhao, E., Yan, R., Li, J., Li, K., and Xing, J. (2022), "AlphaHoldem: High-performance artificial intelligence for Heads-Up No-Limit Texas Hold'em from end-to-end reinforcement learning", in *Proceedings of Thirty-Six AAAI Conference on Artificial Intelligence*.

Zhou, B., Lapedriza, A., Xiao, J., Torralba, A., and Oliva, A. (n.d.), "Learning deep features for scene recognition using places database", in *Proceedings of Advances in Neural Information Processing Systems (NeurIPS)*, pp. 487–495.

Zhu, J.-Y., Park, T., Isola, P., and Efros, A. A. (2017), "Unpaired image-to-image translation using cycle-consistent adversarial networks", in *Proceedings of the IEEE/CVF International Conference on Computer Vision (ICCV)*, pp. 2223–2232.

Zhu, X., Su, W., Lu, L., Li, B. *et al.* (2021), "Deformable DETR: Deformable transformers for end-to-end object detection", in *Proceedings of the International Conference on Learning Representations (ICLR)*.

Ziebart, B. D., Maas, A. L., Bagnell, J. A., Dey, A. K., et al. (2008), "Maximum entropy inverse reinforcement learning", in *Proceedings of the Twenty-Third AAAI Conference on Artificial Intelligence*, Vol. 8, pp. 1433–1438.

Zöller, M.-A. and Huber, M. F. (2021), "Benchmark and survey of automated machine learning frameworks", *Journal of Artificial Intelligence Research* (70), 409–472.

Zweben, S. J., Terry, J. L., Stotler, D. P., and Maqueda, R. J. (2017), "Invited review article: Gas puff imaging diagnostics of edge plasma turbulence in magnetic fusion devices", *Review of Scientific Instruments* **88**(4), 041101.

Index